GREENING INTERNATIONAL LAW

Greening International Law is the first volume in the *International Law and Sustainable Development Series*, established by the Foundation for International Environmental Law and Development (FIELD) and Earthscan in 1993. The series aims to address and define the major legal issues associated with sustainable development, and to contribute to the progressive development of international law.

GREENING INTERNATIONAL LAW

DEDICATION

This book is dedicated to past, present and future generations of the Buchholz family; to the memory of Jean-Pierre, Adrien and Alexis Buchholz; and especially to my grandfather, Leon Buchholz, who is and will always be a figure of courage, strength and inspiration for me.

First published in the UK in 1993 by
Earthscan Publications Limited
120 Pentonville Road, London N1 9JN

Copyright © Foundation for International Environmental Law and Development, 1993

A catalogue record for this book is available from the British Library

ISBN: 1 85383 151 4

Typeset by Media Publishing Services, London
Printed and bound in Great Britain by
Biddles Limited, Guildford and King's Lynn

Earthscan Publications Limited is an editorial independent subsidiary of Kogan Page Limited and publishes in association with the International Institute for Environmental and Development and the World Wide Fund for Nature.

CONTENTS

Foreword   ix
Acknowledgements   xi
List of Contributors   xiii
Introduction   xv

**1. International Environmental Law from Stockholm to Rio:
Back to the Future?**   1
Marc Pallemaerts
    UNCED and the progressive development of law   1
    The never-ending quest for general principles   2
    Sovereignty versus responsibility   5
    Environmental law and human rights law   8
    From 'sustainable development' to 'sustainable growth'   13
    Absorbing environmental law into economic law   16
    Where is the future for environmental law?   18

**2. The Rio Declaration: A New Basis for International
Cooperation**   20
Ileana Porras
    Using the 'environment' to achieve a new globalism   20
    Negotiation of the Rio Declaration   22
    Integrating environment and development   24
    Common but differentiated responsibilities   27
    In defence of sovereignty   30
    Conclusion   32

3. Defending the Global Commons   35
Christopher Stone
    Introduction   35
    A voice for the environment: global commons guardians   39
    Financing the repair: the global commons trust fund   43
    Conclusion   49

4. Enforcing Environmental Security   50
Philippe Sands
    Introduction   50
    Resolving environmental conflicts   52
    Challenges to environmental security   59
    UNCED and beyond   63
    Conclusion   64

5. Greening Bretton Woods   **65**
Jacob D Werksman
    Introduction   65
    Historical overview: incompatible structures and conflicting
      interests   67
    The World Bank and the environment   69
    UNCED: principles for development lending   74
    UNCED and Agenda 21: Institutional Reform   79
    A restructured bank   84

6. Greening the EEC Treaty   **85**
Marina Wheeler
    Introduction   85
    The constitutional position: building environment into the
      Treaty   85
    The practice: reconciling trade and environment concerns   89
    The GATT experience and restrictions on external Community
      trade   96
    Conclusion   99

7. The GATT and the Environment   **100**
James Cameron
    Introduction   100
    A selection of environmental challenges to free trade: in a
      legal context   106
    The elements of sustainable development and the failure of the
      GATT/MTO to accommodate them   116
    Conclusion   119

8. Environmental Law and Policy in Antarctica   **122**
Lee Kimball
    Introduction   122
    The quiet pursuit of science   124
    The resource issues heat up again   125
    Enter the environmentalist   128
    The 1980s: the decade of the environment   130
    Accountability   135
    Conclusion   138

9. Radioactive Waste Dumping at Sea   **140**
Remi Parmentier
    Introduction   140
    Current sea dumping regime: a historical overview   140
    The radioactive waste dumping controversy   142
    Future options   146
    The 1992 Paris convention compromise formula   150
    Amendment conference: toward the 'greening' of the London
      Convention   155

Conclusion   156

10. The Evolution of International Whaling   **159**
Greg Rose and Saundra Crane
Introduction   159
Environmental pressure on the IWC   166
Maintaining the moratorium   169
Revised management procedures   170
Small cetaceans   175
Threats to the IWC   178
Conclusion   179

11. Technology-based Approaches Versus Market-based
  Approaches   **182**
Dan Dudek, Richard Stewart and Jonathan Wiener
Introduction   182
Approaches to environmental policy   183
The need for comprehensive policy   190
Market-based approaches in action   192
Recommendations for environmental policy   206
Conclusion   209

Notes and references   *210*
Glossary   *245*
List of Treaties and Other International Acts   *248*
List of Cases   *252*
Index   *254*

FOREWORD

International responses to global environmental problems are usually founded in law. Law is important because it provides a legitimate basis for action by States and the international community as a whole and translates into legally binding international norms, the dominant international viewpoint on the basic issues of environmental protection. International environmental law represents the juridical articulation of our responses to the threats posed to the integrity of the biosphere and its processes by human activities. A greater recognition has thus been given to environmental law as a tool for promoting sustainable development.

The 1972 Stockholm Conference on the Human Environment was an important watershed in the global environmental awakening. It not only led to the emergence of important legal principles and concepts but also resulted in the establishment of the United Nations Environment Programme (UNEP), an organization which plays a key role in shaping the international legal response to global environmental challenges. Multilateral treaties, agreements and guidelines emerged in such diverse areas as the protection of the marine environment, the prevention of air and water pollution, the conservation of fauna and flora, and the regulation of trade in chemical and toxic substances. The adoption by the UNEP Governing Council in May 1982, of the Montevideo Programme for the Development and Periodic Review of Environmental Law has contributed to the successful negotiation and conclusion of important international legal instruments including those which address the challenges posed by the depletion of the stratospheric ozone layer, transboundary movements of hazardous wastes, climate change, and the loss of biological diversity.

The United Nations Conference on Environment and Development (UNCED) held in Rio de Janeiro in June 1992, has provided fundamental guidance for, and created a new dimension to, future international action in the field of environmental law. Indeed, Chapter 38 of Agenda 21 asks UNEP to take the leading role in international environmental law. In meeting these challenges UNEP will have to consolidate and enhance its legal programme and activities, such as promoting effective implementation of international legal instruments and assessing their adequacy, developing appropriate protocols and guidelines, and elaborating relevant rights and obligations of States. The objective is to reinforce the existing, and to develop new, legal regimes to respond to the imperative of sustainable development. The Programme for the Development and Periodic Review of Environmental Law, adopted by the 17th Governing Council of

UNEP held in May 1993, provides a basis for the relevant activities of the organization in the 1990s.

International environmental law is a rapidly evolving and expanding branch of international law. The development of international environmental law brings in many new and innovative ideas, concepts and principles which constitute an important and unique feature of this branch of international law. Concepts such as common concern of mankind, global partnership, common but differentiated responsibilities, anticipatory and preventive mechanisms, and incentives to compliance, have contributed to the elaboration and adoption of the most recent and significant international legal instruments. A balanced and precise legal formulation of these and other concepts and principles would be beneficial in accommodating the interests of common concern of mankind and those of individual sovereign States in promoting the partnership in the implementation of international legal obligations, in establishing an accurate differentiation of the responsibilities and obligations of States, and in ensuring the application of innovative mechanisms of compliance. All these will greatly contribute to the progressive development of international law.

Legal doctrine has always made important contributions to the understanding and development of law. Doctrinal exposition of emerging concepts and principles facilitates the further development of law. *Greening International Law* traces the evolution of this branch of international law from Stockholm to Rio and examines and reviews its nascent concepts and principles. The book also represents one of the first significant attempts at examining the notion and content of international law of sustainable development. The authors' preoccupation with sustainable development is reflected, in particular, in their analysis of such specific issues as the 'greening' of the Bretton Woods institutions, environment and trade, and environment and economics. *Greening International Law* is an important contribution to the development of international law doctrine and will be of great interest to environmental policy-makers, scholars, and students of international environmental law.

Elizabeth Dowdeswell
UNEP Executive Director
August 1993

ACKNOWLEDGEMENTS

This book is the first volume in a new FIELD/Earthscan series, *International Law and Sustainable Development*, which will address and define the main international legal issues associated with sustainable development and will, I hope, contribute to the progressive development of that new area of law. Many people have contributed in significant ways to the development of the book, which I think of as being among the early fruits of personal and professional contacts and experiences which have taken place over a period of several years. The idea for the book has four sources. David Kairy's edited collection of essays *The Politics of Law* (1981, Pantheon) which is, to my mind, a model of its kind. A lecture given by Phillip Allott in Room No 4 of the Old Schools, Cambridge University, in October 1982 on the subject of law and international society. An essay by Christopher Stone entitled *Should Trees Have Standing?*, which was written in 1972 but which I did not come across until the summer of 1988. And the *Blueprint* series edited by David Pearce and published by Earthscan, of which the first book, *Blueprint for a Green Economy*, is a model for making complex ideas accessible and from which we in the legal community have much to learn. Each has had a profound influence on my work and FIELD's work and this is reflected in the choice of authors and topics.

I am especially grateful to all the authors, for agreeing to submit chapters and for doing so under a tight deadline with such grace and, in the case of at least one, a keen sense of humour. The book has benefited from the support and input of all the administrative and legal staff and interns at FIELD. Louise Rands, my administrative assistant, carried out responsibilities in respect of this book with her usual (amazing) combination of diligence, humour, unflappability and single-mindedness; Kurt Skeete and Jennifer Hunt prepared the tables and index with admirable efficiency at short notice. Jonathan Sinclair Wilson and Jo O'Driscoll at Earthscan provided continuous encouragement in the face of missed deadlines, supplemented by long distance interest and support from the staff of the book's American publisher, The New Press. Lisa Sternlieb and Natalia Schiffrin made helpful editorial input at critical moments.

I would like to gratefully acknowledge the following for permission to reprint previously published material. Blackwell Publishers: Marc Pallemaerts' and Ileana Porras' chapters, in the *Review of European Community and International Environmental Law*, Volume 1, Issue 3, (1992). Reprinted by permission of Blackwell Publishers and the

Foundation for International Environmental Law and Development. *Columbia Journal of Environmental Law*: excerpts from the article 'Environmental Policy for Eastern Europe: Technology-Based Versus Market-Based Approaches' by Richard Stewart, Dan Dudek and Jonathan Wiener, 17 *Columbia Journal of Environmental Law* 1–52 (1992). Published by permission of the *Columbia Journal of Environmental Law* and the Trustees of Columbia University, New York. Also the *Journal of International Affairs*: Philippe Sands' article 'Enforcing Environmental Security: the Challenges of Compliance with International Obligations', in 46 *Columbia Journal of Environmental Affairs* 367–390 (1993). Published by permission of the *Journal of International Affairs* and the Trustees of Columbia University, New York.

LIST OF CONTRIBUTORS

James Cameron is a Barrister and Director of the Foundation for International Environmental Law and Development. He is also Visiting Lecturer at the School of Oriental and African Studies, London University, and a Life Member of Clare Hall, Cambridge University.

Saundra Crane is an ecologist and a lawyer, currently a Research Assistant at Pace University, USA.

Daniel J Dudek is a Senior Economist at the Environmental Defense Fund, Washington DC.

Lee A Kimball is a specialist in international law and institutions dealing with environment and development issues, oceans, and Antarctica. She has served most recently as Senior Associate on Institutions, World Resources Institute; Executive Director, Council on Ocean Law; and Director, Antarctica Programme, IIED – North America. She is a graduate of the John Hopkins School of Advanced International Studies and Stanford University.

Marc Pallemaerts is Lecturer in International Law at the Vrije Universiteit Brussels and Legal Adviser to the Flemish Regional Minister of Environment and Housing.

Remi Parmentier is a member of Greenpeace International's Political Division. He has represented Greenpeace at meetings of the London Convention, ISPRAD and the Paris Commission since 1983.

Ileana Porras is Professor at the University of Utah School of Law, and was Legal Adviser on the Costa Rican Delegation to UNCED and the Intergovernmental Negotiating Committee on a Framework Convention on Climate Change.

Gregory Rose is an Associate Lawyer at FIELD, London, where he is Director of the Marine Resources programme, and Editor-in-Chief of the Review of European Community and International Environmental Law.

Philippe Sands is a Barrister and Legal Director of FIELD. He is also Visiting Lecturer at the School of Oriental and African Studies, London University, and Visiting Professor at New York University Law School. He was Legal Adviser on the St Lucia delegation to UNCED and the

Intergovernmental Negotiating Committee on a Framework Convention on Climate Change.

Richard Stewart is Professor of Law at New York University School of Law. He formerly served as Assistant Attorney-General for Environment and Natural Resources at the US Department of Justice, and as Professor at Harvard Law School.

Christopher Stone is Roy P Crocker Professor of Law at the University of Southern California. His books include the environmental classic, *Should Trees Have Standing? – Toward Legal Rights for Natural Objects* and *Where the Law Ends – The Social Control of Corporate Behaviour*. His latest book, *The Gnat is Older Than the Man*, was published by Princeton University Press in 1993.

Jacob Werksman is a Staff Lawyer at FIELD, London, where he is Co-Director of the Climate Change and Energy programme. He is a member of the California Bar, and was an adviser to the Delegation of Vanuatu at the Intergovernmental Negotiating Committee on a Framework Convention on Climate Change.

Marina Wheeler is an Associate Lawyer with the law firm Stanbrook and Hooper in Brussels, where she specializes in environmental law, state aid and trade with Eastern Europe. She is an associate of FIELD and an editor of the Review of European Community and International Environmental Law.

Jonathan B Wiener is currently Senior Staff Economist/Attorney at the Council of Economic Advisers' Executive Office of the President; from January 1994 he will be Associate Professor at Duke University School of Law and School of Environment.

INTRODUCTION

The international community's recognition that environmental problems transcend national boundaries has resulted in the development of an important new field of public international law know as international environmental law. The realization that ad hoc, disparate and reactive policy responses by individual States or local communities will be wholly inadequate to address the growing environmental problems faced by the international community has been critical to the development of this new field. Environmental threats have grown exponentially with technological advances and thus environmental law – itself a relatively new field – has necessarily grown from a body of national rules, or perhaps rules agreed bilaterally between two States, to an area governed by a large and expanding body of regional and global treaties.

Over-exploitation of natural resources, loss of biological diversity, ozone depletion, climate change, acid rain, deforestation, desertification, air and marine pollution, toxic and other waste and a population explosion are but some of the interrelated threats facing the planet. At the United Nations Conference on Environment and Development, held in Rio de Janeiro in June 1992, poverty and international debt were added to the accepted list of the root causes of global environmental degradation, adding these to the areas considered to be proper concerns for international environmental law. Each of these areas requires international action involving States and other members of the international community at the bilateral, regional and global levels, which means a central role for international law and organization. Indeed, it is already clear that the combination of scientific evidence about what *needs* to be done, public pressure over what *should* be done, and political action as to what *can* be done, has already led to a virtual explosion of new international laws addressing environmental issues. They have gained increasingly wide acceptance, are increasingly broad in their scope and sophisticated in their approach, and penetrate issues which, until recently, were thought to lie beyond the range of environmental legislation and activism.

It is clear that the body of substantive, procedural and institutional rules adopted internationally to protect the environment continues to increase in size and scope and shows every sign of growing ever more intrusively into 'non-environmental' areas of human activity. Indeed, it is now virtually impossible to find any area of activity which is not in some way subject to international environmental regulation. Whereas international environmental law used to be a subject concerned exclusively with the protection of flora and fauna, it developed to address pollution of rivers and seas, industrial emissions into the atmosphere, and the management and disposal of waste. Environmental law now encompasses the development of new biotechnologies, places limits on international trade, development assistance, and intellectual property rights, and even, in the case of a European Community Directive, places limits on free expression (advertising) rights by prohibiting television advertisements which 'encourage behaviour which is prejudicial to the protection of the environment' (EEC Council Directive 89/552/EEC, Article 12(e) on broadcasting activities).

The 'greening' of international law and organizations raises important new challenges for the international community. Phillip Allott has described the principle challenge with admirable clarity:

> Given that the land and the sea and the air spaces of planet Earth are shared, and are not naturally distributed among the States of the world, and given that world-transforming activities, especially economic activities, can have effects, directly or cumulatively, on large parts of the world environment, how can international law reconcile the inherent and fundamental interdependence of the world environment? How could legal control of activities adversely affecting the world environment be instituted, given that such activities may be fundamental to the economies of particular States?[1]

The authors of the 11 chapters of this book identify and explore some, but by no means all, of the critical issues in respect of which international law and its institutions have been called upon to respond to environmental challenges. Without exception each author has played a central role in the development of international environmental law over the past decade, whether as a scholar, legal adviser to government or environmental organization, or environmental activist. *Greening International Law* therefore reflects a range of political perspectives, ideologies and methodologies. Although this book does not seek to harmonize the approach to international regulation, or to present a single, fully developed approach to the green challenges facing international law, it will be clear from each of the contributions that the authors are in broad agreement about the need for some very fundamental changes to the structure and organization of the international legal order. These changes relate to the law-making process, to the type of rules adopted, and to their techniques for implementation.

That said, each author is responsible for the content of her or his selection. Each chapter tells its own tale, and must be considered in the context of the particular social, economic, political and legal contexts in which it is situated, and in respect of which international legal rules have, or have not emerged. Moreover, since this area of international law is in a state of constant flux each chapter should still be understood as reflecting the early stages of the internationalization of environmental law; while many of the rules have now been established, the larger questions related to meeting the economic costs, implementation and compliance are outstanding.

The 11 chapters of this book identify the underlying issues and challenges which the environment poses for the international legal order. In the Foreword, the Executive Director of the United Nations Environment Programme, Elizabeth Dowdeswell, assesses the critical role of international law in the protection of the environment and the leading place which UNEP has in the further development of international environmental law. The chapters break down, very roughly, into the following divisions: Chapters 1 and 2 address the development of general principles and obligations; Chapters 3 and 4 are concerned with institutional change; Chapters 5, 6 and 7 explore the extent to which economic law and organizations have been transformed by environmental concerns and requirements; Chapters 8, 9 and 10 each take a case study concerning a region, a source of pollution, and a biological resource; and Chapter 11 examines the failings at the national level of traditional approaches to environmental regulation and proposes new approaches. This is not a textbook and is not intended to be comprehensive: the fact that important issues of environmental concern (for instance atmosphere, biodiversity and waste) have not been addressed should not be interpreted as diminishing their importance. The contents of the book and each of the chapters reflect personal concerns and expertise, the idea being to draw out principles and conclusions which might be relevant, in a broad sense, to the entire range of international legal issues addressing environmental matters.

In Chapters 1 and 2 Marc Pallemaerts and Ileana Porras consider some of the themes underlying the emergence of new principles of international environmental law, and consider whether the various instruments adopted at UNCED – including in particular the Rio Declaration on Environment and Development – can be considered to be a positive contribution to the further development of international environmental law or, rather, a step back. Underlying the Rio Declaration and all legal instruments in this field are two fundamental tensions: that which exists between environmental objectives and developmental objectives, and that which exists between the impulse to sovereignty and the impulse towards recognizing that resources are shared and part of the global good. Time will tell whether these are fundamental contradictions rather than tensions. With respect to the first of these two tensions, Pallemaerts takes the view that Rio led to a 'skilfully masked step backwards', subordinating the dictates of each State's environmental policy obligations 'to the dictates of its economic policy' (pp 5–6) and representing, as reflected in Principle 1 of the Rio Declaration, 'a triumph of unrestrained anthropocentricity' (p 12). Herein lies the critical challenge for those concerned with ensuring that the international legal order is reformed to assure, even require, the protection of natural resources: is it possible to make incremental changes in the existing structures and arrangements of the international legal order and its institutions to achieve environmental protection, or is the existing international legal order fundamentally and inherently inimical to environmental protection requiring wholesale rejection and re-invention? Ileana Porras's view is marginally more optimistic about the possibilities for change which were thrown up by UNCED, although she clearly believes that UNCED did not produce the hoped-for new globalism or the abandonment of self-interest and short-termism. For Porras, UNCED redefined the relationship between environment and development by suggesting in Principles 3 and 4 of the Rio Declaration, that 'development may sometimes take precedence over environment' (p 22), even though the environment was the dominant organizing motif at Rio.

Unlike Pallemaerts, Porras concludes that those developing countries which once clung to such notions may, ironically, influence the creation of the new globalism which:

> seeks to transform the accepted relationship between a State and its natural resources from one of ownership, in which the State is free to exploit its resources in accordance with its national policies and priorities, into one of trusteeship, where the State would be required to consider the interests of, and probably consult with, the international community before taking any action affecting the resource (p 31).

These concerns with sovereignty go to the very heart of the existing international legal order, and are further explored in Chapters 3 and 4 by Christopher Stone and Philippe Sands. In both chapters the authors turn their attention more directly to the legal and political issues which are raised by current efforts to rethink law-making and law-enforcement at the international level. Underlying both chapters is the recognition that it will not be enough for States simply to adopt international standards and principles. A further shedding of sovereignty will be required to ensure that these international obligations are acted upon domestically and internationally and enforced where there is a failure to comply.

Acceptable and effective methods for the settlement of disputes need to be established. Christopher Stone proposes two answers to address international environmental crises: a system of Global Guardianship and a Global Commons Trust Fund as foundations for an appreciable 'greening of international law'. Underlying both his proposals are maps and boundaries for diplomats which divide the world into two sorts of regions: 'those that fall under *territorial sovereignty* and those that lie outside the political reach of any nation State – the *global commons*', including the atmosphere, outer space and the high seas; it is the simple fact that these degraded areas lie outside anyone's exclusive jurisdiction, and that only some of these areas are (partially and feebly) protected by international law, which presents 'serious obstacles to securing legal and political relief' (pp 35, 37, 39). In his answer to his own question 'What is to be done?', Stone proposes a system of guardians as legal representatives for the natural environment ('an international public service for an international public good') with three tasks: to monitor, to exercise legislative functions, and to act as intervenor-counsel in disputes. With respect to each function he invokes support from precedents found in national legal systems, and this part of his chapter draws upon and internationalizes his classic writing in the seminal piece *Should Trees Have Standing? – Towards Legal Rights for Natural Objects.*[2]

The second limb of Stone's proposal, a Global Commons Trust Fund, is designed to meet some of the costs associated with protecting the global environment including, in particular, the costs of assuring the participation of developing countries in international efforts. There is now broad accept-ance of the need for an appropriate mechanism to ensure that the costs of applying international environmental regulations can be paid for, particu-larly in the developing world, and that economic incentives to influence the behaviour of States and other international persons need to be internation-alized. Both these themes are further developed by Jake Werksman in Chapter 5 and by Dan Dudek, Richard Stewart and Jonathan Wiener in Chapter 11.

Philippe Sands looks beyond the adoption of principles and standards of international environmental law to the question of compliance: how can we ensure that international legal obligations are implemented and translated into actions, principally at the national level? Who has the right to enforce international environmental obligations and what techniques are available to adjudicate upon the myriad of disputes which are bound to occur with increasing frequency? Like the authors of the earlier chapters discussing the Rio Convention, he concludes that UNCED did not fulfil the task set for it by the General Assembly in 1990, namely to recommend measures to assist in the prevention and settlement of environmental disputes.

Nevertheless, the widespread recognition of the need for change which emerged at UNCED, but was not fully acted upon, has been accompanied by tangible developments which go to the core of the traditional legal order. Agreement on the need to provide financial and technical assistance to developing States will 'internationalize the domestic implementation of international environmental obligations' (p 64); international organiza-tions and non-governmental actors are increasingly being granted informal and formal roles in the international enforcement process; and recognition of the need for special adjudication processes to respond to the particular characteristics of environmental disputes is leading to change. This last point is illustrated by the decision taken by the International Court of Justice in July 1993 to establish a Chamber for Environmental Disputes, taking account of the fact that two of the Court's 11 cases have important implica-tions for international law on matters relating to the environment (Ceraftin Phosphate Lands in Nauru (*Nauru* v *Australia*), and Gabcikovo-Nagymaros Project (*Hungary* v *Slovakia*)), and in view of 'the developments in the field of environmental law and protection which have taken place in the last few years'.[3]

Chapters 5, 6 and 7 examine whether, and to what extent, the international legal and institutional arrangements established in the 1940s and 1950s to address and facilitate international economic cooperation (development lending and free trade) have integrated environmental considerations. The evidence offered by the three authors suggests that although environmental reform has begun to take place, there is still a long way to go. From Jake Werksman's perspective the Global Environment Facility – jointly managed by the World Bank, UNEP and UNDP – promises to become 'the crucible for forging the first operational policies for sustainable development, linking the concepts of environment and development, and the institutions of the UN and the Bretton Woods systems' (p 66).

He focuses on the critical issue that has constantly dogged the GEF; the question of governance, illustrating both that the greening of international law must also address reform of process and that, ultimately, process cannot be divorced from substance. This emerges also from his consideration of the relationship between the UN and the World Bank and the World Bank's environmental protection policies to date. While noting the positive changes which have occurred, he concludes that policies have not yet adequately transformed actual practise, and identifies the principle condition for future success and greater legitimacy as *accountability*: empowerment of stakeholders, public participation in decision-making, access to information and the right of challenge before an independent adjudicative authority. While sovereignty limits the prospects for these principles, Werksman departs from the view expressed by Pallemaerts and Porras and sees the efforts of UNCED to strike a balance between sovereign right and global responsibility as 'qualifying the concept of sovereignty in several significant ways', including through the imposition of green conditions on development lending (pp 70, 71, 75).

In Chapter 6 Marina Wheeler traces the evolution of the greening of the EEC Treaty. Originally designed to achieve free movement of goods, persons, services and capital among Member States, and without any reference to environmental protection in the original Treaty, subsequent practise by the Community and its Member States adopted a plethora of environmental legislation in the 1970s and 1980s. This was justified by the desire to address pollution which did not respect national boundaries, to improve living and working conditions, and to remove barriers to trade imposed by differences in national environmental standards.

What stands out from this chapter is the impact of incrementalism, although questions still remain as to how green the Community can be when faced with recession and a backlash against the costs of environmental regulation. Marina Wheeler believes that building on earlier judicial and legislative measures, the Maastricht Treaty should allow the environment to 'rise a notch in the hierarchy of Community aims' by replacing the original primary objective of the EEC (promoting economic growth) with the aim of achieving 'sustainable . . . growth respecting the environment', and giving States 'a freer reign to enact environmental measures to achieve whatever levels of protection they deem fit' (p 96). This view is not, however, shared by all the authors, and Marc Pallemaerts questions whether this constitutes real progress (p 16). Chapter 6 also illustrates the important role which courts play in giving effect to environmental objectives in the legal order, and even primacy over economic objectives, as evidenced by the decisions of the European Court of Justice in the *Danish Bottles* and *Wallonian Waste* cases. The role of law and the courts cuts both ways, however. Marina Wheeler considers that these judgements of the Court reflected a prevailing political mood and illustrated the reality in the Community order that 'legal analysis and the rule of law has its limits' (p 99), which suggests that the greening of the EEC Treaty may require a suspension of legalism and the interjection of pure political process.

To the extent that a greening of the EEC as a regional free trade area has occurred, the outlook seems markedly different for its global parent, the General Agreement on Tariffs and Trade (GATT), for which the EEC could yet provide a model. In Chapter 7 James Cameron considers whether free(er) trade, environmental protection and sustainable development can be mutually supportive, and the evolution of the GATT regime in the context of environmental change. His conclusion is not encouraging, at least for those who speak the language of environmental law. For trade lawyers, on the other hand, who see environmental regulation as '*prima facie* barriers to trade', the proper place of environmental considerations in the trade debate is clearly on the margins, despite the heroic efforts of many governments and commentators to provide assurance that the GATT is not anti-environmental. Clearly there is much still to change if international trade and environment policies are to become mutually supportive, as required by the international community in its various declarations at UNCED (pp 101–2). The GATT itself will also clearly require transformation, if not in the Uruguay Round then in the next Green Round. Cameron argues for wholesale reform: institutional change; the greater use of CITES-type trade restrictions to protect the global commons; change to the substantive law of the GATT, as set out in Articles XX(b) and (g) which led to the infamous decision in the *Yellowfin Tuna* case; greater access to information; and reliance on the precautionary principle. He bemoans the failure of the Uruguay Round, and in particular the proposed new Multilateral Trade Organization, for not having integrated any formal commitment to sustainable development. Cameron cites as examples in which economic organizations have instituted formal changes to their constitutional instruments the EEC and the European Bank for Reconstruction and Development, which is widely considered to have a better record on integrating environmental concerns than its Bretton Woods partners.

Chapters 8, 9 and 10 deal with three specific case studies to examine how international legal arrangements can be transformed by greening over time. Lee Kimball, Remi Parmentier and Gregory Rose examine particular issues, including a region (the Antarctic), a source of pollution (radioactive waste), and a biological species (whales), to explore the extent to which environmental considerations influenced human behaviour through international legal and institutional process. Lee Kimball traces the evolution of environmental protection in the Antarctic from the original 1959 Treaty, via the rejected 1988 Convention – which would have allowed mineral activities subject to stringent environmental regulations – to the superseding 1991 Protocol which bans all commercial and mineral activity over a 50-year period. The Antarctic experience describes, as Lee Kimball herself indicates, a 'microcosm for the evolution of environmental law and policy' at the international level, particularly in relation to institutional change; participation rights of members of the international community in the law-making process; and the adoption of new principles. (The latter include the precautionary approach in the 1988 CRAMRA, which reversed the traditional burden of proof governing the decision to permit human activities by prohibiting minerals exploration and development 'unless it was authorized by consensus and in accordance with requirements for environmental assessment and other safeguards' (pp 132, 138)). Lee Kimball's piece paints a compelling picture of the impact of incremental legal change on international consciousness which culminated in the most draconian act of international environmental legislation yet adopted. Her chapter also describes the power of the environmental movement, the way in which it made use of the international legal process by using international legal arguments in a sophisticated politico-legal strategy which eventually succeeded in killing off the 1988 Convention (which had been negotiated over a six-year period) and replacing it with a new one. Without doubt the Antarctic region stands out as having been greened by international law over a period of three decades in a manner unparalleled elsewhere.

In Chapter 9 Remi Parmentier describes in detail another story which has pitted nation against nation in a particularly acrimonious battle but remains inconclusively subject to imminent denouement: the controversy over radioactive waste dumping under the 1972 London Convention which led to the adoption of a moratorium despite the opposition of powerful nuclear countries, including the United States, the United Kingdom and France. Like the previous chapter, the essay is a lesson in incrementalism and suggests some of the strategies which can be deployed by small and relatively weak countries against more powerful opposition in their efforts to achieve the greening of international legal arrangements. In identifying the seven options available to the international community by addressing this matter in the future (p 146), Parmentier points to the broader issues facing the international community on a range of other subjects, identifies possible regulatory strategies, and indicates the interconnectedness of decision-making under the 1972 London Convention with developments in other fora, such as UNCED. In this regard, it is noteworthy that Agenda 21, which is not a legally binding instrument, nevertheless contains provisions which may be of persuasive authority in influencing legal development.

In Chapter 10 Gregory Rose describes how the International Whaling Commission (IWC) was transformed from a whalers' club into the organization which in 1982 established a moratorium on commercial whaling. He also explains how the IWC is now faced with a variety of claims for the resumption of such whaling as well as the challenges posed to the moratorium by scientific, pirate and aboriginal whaling. The transformation has resulted in the departure of some whaling States from the organization and the creation, in 1992, of a new organization (the North Atlantic Marine Mammal Conservation Organization) whose members produce more whale products than they consume. Gregory Rose's chapter notes that, perhaps remarkably, 'the rules set by the IWC have usually been observed rather than breached', but he concludes with the view that the Convention has not been formally greened, that the instrument remains a fishing rather than a conservation convention, and that it is in urgent need of 'more modern and efficient legal machinery than the 1946 Convention' (pp 179–81).

To conclude, in Chapter 11 Dan Dudek, Richard Stewart, and Jonathan Wiener examine some of the possible new approaches to international regulation based on the national experience of the US. They contrast the existing approach (which they describe as 'technology-based, command-and-control (CAC) techniques that select a technology for industry to install) with the market-based approaches that hope to create economic incentives for industry to reduce the harm to the environment which, in their view, should supplement or supplant the existing approach (p 182). They consider the relative successes and failures of US environmental policy over the past two decades, by reference to air pollution (including transboundary atmospheric pollution), water resources, management of waste, information disclosure, land use and fisheries. In the face of the rather basic advances made in international environmental law in limiting global pollution, the international community is also now looking to alternatives to traditional regulatory approaches, whilst recognising that '[l]egal instruments will not, by themselves, necessarily produce environmental quality – there will also need to be sufficient political will to ensure environmental compliance' (p 206). Their suggestion met with a degree of support at UNCED, and is reflected in Principle 16 of the Rio Declaration, which provides that national authorities 'should endeavour to promote the internalization of environmental costs and the use of economic instruments', although the language indicates that there is still some way to go before this approach meets with broad approval. Additionally, the authors put forward 15 recommendations for environmental policy: these are clearly capable of guiding legal and institutional action at the global, regional, sub-regional, national and local levels.

Although the 11 chapters represent individual views, it is nevertheless possible to discern certain themes which are common to each and which indicate some of the benchmarks which might be taken into account in assessing the extent to which international law has been greened. Pointers for international legal action to address environmental concerns and requirements at the regional and global level are also raised in several chapters. In particular, the contributors make it abundantly clear that the process of legal reform will need to address issues of substance, of procedure and of institutional structure. The interdependence of these aspects of the legal order emerged at UNCED and is reflected, to varying degrees, in each of the chapters, together with the following critical issues.

First, how can international law integrate issues of environment and development? It is now accepted that economic development must take into account and reflect environmental requirements, while environmental concerns must take into account the development needs of all members of the international community. But how is this to be translated into binding, enforceable commitments at the global and grass-roots levels? On what basis should emission rights of carbon dioxide and other greenhouse gases be allocated to developed and developing countries? Which body (national or international), for example, is to determine whether a road being built through a wood situated in a London suburb satisfies international environmental impact requirements? These questions raise legal issues which vividly illustrate the internationalization of environmental decision-making, and suggest that the limits to environmental law-making are yet to be reached. As environmental concerns penetrate the heartland of international economic policy in its efforts to place limits on economic decision-making – including the GATT and the World Bank – new pressures will surely be unleashed calling for institutional reform, the development and application of new procedures (for example environmental impact assessment and access to environmental information) and the integration of principles of economic and social justice.

Second, how can the substantive obligations imposed by international legal obligations be more effectively implemented? Addressing this concern will require new approaches to international legal regulation, including the greater use of incentives and sanctions, as well as the necessary international procedures to monitor, administrate and enforce. Needless to say, there will be strong resistance by those who would consider that this amounts to a radical attack on sovereignty.

Third, what constitutional and administrative reforms are needed to the relevant international organizations, including both those established in the period after the Second World War and those created by international environmental agreements? It is clear to all involved in this field that we now find ourselves with a fragmented institutional structure which is ill-equipped to meet future needs. Although UNCED made a start, the 50th anniversary of the United Nations in 1995 marks an important opportunity to integrate environmental needs fully into the operations of that organization and its Specialized Agencies. The Agencies were established to address issues of a political, economic, social or cultural nature and now find themselves faced with environmental challenges which they were not designed to address. This process of international constitutional reform should also allow an opportunity to rationalize the activities of organizations established by environmental agreements.

Fourth, how should the principles of international environmental law be implemented and balanced against competing interests? New and emerging principles of international environmental law are challenging accepted practises and the tenets of the international legal order. How can the obligation not to cause damage to the environment in areas beyond national jurisdiction be squared with sovereignty over a State's natural resources? How far should the precautionary principle go in requiring States to act to prevent environmental harm where no scientific consensus exists as to the likelihood of that harm? Under what circumstance should the polluter not be required to pay? And how far should the developing States go in requiring the industrialized countries to meet their commitments pursuant to the principle of 'common but differentiated responsibility'? These and other questions address issues which lie at the heart of the existing legal order and require legal responses at the procedural, substantive and institutional level.

Fifth, how can the international community ensure the effective participation of all States in relevant legal processes (including law-making, implementation and enforcement), and what legal measures need to be taken to formalize the role of non-State actors in the international legal order? States can no longer claim to be the sole holders of the right to participate in the international legal order and its processes, having been joined by a range of new actors, including international organizations and non-governmental actors. The international legal order will need to accommodate new actors' participation in the process of law-making, monitoring and enforcement, perhaps on the basis of the model established by the European Community.

Sixth, what procedural and institutional changes should be set in motion to allow the law-making process (principally treaties and acts of international organizations) to be able to respond more promptly and effectively to environmental challenges by establishing binding standards in the face of scientific evidence which often requires immediate and wide-ranging action?

These six issues transcend the 11 chapters of the book, as they did the negotiating process prior to and at UNCED and the negotiation of the related treaties, the Climate Change and Biodiversity Conventions. They suggest that the greening of international law will require, over the long term, fundamental changes to the rules of international law, to international institutions and to the law-making and enforcement process. The institution of legal control of activities adversely affecting the world environment is still in its early stages; the fact that these activities are fundamental to the economies of particular States will raise powerful limits to change. These chapters illustrate that change is under way and that after two decades of frenzied environmental rule-making, attention is now switching to questions of compliance including implementation, enforcement and dispute settlement. Although these new international rules have gone some way towards addressing the early campaigns of environmental groups, much remains to be done in adopting and implementing environmental protection standards.

Philippe Sands
London
2 August 1993

1 INTERNATIONAL ENVIRONMENTAL LAW FROM STOCKHOLM TO RIO: BACK TO THE FUTURE?

Marc Pallemaerts

UNCED AND THE PROGRESSIVE DEVELOPMENT OF LAW

One of the stated aims of the United Nations Conference on Environment and Development (UNCED) was to 'promot[e] the further development of international environmental law', and, more specifically, to 'examin[e] the feasibility of elaborating general rights and obligations of States . . . in the field of the environment'.[1] The purpose of this chapter is to assess to what extent the various instruments adopted by the Rio Conference can be considered a positive contribution to the 'further development of international environmental law', and whether the Conference has indeed succeeded in strengthening the existing body of conventional international environmental law by 'elaborating general rights and obligations of States'.

The Rio Declaration on Environment and Development is the one 'product' of UNCED designed precisely to embody rules and principles of a general and universal nature to govern the future conduct and cooperation of States, and forms the focus of this study. Its provisions are analysed against the background of those of two earlier declaratory instruments of a universal nature, elaborated within the institutional framework of the UN: the Stockholm Declaration, adopted by the UN Conference on the Human Environment (UNCHE) in June 1972, and the World Charter for Nature, adopted by the UN General Assembly (UNGA) in October 1982. Analysis of the Rio Declaration necessarily entails also a consideration of the notion of 'sustainable development' which forms the basis and also pervades all the other instruments adopted by UNCED, namely the Convention on Climate Change, Convention on Biological Diversity, Agenda 21 and the Statement of Principles on Forests.

This study raises interesting questions as to how 'progressive' the development of international environmental law really is – to use a term from the UN Charter, which is both a prescription for action and a statement of faith in the 'progress' of the rule of law in the international community.

THE NEVER-ENDING QUEST FOR
GENERAL PRINCIPLES

It is obvious from their drafting history, form and content that the Stockholm Declaration, World Charter for Nature and Rio Declaration each belong to the realm of soft law.

The Stockholm Declaration

Although Maurice Strong – at that time Secretary-General of the UNCHE – had initially recommended to the UNCHE Preparatory Committee that the Stockholm Conference should adopt a declaration laying down 'rights and obligations of citizens and governments with regard to the preservation and improvement of the human environment',[2] it became clear during the drafting process that many governments were hostile to his ideas as to the scope and legal status of the proposed declaration.[3] While some governments were willing to contemplate a declaration 'embodying general principles elaborating the rights and duties of States with respect to the environment', they were not prepared to go as far as to accept the elaboration of a legally binding instrument.[4] They pointed out that 'by its very nature, the Declaration should not formulate legally binding provisions, in particular as regards relations between States and individuals, or as between the latter'.

The Stockholm Conference eventually opted for a non-binding declaration of principles, reflecting commitments of a political and moral, rather than legal, nature; a document 'embodying the aspirations of the world's people for a better environment',[5] rather than imposing specific obligations on governments in order to fulfil those aspirations. Yet, notwithstanding its non-binding character, the Stockholm Declaration[6] is generally regarded as the foundation of modern international environmental law. Despite its ambiguities, the Declaration eventually acquired not only moral and political value, but some of the principles laid down in it are now considered as part and parcel of general international law and as binding on governments, independent of their specific consent. In particular, Principle 21 has evolved into hard law.[7]

Moreover, the Stockholm Declaration has served as a basis for the subsequent development of international environmental law in the form of numerous bilateral and multilateral conventions and other legally binding instruments. Numerous principles and concepts which were first articulated in the Stockholm Declaration were subsequently incorporated not only in the preambles of international environmental treaties, but also in certain binding provisions, and even in the constitutions or other provisions of domestic law of various States.

World Charter for Nature

The need for a legal instrument of a universal nature setting forth, in general terms, the environmental rights and obligations of States under international law not only *inter se* but also in relation to individuals, and to future generations, or even to other species and the planet itself, is a long-standing subject of scholarly debate.

From time to time, this debate has some impact outside academic circles and 'spills over' in the real world of diplomacy and international law-making. But it hardly ever seems to leave more than a few ephemeral ripples on the surface.

As the Stockholm Declaration fell short of the expectations of environmentalists and legal scholars, they vowed to try again. The second attempt to draw up a world environmental charter was spearheaded by the World Conservation Union (IUCN), which convinced Zaire to put the matter on the agenda of the UNGA. At the Session of a Special Character of the UN Environment Programme (UNEP) Governing Council, held in Nairobi in May 1982 to mark the tenth anniversary of the Stockholm Conference, President Mobutu of Zaire announced that 'his' initiative was nearing adoption by the UNGA and harangued the governments assembled in Nairobi in the following terms:

> The days of the 'law of the jungle' are over. All responsible people on earth have a duty to defend the global heritage, as well as the space in which they live, against the insatiable vultures who will not hesitate to destroy and pollute for personal profit.[8]

The World Charter for Nature,[9] which was adopted by the UNGA a few months after the UNEP Special Session, constitutes another laudable effort to formulate general principles of conduct for States and individuals, but its scope is limited to the conservation and use of living natural resources, and it does not purport to have any greater legal effect than the Stockholm Declaration. Though the UNGA urged that 'the principles set forth in the ... Charter shall be reflected in the law and practice of each State, as well as at the international level', the various provisions of the Charter put as much emphasis on the duties of individuals as on those of governments who fail to clearly identify their addressees and specify their respective responsibilities.

The Brundtland Report

A few years later, the World Commission on Environment and Development (WCED) added its voice to that of earlier advocates of a universal legal instrument and proposed 'to consolidate and extend relevant legal principles in a new charter to guide State behaviour in the transition to sustainable development.'[10] At present, international enviromental law is scattered throughout numerous conventions and other instruments, all of which are limited in scope and only deal with ecological issues in a sectoral, piecemeal fashion.[11] The WCED was clearly aware of the need to strengthen this shoddy edifice by further elaborating and affirming a number of general legal principles in the field of environmental protection, which would constitute the keystone of the system of international environmental law.

The WCED, therefore, recommended that the UNGA 'commit itself' to the elaboration of a universal declaration and, ultimately, a global convention on environmental protection and sustainable development.[12] To this end, the WCED had mandated a group of eminent experts on environmental law to draft a set of legal principles 'which ought to be in place now or before the year 2000' for submission to the UNGA.[13] Unfortunately these principles, although very carefully and skilfully drafted by eminent experts from North and South, were never seriously considered by the UNGA, nor by the Preparatory Committee of UNCED, let alone by the Rio Conference itself.

The Rio Declaration

The very wording of UNCED's mandate, as laid down by the UNGA in Resolution 44/228, already indicated that this third attempt to elaborate 'general rights and obligations of States', was doomed to fail, since the UNGA only half-heartedly agreed to have UNCED 'examine the feasibility' of such an exercise.

What then is the legal significance of the Rio Declaration? Has any progress been made since the Stockholm Declaration and the World Charter for Nature in codifying general rights and obligations of States with respect to the protection of the global environment? Does the Rio Declaration, however 'soft' it may be, contain any principles which could evolve into hard law? The Rio Declaration[14] emerged from the last UNCED Preparatory Committee meeting in New York under the heading 'principles relative to general rights and obligations',[15] and was adopted unchanged by the Rio Conference. It is a far cry from the original ambition of the proponents of an 'Earth Charter', who hoped that UNCED would adopt a declaratory instrument whose moral and political authority would be equivalent to that of the Universal Declaration of Human Rights. [16]

The Preamble of the Rio Declaration solemnly 'reaffirms' the Stockholm Declaration and asserts that the Rio Declaration is 'seeking to build upon it'. However, the operative provisions in fact proceed to unravel the Stockholm Declaration, which it ironically was pretending to reaffirm. The UNCED Secretariat's concern 'to avoid a situation where countries will re-argue documents like the Stockholm Declaration or . . . the World Charter for

Nature' and 'not to go behind the baseline of those documents'[17] obviously fell on deaf ears.

SOVEREIGNTY VERSUS RESPONSIBILITY

The fundamental principle of State responsibility for transboundary environmental harm – enshrined in Principle 21 of the Stockholm Declaration – is regarded by most scholars as part of customary international law.[18] Although worded in a general, even vague way, Principle 21 is clearly formulated as a legal principle which could be interpreted and applied in concrete situations through international mechanisms for dispute settlement. It describes limits to national sovereignty, and thus imposes limits on the pursuit, by States, of economic growth and development. In striking a balance between national sovereignty and environmental responsibility, Principle 21 of the Stockholm Declaration first affirms that:

> States have ... the sovereign right to exploit their own resources pursuant to their own environmental policies,

but this principle of sovereignty is juxtaposed with and balanced against the principle of responsibility. The latter principle imposes on States:

> the responsibility to ensure that activities within their jurisdiction or control do not cause damage to the environment of other States or of areas beyond the limits of national jurisdiction.[19]

What has become of this principle of responsibility in the Rio Declaration? The fact that a clause, virtually identical to Stockholm Principle 21, can be found in Principle 2 of the Rio Declaration, appearing at the beginning of the Declaration and not in the 21st place, gives cause for optimism, but a closer reading of Principle 2 reveals a skilfully masked step backwards. The Rio text is not identical to the one adopted in Stockholm: the Rio version of the principle of responsibility stipulates that:

> States have ... the sovereign right to exploit their own resources pursuant to their own environmental *and developmental* policies (emphasis added),

an addition of two words which is anything but innocent. The stronger emphasis on development in this new version upsets the delicate balance struck in Stockholm between the sovereign use of natural resources and the duty of care for the environment.

In the Stockholm Declaration, the sovereign right of States to exploit their natural resources was affirmed in the context of their national environmental policies, giving 'a more ecological colour' to the principle of sovereignty over natural resources (which was originally established in a primarily economic context).[20] This environmental colour is now neutralized by the parallel stress on national development policies. After Rio, a State's responsibility in the exercise of its sovereign right to exploit its natural resources will no longer be measured first and foremost in terms of its environmental policy obligations, which are now explicitly subordinated to the dictates of its economic development policy.

The Climate Change Convention

The real significance of this downgrading of environmental concerns in the legal discourse appears upon reading the penultimate draft of the Framework Convention on Climate Change, submitted to the last session of that Convention's Intergovernmental Negotiating Committee. In the Preamble of the draft one finds language spelling out the revisionist re-interpretation of the principle of environmental responsibility of States in its crudest version. Indeed the preambular paragraph which recalls Principle 21 and contains a bracketed clause adding that 'accordingly . . . environmental considerations should not be used as a pretext for interference in the internal affairs of developing countries'.[21] This disconcertingly frank and cynical re-interpretation of Stockholm Principle 21, proposed by India and China, shows little concern for preserving even the appearance of logical consistency and formal legal reasoning. Inferring a right to ecological non-interference from the principle of responsibility of States for transfrontier ecological damage is, in fact, the negation of the very essence of that principle, which logically and necessarily implies the existence of certain limits to national sovereignty.

Although we may rejoice that this preambular clause was not included in the final text of the Climate Change Convention, the paragraphs which replaced it achieve the same result, albeit in a more subtle way. In its final, adopted version the Preamble no longer explicitly refers to Principle 21 of the Stockholm Declaration, but only to the 'pertinent provisions' of that Declaration. (Some States obviously do not consider Principle 21 to be all that 'pertinent' to the issue of global warming.) The Preamble reproduces verbatim the principle of responsibility as it appears in Principle 2 of the Rio Declaration.

Thus, the Framework Convention on Climate Change sanctions the silent demise of the principle of responsibility in its 'classical', Stockholm version. To complete this revisionist exercise, the following preambular clause of the Convention yet again:

reaffirm[s] the principle of the sovereignty of States in international cooperation to address climate change.[22]

The precedence of national economic development policies over national and international measures to check climate change is also stressed in several operative provisions of the Convention, which provide, *inter alia*, that such measures 'should be integrated with national development programmes' (Article 3(4)), and should 'tak[e] into account . . . the need to maintain strong and sustainable economic growth' (Article 4(2)(a)).

Convention on Biological Diversity

The Convention on Biological Diversity, at Article 3, reproduces verbatim the terms of Principle 21 of the Stockholm Declaration, without the added reference to 'developmental policies' found in Principle 2 of the Rio Declaration. However, this is not matched by the other substantive provisions, which fail to impose precise and unconditional obligations on contracting parties to ensure their national policies affecting biological diversity do not adversely affect the environment beyond the limits of their national juridisdiction. Almost every single provision of the Biological Diversity Convention specifying the obligations of contracting parties is qualified by the phrase 'as far as possible and as appropriate' or similar language.

It is paradoxical that while the applicability of Stockholm Principle 21 to the conservation of biological diversity is by no means as direct and obvious as to the protection of the world's climate through the reduction of emissions of greenhouse gases, this principle is incorporated in an international legal instrument on biodiversity instead of one on climate change! The extent to which contracting parties to the Convention on Biological Diversity could be considered to be bound by the principle of responsibility, as stated in Article 3 outside the ambit of the Convention, is likely to be much debated.

Statement of Principles on Forests

The highly controversial 'non-legally binding authoritative statement of principles for a global consensus on the management, conservation and sustainable development of all types of forest', deals with the principle of State responsibility in a curious and questionable way. Paragraph 1(a) of that document reiterates Principle 21 in its original Stockholm version, but places it between inverted commas, as if to stress that it constitutes an extraneous element. A remnant of another age, Principle 21 does seem somewhat out of place in this new document, which places heavy emphasis on the sovereignty of States with respect to the use and abuse of their forest resources.

Indeed, it is difficult to understand how paragraph 1(a) can ever be compatible with paragraph 2(a), which affirms that:

> States have the sovereign and inalienable right to utilize, manage and develop their forests in accordance with their development needs and level of socio-economic development and on the basis of national policies consistent with sustainable development and legislation.

Paragraph 2(a) suggests that national forest policies are not subject to any constraints deriving from international law.

Liability and Compensation

As UNCED has qualified and weakened the principle of State responsibility for transboundary environmental harm, there can be little doubt that it has failed completely to meet the recommendation of Stockholm Principle 22 to:

> develop further the *international* law regarding liability and compensation for the victims of pollution and other environmental damage caused by activities within the jurisdiction or control of such States to areas beyond their jurisdiction (emphasis added).

Against the background of Stockholm Principle 22, and two decades of 'progressive development' of international environmental law which never squarely addressed the issue of liability, Principle 13 of the Rio Declaration appears at best as an utterly meaningless and gratuitous exhortation, at worst as yet another regressive provision. Principle 13 provides that:

> States shall develop *national* law regarding liability and compensation for the victims of pollution and other environmental damage (emphasis added),

thus completely removing the issue of compensation for individual victims of environmental harm from the ambit of international law. As regards the liability of States under international law, Principle 13 stipulates that the rules of international law to be further developed are those:

> regarding liability and compensation *for adverse effects* of environmental damage (emphasis added),

thus implicitly qualifying the notion of 'damage to the environment' in Principle 2. In this perspective the pious exhortation to States to 'cooperate in an expeditious and more determined manner' to 'develop further' international law in this field seems altogether cynical.

ENVIRONMENTAL LAW AND HUMAN RIGHTS LAW

The Stockholm Declaration acknowledged that the problem of environmental protection could also be approached from the viewpoint of human rights law. Principle 1 stipulated that:

> [m]an has the fundamental right to freedom, equality and adequate conditions of life, *in an environment of a quality that permits a life of dignity and well-being*, (emphasis added),

and the first paragraph of the Preamble affirmed that the environment is:

> essential to ... the enjoyment of *basic human rights* – even the right to life itself (emphasis added).

The formulation of these principles was rather vague, but it did have the merit of recognizing the existence of certain individual rights with respect to environmental protection – rights which could even be construed as deriving directly from international law.[23]

The Rio Declaration contains no clear affirmation of a human right to a viable environment and no elements which, like those in Principle 1 of the Stockholm Declaration, would constitute a useful basis for the further development of an international legal principle to this effect.

Rio Declaration: Principle 1

Principle 1 of the Rio Declaration contains only an oblique reference to the notion of a human right to environmental protection, where it states that human beings 'are entitled to a healthy and productive life in harmony with nature'. It seems as though the right to health and to a life in harmony with nature is conditional upon the presence of productivity!

Humans – objects of development

On reading Principle 1 of the Rio Declaration, one must also wonder whether human beings, in the perspective of the legal discourse on 'sustainable development', are still considered as a *subject* of law. While 'at the centre of concerns', human beings are reduced to *objects* – objects of soft law on sustainable development, as it is conceived and implemented by a national and transnational elite. Human beings seem no longer to be viewed as autonomous actors who have certain rights and obligations. Although the Rio Declaration still grants them the right to a 'healthy life in harmony with nature', this right is placed explicitly within the perspective of a production-oriented logic.

In contrast, UNCED did, however, affirm the 'right to development' in Principle 3 of the Rio Declaration:

> The right to development must be fulfilled so as to equitably meet developmental and environmental needs of present and future generations.

The right to development is not a new concept, having been a feature of international human rights discourse for some time.[24] However, on reading Principle 3 of the Rio Declaration, one wonders whether it affirms the right to development as an *individual* human right, or as a right of *States*. It establishes a link between the right to development and the needs of 'present and future generations', but does not directly address the needs and rights of individual human beings.

Similarly, the Preamble of the Statement of Principles on Forests mentions 'the right to socio-economic development on a sustainable basis' without identifying its subject. In the Framework Convention on Climate Change, the right to development is clearly envisaged as a right of States and not of individuals: Article 3(4) provides that 'the *Parties* have a right to, and should promote sustainable development' (emphasis added). Viewed from this perspective, the right to development affirmed in Principle 3 of the Rio Declaration appears as yet another way of stressing the precedence of national economic sovereignty over international environmental obligations, rather than as an expression of governmental concern for the fulfilment of social and economic human rights.[25]

Principle 3 and the other provisions of the Rio Declaration recasting concepts taken from the international legal discourse on development, are in fact symptomatic of the ideological character of that discourse. As pointed out by Monique Chemillier-Gendreau in her eloquent critique of 'development law',

> development is a perversion of legal language since there is no object: one does not know who or what must be developed, and up to what point or in which direction.[26]

Individual Human Rights Abandoned

From a human rights perspective, the Rio provisions are once again a step backwards from Stockholm. There was an obvious reluctance at UNCED to accept unambiguously that individuals may be regarded as subjects of international environmental law – that they may have rights and even obligations under international environmental law, independently of any national legal system. Many governments, both from the First and Third World, are confronted from within and without by environmental groups and other popular movements, opposing their environmentally destructive development policies.[27] These governments have obvious reasons to fear the legal implications of the establishment of a direct relationship between international environmental law and the existing international legal mechanisms for the protection of human rights.

WCED and human rights

Building on the elements in Principle 1 of the Stockholm Declaration and other existing international instruments, the WCED Experts Group on Environmental Law had proposed an article stipulating clearly that: 'all human beings have the fundamental right to an environment adequate for their health and well-being.'[28]

The proposed article was designed to establish 'the existence of an international obligation on the part of States *vis-à-vis* other States, if not also *vis-à-vis* individual human beings, to adequately protect the environment for the benefit of individual human beings.'[29] This obviously went far beyond what the governments participating in the UNCED process were willing to accept.

ECE and human rights

The fate of the initiative taken by some Economic Commission for Europe (ECE) countries, to elaborate principles setting forth the rights and obligations of individuals regarding the environment, is symptomatic of the unwillingness of a majority of States to clearly affirm such rights and obligations. Among the principles which these ECE countries – led by the Netherlands and Norway – wished to see universally endorsed by UNCED, one finds the principle of the right of access of individuals to environmental information,[30] the principle of the participation of citizens in decision-making affecting their environment and the right of access to administrative and judicial proceedings.[31] These governments had drafted a proposal for a 'Charter of Environmental Rights and Obligations', which was submitted to and adopted by an experts meeting, convened within the framework of the ECE.[32] However, the draft resulting from that meeting was substantially watered down by the US and UK at later ECE meetings [33] and was never officially transmitted to the UNCED Preparatory Committee by the political organs of the ECE. The efforts of the Charter sponsors to bring their endeavour within the purview of the official conference agenda were aborted at PrepCom II, due to opposition not only from Third World countries, but also from certain ECE members.

Access to Information and Public Participation

The only remnant of this aborted Northern initiative can be found in Principle 10 of the Rio Declaration which touches on the participation of citizens in decision-making and their right of access to information concerning the environment in generally vague terms. These are concepts which did not feature in the Stockholm Declaration and it could be argued that the provisions of the Rio Declaration thus confer a certain 'added value' to those of the Stockholm Declaration. However, on closer examination, it is striking that Principle 10, the only one which uses individual rights discourse in an environmental context, is formulated in manifestly non-juridical language. It states that:

> environmental issues *are best handled* with the participation of all concerned citizens, *at the relevant level* (emphasis added).

From a legal perspective, the expression 'best handled' is rather meaningless and certainly is not intended to confer any right. As to what constitutes the 'relevant level' of decision-making in which citizens should be allowed to participate, the governments who signed the Rio Declaration obviously have very different views.

The second sentence of Principle 10, which deals in more detail with access to information and the right to participation, is formulated as a statement of individual rights, but is again qualified to the extent of rendering it purely symbolic. It provides that:

> *at the national level*, each individual shall have *appropriate* access to information concerning the environment that is held by public authorities, including information on hazardous materials and activities in their communities, and the *opportunity* to participate in decision-making processes (emphasis added).

The reference to 'the national level' clearly and deliberately subordinates the exercise of these rights to domestic law. Moreover, the fact that Principle 10 avoids the use of the word 'right', contrary to Principle 3, where rights discourse is used in a development context, is no coincidence.

Stockholm Principle 1, although just as non-binding as the Rio Declaration's new provisions, was at least written in more juridical language, stated in more authoritative terms and consequently was, and still is, of greater potential value for the further development of international environmental law, especially in its relation to international human rights law.

Increasing Anthropocentricity

Although its very title – 'Declaration on the Human Environment' – and overall tone were undoubtedly anthropocentric, the Stockholm Declaration also contained elements which recognized that human beings are an integral part of the ecosystem and that any human activity is inevitably limited by certain ecological constraints. Indeed, it stressed in its Preamble that 'man is both creature and moulder of his environment'. This 'enlightened' anthropocentric perspective, recognizing the need for a certain humility on the part of human beings in their relations with nature, was even more eloquently articulated in the World Charter for Nature. This not only reiterated that 'mankind is a part of nature' and 'civilization is rooted in nature', but also explicitly recognized the intrinsic right to the existence of other species by stressing that 'every form of life is unique, warranting respect regardless of its worth to man'.

Nature downgraded

By contrast, Principle 1 of the Rio Declaration represents a triumph of unrestrained anthropocentricity. The very first sentence of the Declaration states unambiguously that 'human beings are at the centre of concerns for sustainable development'.

Although Principle 1 goes on to state that the same human beings are 'entitled to a . . . life in harmony with nature', this is secondary. The word 'nature' appears nowhere else in the text and there is no recognition of the intrinsic value of natural ecosystems and wild species.

The Preamble does recognize 'the integral and interdependent nature of the Earth, our home', and Principle 7 affirms the duty of States to 'cooperate in a spirit of global partnership to conserve, protect and restore the health and integrity of the Earth's ecosystem'. But compared to the first principle of the World Charter for Nature, which unambiguously proclaimed that 'nature shall be respected and its essential processes shall not be impaired', and to Principle 4 of the Stockholm Declaration, which stated that 'man has a special responsibility to safeguard and wisely manage the heritage of wildlife and its habitat', this can hardly be called progress.

The Planet Earth, its natural ecosystems and non-human inhabitants are not very prominent in the Rio Declaration, which was originally intended by some as an 'Earth Charter'. In retrospect, it would have been preposterous to give the Rio Declaration that title.

FROM 'SUSTAINABLE DEVELOPMENT' TO 'SUSTAINABLE GROWTH'

The buzzword of the Rio Declaration, indeed of most of the international political and legal debate on environmental issues since the mid-1980s is 'sustainable development'. It is therefore essential to analyse, in the context of the Rio Declaration, the actual meaning and the legal and ideological implications of the concept of 'sustainable development', which appears throughout the Rio Declaration, Agenda 21 and the other instruments adopted by UNCED. This analysis reveals an interesting 'slippage' in international political and legal discourse, beginning with the 1987 publication of the Brundtland Report, and culminating in Rio.

The Brundtland Report

The Brundtland Report defined the concept of 'sustainable development' as:

> development that meets the needs of the present without compromising the ability of future generations to meet their own needs.[34]

Although the WCED did not actually 'invent' the concept,[35] it did redefine and popularize it in an original and inspirational way. The WCED's

13

definition is concise, simple and has symbolic value. It is an undeniable motivator, while remaining sufficiently ambiguous so as not to directly threaten vested interests. Without questioning the principle of 'development' as a method for satisfying the 'needs' of current generations, it explicitly recognizes that future generations also have interests and even rights deserving protection in the (still anthropocentric) new model of development called 'sustainable development'.

It is not surprising that such a concept has received widespread support from leaders of the North and South alike, environmental and Third World movements, international bureaucrats and enlightened managers of financial and economic institutions and structures in both capitalist and socialist countries. This is explained by the artful vagueness which the new paradigm of 'sustainable development' casts upon their respective responsibilities.[36]

Regressing to sustained growth

In legal and political documents, the expression 'sustainable development' is now more and more being used interchangeably with, even equated with, the notion of 'sustainable growth'. In English, the term 'sustainable' also lends itself to subtle slips, since the difference between 'sustainable growth' and 'sustained growth' is a difference of only two letters.

Already in 1987, when Mrs Brundtland, then Prime Minister of Norway, presented her report to the UNEP Governing Council and sought to rally the governments represented there to the cause of 'sustainable development', she stated with conviction that, in the view of the Commission which she had chaired, sustainable development was none other than 'a new concept for economic growth'. While, in her speech and later statements, she continued to use the term 'sustainable development' more often than 'sustainable growth', the WCED certainly bears considerable responsibility for the subsequent debasing of the notion into a vulgar recast of the ideology of economic growth and trickle-down development.

The debate really began to degenerate in the political fora of the UN, when development and growth ideologues from North and South started to realize the full potential of the concept of 'sustainable development' as a vehicle for recasting their traditional ideologies and vested interests in a new, 'green' language. This is reflected in the increasing emphasis on trade, financial resources and other economic concerns in the agenda-setting process of UNCED.

The objective of the Rio Conference was defined as the promotion of 'sustainable and *environmentally sound* development in all countries' (emphasis added).[37] The decision of the drafters to specify that development should be 'environmentally sound' seems odd; in the view of the Brundtland Commission, 'sustainable development' was by definition environmentally sound. The reason for this apparently redundant qualification becomes obvious upon reading the rest of the resolution. It contains numerous explicit and implicit references to a traditional, 'business-as-usual' view of economic growth and development, which hardly pays lipservice to the concept of 'sustainability'. Thus, the resolution not only

> affirms that the promotion of economic growth *in developing countries* is essential to address problems of environmental degradation,

it also,

> affirms the importance of a supportive international economic environment *that would result in sustained economic growth and development in all countries* (emphasis added).[38]

Whereas the Brundtland report specified that the revival of economic growth was necessary above all in developing countries in order to meet the basic needs of their populations, it certainly contained no call for 'sustained economic growth' in *all* countries. This important nuance was completely eliminated in the UNGA Resolution, and the subsequent texts adopted at UNCED. It was this disputable re-interpretation of the concept of 'sustainable development', which led more enlightened members of the international community to add the qualifier 'environmentally sound', as the notion of sustainability no longer automatically incorporated ecological viability.

'Sustainable growth' in the EC

The new ideology of 'sustainable growth' in the North found its first legal expression in the Treaty of Maastricht, which was adopted in December 1991 by the heads of State and government of the member States of the European Community (EC) at their Maastricht summit. This new Treaty[39] will establish a new European Union and reformulate the basic objectives of the EC by amending Article 2 of the 1956 Treaty of Rome.

When the European Economic Community (EEC) Treaty was first modified in 1987 by the Single European Act, introducing a new chapter establishing a solid legal basis for 'Community action in the field of the environment', many commentators deplored that this legal recognition of environmental protection as one of the areas of EEC policy had not been matched by a change in Article 2 of the Treaty, which still spelled out the fundamental objectives of the Community in exclusively economic terms, dating from the pre-Stockholm era. The Maastricht Treaty now reformulates the objective of the EC as the promotion of: 'a harmonious and balanced development of economic activities [and] sustainable and non-inflationary *growth* respecting the environment'.

Thus, the notion of 'sustainable growth' has usurped the notion of 'sustainable development' in the North. While the European Union sets itself the objective of promoting 'economic and social progress which is balanced and sustainable', Article B of the Maastricht Treaty [40] does not even mention environmental protection as one of the essential means through which, what it calls 'sustainable progress', is to be achieved. Have we really made progress since 1956, when the founding fathers of the EEC pledged allegiance to the goal of 'continuous and balanced expansion'?

Traditional economic growth re-instated
Against this ominous background the true meaning of the anthropocentric, production-oriented and technocratic discourse of the Rio Declaration stands out starkly. 'Sustainable development' has become synonymous with 'sustainable growth', not only in Europe, but throughout the world, and, eventually, may very well end up meaning little more than 'sustained growth'.[41]

Rio Principle 12, echoing UNGA Resolution 44/228, proclaims that:

> States should cooperate to promote a supportive and open international economic system that would *lead to economic growth and sustainable development in all countries.*

While the Stockholm Declaration also stressed that 'economic and social development is essential for ensuring a favourable living and working environment for man' (Principle 8), called for 'accelerated development through the transfer of substantial quantities of financial and technological assistance' (Principle 9), and emphasized that 'for the developing countries, stability of prices and adequate earnings for primary commodities and raw material are essential to environmental management' (Principle 10), the traditional term 'economic growth' is not used in any of its provisions. Neither is the term used in the World Charter for Nature. The Rio Declaration rectifies this 'omission'.

Political leaders from industrialized countries, as well as the leaders of transnational business and financial institutions, are no doubt just as delighted as their counterparts in the Southern elites to see the mythology of economic growth restored, not only for Third World countries but for the entire planet. This has been achieved in one fell swoop, and this under the pretext that growth is not actually harmful to the environment but, to the contrary, essential to its very protection.

ABSORBING ENVIRONMENTAL LAW INTO ECONOMIC LAW

The Rio Declaration smothers international environmental law and policy by merging it, as it were, with international economic law and development law. This may well be the eventual result of the much-hailed process of 'integration' of environmental and economic policies, as epitomized by Principle 4 of the Rio Declaration which proclaims that:

in order to achieve sustainable development, environmental protection shall constitute an integral part of the development process and cannot be considered in isolation from it.[42]

The Rio Declaration Preamble even refers to the need to protect 'the integrity of the *global environmental and developmental system*'. Admittedly, Principle 7 refers to the duty of States to cooperate:

to conserve, protect and restore the health and integrity of the Earth's ecosystem,

but the preambular reference to the protection of the 'integrity of the global environmental and developmental system' seems to counterbalance the emphasis on ecological integrity in Principle 7 with a matching reference to the fact that the 'development system' too, is entitled to 'integrity'. This subverts the primary objective of international environmental law which is still described in scholarly manuals as the protection of the integrity of the *biosphere* and the *ecosystems* which compose it.[43]

Subordinating Environmental Law

The new discourse of 'integration' suggests that there is no longer any conflict between environmental protection and economic development, and that the latter has become a necessary complement, condition even, of the former. This obfuscates the very real and increasing conflict between the dominant view of 'development' and prevailing patterns of economic growth on the one hand, and the imperatives of environmental protection on the other. It ambiguously stands as much for the subordination of environmental policies to economic imperatives in the eyes of some, as for the converse to others. The opportunities it presents to subordinate environmental law are reflected in several provisions of the Rio Declaration and other instruments adopted at UNCED. For example, Rio Principle 11 provides that:

environmental standards, management objectives and priorities should reflect the environmental *and developmental context* to which they apply,

and goes on to specify that

standards applied by some countries may be inappropriate and of unwarranted economic and social cost to other countries, in particular developing countries.

The latter sentence echoes a similar clause in Principle 23 of the Stockholm Declaration, which recommended that:

> the extent of the applicability of standards which are valid for the most advanced countries but which may be inappropriate and of unwarranted social cost for the developing countries

should be considered in the determination of environmental standards. There is, however, an important difference between the Rio and Stockholm principles. Whereas the latter seemed primarily intended as a guideline to be taken into account in the formulation of international environmental standards and of national environmental standards in developing countries, Rio Principle 11 is formulated so as to suggest that the freedom of developed countries to set stringent national environmental standards is limited by the duty to avoid causing 'unwarranted economic and social costs' to developing countries.

Another provision of the Rio Declaration implicitly subordinating international environmental law to international economic law, can be found in Principle 12 which addresses the issue of 'trade policy measures for environmental purposes'. Paraphrasing Article XX of the General Agreement on Tarrifs and Trade (GATT), it emphasizes that such measures:

> should not constitute a means of arbitrary or unjustifiable discrimination or a disguised restriction on international trade.

In an apparent attempt to generalize the holding of the GATT panel in the recent dispute between the US and Mexico on tuna import restrictions,[44] it recommends that 'unilateral actions to deal with environmental challenges outside the jurisdiction of the importing country should be avoided'.

Statement of Principles on Forests
A concrete application of these general principles enounced in the Rio Declaration is to be found in the UNCED Statement of Principles on Forests, which explicitly condemns any unilateral measures that may be envisaged to restrict trade in tropical hardwood harvested in a non-sustainable manner.[45] Another provision urges that 'open and free international trade in forest products should be facilitated.' Through such language, the UNCED statement actually suggests that unrestrained trade in forest products is a prerequisite for sustainable forest use, a highly disputable proposition.

WHERE IS THE FUTURE FOR INTERNATIONAL ENVIRONMENTAL LAW?

I have shown how the new ideology of 'sustainable development' undermines the autonomy of environmental law as a body of rules and standards designed to restrain and prevent the environmentally destructive effects of certain kinds of economic activity. There may even be some reason to fear that the Rio Conference constitutes the beginning of the *decline* of international environmental law as an autonomous branch of international law, as a body of 'international juridical norms whose purpose is to protect the environment'.[46]

The Rio Declaration, elaborated pursuant to UNCED's mandate from the UNGA to 'promote the further development of international environmental law', does not even use the term 'international environmental law' and instead the final Principle 27, calls for 'the further development of international law *in the field of sustainable development*'.

The new 'international law of sustainable development' presumably comprises those rules of law until now understood to constitute international environmental law, mixed in with various strands of what was formerly described as international development law. Thus, international environmental law risks being reduced to a mere appendage of international development law,[47] and subordinated to economic rationality.

Chapter 39 of Agenda 21 provides that 'the further development of international law on sustainable development' will have to pay 'special attention to the delicate balance between environmental and development concerns.'[48] What does this 'delicate balance' imply? Clearly it means international environmental law must be 'rebalanced' to take better account of the priority of economic development over environmental protection. A few paragraphs later, Agenda 21 flatly states that:

> many of the existing international legal instruments and agreements in the field of environmental law have been developed without adequate participation and contribution of developing countries, and thus *may require review* in order to reflect the concerns and interests of developing countries and to ensure a balanced governance of such instruments and agreements.

It is ironic that while the legitimacy, indeed the very existence of international environmental law as an independent branch of international law, a critical discipline standing in a dialectical relationship to other branches of international law, was being called into question, some UNCED participants continued to make pious statements of faith in the further development of international environmental law. Thus, the representative of Canada suggested that the newly established United Nations Commission on Sustainable Development 'could negotiate an Earth Charter'.[49] International environmental law, luckily, still has true believers.

2 THE RIO DECLARATION: A NEW BASIS FOR INTERNATIONAL COOPERATION

Ileana M Porras

USING THE 'ENVIRONMENT' TO ACHIEVE A NEW GLOBALISM

When the dust settles, the Rio Declaration on Environment and Development (the 'Rio Declaration'), a statement of general principles and obligations, is likely to prove the most influential of the numerous international instruments adopted during the United Nations Conference on Environment and Development (UNCED or 'the Conference'), held at Rio de Janeiro from 3 to 14 June 1992. This unprecedented and ambitious international event, better known to the English speaking public by the catchier name 'Earth Summit '92' (and to its Brazilian hosts as 'ECO '92'), required two years of intense preparation, and proved to be an extraordinary mix of international negotiation and international media event.

The 'Environment' as Dominant Motif

Although the Conference had been slated as an 'environment and development' conference, 'the environment' was the dominant organizing motif and provided much of the imaginative force, driving not only the media event but the negotiations. As organizing motif, the environment seemed to perform two distinct but complementary functions at the Conference: an internationalizing function and a romantic-utopianizing function.[1]

A common atmosphere, oceans without frontiers, delicately balanced ecosystems, human interdependence with the natural world, a shared planet, seemed to require a new way of constructing international relations. The doomsday rhetoric of limited resources, environmental crisis and irreparable harm, provided the urgency. 'Saving the planet' became the goal of the conference in the public imagination and the recurrent theme running through official government and UNCED secretariat pronouncements.[2] Hopes ran high that the environment would prove the necessary catalyst for radical change. The Earth Summit was to provide the utopian moment when all nations and all people would recognize their mutual responsibility for preserving our planet for present and future generations.[3] Invoking the environment thus inspired a general call for a 'new globalism' based on an ideology of sharing, common interests and long-term perspectives.

Unfortunately for those with utopian ambitions, the Conference did not, in the end, produce the hoped-for new globalism. The negotiations and the resulting agreements reflected the self-interest and short-term perspectives of the participating governments. Failure in the face of so much ambition and raised expectations was predictable. International conferences, regardless of the subject matter, seem pre-determined to be characterized as 'good beginnings' and to end with an inevitable call for more law or more institutions.[4] UNCED was no exception. Even the Rio Declaration, envisaged as an inspiring and poetic 'Earth Charter' by the UNCED secretariat and the majority of Northern industrialized countries, failed to provide the new globalism vision, demanded by the environment.

The Rio Declaration

The text of the Rio Declaration and the process which produced it provide a unique insight into the debates, compromises and achievements of UNCED. As an international statement of general principles and obligations, which was negotiated in detail by a large and representative number of delegations, it must be taken to reflect – to the extent any international instrument can do so – the current consensus of values and priorities in environment and development. As the manifesto of a conference permeated by the environment motif, the Rio Declaration predictably endorses many of the international environmental principles that have recently been devised for, or accepted in, other contexts such as: the precautionary principle (Principle 15); the polluter pays principle (Principle 16); environmental impact assessment requirement (Principle 17); principles on emergency notification (Principle 18); and prior consultation (Principle 19). Predictably also, the Rio Declaration boasts principles which seek to promote international cooperation and peace, such as: Principle 9 on transfer of technology; Principle 12 calling for the establishment of an open and supportive international economic system; Principle 25 on the interdependence of peace, development and environmental protection and Principle 26 on the peaceful resolution of environmental disputes. Although the 'predictable' principles are themselves extremely interesting, this chapter will focus on aspects of the Rio Declaration that appear paradoxical in light of the prevalent environment motif of UNCED.

The Rio paradox
One paradoxical feature of the Rio Declaration is its handling of what, to many people, was the crucial challenge of the Conference, that of fully and

indissolubly integrating environment and development because 'development and environment must be one'.[5] The Rio Declaration's response to this challenge and to the dominant environment motif was instead to redefine the relationship between environment and development, expressing it in such a way as to suggest that development may sometimes take precedence over environment. The most paradoxical feature of the Rio Declaration, however, is that in answer to the call for a new globalism it reaffirms 'sovereignty', while highlighting 'different contributions to global environmental degradation' as the basis for international cooperation in sustainable development. To explain how the Rio Declaration came to incorporate features which seem to challenge the environment's appeal for a new globalism, it is necessary to look at the negotiation process and to examine the function of the development motif at the Conference. This latter motif appeared to be no more than a strong under-current flowing through the conference, and its presence was attributed to the environment imperative of curbing unrestrained development in favour of environment-friendly sustainable development.[6]

NEGOTIATING THE RIO DECLARATION[7]

Negotiations of the Rio Declaration were, except perhaps those on the financial resources chapter of the UNCED action plan, Agenda 21, the most overtly political of the UNCED process. While the battle was over ideologies, priorities and visions, the negotiations also served as a testing ground for developing countries to explore the potency of what they perceived as a new bargaining chip. That is, the desire of industrialized countries to ensure that developing countries adopt sustainable models of development, due to their conviction that their own survival is conditional on it. Developing countries perceived that what developed countries feared most was that they should 'blindly' follow the historical development example of the wealthy industrialized States and thereby impose unsustainable pressures on the environment.

Polarized Political Positions

Despite the steadfast resistance of many industrialized countries to being pressured into adopting a common developed country position, negotiations of the Rio Declaration took on an essentially bipolar North–South character, with a newly revitalized *Group of 77* and *China* (G-77) presenting the developing country position. Given the variety of often conflicting or intersecting interests prevalent among the 128 countries now represented by the G-77, their success in producing a common position on the Rio

Declaration was somewhat unexpected.[8]

Most developing countries had agreed to participate in an international environmental conference only because the theme of development was to be linked to that of environment. Their primary goal was to ensure their urgent development needs were not impeded by a focus on international environmental concerns. These countries felt threatened by the environment motif. Recent experiences with international lenders such as the World Bank, had already raised fears that new environmental conditionalities would be imposed on development projects. The US–Mexico dispute in the GATT over US tuna import regulations (which seek to impose dolphin-friendly tuna production techniques on non-US fishing fleets) was seen by developing countries as further evidence that they were threatened by a new wave of environmental colonialism.[9] In the face of this new colonialism developing countries took a unified stance, certain that to fail to do so was to allow developed countries to use the environment to constrain them.

By exacerbating developing countries' suspicion of developed country motives, the environment motif of the Conference thus reinforced the bipolar nature of the negotiations. The development focus, favoured by the G-77 negotiators, was taken by their developed country counterparts as evidence that developing countries were not concerned with protecting the environment. In a world constructed on the basis of binary oppositions, logic dictated that to be pro-development was necessarily to be anti-environment and vice-versa. By extension, a country had to be either a developed or a developing country and was assumed to hold a developed (pro-environment/anti-development) position or a developing (anti-environment/pro-development) position.[10] Even when such categories flew in the face of reality, the capacity of the dichotomies to influence the debate seemed undiminished. Thus, States found themselves aligned across a single divide and were made to repress most of the other possible dichotomies and available alignments, if those did not fit in with the primary North–South divide.

An uneasy compromise

In the end, despite the enormous distance which existed at the beginning of negotiations between the two trends, agreement was reached on the text of the Rio Declaration. Consensus was achieved in large measures because all parties to the negotiation believed that the entire Conference would be deemed a failure if they could not agree. The Rio Declaration as adopted is a text of uneasy compromises, delicately balanced interests, and dimly discernible contradictions, held together by the interpretative vagueness of classic UN-ese. Although all interests are represented in the text, the Rio Declaration may, on balance, be judged as a victory from the developing country perspective, in so far as there is evidence of a shift away from the practice of developed country dominance of the process of dictating international norms and priorities.

INTEGRATING ENVIRONMENT AND DEVELOPMENT

The shift away from an absolute domination of the field of interpretation of international norms and priorities by developed countries is evident in the Rio Declaration's treatment of the critical issue of the integration of environment and development. In many ways, the whole UNCED process could be described as an international mechanism to determine how that relationship was to be characterized.

Human Beings at the Centre

To the dismay of most developed country delegates, 'human beings' rather than 'the environment' open Principle 1 of the Rio Declaration:

> Human beings are at the centre of concerns for sustainable development.
> They are entitled to a healthy and productive life in harmony with nature.

Structurally, as well as in the terms of the principle itself, human beings are thereby placed at the centre of the twin concerns of the Conference. Furthermore, in this first principle, human beings are given an entitlement to a healthy and productive life, in harmony with nature. Neither here nor anywhere else in the Rio Declaration are human beings specifically given a right to a healthy or clean environment. The very strong anthropocentric focus of Principle 1 is particularly significant given that it begins to contradict the environment motif of the Conference and because most developed countries were opposed to it.[11]

Developed countries opposed placing human beings squarely at the centre of environmental and developmental concerns because they preferred to stress that human beings should be at the service of the environment rather than to suggest that the environment was at the service of human beings. They therefore proposed principles in which human beings were held responsible for the well-being of the environment or provided with an individual right to a healthy environment. To the G-77, however, placing human beings at the centre was of fundamental importance. To allow human beings to be placed at the service of the environment was to subjugate development needs to environmental needs. To provide for an environmental right or admit to an environmental responsibility was to open the door to international interference with their development plans.

Development and/or Environment?

It is Principles 3 and 4 of the Rio Declaration, however, which provide the key defining concepts for the integration of environment and development.

In Principle 3, the international community recognizes an unconditional right to development:

> The right to development must be fulfilled so as to equitably meet developmental and environmental needs of present and future generations.

In Principle 4, the community then asserts that:

> In order to achieve sustainable development, environmental protection shall constitute an integral part of the development process and cannot be considered in isolation from it.

Many developed country delegates opposed the recognition of a right to development implied in Principle 3. There were two main lines of argument:

(1) no such right existed (ie no such right had yet been recognized by the international community);
(2) even if there were such a right, it was a limited right, constrained by natural limits (ie the limit of natural resources and that of the ecosystem to restore itself) and constrained by the principle of equity which required sustainable development.

Finally, developed countries argued that Principles 3 and 4 should be combined. In insisting on their separation, developing country negotiators intended to ensure that the right to development would not be transformed into a right to 'sustainable' development.

The meaning of these two principles is likely to be debated for years. On the one hand, Principle 4 provides that 'environmental protection *shall* constitute an integral part of the development process' (emphasis added). On the other hand, this mandatory requirement is qualified by the preceding phrase '[i]n order to achieve sustainable development'. Ambiguity remains as to whether the phrase '[i]n order to achieve sustainable development', is intended to be read as requiring States to pursue 'sustainable development' or whether it simply sets up the definition of 'sustainable development' in the mode of an aspiration. The juxtaposition of the two principles, however, suggests that not all development need be 'sustainable' as the right to development set out in Principle 3 is unconditional, except to the extent that the purpose of the right to development is described as 'to equitably meet the developmental and environmental needs of present and future generations'. In considering the relationship between development and environment, the Rio Declaration thus appears to give pre-eminence to development. Environment and development are equal partners in 'sustainable development' but the right to development comes before sustainable development.

'Sustainable Development'

With the Rio Declaration, developing countries also begin to influence and take over the definition of the popular and new, but as yet indeterminate, concept of 'sustainable development'. Since its inception in the Brundtland Commission's Report of 1987,[12] the term 'sustainable development' has been widely used. Usually, the term describes, in the abstract, an ideal model of development that takes into account and respects the environmental needs of both present and future generations. Definitions of the term do not, however, explain what those environmental needs are, nor how to measure when they have been met. They do not suggest how, in practice, policy-makers are to balance present needs against future needs; much less do they explain how to achieve intra-generational equity.

In the Rio Declaration the international community takes on the challenge of adding content to the term 'sustainable development'. The term is never itself defined but appears persistently through the text, each appearance providing clues to its interpretation. As has been seen, the term appears in Principles 1 and 4 of the Rio Declaration. It is Principle 5, however that provides the greatest interpretative spin to the term sustainable development:

> All States and all people shall cooperate in the essential task of eradicating poverty as an *indispensable* requirement of sustainable development, in order to decrease the disparities in standards of living and better meet the needs of the majority of the people of the world (emphasis added).

Armed with this principle, developing countries could well argue that sustainable development is development that, as a priority, seeks to eradicate poverty in order to decrease the disparities in standards of living.

Since this principle does not specifically mention future generations, it could even be argued that present generations are given precedence over future ones. From the perspective of developing countries, such an argument would be compelling: in those countries, unless you fulfil the needs of present generations, the chances of providing for future generations are slim. As one developing country delegate put it, you cannot ask a starving man who needs firewood to warm his young children to spare the mango tree that may one day feed his grandchildren.[13]

Reducing developed country consumption
The term sustainable development is further elucidated in Principle 8 of the Rio Declaration:

> To achieve sustainable development and a higher quality of life for all people, States should reduce and eliminate unsustainable patterns of production and consumption and promote appropriate demographic policies.

This principle achieves one of the most delicate balancing acts of the entire Rio Declaration. Without adopting an accusatory tone, this principle clearly addresses itself to developed countries when it refers to '[the need to] reduce and eliminate unsustainable patterns of production and consumption' and, just as clearly, it addresses itself to developing countries when it refers to '[the need to] promote appropriate demographic policies'.

With its reference to patterns of production and consumption, Principle 8 addresses one of the most problematic inadequacies of the term sustainable development: because the term sustainable development refers to development as opposed to 'growth' or 'economy', it appears to apply exclusively to developing countries. Industrialized countries rarely refer to their activities as development activities, and, therefore, seem to be outside the scope of the term. The Rio Declaration provides a reminder that the intra-generational equity goal of sustainable development can only be achieved if industrialized countries cease to benefit, to the detriment of developing countries, from their ongoing unsustainable practices. With Principle 8, developed countries become full partners in the quest for sustainable development.

Reducing developing country population growth

Principle 8 also asserts that to achieve sustainable development, States must promote appropriate demographic policies. The fact that population and unsustainable patterns of production and consumption are given equal prominence in a single principle reflects one of the most difficult compromises of the negotiations. Developed countries hoped that the Declaration would pronounce that in order to achieve sustainable development it was essential for States to address the problem of population growth.[14] Developing countries, on the other hand, argued that the unsustainable patterns of production and consumption of developed countries were historically and currently the major cause of global environmental degradation[15] and that the focus on population pressures was unwarranted and would only serve to obscure the real problems. The compromise did not fully satisfy either group. Despite its failure to satisfy the distinct interests of each group, however, Principle 8 provides significant additional elements to the interpretation of sustainable development and to an understanding of the relationship between environment and development.

COMMON BUT DIFFERENTIATED RESPONSIBILITIES

Another important modification or restructuring of international constructs achieved in the Rio Declaration concerns a number of issues implicated in the international environmental concept of 'common but differentiated responsibilities', consecrated in Principle 7:

> States shall cooperate in a spirit of global partnership to conserve, protect and restore the health and integrity of the Earth's ecosystem. In view of the different contributions to global environmental degradation, States have common but differentiated responsibilities. The developed countries acknowledge the responsibility that they bear in the international pursuit of sustainable development in view of the pressures their societies place on the global environment and of the technologies and financial resources they command.

'Common responsibilities'

This principle was the cause of the most acrimonious (and most strictly bipolar) debate during the negotiations of the Rio Declaration. The concept of 'common but differentiated responsibilities' had been debated shortly before, in the context of negotiations for a Framework Convention on Climate Change.[16] In that context, the concept had been proposed to emphasize the shared character of the Earth's atmosphere and the consequent need for a global partnership to address effectively the dangers of continuing degradation, while recognizing that not all members of the partnership had contributed equally to the problem. During the 4th UNCED Preparatory Committee (PrepCom) meeting, the debate over 'common but differentiated responsibilities' centred around two related issues:

(1) whether or not the Rio Declaration should embrace the concept of 'common' responsibility at all; and
(2) whether it was appropriate for the Rio Declaration to become specific and accusatory in order to explain the basis for the 'differentiation' of responsibilities.

In the context of the Framework Convention on Climate Change, the practical argument for accepting 'common' responsibility, had been that everyone would be worse off (in the long run) if all States did not agree to share responsibility for protecting common resources. Developing countries, which had accepted the idea of 'common but differentiated responsibility' in the context of a legally binding and limited Framework Convention on Climate Change, nevertheless questioned the wisdom of accepting it in the context of a general statement of principles and obligations. They felt uncomfortable about accepting a general 'common' responsibility, when they were unclear about the implications. Having set a precedent in the Framework Convention on Climate Change, however, developing countries, in negotiating the Rio Declaration, did not refuse to adopt the idea of common responsibility altogether, but addressed the basis for and meaning of the 'differentiated responsibility' segment of the concept.

'Differentiated' responsibilities

There are two distinct ways in which Principle 7 of the Rio Declaration begins to define 'differentiated responsibility'. First, it imputes differentiated responsibility to States in accordance with their different levels of responsibility for causing the harm. Second, it ties differentiated responsibility to the different capacities of States, by referring to the differentiated responsibility for sustainable development, acknowledged by developed countries in view of 'the technologies and financial resources they command'. Together, these two elements of differentiated responsibility provide the beginnings of a philosophical basis for international cooperation in the fields of environment and development. It is a basis that allows the characterization of the transfer of resources from developed to developing countries as 'obligation' rather than as 'aid' or 'assistance' and provides a theoretical basis to justify different environmental standards, in view of the different capacities of States and their different contributions to environmental degradation.

Transfer of resources as an obligation
The prospect of characterizing the transfer of resources from developed countries to developing countries as an 'obligation' rather than as 'aid' offered by Principle 7, was extremely important to developing countries. All parties involved in the UNCED process agreed that it would be more costly, in the short term, for a State to adopt sustainable models of development, than it would be to pursue traditional (unsustainable) development. For developing countries, achieving sustainable development would often require leapfrogging over cheaper, locally available, but 'dirtier' technologies to acquire expensive state-of-the-art safe and sound 'cleaner' technologies. Negotiations during the UNCED process, were based on the assumption that, since developing countries could not afford the entire burden of the incremental cost, developed countries would have to help finance their efforts to achieve sustainable development. In the absence of Principle 7 of the Rio Declaration, the transfer of resources from developed to developing countries would have had to be justified on the basis of the 'need' of developing countries. Developing countries would then have been placed in a posture of soliciting aid from their wealthier neighbours. With Principle 7, developing countries can instead assume the more appealing position of entitlement to assistance from their guilty neighbours.

Different environmental standards
The emphasis on the different technological and financial capacities of

States in Principle 7 provides a theoretical basis for the endorsement, in Principle 11, of different environmental standards reflecting the different environmental and developmental contexts of States.

> States shall enact effective environmental legislation. Environmental standards, management objectives and priorities should reflect the environmental and developmental context to which they apply. Standards applied by some countries may be inappropriate and of unwarranted economic and social cost to other countries, in particular developing countries.

The reference to the appropriateness of different standards in Principle 11 was sponsored by developing countries. The focus on different capacities in Principles 7 and 11 provides at least a partial answer to an important question which arises each time an international forum addresses an international environmental issue: whether all States should be required to adopt similarly stringent environmental standards or regulations.

By endorsing the notion that identical environmental standards may not be appropriate in all contexts, the Rio Declaration takes a stance favourable to developing countries. The main arguments in favour of identical environmental standards are trade related. The first argument is that similar standards would facilitate international trade. For example, if all States are required to ban the same pesticides and to adopt similar pesticide management regulations, produce will not be stopped at a border because it fails to meet the importing country's standards on pesticide residues. Thus, identical standards reduce the need for technical barriers and procedural hindrances to trade across borders. The second argument is that lower environmental standards distort trade, by providing a competitive trade advantage to the State adopting the lower standard: since States with lower standards can produce cheaper goods, the incentive will be for all States to lower their standards. This 'slippery-slope' argument, favoured by developed countries, was rejected by developing countries. Instead, developing countries argued that stringent environmental standards might not be technically appropriate in their context, because, for instance, they had lower existing base-levels of hazardous wastes production. Further, they argued, stringent standards might not be appropriate because they were costly and a country's limited resources were needed for other priorities. In support of their arguments for the right to different standards, developing country negotiators pointed to the European Economic Community's own solution to a similar problem, presented by the different economic conditions of its member States.[17]

IN DEFENCE OF SOVEREIGNTY

One of the most striking results of the Rio Declaration is its reaffirmation of traditional 'sovereignty' in the face of the appeal for a new globalism called forth by the dominant environment motif of the Conference:

States have, in accordance with the Charter of the United Nations and the principles of international law, the sovereign right to exploit their own resources pursuant to their own environmental and *developmental* policies, and the responsibility to ensure that activities within their jurisdiction or control do not cause damage to the environment of other States or of areas beyond the control of national jurisdiction. (Principle 2) (emphasis added).

During the negotiations, developed countries opposed the restatement of what was essentially Principle 21 of the Stockholm Declaration, arguing that it would be redundant, since all of the Stockholm Declaration was to be reaffirmed in the Preamble. Although already contained in the major existing international environmental law instruments, and despite the fact that over the past 20 years it had achieved broad acceptance as a norm of international environmental law, the G-77 insisted on its inclusion in the Rio Declaration. This insistence was due, in large part, to their perception that developed country rhetoric was shifting dangerously in the direction of globalizing certain selected environmental resources, such as tropical forests.

Responding to 'Globalization'

This new globalizing rhetoric, in which natural resources become a common good of humankind, turns the State where the resource is located (the home-State) into a guardian of the resource – a guardian on behalf of all the people of the planet. It seeks to transform the accepted relationship between a State and its natural resources from one of ownership, in which the State is free to exploit its resources in accordance with its national policies and priorities, into one of trusteeship, where the State would be required to consider the interests of, and probably consult with, the international community before taking any action affecting the resource. Developing countries were not ready to accept the erosion of traditional sovereignty implied by such a shift, especially given that the resources appearing subject to globalization were resources held primarily by developing countries. By restating an old-fashioned and unambiguous claim of sovereignty, developing countries hoped to halt and reverse this erosion.[18]

If the rhetoric of globalizing resources, with its questioning of traditional concepts of sovereignty, is one of the components of the new globalism called for by the environment motif, then it seems that the environment motif does not exert as strong an attraction on all States. On second glance, developing countries' focus on sovereignty is not as surprising as it first appeared. Weaker entities often find their protection in formal legal concepts and it appears that the most vulnerable elements of a group 'entitled' to a right, are the most reluctant to let go of the constraints imposed by the boundaries of the right.[19] The response of developing countries to the possibility of rethinking sovereignty could be characterized as suspicion, that if developed countries are willing to forego the traditional comforts offered by sovereignty it is because it is no longer beneficial to them. Following the logic of binary opposites, developing countries assumed that if it was no longer beneficial to developed countries it must now be beneficial to them.

Protecting autonomy

The reassertion of sovereignty in the Rio Declaration had a subsidiary effect of importance to developing countries. From the point of view of developing countries, the main problem with the 'new environmental conditionalities' imposed by international lenders in the name of sustainable development was not that these conditionalities require them to address the environmental impact of proposed development projects, but that those making the determination that a project was unacceptably unsustainable were outside of the national context. Developing countries were, therefore, concerned to preserve the maximum autonomy to determine their own environmental policies based on their particular situation. The reassertion of sovereignty in Principle 2 reinforces the view that it is ultimately the responsibility of each State to identify its own priorities, and adopt national environmental and developmental policies based on those priorities. The decision on the sustainability of a development project and whether, if unsustainable, it is acceptably so, becomes, in the light of Principle 2, more clearly a question for each State to answer for itself.

CONCLUSION

As the most recent international statement of principles and obligations in the fields of environment and development, the Rio Declaration will probably be given great deference by legal interpreters and policy-makers and is therefore likely to influence the future shape of environmental and developmental law and practice.

Should the Rio Declaration be judged a disaster for the environment, a reactionary step backwards, attributable to the disruptive role played at the Conference by the development motif? Before answering this question, the Rio Declaration must be examined in its broader context: the momentum worldwide is already directed towards greater environmental protection and sustainable development. This trend is likely to continue unabated for two reasons: developed countries will continue to have virtual control of international purse strings and developing countries have begun to recognize that protecting the environment may also serve their own best interest. By endorsing principles of international environmental law in addition to those which construct a framework from which to address their development needs, developing countries assent to the necessity of addressing environmental protection in the context of development. Indeed, after the Rio Declaration, it will be difficult to separate environment and development concerns.

To the extent that the development-focused principles, including the reassertion of sovereignty over their natural resources, give comfort and reassurance to developing countries, they may facilitate the transition to sustainable development. In practice, most countries understand that repeating the mistakes of the past is not the answer to their development or growth needs. Furthermore, as people become aware of the detrimental effects of environmental degradation on their local communities, they will demand changes in State environmental policies and practices. It is, therefore, likely that most countries will be willing to explore new models of development, so long as they do not perceive that they are being asked to make impossible sacrifices, or to forego the short-term benefits of unsustainable development in order to make it possible for another State to continue to benefit from its entrenched unsustainable patterns of production and consumption.

What of the new hope that the environment would serve as a catalyst for a new globalism? At this time it appears that developing countries feel more comfortable retaining the boundaries of the traditional concept of sovereignty. It is, however, by no means clear that they will in the long run be better off under that model than under a model of globalized resources. Indeed there is little to suggest that developed countries will not continue to benefit disproportionately from continuing under the old rules devised by them. Before the developing countries can begin to be receptive to the call for a new globalism, they will have to reach an, as yet, unachieved level of comfort and security within the international community. Before they can let go of the 'rights' implied by sovereignty, developing countries will have to feel like equal players, able to influence and assent to the rules, rather than the receivers of dictates from stronger players. Developed countries must agree to play according to modified rules in which they are not guaranteed to win. The very rhetoric of winners and losers must be called into question. The apparent ability of developing countries to influence international environmental norms in the context of the Rio Declaration may serve to create a real opportunity for creation of the new globalism. If it is capable of responding to and embracing development, the environment motif may yet serve as a force to progress beyond the rhetoric and logic of binary oppositions towards a new way of understanding international relations.

3 DEFENDING THE GLOBAL COMMONS

Christopher D Stone

INTRODUCTION

Across the world, the environment is in peril. Forests are being stripped, stressed and burned. Natural habitats are vanishing. Deserts are advancing. Croplands suffer from waterlogging in some regions, overgrazing and salinization in others. The atmosphere and ozone shield are under assault. The oceans are being loaded with pollutants and swept of marine life. We are sullying the polar regions, perturbing the climate, and eradicating species.

All these alarms, and more, have been widely sounded. There is no reason to belabour them: what we need now are answers. I have two to put forward: a system of Global Guardianships, and a Global Commons Trust Fund. They alone will not *solve* our complex environmental predicaments,[1] but together they would constitute a major stride forward, a foundation for an appreciable 'greening' of international law.

To understand these proposals, a good start is to mark the distinction in outlook between the scientist, on the one hand, and the international lawyer and Statesperson, on the other. Scientists – such as geophysicists, geochemists and the like – have the luxury of contemplating the planet from the grand panorama of astronauts. From such a removed state, national boundaries fade and the mind can be struck by the marvellous wholeness of the Earth and the interconnection of globe-spanning phenomena that sustain its tenants: one great swirling envelope of atmospheric gases, the great body of ocean, and the broad globe-spanning belts of weather and vegetation.

International lawyers and Statespersons operate from a more cramped and mundane vista. Ours is an inherited world in which all that grand unity has been disrupted into political territories. We all know that most of these pencilled borders have little to do with the great natural processes that the scientist is drawn to; that they are often the legacies of chance, intrigue, vanity, avarice, and military battles that could have gone either way. But for all their caprice and impermanence, the boundaries that mark the diplomats' world, hardened as they commonly are, by pronounced cultural, religious and socio-economic differences, are no less to be reckoned with than carbon.

Broadly speaking, the diplomats' maps (the foundation for received international law) divide the world into two sorts of regions: those which fall under *territorial sovereignty*, and those that lie outside the political reach of any nation State – the *global commons*.

In this view of things, the territorial sovereignty each nation enjoys is co-extensive with its geographic boundaries, extends upwards through its air traffic space, and, in the case of the many nations with coastal borders, extends across an Exclusive Economic Zone (EEZ) running 200 nautical miles seaward.[2]

The global commons refers to those portions of the planet and its surrounding space which lie above and beyond the recognized territorial claims of any nation. That includes the atmosphere, outer space, and the high seas, together with the potentially valuable seabeds and subsurfaces that have yet to be 'enclosed' by any coastal State as part of its territorial extension. On some accounts, much the same commons status does, or should, apply to the resource-rich Antarctic, which comprises 10 per cent of the planet's land mass, and whose ownership is currently in limbo.[3]

Viewed within the constraints of traditional international law, this two-fold division into national territories and commons areas has crucial significance for all efforts to defend the environment. Within its sovereign territory, a nation can, by and large, do whatever it wants. Each nation, and it exclusively, has the right to pull up its forests, bulldoze habitats, wipe out species, fish, farm, and mine – and not have to answer to any 'outside' authority for any repercussions on its own environment.[4]

If the 'outside' world wishes to influence a country's internal behaviour – to constrain deforestation, for example – its recourse is limited. International organizations can try to persuade a developing country's leaders of the long-term benefits of a scale and pace of development which is environmentally kind. Funding sources, pre-eminently the World Bank, can withhold support from massive projects that are environmentally disruptive.[5] Wildlife groups have been known simply to pay a country to set aside an exotic habitat as a wildlife reserve, often arranging so-called 'debt-for-Nature swaps'.[6] However, as long as a nation is chewing up only its own insides, it is not, in the eyes of international law, doing anything it can be sued over. It is true there are *declarations* that all the environment, including internal environments, are to be valued;[7] but they are consistently undermined by conflicting declarations that a nation's use of its own resources is a matter of sovereign prerogative.[8] The counterbalance could be resolved in a 'green' direction: that is, conceivably, grave damage to internal environments could someday come to be considered a sort of 'ecocide', and, likened to human rights violations, made a violation of international law. Unfortunately, such a development does not appear imminent. In the meantime, 'outside' influence is constrained to such tactics as bargaining, loan conditions, and perhaps trade pressures. As we know all too well, desertification and deforestation continue, and thus far neither these tactics nor any others have been able to arrest the degradation of internal environments.

As frustrating as one finds it to have an affect on the 'internal' scenarios, the situation in the commons areas is, in many regards, even worse. All the nations of the world are faced with deterioration of their internal environments, with the result that resources required for cleaning up the commons have to compete with resources required to clean up internal environments. This is a competition in which the domestic demands have a clear advantage. When a country's interior deteriorates – as urban areas become smoggy, or fish die in lakes – there is at least a political constituency of directly aggrieved voters to focus pressure on whichever government – State, federal or local – to provide relief. In contrast, when we turn to the commons, the areas lack, by definition, their own 'citizens' to complain, and those who do in fact have complaints cannot locate a competent authority to complain to.

However, the plight of the commons reflects more than a jurisdictional vacuum. Important economic and bargaining considerations reinforce the inclination to give the commons short shrift. When a nation turns its attentions inward, it can select the most pressing problem on its own political agenda, be it water quality or soil treatment. Since a nation has full control over its domestic programmes, it can arrange to fund only those projects for which it receives at least a dollar benefit for each dollar it spends. However, suppose we were to ask the same nation to invest a million dollars in mending the commons – to restrict carbon emissions, for example, and thereby reduce the risks of climate change. In expenditures to clean up the commons, the nation stands to capture some fraction of the benefits (the reduced risks of climate change). But most of the benefit will be diffused among all 180 or so members of the world community, some of whom will fail to shoulder their proportionate share of the burden.

One can put the point in familiar public finance terms: the maintenance of the commons is a public good, and efforts to provide for the public good are notoriously dogged by the manoeuvers of those who wish to 'free ride' on those who contribute. Of course, domestic governments face the same problem when they undertake any public finance project: parks, police and so on. The problem is that combatting strategic behaviour and securing cooperation in the international arena is considerably more difficult than overcoming the analogous obstacles in domestic contexts. In domestic democratic societies subject to majority rule, dissenters – potential free-riders – can be simply forced to pay their share by law. In the international community, however, a corollary of sovereignty is that no nation can be forced into any agreement to which it does not assent: in essence, unanimity,

Furthe,

1 Rethinkin
Industrial E

2 Managem
2645, £12.0

not majority, is the collective choice rule. As a consequence, every country is wary of getting drawn into a fragile multilateral agreement in which it may find itself under pressure to pay out a larger share of the costs than its benefits warrant. (This is one basis for the United States's reluctance to put teeth into a Climate Change convention). Each nation may incline to mend its own local disorders even when it would make more sense overall (if cooperation could be ensured), for all the nations of the world to turn their joint attention to more ominous problems they face in common.

This 'no man's land' feature of the commons has important implications for the design of institutional remedies. The fact that the degraded area lies outside anyone's exclusive jurisdiction presents impediments to *monitoring* deterioration, and presents even more serious obstacles to securing legal and diplomatic *relief*.

Invasion of Territories

Speaking realistically, international law does not enter the picture until something a nation does – releasing a radioactive cloud, for example – sweeps across its boundaries and damages a neighbouring country. In those circumstances it is generally agreed, at least it is universally verbalized, that the injured neighbour has grounds for diplomatic and legal remedies. In the 1940s the US successfully sued Canada over sulphur fumes from a Canadian lead smelter that were wafting across the boundary into the State of Washington.[9] The US once even acquiesced to a Mexican diplomatic demand that it eliminate offensive transboundary odours that were blowing south from a US stockyard.[10] Such results in transboundary contexts are rare; but relief is at least a theoretical option that potential polluters have to consider in the design of factories etc.

When, however, fumes blow across a frontier not into a neighbouring nation, but up into the commons region of higher atmosphere, or out across the sea, however many soft declarations may denounce it,[11] resort to law becomes appreciably more problematic. In a typical nation-to-nation transboundary conflict, such as the US–Canada case referred to, one can assume there are officials of the injured state on hand at the site of the harm to inspect the damage and determine where it is coming from. In that dispute, the fumes could be characterized as an 'invasion' (however modest) of US sovereignty, the sort of thing international law has customarily sought to mend.

By contrast, when the open sea or the atmosphere is degraded, who is on hand to keep watch? Are significant loadings of heavy metals working their way into the deep seas and seabed? If so, are the levels dangerous and are they insinuating their way into the food cycle? Who is responsible for cleaning them up? To answer these questions, even to gather the relevant facts in a scientifically and internationally credible way, goes beyond any single nation's ordinary motivation and competence; it practically necessitates a multi-national coordinated effort.

Even then, if the appropriate institution *could* be established, and the monitors *could* identify substantial and worrisome changes in the environment and pin down their source, there would remain judicial obstacles of legal interest and standing. If someone should come onto your yard, and steal your pet turtle from your pond, you would have a suit because it would be a trespass and injury to your property. But if some nation's fleet of fishing vessels, sweeping the high seas with nets, obliterates scores of rare sea turtles or dolphins, customary international law – that is, international law as it stands absent some specially-tailored treaty – is unlikely to grant a remedy to any nation that objects.[12] Who can prove that the destroyed creatures would have been captured by the objecting nation? On the high seas, because the turtles do not belong to anyone, it is unclear that anyone has the legal interest which the law requires to complain. Besides, what is the market value (the law would want to know) of turtles and dolphins? Where was the legal damage?

Who is Responsible?

One should understand that the liberty of each State to impair the commons is not a principle that is condoned. There are, in fact, any number of lofty declarations of international conferences and commentators which solemnly (although usually with saving double-speak qualifications) renounce abuse of the commons areas. There are even scraps of legal doctrine from which a suit to protect the commons areas might be constructed. Some government could argue that a country responsible for a massive injury to the commons had committed a wrong *erga omnes* (crime against the community of nations), a notion historically invoked to legitimate the power of any nation to punish piracies on the high seas. But the fact is, aside perhaps from the special case where the complaining nation was able to show that the offender violated an express agreement (such as a treaty), no claim arising out of commons despoliation has yet to be pressed, and the prospects of such a suit would have to be regarded at present as rather doubtful.[13]

Thus, whatever lip service environmental diplomats will pay the commons areas at great Earth Summits, nations still find it expedient to let vast proportions of their pollutants simply blow away into the global atmosphere or run off untreated into the open sea. Each year, humankind pumps into the atmosphere over eight billion tons of carbon, together with hundreds of millions of tons of nitrogen oxides, sulphur dioxide, particulate, and other such airborne junk. Into the oceans, their marine life already pillaged by modern fishing technology, go hundreds of millions of tons of sewage, dredge spoils, agricultural run-off and industrial wastes. To this we add millions of tons of marine litter – no longer your ordinary biode-gradable garbage, either. Each year, tens of thousands of marine mammals, turtles, and seabirds die from entanglement with or ingestion of plastics and abandoned fishing gear ('ghost nets'), some of which will not disintegrate for centuries.

Some of the stuff that has been dumped is even worse. Sitting on the seabed right now are hundreds of thousands of tons of World War II munitions, including unfired chemical weapons,[14] to which we have more recently added untold canisters of nuclear waste that were deposited in the sea for 'safe storage', which are already showing signs of fatigue.[15] An ex-Soviet official recently admitted that for nearly 30 years the Soviet military had been jettisoning its nuclear wastes (including thousands of canisters, 12 old reactors and one damaged submarine) into the Arctic Sea in the most heedless way imaginable.[16] The important thing now is, no one is responsible for cleaning up the whole mess.

This does not mean that the commons are utterly undefended. While no nation can be compelled to protect the commons, various protective conventions and declarations have garnered the cooperation of enough countries to monitor the rate of deterioration. The 1985 Vienna Convention on Substances that Deplete the Ozone Layer is achieving a dramatic reduction in the release of ozone-depleting agents. The 1991 UN General Assembly Resolution against Driftnetting is, technically, no more than that, a legally nonbinding 'resolution'. Yet, the announced willingness of the major driftnetting nations, Japan, Taiwan and Korea, to respect it is a promising development of some significance. Also there is a whole patchwork of other conventions in other areas, each with its own aspirations and attainments. These include the ban on weapons testing in space, the International Whaling Convention (IWC), the Antarctic treaty system, and the London Convention on the Prevention of Marine Pollution by Dumping of Wastes.

The present picture can best be summarized as this: if one looks behind the various lofty declarations and examines the prevailing practices – the law in action – one finds that, aside from a few areas provided for by special treaty, much of the commons is only partially and feebly protected. In essence, since the commons are available for purposes of wealth exploitation – anyone can sweep it for fish or scoop up deep seabed minerals without answering to the world community – questions about the pollution of the commons are going unanswered. What is to be done?

A VOICE FOR THE ENVIRONMENT: GLOBAL COMMONS GUARDIANS

One approach is to negotiate more and stronger multinational treaties specially tailored to protect designated portions of the commons, along the lines of the Ozone Agreements, and the more recent, still nebulous, FrameWork Conventions on Climate Change that emerged from the Earth Summit at Rio. Those efforts deserve further support.

Yet, there is another approach, in some ways bolder, and in some ways integral and supplementary to the treaty efforts. As we saw, one of the reasons for over-exploitation of the commons is the lack of a plaintiff clearly qualified to demonstrate both standing and injury. Hence, the first proposal; to establish a system of guardians who would be legal representatives for the natural environment. The idea is similar to the concept of legal guardians (sometimes 'conservators') in familiar legal systems. Presented with possible invasions of the interests of certain persons who are unable to speak for themselves as such, unrepresented infants, the insane, and the senile, courts are empowered to appoint a legal guardian to speak for them. So too, guardians can be designated to be the legal voice for the otherwise voiceless environment: the whales, the dolphins, important habitats, and so on.

The guardians could either be drawn from existing international agencies that have the appropriate focus, such as the United Nations Environment Programme (UNEP) and the World Meteorological Organization (WMO), or from the many non-governmental organizations (NGOs), such as Greenpeace or the Worldwide Fund for Nature (WWF). Certainly the guardians would not be given plenary and unreviewable powers to halt any activity they disapproved of. Rather, the guardian would be built into the institutional process to ensure that environmental values were being identified and accounted for. Take the oceans, for example. To ensure that oceanic ecosystems were being adequately accounted for, an Ocean Guardian might be designated, perhaps the Joint Group of Experts on the Scientific Aspects of Marine Pollution (GESAMP), with supplementary legal staffing.

As guardian, its first chore would be to *monitor*. It would review ocean conditions not just to gather facts 'scientifically', but with a specific eye towards assuring compliance with conventions already in place. One weakness of the 1972 London Dumping Convention (LDC) and many fishing agreements is that compliance depends almost entirely on 'self-monitoring', without any independent effort to survey the activities of signatories. The guardian could provide that monitoring. By doing so, it would improve the willingness of every State to comply, since each country will no longer feel hesitant that if they observe the rules, they will be the only nice, law-abiding 'sucker'. Everyone would benefit from the mutual assurances.

Second, the guardian would exercise *legislative functions*, not as a legislative body, but as part of the complex web of global policy-making institutions. In exercising the monitoring function it would undoubtedly come across problems uncovered by existing agreements, which would prompt it to recommend and stimulate formation of new multinational agreements. The guardian could appear before international agencies and even the domestic legislatures and administrative agencies of nations considering ocean-impacting actions to counsel moderation and to suggest alternatives on behalf of its 'client'.

Third, it could be authorized to appear as a special *intervenor-counsel* for the unrepresented environmental 'victim' in a variety of bilateral and multi-lateral disputes. For example, whenever there is a proposal to dam an international river, one or more of the nations along the river may initiate international negotiations to assure the fair division of the water flow, electric and irrigation benefits, etc. However, we have learned, often too late and to our chagrin, that such dam projects inevitably affect the environment, including life in the oceans to which they feed. The ocean guardian would appear as a 'third party' before the appropriate body to assure, not necessarily that the viability of the ocean environment was the conclusive issue, but at least that it was raised in the most effective manner possible.[17]

The final function simply takes the intervenor concept one step further. International treaties should endow the guardian with standing to initiate legal and diplomatic action on the ocean ecosystem's behalf in appropriate situations; to sue at least in those cases where, if the ocean were a sovereign State, the law would afford it some prospect of relief. The law could be arranged so that, even if a violating nation refused to appear, the guardian could secure a declaratory judgment that the conduct in question was indeed unlawful. Such a judicial pronouncement is far less steely than an injunction, but is not the sort of thing members of the world community would simply brush off either.

The notion of legal standing for nature is hardly farfetched. Indeed, many guardianship functions are currently recognized in US environmental laws on a more modest scale. For example, under the Superfund Legislation, the National Oceanic and Atmospheric Administration (NOAA) is designated trustee for fish, marine mammals, and their supporting ecosystems within the US fisheries zone. NOAA has authority to institute suits to recover restoration costs against any party that injures its 'ward'.[18] A major law suit is presently proceeding in a federal court in Southern California, in which NOAA attorneys are suing local chemical companies allegedly responsible for seepage of PCBs and other chemicals into the coastal water ecosystem.[19] There is no reason such a system could not be replicated internationally.

A Case for Seals

A recent case in Germany even invoked the guardianship concept in a case with global commons implications.[20] In 1988, approximately 15,000 dead seals mysteriously washed up on the beaches of the North and Baltic Seas. Widespread alarms were sounded, amid considerable concern that the massive deaths were a portent of an impending ecological disaster. This most flagrant insult to the North Sea's chemistry was widely considered to be titanium and other heavy metals that were being produced by incineration and dumping on the high seas by permit of the West German Government.

Conceivably, any of the States bordering the sea might have tried to challenge Germany's actions. However, recall that, so long as the harm was being done on, or affecting life only in, the high seas, the authority of any nation to sue was (and is) doubtful. For Poland, say, to trace through a legally compensable injury would have been nearly hopeless. From the point of view of national fishing interests, the reduction, or even elimination, of the seals might even have been regarded as an economic *benefit*. (The harbour seals involved, unlike fur seals, are themselves commercially valueless but compete with fishermen for commercial fish stocks.) Moreover, all the sea-bordering nations were contributing to the pollution, and thus, had any of them objected, their case might have been be met by Germany with an 'unclean hands' defence: 'you can't complain, because you're as guilty as we are'.

Who then, was to speak for the seals, and, in so doing, represent all the elements of the ecological web whose hazarded fortunes were intertwined? In comparable situations in the US, courts have shown willingness to interpret the Administrative Procedure Act and other laws as giving a public interest group standing to challenge the government's actions. German law, however, is much more stringent about allowing 'citizen's suits'.

The solution was for a group of German environmental lawyers (with the encouragement and advice of the author) to institute an action in which the North Sea Seals were named the lawsuit's principal plaintiffs, with the lawyers appearing essentially as guardians, speaking for them. What better plaintiffs? No one could accuse the seals, surely, of unclean hands (or fins). The injury to them, furthermore, did not appear as problematical as it was one step less removed from the harm that the other littoral nations might have raised.

The administrative law court rejected the seals' standing on the grounds that seals were not 'persons' and no specific legislation had authorized standing on their behalf. There were two lessons. First, the very filing of the case and attendant news media coverage was considerable and favourable. When the time came for the government to renew the ocean dumping permit, the authorities who initially gave their permission were forced, by a kindled public opinion, to revoke it. Germany has committed to limit or phase-out disposal of heavy metals in the North Sea. The seals lost the battle in court, but emerged hardier in the war.

On the other hand, the technical defeat underscored the advantage of institutionalizing any system for commons guardians in advance. When local (länder) statutes so provide, even German courts will allow specially designated environmental groups to challenge forest-threatening actions.

In the international context, formal recognition of commons guardians could be achieved through reforms within existing legal frameworks – for example, appropriate amendments of the charters of the United Nations and of the International Court of Justice.

The institutionalization of guardians would have the virtue of designating one responsible voice for each part of the environment. There is at least one drawback that grows out of that virtue, however. The more power a guardian were to have, and the more exclusively its voice were made to be the voice that counted, the greater the political pressures to compromise its scientific and legal integrity.

Furthermore, while a system of commons guardians would be a step forward, it would be no panacea for biosphere degradation. Those commons areas that were placed under guardianships, such as living ocean resources, would be elevated to a legal and diplomatic standing on a par with a sovereign. But unfortunately, under present law the powers even of sovereign States are limited when it comes to protecting themselves from transfrontier pollution. Hence, the success of a guardianship regime would depend not only upon legitimation and institutionalization of the guardians as legal representative, but upon significant changes in the substantive law which the guardian would be empowered to invoke – for example, conventions proscribing levels of pollution hazardous to sea life. The oceans not only need their own independent voice, they need the world community to adopt more diligently protective standards.

FINANCING THE REPAIR: THE GLOBAL COMMONS TRUST FUND

Supporting a system of guardianships – indeed, any counterattack on global degradation – will cost money. Where will it come from? I have already observed the understandable inclination of political leaders to give priority to their hard-pressed domestic agendas before they address the commons areas. If any nation unilaterally and voluntarily lays out a hundred million dollars to clean up the ocean floor or atmosphere, it just relieves the pressure on other nations to pay up, if they can bank on getting a 'free ride' on the benefits of others' expenditures. Meager or non-cooperation becomes a dominant strategy.

Of course, as noted above, problems of 'free-riding' confront any domestic society when it plans the provision of any public goods, such as the payment for police and fire protection, and the maintenance of public parks. But the difference, once more, is that domestic democratic societies have the power to tax. When the majority decides on a programme for the general welfare, it can compel a raising of the needed funds. The world community enjoys no comparable power to levy a 'world tax' for world public welfare.

While 'One World' idealists have proposed such a tax, it is not presently a viable alternative.

There already exists one financial mechanism to tackle the job without appeal to taxes: the Global Environmental Facility (GEF). The GEF is a pilot programme originally conceived to support energy conservation, preserve ecological diversity, arrest depletion of the ozone shield, and protect the marine environment. It has been able to garner $1.3 billion in voluntary financial commitments from the industrialized countries for the years 1991, 1992 and 1993. As a financial mechanism, however, purely voluntary contributions are not a dependable basis on which to build a stable infrastructure. In fact, the pilot phase of GEF is soon to expire and its future level of funding is highly uncertain.

Exacerbating the GEF's problems has been a continuous conflict over how the fund is to be governed. The developed countries, as donors, want a proportionately stronger voice. They, therefore, favour governance somewhat along the lines of the World Bank, which allots each nation voting power in proportion to its contributions. In 1987, the World Bank formula gave the US 19.47 per cent of the voting power; Egypt had just 0.52 per cent. Such a weighted-voting plan may be explained on pragmatic grounds: it induces the wealthy to keep giving. But the unevenness rankles the Third World as being clearly undemocratic, and unresponsive to a pattern of historical wrongs that make wealth transfers now a matter of compensation and obligation, not of largesse. Hence, Third World countries resist transporting the same standards into the environmental field; even more specifically, they fear any such formula will slant funding towards projects favoured by the developed countries, such as ozone depletion, and away from the more immediate concerns of the Third World, notably desertification and treating water. All parties have agreed in principle to come up with 'some other' formula. However, friction over the issue, and the continued inability of anyone to produce a mutually acceptable alternative, is one more impediment to the GEF's long-range viability.

Implenting a Global Commons Trust Fund

These considerations suggest the advantages of a fund that is not wholly dependent on voluntary contributions. More specifically, a financial mechanism that sought levies from legal obligations would both make the flow of funds relatively dependable from year to year, and, by removing the present element of 'largesse', perhaps eliminate the governance element that arises out of donor-donee frictions. That is what the proposed Global Commons Trust Fund (GCTF) aims to achieve. The idea is that in order to finance the repair of the global commons, we look to levies on uses of the commons areas themselves.

Let us expand on how this might be accomplished. As I have already observed, under present practice all the commons areas can be used and abused with relative impunity – free of charge. If we were to rectify this practice, and charge even a fraction of the fair worth for the various uses to which nation-States put the global commons, we would advance two goals at once. The charges would dampen the intensity of abuse, and at the same time underwrite the costs of providing public order such as marine resources management and the repair of environmental damages. Because the resources raised would not be founded on 'largesse' but on what could be presented as legitimate obligations, the supply of funds would be relatively more stable from year to year.

The revenue, while difficult to estimate, is potentially enormous. Consider some rough projections.

The oceans

The world harvests 185 billion pounds of marine fish annually. A tax of a mere one-tenth of one per cent of the commercial value would raise approximately $200 million for the proposed fund.[21] The same token rate on oil and gas produced in the EEZs would add perhaps $80 million more.[22] As for the use of the oceans as a dump-site, the official figures, almost certainly under-reported, amount to 212 million metric tons of sewage sludge, industrial wastes, and dredged materials yearly.[23] A tax of only a dime a ton would raise an additional $20 million. A charge on ocean transport – particularly uses such as tanker traffic that imperil waters and beaches – would swell the fund further.[24]

The atmosphere

By burning fossil fuels and living forests, humankind thrusts 22 billion metric tons of carbon dioxide (CO_2) into the atmosphere annually.[25] A CO_2 tax of only ten cents a ton would raise $2.2 billion each year, 30 times the current budget of the United Nations Environmental Programme (UNEP). Taxing other greenhouse gases (GHGs) such as nitrous oxides at a comparably modest (dime-a-ton) rate, indexed to their 'blocking' equivalent to CO_2, would bring the total to $3.3 billion.[26] The same ten cents a ton tax could be levied on other (non-GHG) transfrontier pollutants; a sulphur dioxide levy, for example, would produce $16 million more.

Space

Tapping the wealth of the planets may still be far off, but the rights to 'park' satellites in the choice slots is a potential source of enormous wealth right now. Most valued are points along the 'geostationary orbit', the volume of space 22,300 miles directly above the earth's equator in which a satellite can remain in a relatively fixed point relative to the surface below. The number of available points is restricted by minimal distances required between satellites to avoid interference. Rights to spots directly above the Earth's equatorial belt are also valued because they are exposed to exceptionally long hours of sunlight, and are therefore ideally situated for production of energy from solar radiation, as a support for special operations such as high-tech gravity-free manufacturing, and, perhaps, ultimately for commercial redirecting to Earth.

These positions, and ancillary frequencies in space, 'the most precious resource of the telecommunication ages' – worth to users an estimated $1 trillion globally over the next decade – are now parcelled out free of charge in a system that can only be labelled absurd. The tiny island nation of Tonga, after being awarded 3–6 orbital positions gratis, subsequently put them up for auction, recently striking a deal with a satellite company for $2 million a year 'rental'. It is reportedly seeking more such deals. Why should the rights to any of these slots and spectrum positions, a limited resource that is the legacy and province of all humankind, and worth trillions of dollars to users, be doled out like free lottery tickets, while those who would mend the planet are severely limited by a lack of resources? An auction of slots and frequencies would yield several hundred million dollars annually.

Biodiversity

I am a little more ambivalent about including biodiversity as part of the Common Heritage of Humankind in the sense of making it a tax base for the fund. While tuna are (often) in the high seas, beyond any nation's exclusive jurisdiction, many biological riches lie within the territories of nations. Of course, when we talk of biotechnological potential, we are not talking about seizing physical matter from forests, trees, and so on, as much as copying and exploiting *genetic information*. It presumably makes small difference to the biologically rich nations such as Columbia and Brazil, who would regard global demands to share the fortune of their biological wealth about the same way the Saudis would react to arguments that the world should co-own its oil. The proposal may simply intrude too far into their sovereign space and prerogatives, which is why the Rio negotiators rejected labelling biodiversity part of the Common Heritage in favour of the limper 'common concern'.

On the other hand, perhaps a compromise could be worked out whereby the industrial world's pharmaceutical companies, which will presumably manage the exploitation of the potential, would pay a royalty into the GCTF.

Even if we do not include biological diversity in the base, the total thus far is about $4 billion a year. That is before adding the yield of a surcharge on uneliminated ozone depleting agents, on toxic incineration at sea, or on the liquid wastes that invade the oceans from rivers. Consider also fees on the minerals that someday will be harvested from the sea and seabed, and, perhaps, depending upon the staying power of the conservation movement which is fighting the efforts, the Antarctic.[27]

Another way to bolster the fund would be to make it the receptacle for legal judgments assessed under various commons-protecting treaties. For example, the oils spills conventions could easily be amended to provide that some measure of ecological damages to the high seas (and not merely local waters) be paid into the trust fund and marked for the benefit of the environment. There are precedents: the Exxon Corporation established an environmental repair fund in the wake of the *Exxon Valdez* disaster in Alaska. After the spill of the highly dangerous pesticide Kepone into the James River in the US, Allied Chemical, which was responsible, agreed to establish such a fund for the James River, and Sandoz Corporation did the same in the wake of the catastrophic 1986 accident in Basel, Switzerland, which devastated marine life in the Rhine.

Areas in Need of the Global Commons Trust Fund

That brings us to the functions of the GCTF: what would the raised revenue be used for? To begin with, the GCTF would pay the costs of the Guardianship system, previously described. Any number of potentially critical treaties, including the 1972 London Dumping Convention, the 1973 Convention on International Trade in Endangered Species, the 1987 Basel Convention on the Movement of Transboundary Wastes, and the 1992 UN Resolution on Driftnetting, are simply under-policed; the GCTF would make policing viable. The monies would support improved scientific monitoring and modelling of the commons areas, and underwrite the transfer of environment-friendly technology to developing nations. They could also promote institutional readiness to respond to various sorts of crises with the global equivalent of 'fire fighters'. To illustrate, no single nation anticipates incidents in its own waters enough to warrant keeping on alert a full-time staff trained and equipped to contain oil spills. But a force with global responsibilities, financed out of the fund, might well be cost-effective. It has been estimated that $150 million a year would underwrite an effective world-wide system to ensure early detection of major new viral diseases, for instance, so that the next AIDS-type epidemic does not catch us off-guard.

Notwithstanding the mutual and widespread value of such measures, not every country would readily submit: one can anticipate resistance among the already struggling developing nations, in particular. Yet they do not face the highest levies, and the fund therefore does not depend on them. For the developed countries, the four–five billion dollars or so is a lot more realistic than many of the figures that have been bandied around in the wake of Rio.

Some countries will object to any tax on activities within their territories or, in the case of the coastal States, within their self-proclaimed EEZs.

47

However, the charges are not for what nations do within their sovereign territories; they are levied largely for the effects of their activities on the 'outside' world.[28] Moreover, many non-coastal, landlocked nations – along with many scholars – continue to regard as semi-legitimate, at best, the coastal States's proclaimed EEZs of 200 miles and more from their coasts. Allowing the coastal States to supply exclusive management across these zones makes a certain amount of sense; some management of ocean resources is better than none. But allowing the coastal States to snatch all the wealth without any accounting to the rest of the world, just because it happens to be closer to them, is indefensible. That is why I would incline to tax activities such as fishing and oil production undertaken anywhere beyond the traditional territorial boundaries of three or 12 miles from the coastline, and not merely in the smaller region beyond their EEZs.

Many people will object to the pollution charge component of the proposal, calling it immoral to permit pollution-for-pay. The answer is that some pollution is inevitable, and it is more of an outrage that the polluters get away with it, as they presently do, free of charge.

Indeed, if there is a real objection to the proposed GCTF, it is that the initial rates I have suggested are probably too paltry. Many would say that, viewed as a strategy for reducing environmental damage, the levels advanced for discussion – ten cents a ton for carbon usage – are unlikely to confront the polluting nations with the full costs of the damage they are causing, and therefore will fall short of inducing the 'right' amount of conservation and pollution control.[29] Viewed from the reverse side, as a strategy for maximizing revenues for the environmental infrastructure, the proposed rates will often fall short of extracting the full value of what users would pay if they were required to bid for restricted rights at an internationally conducted auction.

It is true that, superficially, similar proposals have been advanced in the past, without making much political headway. But the GCTF can be distinguished from the other similar sounding plans – distinguished in ways that may make the GCTF both more effective and more 'saleable' politically.

First, the GCTF can be differentiated from a host of plans, such as that put forward by the late Rajiv Gandhi of India, to tax each developed nation a fraction of its Gross National Product and to distribute the funds to less-developed countries. While Gandhi called his proposal a Planet Protection Fund, the transparent intent was to redistribute wealth from rich countries to poor. The aim may be noble, but it ought not to be confused with the GCTF, which would link levies not to each nation's wealth per se, but to its *use of the commons*, and would restrict application of the revenue raised to the *maintenance and repair of the commons*.

Second, most proposals have been limited to a single source or activity. Recently the focus has been on carbon use. Years ago, during the Law of the

Sea, negotiations were advanced, unsuccessfully, to tax users of ocean space. Although the ocean tax proposals failed the public atmosphere, in terms of environmental consciousness, is more sympathetic today than 20 years ago. The proposed ocean taxes, moreover, were designed to pay off third world countries, rather than being earmarked to repair the ocean environment. By contrast both with the carbon and ocean tax, the idea of the GCTF is comprehensive: to bring all economic uses of the commons under an overall plan, from uses of the ocean to uses of the atmosphere and of space.

CONCLUSION

It is true that the GCTF, by focusing on the global commons, would leave unaffected many pressing problems that occur wholly within sovereign boundaries. The answer is that these 'internal' problems, bad as they are, are better attended to by existing institutions. In fact, the International Development Agency (a subsidiary of the World Bank) has had no trouble collecting a $3 billion 'earth increment' to provide virtually free grants to help poor nations protect their internal ecological systems.[30] To some extent, the relative disadvantage of the commons is a question of out of sight, out mind; and partly, while dolphins may have friends in Greenpeace, they don't vote or form potentially irksome alliances. For both reasons the commons is, once more, a low priority.

The guardianship proposal would help fill the void. It would establish a 'police' mechanism for the global commons areas, an international public service for an international public good. The GCTF is the mechanism to pay for it. The Global Commons Trust Fund is not merely a roundabout scheme to take wealth from the rich nations and redistribute it to the poor. It simply seeks, from users of the global commons, a reasonable fee for their use of the commons so as to apply it back to the commons, for its maintenance and repair. What could be more reasonable? Or, given the afflictions of our planet, more crucial?

4 ENFORCING ENVIRONMENTAL SECURITY

Philippe Sands[1]

Humanity stands at a defining moment in history. We are confronted with a perpetuation of disparities between and within nations, a worsening of poverty, hunger, ill health and illiteracy, and the continuing deterioration of the ecosystems on which we depend for our well-being.[2]

Agenda 21

INTRODUCTION

The emerging importance of environmental concerns to international security[3] was emphasized in a January 1992 statement by the 15 members of the United Nations Security Council, declaring that 'non-military sources of instability in the economic, social, humanitarian and ecological fields have become threats to peace and security.'[4] Six months later, the majority of the world's nations gathered in Rio de Janeiro for the UN Conference on the Environment and Development (UNCED), which had, as one of its major objectives,

> to assess the capacity of the UN system to assist in the prevention and settlement of disputes in the environmental sphere and to recommend measures in this field, while respecting existing bilateral and international agreements that provide for the settlement of such disputes.[5]

Implicit in the international legal instruments adopted at UNCED is the recognition that the members of the international community must act together to address global environmental challenges and to prevent the occurrence and escalation of international environmental conflicts.[6]

In this broader security context, States' compliance with their international environmental obligations has become a more critical issue in international affairs than ever before. This is evident from the attention the subject received during UNCED as well as the negotiation of recent landmark environmental treaties, including the 1987 Montreal Protocol on Substances that Deplete the Ozone Layer and the 1992 Conventions on Climate Change and Biological Diversity.

Three factors underlie this increased concern with compliance. First, the growing demands and needs of States for access to and use of natural resources, coupled with a finite, and perhaps even shrinking, resource base, lay the groundwork for increasing interstate tension and conflict. Second, as international environmental obligations increasingly affect national economic interests, States that do not comply with their environmental obligations are perceived to gain unfair competitive economic advantage over other States. Finally, the nature and extent of international environmental obligations have been transformed in recent years as States assume greater environmental treaty commitments.

Despite the recent emergence of the concept of environmental security, the challenges it poses are not new to the international legal order. Indeed, the legal issues facing the international community today in relation to the environment are remarkably similar to those addressed one hundred years ago.[7] Over the past century, the international legal system has developed institutions, mechanisms and techniques for preventing and resolving international environmental disputes that have emerged as certain natural resources diminish. The controversial issues include transboundary air pollution, the diversion of international rivers, conservation of fisheries resources, national import restrictions adopted to enforce environmental objectives and responsibility for rehabilitation of mined lands.[8] The existing institutions that deal with environmental security are the United Nations, regional and other organizations established by UNCED and earlier environmental agreements. Furthermore, in the last two decades since the 1972 Stockholm Conference on the Human Environment – which was the precursor of today's environmental movement – the international community has created a large body of international environmental law to establish standards and procedures on handling disputes. The current dispute between Hungary, the Czech Republic and Slovakia over the diversion of the Danube, illustrates the range of enforcement and dispute settlement options available: Hungary is seeking to prevent further dam construction by taking the case to the International Court of Justice (ICJ), as well as to arbitration and the emergency procedures of the Conference on Security and Cooperation in Europe (CSCE).[9]

Although the legal mechanisms for ensuring compliance and resolving environmental disputes have developed significantly, these mechanisms are still used infrequently and have yet to be tested by a major conflict. In the absence of clear rules establishing acceptable global and regional standards of environmental behaviour with regard to such areas as atmospheric emissions, waste disposal and production of hazardous substances, interstate disputes will occur with increasing frequency. Similarly, the failure to comply with minimum standards of good neighbourliness – carrying out transboundary environmental impact assessments, exchanging information or consulting on projects likely to have transboundary effects – will cause significant tension. It is unclear whether the international legal system has the resources to meet these and other imminent challenges to environmental security. UNCED provided an opportunity to develop stronger enforcement mechanisms, but it now appears that this opportunity was not fully utilized. Achieving international environmental security thus demands setting firmer standards and procedures to enforce compliance with these obligations. Non-compliance by States and international institutions limits the overall effectiveness of environmental treaties, undermines the international legal process and contributes to conflict and instability in the international system.[10] Non-compliance raises three separate, but interrelated, legal questions regarding implementation, enforcement and conflict resolution:

(1) What formal or informal steps must a State or international institution take to implement its international legal obligations?
(2) Who may seek to enforce the international environmental obligations of a State or international organization?
(3) What techniques and bodies exist under international law to settle disputes over alleged non-compliance with international environmental obligations?

This chapter briefly considers these three questions, and then identifies some of the more critical issues that are likely to face the international legal system in the near future. Case examples highlight possible techniques to resolve those disputes. The chapter concludes with a brief assessment of UNCED and the capacity of the international legal system to respond effectively to growing threats to environmental security. The discussion notes that although considerable precedents exist with regard to environmental law, the international legal system does not yet have the institutional capacity to deal with new environmental challenges that transcend national boundaries and require a supranational response. Recent developments, however, suggest that the international community recognizes this problem and is preparing to address it.

RESOLVING ENVIRONMENTAL CONFLICTS

International environmental conflicts arise when States conduct or permit activities that other States consider to have adverse or illegal environmental consequences. At the root of international environmental conflict lies the actual or perceived failure of a State to fulfil its international environmental obligations under customary law, as codified for example in Principle 21 of the 1972 Stockholm Declaration[11] or international treaty obligations.[12] State compliance requires action in three ways: it must adopt national enabling legislation, policies and programmes; it must ensure compliance within its jurisdiction and control; and it must fulfil any obligations to the appropriate international institutions, such as reporting the national measures taken to give effect to the obligations.

National Enforcement

A State formally accepts an international environmental obligation through ratification of a treaty or acceptance of the act of an international institution. Subsequently, the State will need to develop, adopt or modify relevant national legislation, policies and programmes through administrative, legislative or other means. Some treaties require States to take appropriate measures to ensure the implementation of obligations,[13] or to 'take appropriate measures within its competence to ensure compliance with [the] Convention and any measures in effect pursuant to it.'[14] Most also require States to designate a competent national authority or focal point for liaison purposes.[15]

Once an environmental commitment has been mandated by national legislation, the State then has the obligation to ensure full and effective compliance. A number of treaties attempt to enforce compliance either by those measures existing within the State's jurisdiction or control, or through the application of national sanctions or other such punishment.[16] Enforcing national compliance is a matter for the public authorities of each State; some States also allow private enforcement through suits brought by citizens.

Like other international legal obligations, almost all environmental treaties now require that signatory States report certain information to a designated international institution. This information varies with each treaty, but typically includes: statistical information on production, imports and exports; the grant of permits or authorizations to pollute; measures adopted for implementation and enforcement of the treaty's provisions; relevant judicial decisions; scientific information; and breaches or violations that occurred under a State's jurisdiction or control.[17] These reports provide the international community with a means for assessing the implementation of a State's obligations. It has become quite clear, however, that many States are unwilling to meet even the basic obligation to provide a regular report of their activities, suggesting that other obligations also may be ignored.[18]

International Enforcement

Once there is evidence that a State has failed to uphold an environmental obligation, it becomes necessary to determine who has the right to seek its enforcement at the international level.[19] Enforcers may include a State or group of States, international institutions or non-governmental organizations (NGOs). In practice, international enforcement involves a combination of the three. The extent to which any of these parties actually can initiate or participate in enforcement measures, will depend on the nature of the alleged violation, the topic and the terms of the international legal instruments available. This section will examine in more depth each party's potential role as international enforcers.

State enforcement powers

As the principal subjects of international law, States have the primary role in enforcing international environmental rules. A State must show that it has a legal interest in the obligation at issue and that non-compliance by another State violates its international legal rights under customary or treaty law.

With respect to alleged breaches of treaty obligations, the right of a State to enforce obligations will usually be settled by the terms of the treaty. For example, various human rights treaties permit any party to that treaty to enforce the obligations of any other party to the same treaty.[20] Environmental treaties are sometimes less explicit, although many do establish dispute settlement mechanisms that settle the question of enforcement rights in accordance with the provisions available under the treaty. It is strongly arguable, however, that as a general matter any failure to comply with the terms of an environmental treaty is actionable by any signatory parties through the established mechanisms. This is particularly appropriate where treaties regulate issues of concern to all mankind – such as the protection of the global commons – or where violation results in economic disadvantage to a State.[21]

A more difficult question is whether or not an individual State has the right, on behalf of the entire international community, to enforce legal measures taken to protect the global environment. This point has not been well-developed under the law.[22] Two situations where this could apply are: when the activities of a State are alleged to be causing harm to the commons, and when a State is unable to show that it has suffered direct loss as a result of another State's violation of environmental law.

Unfortunately, there are many cases where States have been unwilling to enforce obligations of environmental protection. Perhaps the best example is the failure of any State to force the former Soviet Union to comply with its international legal obligations arising out of the consequences of the accident at the Chernobyl nuclear power plant in 1986.[23] This case suggests the need for an increased enforcement role for international institutions as well as NGOs, particularly where the mere attempt to enforce obligations establishes a precedent that will subsequently bind the enforcing State to the same obligations.[24]

International institutions' enforcement powers

While international institutions play an important legislative role in the development of international environmental law, their actual enforcement role is limited. As persons under international law, international institutions may seek to protect their own rights and to enforce the obligations that others have toward them.[25] Sovereign interests, however, have resulted in a general unwillingness of States to transfer much – if any – enforcement power to international institutions. This unwillingness highlights the fundamental tension between the juridical reality of States' territorial sovereignty over their natural resources and the physical reality of ecological interdependence. In a world of shared natural resources it becomes increasingly difficult to justify international constitutional arrangements that narrowly define States' abilities to enforce either environmental rights or minimum international standards of environmental behaviour.

Nevertheless, some international institutions have been endowed with enforcement or quasi-enforcement functions. In relation to weapons agreements, for example, the UN Security Council has a more or less unlimited right to 'take action in accordance with the [UN] Charter,' if the consultation and cooperation process leave doubts about a State's adherence to certain nuclear weapons treaties.[26] Many international bodies were established precisely to promote the effective implementation of their governing treaties.[27] This function could easily be interpreted to allow these institutions to expand their roles to be enforcers as well.[28] For example, the European Community Commission has the power to ensure that the provisions of the EEC Treaty and subsequent measures are applied.[29] In September 1992, the new commission to be established under the Convention for the Protection of the Marine Environment of the Northeast Atlantic was granted the right to 'decide upon and call for steps to bring about full compliance with the Convention.'[30]

NGOs' enforcement powers

NGOs, however, are not widely accepted as international legal persons except within the limited confines of international human rights law.[31] This limitation would appear to bar their participation in the international environmental legal process. Yet in practice, environmental NGOs participate actively in the negotiation of environmental treaties and at other key international meetings, serving as members of official State delegations, official observers or simply as private participants. Since the 1972 Stockholm Conference – convened primarily as a result of pressure by environmental groups – NGOs have played an important role in the great increase in international environmental legislation. Their impact is greatest at the national level, enforcing compliance through political means or by recourse to national administrative or judicial procedures. While at the international level the formal opportunities for NGOs to play an enforcement role are limited, it is in their informal capacity as watchdogs that NGOs play an important role in the development, application and enforcement of international environmental law. The unwillingness of States to act as guardians of the environment has created an important role for NGOs, who seek to force governments to adopt measures to protect the environment, to identify threats and signal breaches of existing international environmental regulations. NGOs' formal role as partners in the international process was recognized at UNCED.

Diplomatic and Legal Means of Dispute Settlement

An international set of guidelines is needed to help resolve environmental disputes among States. Article 33 of the UN Charter, which identifies the traditional mechanisms for the peaceful settlement of disputes, provides that the parties to any dispute, the continuance of which is likely to endanger the maintenance of international peace and security shall, first of all, seek a solution by negotiation, enquiry, mediation, conciliation, arbitration, judicial settlement, resort to regional agencies or arrangements, or other peaceful means of their own choice.[32]

These different techniques can be divided into two categories. The first includes diplomatic means – negotiation, consultation, mediation or conciliation – whereby the parties retain control over the dispute insofar as they may accept or reject a proposed settlement. The second encompasses legal means – arbitration and judicial settlement – that result in legally binding decisions for the parties to the dispute. Having regional and international institutions to act as mediators and conciliators provides something of a middle way. In the latter case, the legal consequences of any decision taken by the institution will depend upon its governing treaty.

Many of the earliest environmental treaties did not provide for any means of dispute settlement, whether of a diplomatic or legal nature, or of a voluntary or mandatory character.[33] Initially, the trend was toward the use of informal and non-binding mechanisms, such as negotiation and consultation, supplemented by the use of more formal mechanisms, such as conciliation, arbitration and judicial settlement. Today, the trend is toward the use of non-adversarial conciliation and non-compliance mechanisms, supplemented with the right to go to arbitration or the World Court.

Negotiation as a technique of dispute settlement has early roots in the environmental sphere, dating back more than 100 years. This widely used technique has been applied to defuse a broad range of environmental disputes before they led to serious conflict.[34] Negotiations frequently take place at the bilateral level on a range of issues, including: access to and use of shared natural resources, location of facilities and joint cooperation on transboundary resources. As a matter of more or less standard practice, environmental treaties refer to the need to ensure that parties resort to negotiation and other diplomatic channels to resolve their disputes before making use of other, more formal approaches.[35] In a similar fashion, *consultation* between States is also encouraged in environmental treaties as a way to avoid and resolve actual and potential disputes. Many treaties now provide for this measure.[36]

When negotiation and consultation fail, a number of environmental treaties provide for the use of mediation,[37] conciliation[38] or the establishment of a committee of experts[39] to resolve disputes. Both mediation and conciliation involve the intervention of a third person. In the case of *mediation*, the third person is involved as an active participant in the dialogue and interchange of proposals between the parties, and may even offer informal proposals of his or her own, but is unlikely to make a formal recommendation. In the case of *conciliation*, the third person assumes a more formal, detached role, often investigating the details of the dispute and making formal proposals for its resolution.

The political organs of international institutions and regional agencies also play an important role in dispute settlement. Such bodies may either be granted an express mandate to consider disputes between two or more parties to the treaty[40] or – as is more often the case – seek to resolve disputes between parties although absent a specific mandate to do so.

Neither mediation nor conciliation, however, produces legally binding decisions. If the parties to a dispute seek such a result, they must opt for arbitration or recourse to an international judicial body. *Arbitration* has played an important role in the development of international environmental law; it is a procedure for the settlement of disputes between States by a binding award on the basis of law and as a result of an undertaking voluntarily accepted. In earlier disputes, arbitral tribunals were established to deal with the particulars of each case.[41] In recent years, however, States negotiating environmental treaties have favoured the inclusion of a specific language that provides for the establishment of an arbitration tribunal with the power to adopt binding and final decisions. Often this step will be a last resort, following unsuccessful negotiation, mediation or conciliation.

Judicial settlement involves referring the dispute to a permanent tribunal for a legally binding decision. With regard to environmental disputes, three international judicial bodies have played, and will continue to play, an important role: the International Court of Justice (ICJ), the European Court of Justice (ECJ) and the constitutions established under the UN Convention on the Law of the Sea (UNCLOS). In addition, the courts established under the various regional human rights treaties have begun to play a role in the resolution of certain environmental disputes. As the principal judicial arm of the United Nations,[42] the ICJ is a dispute settlement body available under many environmental treaties, including the Climate Change and Biodiversity Conventions. Occasionally treaties will establish the compulsory jurisdiction of the ICJ in the dispute,[43] but more often the reference of a dispute to the ICJ requires the consent of all parties.[44] While the ICJ has never dealt fully with a major international environmental dispute, it has had the opportunity to consider matters related to natural resource conservation and to hand down judgments that establish important general guiding principles.[45] In the 1949 *Corfu Channel* case, the ICJ underlined the basis for Principle 21 of the 1972 Stockholm Declaration when it affirmed 'every State's obligation not to allow knowingly its territory to be used for acts contrary to the rights of other States.'[46] This finding has subsequently been relied upon in international treaty negotiations and environmental disputes as the basis for establishing limitations on the rights of a State over the use of its natural resources.[47]

The UN Charter also allows the General Assembly or the Security Council to request the ICJ to give an advisory opinion on any legal question.[48] Furthermore, the Charter authorizes other UN agencies to request advisory opinions by the ICJ on legal questions arising within the scope of their respective activities.[49] Advisory opinions are not binding in law upon the requesting body, yet they are accepted in practice. This route could provide an important way to obtain independent international legal advice on environmental matters.

The ECJ is the judicial institution of the EC and is required to ensure the observance of law in the interpretation and application of the EEC Treaty.[50] This translates to a stronger role for the ECJ, as the rights and obligations conferred by EC law – provided they are clear, unambiguous and unconditional – are enforceable before national courts.[51] The failure of EC member States to adopt national legislation or other measures to implement Community environmental law has been the frequent object of enforcement measures brought before the court by the EC Commission. In dealing with these cases, the ECJ has rejected different arguments by States seeking to justify their non-implementation.[52]

Environmental cases reach the ECJ in a number of ways. The most frequent route is under Article 169 of the EC Treaty. Since 1980, the EC Commission has brought more than 50 cases before the Court, alleging the failure of several member States to comply with their environmental obligations. These cases have been useful in determining that member States may not plead provisions, practices or circumstances existing in their internal legal system to justify the failure to comply with an international environmental obligation.[53] Furthermore, practices that may be altered at the whim of a national government do not constitute the proper fulfillment of an environmental obligation.[54] Article 173 of the EEC Treaty permits the ECJ to review the legality of certain acts of the EC Council and Commission, on the grounds of: lack of competence, infringement of an essential procedural requirement, infringement of the Treaty or any rule relating to its application, or misuse of powers.[55] More recently, the ECJ has considered the legality of environmental measures taken in the context of free trade obligations,[56] as well as the failure of a State to execute a judgment of the ECJ.[57]

An example of a comprehensive approach to compliance is provided by UNCLOS, which has elaborate provisions against pollution from atmospheric and land-based sources, seabed activities and dumping. UNCLOS also addresses the enforcement by States of their laws and regulations adopted in accordance with the Convention and the implementation of applicable international rules and standards.[58] Part XV of UNCLOS contains detailed provisions on compulsory dispute settlement, allowing States to choose one or more of the following mechanisms to decide disputes under UNCLOS: the International Tribunal for the Law of the Sea, the ICJ and arbitral tribunals.[59]

CHALLENGES TO ENVIRONMENTAL SECURITY

Today, international law is concerned with environmental challenges at national, regional and global levels. Whereas international environmental law was developed to address traditional concerns such as the protection of flora and fauna, the conservation of fisheries resources and oil spills – all of which had a somewhat localized interest – the fundamental challenges of the late twentieth century are of a different order. The Rio Declaration and Agenda 21 – so called for its prescriptions for the next century – advocate the integration of environmental considerations into all development activities, thus creating an enormous new agenda for international environmental law. The number of environmental disputes undoubtedly will rise as the international community seeks to reconcile the conflicting demands of economic growth and environmental protection.

Atmospheric issues are now at the top of the agenda, as scientific evidence mounts about the consequences of the depleting ozone layer and increased atmospheric concentrations of greenhouse gases to human health and the environment. In addition, the massive loss of biological diversity, deforestation, increased soil degradation, drought and desertification are issues now considered to be the common concern of all States and peoples, and thus ripe for international action.

Moreover, hazardous substances and activities, including pesticides and nuclear power, are matters demanding increased international attention and new regulatory treaties. Minimizing the generation and international transport of waste will require new legal instruments, and techniques for the disposal of waste must be found as international legal prohibitions on dumping at sea and incineration begin to take effect. Finally, and perhaps most challenging of all, the adverse environmental consequences caused by activities within the international trading system and multilateral development banks require the so-called greening of such institutions as the General Agreement on Tariffs and Trade (GATT). These challenges threaten to place immense strains on the existing international legal system.

On a more positive note, however, there now exists a sufficiently well-developed body of precedent to suggest that the international legal system does have available a number of mechanisms to deal with environmental disputes that constitute a threat to international peace and security. The following cases illustrate the availability of certain international institutions and implementation techniques that may offer the most optimism in addressing new challenges.

Indicative Cases

An important and long-standing source of international tension between North and South is the belief of people in many less-developed countries (LDCs) that their former colonial occupiers were responsible for the plunder of natural resources, and thus are obligated to rehabilitate lands and restore natural resources that were damaged or removed during colonial occupation. The ICJ has now been called upon to resolve a dispute between the island nation of Nauru and the trustee governments who managed Nauru's affairs prior to its independence in 1968. The dispute concerns damage to the territory of Nauru caused by the mining of phosphate on a massive scale, an act that has made more than one-third of the island uninhabitable. The claim is based, in part, on the principle of general international law that a State responsible for the administration of a territory must not bring about changes in the condition of the territory that will cause irreparable damage to the legal interests of a future successor State. Nauru is seeking a declaration of its legal entitlement to the proceeds of the phosphate sales, and to reparation for losses due to breaches of international legal obligations. The claim presents the ICJ with an important opportunity to consider, *inter alia*, the environmental responsibilities of an administering State, and to lay down principles that could be applied to similar disputes between other States. The ICJ could also lay down principles of more general application, concerning States' responsibilities relating to the environment and natural resources.

The *Nauru* case is potentially important in determining responsibility for environmental damage in the newly independent States of East Central Europe, and whether – and to what extent – the governments of the Commonwealth of Independent States might be responsible for environmental damage in the former Soviet satellites. Similarly, this case may help ascertain the liability of the United Kingdom for the effects of nuclear tests that were performed in Australia prior to independence.

With regard to ozone depletion and climate change – another critical environmental issue – new environmental treaties have begun to establish environmental standards that have significant economic implications for signatory States. The 1987 Montreal Protocol, as amended, requires the total phase-out in production and consumption of certain ozone-depleting substances. This was the first time that the international community had banned the production and consumption of any product. The 1992 Climate Change Convention now requires industrialized countries to return their emissions of greenhouse gases to 1990 levels by the year 2000 – a move that has significant implications for transport and energy sectors. The fear of the effects wrought by non-compliance with those obligations, and the consequential economic benefits to be gained from ignoring obligations, has led to the establishment of important new techniques for ensuring compliance.

In June 1990 the State parties to the Montreal Protocol established an Implementation Committee to consider and report on submissions made by one or more States concerning reservations about another State's implementation of its obligations under the Protocol.[60] The Committee is required to try to secure 'an amicable resolution of the matter on the basis of respect for the provisions of the Protocol'[61] and report to the Meeting of the Parties, which may decide upon and call for steps to bring about full compliance with the Protocol. In November 1992 the non-compliance procedure under the Montreal Protocol was amended to include an indicative list of measures that might be taken by a Meeting of the Parties with respect to non-compliance with the Protocol.[62]

In another significant move, the 155 signatories to the 1992 Climate Change Convention created a subsidiary body for implementation to help assess and review State implementation of the Convention. It also provided for the possibility of establishing a 'multilateral consultative process' for the resolution of implementation questions, to be available to the Parties on their request.[63] These important and innovative developments are evidence of a broadly held belief that compliance mechanisms need to be strengthened to make these treaties workable. The participation of NGOs in the negotiation of these treaties also suggests that they could be an important source of information on non-compliance; indeed, the reluctance of States to engage in whistle-blowing will require international institutions or NGOs to play a greater role in enforcement.

The impact of trade on the environment has also become a growing source of conflict among States. In the absence of international environmental standards for products and manufacturing processes, States will resort to unilateral measures of environmental protection, including import bans on products that they consider to be environmentally harmful or produced by environmentally harmful processes. Given the often severe economic consequences that result from such bans, those States whose products have been subject to an import ban have considered such an act to be an unwarranted incursion into their internal affairs.

In August 1990 the United States imposed a ban on the importation of yellow-fin tuna and yellow-fin tuna products from Mexico and intermediary nations that had been caught with purse-seine fishing nets. Use of these nets resulted in the incidental killing of dolphins in excess of US standards. In January 1991 Mexico requested the GATT to establish a Dispute Settlement Panel to examine the compatibility of the import prohibition with the GATT rules on free trade. The following September, the Panel ruled in Mexico's favour that the import ban contravened the GATT, since it amounted to the extrajurisdictional application of US law; the measures had not been shown to be necessary; the US had not exhausted all options reasonably available to it to pursue its dolphin protection objectives, neglecting negotiation through international cooperative arrangements; and finally, the measures taken were too unpredictable.[64]

Although the US has not yet complied with the ruling of the Panel – which is not legally binding – the ruling provided Mexico with important leverage for subsequent negotiations and an eventual solution between the two countries. In effect the Panel, which fulfilled the role of conciliator, provides another example of a mechanism available under international law for defusing environmental tensions between States.

Establishing international standards, such as trade bans, also leads to conflict, as evidenced by attempts to reduce the threat to the survival of the African elephant. This has been a controversial issue for a number of years. The main institutional forum for resolving disputes over measures to restrict international trade in ivory has been the Conference of the Parties to the Convention on International Trade in Endangered Species (CITES), which meets every three years. In 1989 NGOs played a key role in the decision to ban international trade in ivory: Environmental NGOs for many years raised public consciousness about the issue and – relying on international law, including their observer status at CITES – forced the issue on to the international agenda. The World Wide Fund for Nature (WWF) dismissed the argument that the proposed ban would amount to a retroactive application of law or constitute a wrongful interference with the legitimate expectations of existing ivory stockpile holders. The WWF did this by obtaining, and then circulating to all 103 States present at the CITES meeting in Lausanne, an independent and formal legal opinion challenging the basis of the 'retroactivity' and 'legitimate expectation' arguments.[65] While the effect of WWF action cannot be quantified with certainty, it is interesting to note that following the circulation of the legal opinion, those legal arguments did not reappear. A former member of the CITES Secretariat has indicated that this outcome was a direct result of WWF action.

The complex legal saga of the attempt to save the African elephant did not, however, end with the overwhelming vote of the Conference of the Parties to CITES. On 17 January 1990, shortly before the 90-day period for entering reservations to the CITES amendment had expired, the United Kingdom entered a reservation excluding the application of the ban to the territory of Hong Kong. The task was left to environmental NGOs to consider the legality of that reservation under English law, under CITES and EC law. Immediately after the reservation was entered, a group of US environmental NGOs, led by Greenpeace, obtained an independent and formal legal opinion from another NGO. On 25 April 1990 they formally petitioned the US Secretary of the Interior to certify that China, the United Kingdom (on behalf of Hong Kong) and Zimbabwe were 'diminishing the effectiveness' of the CITES programme for the protection of the African elephant.[66] If it had been successful, President Bush would have been required to impose appropriate economic sanctions against the named countries. In July 1990 the reservation expired and was not renewed, bringing the issue to a close and illustrating the effective use of informal legal opinions and NGO advocacy.

UNCED AND BEYOND

Whereas the 1972 Stockholm Conference did not address the issue of State compliance in any depth, the subject was clearly an important one in the preparations for UNCED in 1992 – yet this task was only partially fulfilled. The Rio Declaration goes part way toward identifying some of the inadequacies in the institutional and legal arrangements for the maintenance of environmental security. The Declaration calls on States to provide 'effective access to judicial and administrative proceedings, including redress and remedy,' to 'enact effective environmental legislation' and to 'resolve all their environmental disputes peacefully, by appropriate means and in accordance with the Charter of the United Nations.'[67] Agenda 21 goes even further. It recognizes the limitations of existing arrangements, including inadequate implementation by States of their obligations, the need to involve multilateral organizations in the implementation process, and gaps in existing dispute settlement mechanisms.

Agenda 21 also recognizes the role of various international institutions as central to the maintenance of environmental security. The UN Environmental Programme is called upon to promote the general implementation of international environmental law, while the UN Development Programme will play a lead role in supporting the implementation of Agenda 21 and capacity building at country, regional, inter-regional and global levels.[68] The newly created UN Commission on Sustainable Development will evaluate information supplied by States with regard to their progress in implementing environmental conventions.[69] The role of the UN General Assembly and other agencies concerned with international environmental issues will continue to expand. Moreover, the World Bank will become an increasingly dominant presence through the activities of the Global Environment Facility, which now serves as the interim financial mechanism to disburse resources under the Climate Change and Biodiversity Conventions. Regional organizations, including the EC and the regional development banks, have also signalled their intention to promote activities that will contribute to the maintenance of environmental security. The effectiveness of these organizations, however, will ultimately depend on the extent to which States are willing to cede sovereignty in the establishment, monitoring and enforcement of international standards.

The international community must study and consider ways in which the capacity of current enforcement mechanisms can be broadened and strengthened to promote the prevention and peaceful settlement of environmental disputes.[70] Agenda 21 does not provide any details about such mechanisms, yet it does address the need for mechanisms and precedents to improve the exchange of data and information, notification and consultation regarding situations that might lead to disputes with other States. This is particularly important in the field of sustainable development and for effective peaceful means of dispute settlement in accordance with the Charter of the United Nations including, where appropriate, recourse to the ICJ, and their inclusion in treaties relating to sustainable development.[71]

Will UNCED make a difference? Certainly, it helped to secure a place for environmental security on the international agenda. The international legal and institutional responses to deal with challenges to environmental security will be channelled principally through the General Assembly as well as through the Commission on Sustainable Development. As discussed in this chapter, however, there are many limitations inherent in the ability of international arrangements to ensure widespread compliance with international environmental obligations.

CONCLUSION

Developments in international law alone will not be sufficient to overcome the political, economic and social reasons underlying non-compliance. Nevertheless, the law itself, legal processes and institutions can make a difference, and recent developments suggest strong recognition of the need to make changes in the very structure of the traditional international legal order. To begin with, the provision of technical, financial and other assistance to States, particularly LDCs, will internationalize the domestic implementation of international environmental obligations. In addition, the expanded role granted to international institutions and, to a lesser extent, NGOs in setting international standards, monitoring and enforcement, broadens the scope of actors formally entitled to identify and remedy violations. This should facilitate early warnings of activities that pose significant threats to environmental security. Finally, the establishment of a wider range of mechanisms for dispute settlement suggests an important and growing role for independent international adjudication. These are all important developments and – however inadequate they might appear – should be welcomed as a basis for further efforts toward environmental conflict resolution.

5 GREENING BRETTON WOODS

Jacob D Werksman

INTRODUCTION

Through the gun sights of an eco-activist few international institutions appear in greater need of greening than the World Bank. The Bank and the affiliated international financial institutions known as the Bretton Woods group,[1] have been accused of bankrolling ecological and economic disaster in the developing world, by promoting development projects that have denuded forests, depleted soils, and increased dependence on unsustainable energy sources. Gestures by the Bank to introduce greener policies in response to these criticisms have been met with deep scepticism and accusations of superficial 'greenwashing'.[2]

The Bank's most vocal critics, the non-governmental organizations (NGOs) with interests and constituencies in the area of environment and development, claim that the source of the Bank's ecological disasters lies far deeper than the reach of recent reforms. In order for the Bank to become truly responsive to environmental concerns it must be accountable for its policies and actions, not merely to its shareholders, but to the stakeholders in its projects – the countries, communities and individuals most affected by Bank activities.

Mounting criticism of Bank activities, despite its efforts at reform, has led some to conclude that the Bank is incapable of reforming itself from within. Accountability will require not merely internal reform, but review of Bank activities by an external authority.

In this context, many have looked to the United Nations (UN) to provide a framework for setting and monitoring compliance with internationally agreed environmental principles and standards. The 1992 UN Conference on Environment and Development (UNCED), demonstrated an ambitious global initiative in international policy-making aimed at integrating responses to environment and development concerns. Prominent on UNCED's agenda for the future is the use of international legal agreements on principles and standards for the achievement of environmentally sustainable development; and the strengthening of the UN's role in monitoring compliance with these agreements, including the compliance of the World Bank.

The first test for this new relationship will be the operation of the Global Environment Facility (GEF). The GEF was established by the World Bank, the United Nations Development Programme (UNDP) and the United Nations Environment Programme (UNEP) with the hope of playing a central role in the implementation of the international legal agreements or 'conventions' entered into at UNCED. The UNCED negotiators, wary of ceding policy-making control to the Bank, yet anxious for the Bank's resources, approached the new relationship tentatively, and on the condition that the GEF be held accountable to the Parties to the conventions and comply with UNCED principles.

As the GEF is gradually restructured to conform to UNCED principles it promises to become the crucible for forging the first operational policies for sustainable development, linking the concepts of environment and development, and the institutions of the UN and Bretton Woods systems.

The debate over how these links should be made has prompted policy-makers to reconsider the nature of the relationship between the World Bank group and the UN, to consider why Bank environmental polices have failed in the past, and to explore whether the principles for sustainable development, agreed at UNCED, could be better achieved through a closer legal relationship between the UN and the Bretton Woods systems. While there are significant barriers to linking the two fundamentally different systems, UNCED has raised hopes that the set of principles and procedures for sustainable development, agreed at Rio, will produce a momentum towards institutional reform.

UNCED challenges international law to establish the process whereby the conflicting interests raised by environment and development concerns, and the struggles between the UN and the Bretton Woods systems of governance, can be confronted and resolved. This process will involve an attempt to incorporate the cornerstones of sustainable development identified at Rio: the integration of environment and development on a transparent and equitable basis through the empowerment of all the stakeholders in the development process. In the context of the World Bank and the GEF, this process will encourage the empowerment of the people of developing countries, at both the governmental and non-governmental level, with the right to participate in and have access to information on the environmental and developmental design and assessment of Bank projects.

This chapter begins with an overview of the history of the relationship between the UN and the Bretton Woods systems. It then turns to a brief review of the Bank's relationship with the environment and environmental policy. The shortcomings in the Bank's environmental policies are suggested by a description of the Bank's involvement in the ill-fated Narmada Dam project in India. The principles and standards developed at UNCED are reviewed generally, and in the specific context of the relationship between the GEF and the Climate Change Convention. Finally, this relationship is described as offering an opportunity for putting the UNCED principles to test, by making the GEF legally accountable to the stakeholders in GEF funded projects.

HISTORICAL OVERVIEW: INCOMPATIBLE STRUCTURES AND CONFLICTING INTERESTS

International law and international governance, like any legal system, can be seen as a framework for resolving conflicting interests in pursuit of the common good. The spirit of international cooperation, prolific in the 1940s, engendered two fundamentally different international legal structures for sorting out the world's problems: the United Nations and the World Bank.

The United Nations and the World Bank: Creation and Constitution

The United Nations and its affiliated agencies have since provided a political forum for pursuing the common good by working to avoid and settle armed conflicts, alleviate sickness and hunger, protect human rights and, with increasing intensity of effort, to protect the environment. The United Nations Charter was based loosely on the constitutions of the Western democracies that won the war. Each member State in the UN's principal political organ, the General Assembly, following the paradigm of representative democracy, holds the sovereign right to cast an equal vote. NGO representatives are routinely allowed to observe, to have access to information and to contribute their expertise and the concerns of their constituents. As the only intergovernmental organization with universal membership, the UN has been recognized as having a special authority to speak on issues, such as environment and development, that concern all the world's citizens.[3]

The World Bank has focused its resources on alleviating poverty and promoting development in an effort to raise the standard of living in developing countries. The Bank's Articles of Agreement are based on an equally venerable institution of Western democracy – the commercial bank. Within the Bank's Executive Boardroom, respectful of the investors' right to protect their investment, Directors' votes are weighted by the number of shares held in the Bank, ie, by the number of dollars each shareholder contributes to the Bank's capital. Following the model of the traditional banker/client relationship, the Bank closely guards much of the information it holds on its clients' projects. NGO participation in the design and implementation of Bank policy and projects is minimal.

Although members of the same UN 'family', the UN and the Bank were intentionally separated at birth. They continue to be governed by a 1947 Agreement, which expressly walls off the Bank as an 'independent international institution', entitled to keep information confidential and to make loan decisions through the independent exercise of its own judgment.[4] The UN was expected to be the world's central political organ, while the World Bank's Articles forbid it from making loans with 'regard to political or other non-economic influences or considerations'.[5] For most of the history of these institutions, environmental concerns have been left for the UN's politicians and have been considered beyond the scope of the Bank's 'economic' considerations.

Since their creation, these two international legal 'persons' have pursued their often overlapping development goals with limited success, in part due to their disjointed legal heritage. The United Nations struggles along like a legislature stripped of its power to tax and spend and unable, on its limited budget, to finance the ambitions of its resolutions and the wide scope of its mandate. The World Bank, self-regulating and largely unaccountable to the communities it aspires to help, manages its $140 billion portfolio with a project failure rate staggering even by internal assessments.[6]

Cooperaton or discord?

To some extent the distinction between the UN and the World Bank is an artificial one in that membership in the two institutions closely overlap.[7] However, as has been frequently noted, structural differences at the international and the domestic level prevent the two institutions from speaking with the same voice.[8]

The Bank's decision-making system of 'one dollar, one vote' precludes some of its members – ie, the developing countries in which the Bank's projects are implemented – from participating in Bank policy decisions to the full extent they can in the UN General Assembly. Furthermore, because the individuals in the ministries responsible for environmental matters in the UN system are often distinct from and subordinate to those dealing with financial matters through the Bank's system of governance, member countries of both institutions appear to have difficulties in coordinating their environmental and development assistance policies on the international plane.

Thus, some countries who are shareholders in the Bank may vote to adopt resolutions in the General Assembly and enter into treaties negotiated under the UN's auspices and find themselves without the voting power to carry through these policies at the Bank. Similarly, other countries may undertake certain obligations under the political pressures of an open and more democratic UN, and then use their financial voting power to downplay the same obligations while closeted in the Bank's Boardroom. As a result, both the Bank and its shareholder countries remain essentially unaccountable to UN policy-making.

As this discussion suggests, the power struggle between the two institutions masks a more fundamental conflict between the developed and the developing countries over the size and shape of the global development agenda. The disjunction between the UN and the Bank allows both groups to evade responsibility, by pointing to inadequacies in the institution over which they have less political control. The question is raised whether greater cooperation and accountability can be achieved by linking these two fundamentally incompatible systems, and if so, what role an emerging international law of sustainable development can play in forging that link. Ideally such a link would ensure the integration of an internationally determined set of environmental principles and standards into the Bank's development assistance at both the policy-making level and at the level of project implementation.

As discussed below, in the context of the GEF, accountability may best be achieved through international legal agreements based upon UNCED principles that establish procedures to oversee and assess whether the Bank's governance, its management and its staff carry out policies as set by the international community. In order to operate effectively, such procedures would have to assure access to information about Bank activities, and to input from communities affected by these activities.

A review of the Bank's attempts to set and implement environmental policy will suggest that the UNCED's principles for the future are based, in part, upon lessons learned from the Bank's relationship with the environment in the past.

THE WORLD BANK AND THE ENVIRONMENT

Past efforts to integrate environmental concerns into Bank policy have fallen short of expectations. Bank policies first began to address environmental concerns in the 1960s by lending on a relatively small-scale for particular environmental projects. The Bank made considerable progress in designing projects to promote water sanitation, reduce urban pollution, prevent soil erosion and manage wildlife. But the Bank's critics contended that the effect of this small-scale lending for environmental projects paled in comparison with the impact the Bank's regular development lending was having on the environment. Real progress could only be made by integrating environmental concerns into all aspects of Bank lending, not just those aimed specifically at improving the environment.

The effort to integrate the environment and development gained political momentum through various UN initiatives at developing international environmental law and policy including the 1972 United Nations Conference on the Human Environment (UNCHE), the negotiation of the 1980 Declaration of Environmental Policies and Procedures Relating to

Economic Development, and the work of the World Commission on Environment and Development (WCED). To some extent the Bank has responded, by implementing both procedural and institutional reforms.

The Bank's first attempt to integrate environmental concerns into the procedures of the Bank project cycle was made with the introduction of Environmental Guidelines, in 1970. These guidelines were monitored internally by the Bank's Office of Environmental Affairs (OEA). Institutional inertia and a failure to commit resources at the appropriate stages of project selection and development have led many to conclude that these guidelines proved largely unsuccessful.[9]

A more sophisticated attempt, intended to 'apply state of the art practice on environmental assessment . . . to the subtleties of the Bank's relationship with clients' and to 'bring in the legitimate interest of various groups at the local level' was launched in 1989 by the Bank's Operational Directive on Environmental Assessment (EA).[10] Under this Directive, the Bank requires a preliminary screening of all projects for their environmental consequences as soon as a possible project is identified. Projects are then categorized by their potential environmental impact and subjected to varying degrees of Environmental Assessment, or to none at all.[11]

The Bank's EA Directive conforms in principle with UNCED's recommendations for integrating environmental concerns into development policy; it fails, however, to incorporate opportunities for meaningful public participation. The concept of environmental assessment as a precondition for project approval derives from national laws, where it has worked to block government and private projects that threaten to damage the environment. The success of national application of this concept depends largely on the right to public participation in the EA process, and the right to challenge the EA's conclusions before an adjudicative authority. Thus, while the Bank's EA process has, in theory, great potential for promoting environmentally sustainable development,[12] it has already come under sharp criticism. Internal Bank and NGO evaluations of the EA Directive in practice, have revealed that the EAs are often superficial, underestimate and miscategorize the potential environmental impact of projects and fail to take into account the concerns of local peoples.[13]

The Bank's apparent inability to carry out its own policy directives has been consistently linked to the need for institutional reform to complement policy initiatives within the Bank. The WCED, commissioned by the UN Secretary-General to propose a 'global agenda for change', identified the World Bank as especially influential in achieving sustainable development for providing 'the largest single source of development lending and for its policy leadership which exerts a significant influence on both developing countries and donors'. The WCED called for the establishment of a high level office within the Bank with the authority to ensure the incorporation of sustainable development objectives and criteria into the Bank's policies and programmes.[14]

Bank President Barber Conable, acknowledging that major institutional reform was necessary to truly integrate the environment into project development established, in 1987, the Bank's Environment Department. The department, however, was relegated to the policy and research complex of the Bank, and has not reached directly to the core of the Bank's lending operations. Instead its role has been seen as being a 'monitor and mentor' to regional operations.[15]

It is, perhaps, not surprising that in 1992, at the UN Conference on Environment and Development, the Bank found itself, once again, the target of reformist criticism. In the months following Rio, the Bank has restructured its Environment Department. The department, still focused on policy and analysis, has now been given a tool with which to shape project selection. The various divisions of the department will design 'best practice papers' to help policy-makers and project designers to conform projects to what the Bank considers the most environmentally friendly approaches.

Most recently, since January 1993, the restructured department has been placed under the authority of a newly created Vice Presidency for Environmentally Sustainable Development. Within the Bank's pyramidical structure, the Environment Department will be on the same level and under the direction of the same Vice Presidency as the Agriculture and Natural Resources Department and the Department on Transport and Urban Development.[16] It remains to be seen whether this reshuffling will produce a better integration of policy into practice.

Although the Bank can be said to have made significant progress in establishing policies that are designed to promote sustainable development and environmental protection, and to establish institutional structures within the Bank for monitoring the implementation of these policies, the conclusions of UNCED suggest that the degree to which these policies are implemented and enforced will depend on deeper institutional reforms that open the Bank's governance to accountability to those outside the Bank. Without accountability, the Bank's EAs and best practice papers may remain severed bits of policy, borrowed from domestic legal frameworks that depend on public participation and challenge for their legitimacy.

UNCED can be seen as an effort to provide this legitimacy by establishing a framework for external participation and accountability. The UN's past efforts toward this end have failed, primarily because of the largely symbolic nature of these initiatives that have produced only weak links between the World Bank and the UN.

Weak Links

The United Nations has made efforts in the past to influence the World Bank's lending policies through its own initiatives in environmental policy-making. As outlined above, these efforts, focusing international attention on the need to integrate environment and development policy, can be said to have had some influence on Bank behaviour. However, as has also been pointed out, direct accountability of the Bank to the UN has remained elusive, in part because of the 1947 Agreement, which establishes the institutional independence of the Bank. In lieu of a direct oversight role, UN agencies have established mechanisms which have sought, on a cooperative basis, to coordinate environment and development policy and activities between the UN and the Bretton Woods family.

To encourage implementation of the Stockholm Principles, enumerated at the 1972 UN Conference on the Human Environment, the UN agencies and several multilateral financial institutions including the World Bank signed, in 1980, a joint Declaration of Environmental Policies and Procedures Relating to Economic Development. The Declaration established a Committee of International Development Institutions on the Environment (CIDIE). Since then UN agencies and multilateral financial institutions have been meeting and consulting on environmental issues.

In the Declaration, the participating agencies affirmed their commitment to follow through on the Stockholm principles and to ensure that their policies and programmes would comply. Most relevant to Bretton Woods activities is the Declaration's undertaking to ensure the integration of appropriate environmental measures in the design and implementation of economic development activities.[17] Despite these ambitious aims, the CIDIE has been said to have achieved little. In 1987 UNEP's Executive Director found that in its first five years 'CIDIE has not yet truly succeeded in getting environmental considerations firmly ingrained in development policies'. Similarly, the WCED concluded that CIDIE members had gone along with the Declaration in principle more than in major shifts in action.[18]

A parallel mechanism for coordinating policy within the UN system at a higher, administrative level is the UN's Administrative Co-ordination Committee (ACC) which brings together the heads of all the institutions within the UN system. Although the ACC has not focused specifically on environmental concerns in the past, the UNCED negotiators recognized the potential for the committee, which is headed by the UN Secretary-General 'to provide a vital link and interface between the multilateral financial institutions and other United Nations bodies at the highest administrative level.'[19]

Past practice suggests, however, that loosely structured efforts at policy coordination without accountability, monitoring or implementation review, are unlikely to lead to substantive reform. Like the Bank's unilateral procedural arrangements, which do not open lending procedures to outside scrutiny, systematic public participation, or opportunities for external challenge of the Banks conclusions, CIDIE and the ACC will continue to be subject to accusations of greenwashing.

Greater levels of accountability have been promised by the agreements resulting from UNCED, which offer opportunities for providing crucial and strengthened links between democratic policy-making and development funding procedures. Before turning to the UNCED agreements, it may be helpful first to review a particular example of the conflicts between environment and development that have arisen in the recent pre-UNCED operations of the Bank, and the challenge these conflicts present to the principles of sustainable development.

The Narmada Dam: A Case Study for Sustainable Development

The formidable nature of this challenge is illustrated by the controversy surrounding the Bank's involvement in a hydroelectric and irrigation dam project on the Narmada River in north-western India. First proposed by the Indian Government in 1946, this massive undertaking is intended to bring hydroelectricity, irrigation and drinking water to some 30 million people. The Bank first became involved in the project in 1985 and committed $450 million in loans and credits, or about 15 per cent of the total estimated cost of the project.

Although the Bank's financial contribution represents a relatively small portion of the project's overall cost, it is generally recognized that Bank involvement in any project is crucial to attracting financial resources from additional multilateral, bilateral and private sources of aid and loans.

As has been described, by the 1980s, the Bank had begun to develop internal procedures for assessing the potential social and environmental impact of its projects. Accordingly, the Bank negotiated with the Indian Government what it claimed to be a comprehensive assessment of the environmental impact of the project and a plan for resettling local people who would be displaced by the dam's reservoir.

Soon after the project was under way, local communities, Indian NGOs and, later, the international NGO community, began to assess a social and environmental catastrophe well beyond what the Bank's assessment procedures had revealed. Estimates now place the number likely to be displaced by the dam at over 100,000, a population described as impossible to relocate humanely.[20]

In response to growing local and international pressure, revelations of civil uprising, government crackdowns and human rights abuses among the villages in the dam's flood plain, the Bank's President commissioned an unprecedented independent review of the Bank's involvement in the project. The review, known as the Morse Commission Report and published in June 1992, found the Bank management had abused and neglected stated Bank policies on environment and resettlement, and that this attitude pervaded the Bank's hierarchy of decision-making and project implementation. The review concluded that the primary cause was that 'the Bank is more concerned to accommodate the pressures emanating from its borrowers than to guarantee implementation of its policies.'[21]

In March 1993, the Bank, bowing under pressure, enforced its policies and drew up a newly negotiated series of 'benchmark' conditions for continued Bank involvement. The Indian Government, unable to meet new requirements on environmental protection and resettlement, was forced to withdraw from the remaining $170 million of the loan package. There are, however, indications that the Indian Government will continue with the project, without the Bank's support, but free from international intervention.[22]

The Narmada project reveals the outlines of the conflicts thrown up by the interface between environment and development, conflicts that UNCED suggests the international law and policy of sustainable development will play a role in resolving. It provides a concrete example of the attitudes that contributed to the atmosphere and outcome of Rio, and to the articulation of the principles, standards and structures of UNCED.

UNCED: PRINCIPLES FOR DEVELOPMENT LENDING

Perhaps the most prolific and sustained effort at international law making for the global environment, UNCED produced a large volume of international agreements. These include a non-binding 'soft-law' ministerial declaration on environment and development (the Rio Declaration), 40 detailed chapters forming an agenda for action on sustainable development into the twenty-first century (Agenda 21), and two legally binding treaties: one aimed at responding to the threat of human-induced climate change and one at preserving biological diversity.

In the context of the Narmada project and the questions it raises about the relationship between the UN, the World Bank and development lending, the most relevant of the UNCED documents are the principles for sustainable development, outlined in the Rio Declaration;[23] the chapters of Agenda 21 on International Institutional Arrangements, and Financial Resources and Mechanisms; and the articles on financial mechanisms within the Conventions on Climate Change and Biodiversity.

As has been suggested previously, the primary recommendations for the Bank that can be distilled from UNCED's principles, call for the empowerment of stakeholders in the design and implementation of Bank policy and projects. UNCED recognizes that the tools of empowerment are fundamentally linked to rights of access to information and of participation in policy-making. At an international level this means the empowerment of developing country governments and non-governmental actors with greater participation in, and review of, the Bank's overall policy-making. At ground level this means the empowerment of local citizens to participate in a meaningful and informed manner in the design and implementation of Bank projects.

To this end, the UNCED participants placed considerable faith in the role of international agreements and international law in setting the standards and procedures for achieving these goals on the road to promoting sustainable development. The Rio Declaration and Chapter 39 of Agenda 21 encourage members of the international community to respect and to further develop the international law of sustainable development.[24] The iteration of UNCED's principles in international legal instruments is only the beginning of a process that is bound to raise conflicts and evade implementation.

This discussion will briefly sketch some of the principles of sustainable development contained in the UNCED documents and suggest areas of conflict that may arise when these concepts are applied to specific examples of development lending, such as the Bank's Narmada project.

Sovereignty and Conditionality

The Rio Declaration and the Rio Conventions reaffirmed the centrality of the principle of sovereignty in the context of environment and development. Principle 2 of the Rio Declaration recognizes that all States have the 'right to exploit their own resources pursuant to their own environmental and developmental policies'. That right, however, is qualified by States' responsibility to ensure that activities within their jurisdiction or control do not cause damage to the environment of other States or of areas beyond the limits of national jurisdiction, or what has become known as the 'global commons'.[25]

UNCED's attempt to strike a balance between sovereign right and global responsibility, operating in the context of development lending, can be seen as qualifying the concept of sovereignty in several significant ways. All Bank projects have and will continue to require the approval of the sovereign State in which they are carried out. However, development decisions that effect neighbouring States or the global commons, may trigger the operation of internationally agreed standards which would place conditions on the way in which the project is designed and implemented within the putative sovereign territory.

Were the Bank to impose these environmental standards and procedures, or 'conditionalities', it might interfere with the borrower's national policies and thus infringe on the sovereign right to pursue nationally determined environmental and developmental policies. Resistance to these conditionalities can result in a breakdown in loan agreements that neither benefits the environment nor promotes development. It was, after all, the benchmarks established by the Bank's intergovernmental Board that, when finally enforced, lead to the withdrawal of the Indian Government from the Narmada loan agreement. Narmada serves to demonstrate that in the balance between sovereignty and international efforts at environmental protection, the borrowing country continues to hold the sovereign power of withdrawal.

Under current Bank procedures, the trump may be well justified. The Bank's use of conditions in its loan agreements gives its majority shareholders considerable power in setting the fiscal and development agendas for its borrowers, further provoking the outcry of injured sovereignty. The UNCED principles suggest debacles like Narmada and the consequent Indian withdrawal could have been avoided by enabling universally agreed international environmental and development standards to play a constructive role in the Bank's relationship with its clients. Widespread participation may help to legitimize Bank policy-making through a more open and accountable decision-making process, rendering such policies more politically palatable and more difficult to avoid.

Although the principle of sovereignty can be used to justify greater developing country participation in Bank policy-making, it is essential to note that soveriegnty has also been used by the borrowing countries as a basis for withholding information on Bank projects from the public, thus undermining UNCED's concern with regard to the accessibility of information. Again, internationally agreed upon rules for the disclosure of information may help ease political objections.

Democracy and Equity

Universality, democracy and equity are principles central to the Rio Declaration and the institutional arrangements envisaged by Agenda 21 and the Conventions. Closely linked to the concept of sovereignty, democracy, on the international plane, entitles each sovereign State to an equal say in international governance. The relatively democratic institutions of the UN are based on the premise that the political unit of the nation State, regardless of its internal form of governance, adequately represents its citizens. While all stable forms of government, in the context of the debate on environment and development, demonstrate tenacity in protecting the territorial integrity of borders and the value, on the international market, of national resources, international law is beginning to recognize that governments – whether democratic or otherwise – may not be the most effective channel for voicing the concerns of individual citizens. Even the Indian Government, which may justifiably lay claim to representing the world's largest democracy, can be said to have failed to protect the interests of its local peoples to the extent that it found itself quelling riots in the Narmada flood plain.

The Rio Declaration, while confirming the principle of sovereignty, proclaims as its first principle that the human being, and not the nation State, deserves priority in the international debate over sustainable development. UNCED further tacitly acknowledges that NGOs, which gather their constituencies according to issues rather than according to State boundaries, have a legitimate role to play in international democracy. Thus, UNCED suggests that international democracy must extend beyond the concept of one State one vote, to allow input from people. NGOs claim to speak directly for the people, and demand a voice in international governance based on direct representation of individuals without the interference of governments.

As has been noted, the other essential aspect of democracy is access to information. In UNCED parlance the importance of information is captured in the principle of transparency. Like light passing through glass, transparency suggests the free flow of information into and out from the Bank operations. The principle of transparency would allow input into the process at the earliest levels in project development, from all interested segments of society: from international organizations, to the borrowing government, to grassroots NGOs and the individuals effected by the project; and allow free access to information with regard to the environmental and social impacts of proposed and ongoing projects.

The broad principles of democracy as articulated at UNCED, when applied to the specific circumstances of the Bank, raise the question as to whether the appropriate response is to demand that the Bretton Woods institutions open themselves to direct democratic governance, or to oversight by institutions based on one nation one vote.

The Bretton Woods donor countries defend its system of shareholder voting on the grounds that equity or fairness entitles them to control how money, raised from their own taxpayers, is spent. Commentators have questioned whether the imposition of a fully democratic system on the Bank would not 'jeopardize the ability of Bretton Woods institutions to raise large funds on commercial markets by subordinating Bank decisions by shifting decisions . . . from weighted-vote procedures that favour governments who back the World Bank with hard credit, to one-State, one-vote procedures . . . that favour recipients'.[26]

Furthermore, the UN with its relative democracy has generated an inertia and bureaucracy of its own. Wider participation can lead to the proliferation of conflicts of interest and the breakdown of consensus. This has led some environmentalists, who see the need for as rapid a deployment of funding as possible, to call for a funding mechanism separate from both the UN and the Bretton Woods systems.[27]

Nevertheless, the experience of Narmada, and the failure rate noted by the Bank's own internal assessment, raise serious questions as to whether the status quo is the best way to guarantee the success and creditworthiness of Bank projects. A more evenly balanced power sharing arrangement within multilateral finance institutions may offer other benefits beyond the legitimacy of democracy. Full participation of the international community in project decisions allows consensus to build within the developing world as to how spending priorities are to be set globally. This might encourage recipient countries to think globally rather than locally and to discourage a tendency of the donor countries to divide and conquer developing countries by appealing to their desire to secure funding for themselves rather than thinking in terms of global priorities. An open and democratic system of project selection would allow all developing countries to compete for funding at the project approval level, using internationally agreed upon standards for sustainable development, that would, hopefully, avoid the channelling of precious development resources into projects like Narmada.

Common But Differentiated Responsibility

Greater participation by developing countries in Bank policy-making is further justified by the implication of yet another principle that found expression in the Rio Declaration and the UNCED legal agreements. As has been stated, the Bank's one dollar one vote system is based upon a recognition of the generosity of Bank donors, reciprocated by their right to determine the way in which their money is spent. UNCED has begun to view development funding, at least in the context of global environmental issues, as a 'responsibility that [developed countries] bear in the international pursuit of sustainable development in view of the pressures their societies place on the global environment and of the technologies and financial resources they command'.[28]

In the light of this reasoning, which views areas of development assistance as the responsibility rather than the generosity of developing countries, traditional justifications for allowing donor countries to dominate decision-making within the Bank dissolve.

Public Participation

Finally, as has been stated previously, UNCED principles expressly recognize that:

> [e]nvironmental issues are best handled with the participation of all concerned citizens, at the relevant level. At the national level, each individual shall have appropriate access to information concerning the environment that is held by public authorities, including information on hazardous materials and activities in their communities, and the opportunity to participate in decision-making processes. States shall facilitate and encourage public awareness and participation by making information widely available.[29]

While political realities may prevent these aspirations from being realized in all countries, rules of procedure at the international level may allow, through the participation of non-governmental and grassroots organizations, individuals to have a voice when local rules of procedure and forms of government might have silenced that voice. Had the Bank's procedures allowed local people to participate in a meaningful way in the review of the Narmada project prior to the loan approval, the disaster that resulted might have been avoided.

UNCED anticipated that the implementation of each of these principles will require institutional reform within and between international organizations.

UNCED AND AGENDA 21:
INSTITUTIONAL REFORM

The process that led to UNCED caused policy-makers within the UN agencies and the World Bank to consider, once again, the relationship between the environment and development, and the relationship between the two institutions. As chapter after chapter was added to Agenda 21, the estimated need of developing countries, in grant and concessional financing, to implement Agenda 21's policies rose to $125 billion a year between 1993 and 2000. It became clear that a new level of cooperation would have to be sought to ensure that unprecedented levels of resources could be directed towards environmental protection and that all resources dedicated to development were in harmony with the principles of sustainability.

Agenda 21, which establishes a programme for action on sustainable development for the international community, is largely hortatory and recommendatory in nature and does not purport to bind directly UNCED participants to particular actions. It does, however, contain a remarkably detailed consensus of over 170 countries reflecting a general commitment to pursue the goals of sustainable development. Most significantly, it calls for the establishment of a high level Commission on Sustainable Development (CSD) to ensure the effective follow up of Agenda 21.

Agenda 21 contains extensive recommendations for the redirection and revitalization of the UN system, including the Bretton Woods institutions, towards the achievement of sustainable development. Central to these commitments is that the implementation of Agenda 21 shall be 'based on an action- and result-oriented approach and consistent with the principles of universality, democracy, transparency, cost-effectiveness and accountability.'[30]

While virtually every aspect of Agenda 21's outline for sustainable development has implications for the Bank's lending policies, the principles of Agenda 21, like the Stockholm principles of 20 years ago, will likely

remain unimplemented without new and powerful structural and procedural mechanisms. To this end, the negotiators dedicated a subchapter to
govern the 'cooperation between United Nations bodies and international
financial organizations, recognizing that:

> [t]he success of the follow-up to the Conference is dependent upon an effective
> link between substantive action and financial support, and this requires close
> and effective cooperation between United Nations bodies and the multilateral
> financial organizations.[31]

To ensure that the policies of Agenda 21 are followed, the Conference
recognized the need for institutional arrangements within the UN system
to implement Agenda 21 and called upon the General Assembly, as the
'supreme policy-making forum' of the UN system, to establish the CSD.

In response to UNCED, the UN General Assembly adopted verbatim the
Conference's recommendations on the primary task of the CSD, which will
be:

> [t]o monitor progress in the implementation of Agenda 21 and activities
> related to the integration of environmental and developmental goals *through-
> out the United Nations system* through analysis and evaluation of reports from
> all relevant organs, organizations, programmes and institutions of the United
> Nations system dealing with various issues of environment and develop-
> ment, *including those related to finance* . . . [32](emphasis added).

Specifically, the General Assembly empowers the CSD to monitor the
World Bank's activities and plans to implement Agenda 21, and invites the
Bank to submit regular reports to the CSD on the Bank's progress.[33]

Agenda 21 envisages the NGO community playing a central role in this
review process and recognizes that the United Nations system, including
international finance and development agencies, should:

(1) design open and effective means to achieve the participation of
non-governmental organizations, including those related to major groups,
in the process established to review and evaluate the implementation of
Agenda 21 at all levels and promote their contribution to it; and

(2) take into account the findings of non-governmental organizations' review systems and evaluation processes in relevant reports of the
Secretary-General to the General Assembly and all pertinent United
Nations agencies and intergovernmental organizations and forums concerning implementation of Agenda 21 in accordance with its review
process.[34]

Whether, and how effectively the CSD will monitor the Bank's compliance
with Agenda 21 remains to be seen. Hopefully the wide consensus reached
at Rio signals a genuine commitment among the Bank's controlling share-

holder countries to open up the Bank's operations to greater scrutiny, participation and oversight.

The first indications as to the sincerity of this commitment are likely to come from the specific relationship established at Rio between the Parties to the UN Framework Convention on Climate Change and the Bank's Global Environmental Facility (GEF).

The Global Environmental Facility

The initial testing ground for the post-UNCED relationship between the UN and the Bank, has become the Global Environmental Facility (GEF), set up by the World Bank primarily in anticipation of new financial commitments arising out of UNCED. Since UNCED, the GEF has been designated the operator of the interim financial mechanism for the Climate Change Convention. The nature of this relationship has not yet been fully elaborated, but the legally binding nature of the Convention, and the specific requirements it demands of the GEF, represent the first significant attempt to use international law to force the greening of a Bretton Woods offspring.

In 1987, the WCED's report had suggested that the Bank develop a 'special banking programme or facility linked to the World Bank [that] . . . could provide loans and facilitate joint financing arrangements for the development and protection of critical habitats and ecosystems, including those of international significance,' and strongly recommended that additional financial resources be earmarked for the protection of the global commons.[35]

Following the outlines of the WCED's suggestions and the encouragement of donor countries, the Bank's Board of Executive Directors established the GEF in 1991.[36] The GEF was launched with a budget of approximately $1.3 billion to be allocated on a grant basis, over a three-year period. During these three years, known as the GEF's Pilot Phase, GEF funding was to be focused on four areas of global environmental concern that were becoming the focus of UN driven policy-making: climate change, biodiversity, pollution of international waters and ozone depletion.

Intended to be a model of cooperation between UN and Bretton Woods institutions, the GEF is described as a joint project between the United Nations Development Programme (UNDP) the United Nations Environment Programme (UNEP) and the World Bank. UNDP is to provide technical assistance, capacity building and project preparation, while UNEP is to provide strategic planning and to assure the scientific, technical and legal integrity of GEF projects. The Bank describes its own role as managing the GEF's investment project cycle, acting as trustee, nominating the Chairman to the GEF's governing body, and housing the GEF Secretariat.[37]

GEF documentation nobly recites many of the same principles contained in Agenda 21. It promises that the GEF will be transparent and accountable to contributors and beneficiaries alike and that it will ensure universal membership and a broad and equitable representation of developing and developed countries in its decision-making procedures.[38] Furthermore, the GEF promises to establish new structural mechanisms designed to guarantee follow through on these principles. Projects are to be overseen, directed and reviewed by a Participants' Assembly (PA) comprising all developed and developing countries participating in the GEF. To assist the PA and the GEF administration, an independent scientific and technical advisory panel (STAP) composed of experts from developed and developing countries, acting in their personal capacities, will provide advice on every stage of project selection and development.[39] Finally, NGOs are to have a 'major role to play in the identification, design and implementation of projects'.[40]

Critics maintain that the GEF, in practice, has thus far fallen seriously short of its noble aspirations. Much of the criticism of the first stages of the GEF's operations surround the continued domination of the World Bank and its policies in the running of the GEF. During the GEF's Pilot Phase, membership in the GEF was limited to those countries wealthy enough to contribute a minimum of $4 million to the GEF's trust fund. As a result the GEF, just like the Bank's Board of Executive Directors, was dominated by developed countries during the period when much of the GEF's operational policy was being developed. Furthermore, the GEF's 'democratic' governance procedures were under the direction of the GEF's powerful Chairman, appointed by and an employee of the Bank. Decisions were taken by consensus, as perceived and summarized by the Chairman in his report.

Critics claim that the independent STAP, and the UNDP and UNEP, have had only a limited opportunity to influence project selection. As many as 80 per cent of the GEF's projects were prepared and approved by World Bank staff and are linked in some way to larger Bank projects. STAP apparently has been denied access to relevant information about the World Bank projects to which GEF projects are linked.[41] Furthermore, the GEF participants have thus far failed to reach a consensus on allowing NGOs to participate, even as observers. Instead, NGOs are limited to consultations held just prior to the GEF meetings, attended by the GEF administration but generally avoided by the participants. Some of the GEF's documentation of claims of having involved local NGOs in project development and implementation have proved difficult to verify.[42]

The GEF's fulfilment of the promise of universal membership has been gradual, and has been seen as an attempt to allow the donor countries to set the rules before the game begins. Even as larger numbers of developing countries are added to the roles of the GEF participants, traditional power struggles are emerging, blocking consensus on voting procedures and raising genuine fears that a newly democratized GEF will not yield UNCED's vision of an accountable and equitable cooperation, but political deadlock.

Hope that this deadlock could be broken, and that genuine reform will be introduced to the GEF, can be drawn from the legal force of the Climate Change Convention, which provides specific guidance on how the GEF, as the operator of the Convention's financial mechanism, is to conform with UNCED principles. The political relationship between the main organ of the Convention – the Conference of the Parties (COP) – and the GEF can be seen as roughly parallel to the political relationship between the UN and the Bank. Just as in the UN General Assembly, developing countries will numerically and politically dominate the COP. Legally, however, the relationship is not parallel. Far from being an independent institution, the GEF is intended to serve the COP, which will determine the GEF's climate-related funding policies. Developed countries party to the Convention, whether they are operating within the GEF's PA or through the World Bank's governance, must respect the text of the Convention when discussing matters related to it. Thus, while the GEF as an institution is not a 'party' to the Convention, States party to the Convention participating in the GEF are bound by international law to ensure that, in restructuring the GEF, they comply with the requirements and the principles of the Convention.

Furthermore, the text of the Convention codifies the developing countries' collective sovereign right to withdraw from the GEF. In an unprecedented move, the developing countries negotiating the Convention accepted the GEF on the condition that the GEF be reformed if it is to maintain a relationship with the Convention. Thus, the Convention provides that, within four years of entry into force, the COP may sever its relationship with the GEF and seek a different entity to operate its financial mechanism.[43]

To prevent such a result and to shore up this new relationship, the specific terms of the Convention can be read to require the Parties to the Convention to enter into an international legal agreement with the GEF to ensure the accountability of the GEF to the Parties and a long-term relationship between the GEF and the Convention. The closely negotiated text of the Convention illustrates an attempt to use international law to translate UNCED principles into operational procedures.

Strong Links: An Agreement for Accountability

Article 11(1) of the Convention requires that the Convention's Financial Mechanism (FM) be 'accountable' to the COP. The Convention anticipates this relationship will be established through an Agreement between the COP and the GEF, as the entity entrusted with operating the FM.

Article 11 empowers the COP to decide on virtually every aspect of the FM's operational mandate, including the FM's 'policies, programme priorities and eligibility criteria'.[44] This suggests that the COP will have to maintain a high degree of oversight and direction over the FM. Accordingly, the Convention calls for the Agreement between the COP and the GEF to establish modalities for the provision of regular reports to the COP.[45] The Agreement will also provide for the GEF to be made accountable to the COP through the assessment and review of particular funding decisions.

Thus, the general concept of accountability in Article 11(1), is supported by the broad procedural guarantees outlined in Article 11(3), which empower the COP to enter into an Agreement with the GEF, to ensure that the Convention's funding decisions conform with COP policies and that these decisions can be reconsidered in light of COP policies.[46]

It will be recalled that as the Convention enters into force and the GEF's membership is made universal, Parties to the Convention may also become Participants in the GEF.[47] Legally, this relationship will provide an additional level of accountability, as the requirements of the Convention will guide and bind the GEF's Participants' Assembly in Convention-related decisions.

In negotiating the Agreement under Article 11(3), the COP is empowered to put in place procedures that bind the GEF at an institutional level, to ensure that the Parties can exercise meaningful control over funding decisions to a degree that may not be provided through the Participants' Assembly. Such an Agreement would provide a concrete legal link between a democratic body operating under the auspices of the UN and a Bretton Woods institution. Projects implemented by World Bank management would for the first time be subject to policy direction, review and revision by an open and democratic process.

A RESTRUCTURED BANK

In the hope of rallying the support of a sceptical NGO audience, the GEF's Chairman, Mohammed T El-Ashry once described the GEF as a Trojan Horse, capable of seductively breaching the walls of the World Bank and unleashing progressive environmental policies on the Bank's establishment. There is hope that Mr El-Ashry's metaphor will not prove hollow, if the GEF is allowed the opportunity to demonstrate that greater success can be achieved through openness, democracy and accountability, than through traditional World Bank operations.

A great deal of work will have to be done to devise the appropriate procedures and institutional arrangements to give shape to UNCED's vision of 'accountability'. The concept can encompass a wide range of meanings but certain elements have been recited often in the debate and have become a mantra for those restless for institutional reform. Universality, accountability, transparency, democracy and equity: close examination will have to be made of the implications of these words, as policy-makers explore ways in which the catch words of UNCED can be translated into action, both at the level of the relationship between the GEF and the Convention and between the Bank and the UN.

6 GREENING THE EEC TREATY

Marina Wheeler

INTRODUCTION

At the international level, the conflict between free trade and environmental regulation is becoming acute. Technical standards are being developed, for example, to limit the use, and trade, in hazardous substances. Many countries have now enacted regulations banning products from their markets on environmental grounds. In the *Mexican Tuna* case the United States was condemned by the GATT panel for banning imports from Mexico of yellow-fin tuna caught using technology and practices which resulted in the deaths of dolphins. This ruling served to illustrate that at the international level, protection of the environment is not always recognized as a legitimate limitation on the principle of free trade.

The GATT, to date, remains committed only to liberalize world trade. The same trends and tensions are visible within the European Community. For example, Belgium and France have both instituted bans on imports of foreign waste. Germany recently banned the import or use within Germany of pentachlorophenol (PCP) or PCP-treated products. However, in contrast to the international level, the EC has developed a legal framework, however imperfect, which attempts to reconcile trade and environment concerns. This chapter examines this framework and recommends that similar mechanisms be adopted at the international level.

THE CONSTITUTIONAL POSITION: BUILDING ENVIRONMENT INTO THE TREATY

The EC was established in 1957 as an *economic* community. In the aftermath of the Second World War, the aim of the founding fathers was twofold: to bring prosperity back to a devastated continent, and to avoid future wars by weaving the economies of Europe so closely together as to make them mutually dependent. The Treaty of Rome, which set up the EEC, was designed to establish a 'common market' and ensure the free movement of goods, services, capital and people. The first step was to remove all tariff and non-tariff barriers to trade, and construct a common commercial policy. At this early stage, however, no one envisaged the need for an environment policy. Consequently, the Treaty of Rome, as adopted in 1957, contained no provision for Community action on the environment.

The first decades of the Community were enormously successful. With the aid of the Marshall Plan, prosperity returned to Europe amidst unprecedented economic growth. However, by the early 1970s the environmental effects of rapid expansion were becoming visible. As acid rain ravaged the European forests, public protest was mobilized. In West Germany, home of the post-war 'economic miracle', the outcry was loudest and transformed protection of the environment into a political issue. The EC could not ignore these events. In 1972 at a meeting in Paris, (shortly after the 1972 UN Conference on the Human Environment), the EC Heads of State formally acknowledged the need for a Community role in protecting the environment. Certainly the arguments for doing so were pressing.

First, it was obvious that pollution did not respect national borders. The close geographic cohesion of the Community meant that one country's waste easily became anothers' pollution, especially water and air-borne pollution. With member States sharing borders and waterways, a regional solution to regional problems, therefore, seemed logical. The state of rivers such as the Rhine and Meuse pressed home the urgency of the matter.

Further justification was found in the commitment stated in the Treaty Preamble to achieve 'the constant improvement of the living and working conditions of [its] people . . .' This led the Heads of State to assert that:

> Economic expansion is not an end in itself . . . It should result in an improvement in the quality of life as well as in standards of living. As befits the genius of Europe, particular attention will be given to intangible values and to protecting the environment, so that progress may really be put at the service of mankind.

This argument was strengthened by the growing belief that the Community itself bore, and continues to bear, large responsibility for the deteriorating environment at the regional and global levels. This has been the result not only of increased growth, but the Community's policies on agriculture, energy, transport and regional development. In the light of this, it seemed right to give the Community the power to prevent further environmental damage.

Furthermore, an EC environment role could also be justified on classic economic grounds. Differences in national environmental standards were seen to distort competition and erect barriers to trade, thereby disrupting the smooth functioning of the Common Market. For example, national legislation requiring companies to install purifying or emission control devices, would raise production costs and impair a company's ability to compete. Similarly, tough noise control standards for construction equipment, or tighter exhaust emissions curbs on cars in one member State, might restrict imports from other member States and thus limit free trade. Only harmonization of environmental standards could avoid these pitfalls, so the argument went.

On this basis, measures protecting the environment had been adopted before the 1972 Resolution in Paris. For example, the 1967 Directive on the classification, packaging and labelling of dangerous substances,[1] and the 1970 Directives on noise levels and pollutant emissions of motor vehicles,[2] were presented as 'harmonization measures', designed to ensure the smooth functioning of the Common Market. But the Paris Resolution, in 1972, was the first time that protection of the environment was openly acknowledged as a legitimate Community goal. This extended enormously the potential scope of Community action. However, at this stage there was no question of amending the Treaty to include this new area of concern. The EC Commission would draw up 'action plans' for environmental action, and specific legislation would be adopted either under the Treaty at Article 235, reserved for residual matters, or under the old harmonizing provisions (ie Article 100A).

At the end of 1973, the Community adopted its first action plan for the environment. This set out the basic principles on which Community action would be based and served as a legislative agenda. During the coming decade over 100 Acts of EC environment legislation were adopted on the basis of the 1973 plan and three subsequent ones.[3]

In spite of this respectable volume of legislative activity, however, the 1980s signalled a realization that in concrete terms, little had been achieved to protect the environment. Scientific evidence that the ozone layer was, perhaps irrevocably, damaged brought some to their senses. Governments which had previously dragged their feet, became converts to the environment cause – witness Mrs Thatcher's speech in 1982 at the World Conference on Ozone Protection. Concern for the environment spread across Western Europe and Green parties emerged in countries other than West Germany. Indeed, in the European Parliamentary elections of 1989, the Green parties won 30 of the 518 seats, and gained a significant percentage of the total vote, including 15 per cent in the UK. The Green vote became a force to be reckoned with.

The Single European Act: A New Environment Chapter

It was in this context that, in 1986, Community involvement in environmental protection was given a proper legal basis within the Treaty of Rome. The

Single European Act, which entered into force in 1987, introduced a specific chapter on the environment into the Treaty.[4]

Political pressure required a specific environmental competence within the Treaty of Rome. To the extent that it spurred on the development of EC environment policy, it was certainly a move to be welcomed. The new environment chapter clarified the principles of EC environment policy (that should preventive action be taken, the polluter should pay) and provided that environmental protection should be a component of all other EC policies. It also provided a basis for Community action at the international level and granted specific authority for EC environmental legislation. However, slotted into the existing Treaty structure, the introduction of the environment chapter has created confusion. The Single European Act granted the Community the power to legislate in a number of areas not traditionally considered economic. These non-economic areas, of which the environment was one, were bound, at times, to conflict with the creation of the internal market and free trade principles. This conflict has surfaced in two particular situations: in deciding the legal basis on which environmental measures are adopted; and in determining a priority where trade and environmental objectives conflict. These are examined below.

Articles 100A and 130S

Under the amended Treaty, environmental protection measures can now be adopted principally under one of two Articles: Article 130S or Article 100A. Article 100A is intended for measures 'which have as their object the establishment and functioning of the internal market'. Article 130S is essentially devoted to measures designed to protect the environment.[5] However, while most proposed measures could fall equally well under Article 100A or 130S, the procedures for adoption differ depending on which Article is chosen. Article 100A permits qualified majority voting and substantial input from the European Parliament, significantly limiting the power of veto of individual member States. Article 130S, by contrast, requires unanimous voting and allows member States almost unfettered powers to adopt national standards stricter than the agreed Community norm. This division has led to serious institutional conflict within the Community, with the EC Commission and Parliament favouring Article 100A, and the Council (ie member States) pushing Article 130S.[6]

The creation of a specific environmental competence under the new Articles 130R–T, has also made concrete the need to prioritize different policies within the hierarchy of Community objectives. The European Court of Justice (ECJ) has had the task of setting out criteria on the basis of which this calculation will be made. The EC Commission, in turn, has had to apply this analysis in a number of difficult factual cases. The nub of the problem is set out below.

THE PRACTICE: RECONCILING TRADE AND ENVIRONMENT CONCERNS

Article 30 of the EEC Treaty is the provision which guarantees the free movement of goods. It does so by prohibiting member States from imposing import quotas ('quantitative restrictions') and other trade restrictions which have a similar effect of hindering imports ('measures having equivalent effect').[7] The ECJ has interpreted this provision as prohibiting 'all trading rules enacted by member States which are capable of hindering, directly or indirectly, actually or potentially, intra-Community trade'.[8] Potentially, this formula could embrace an enormous variety of national measures. For example, it might prohibit national rules relating to advertising or the marketing of products. Decided cases have classified trading rules for commodities which are capable of hindering intra-Community trade requirements, such as including the requirement that margarine be marketed in cube shaped packs,[9] a prohibition on the sale of silver goods without hallmarking,[10] and the roadworthiness testing of imported vehicles.[11]

However, in spite of this, some trading rules may be permitted under Article 36, which lists four grounds on which a trading rule may be justified. These are on grounds of:

- public morality, public policy or public security;
- the protection of health and life of humans, animals and plants;
- the protection of national treasures possessing artistic, historic or archaeological value; or
- the protection of industrial and commercial property.

Provided, therefore, that a member State can show that its trading rule is intended to further one of these four objectives, it will not be struck down as contrary to Article 30.

The Court, however, has interpreted these exceptions restrictively. It has, for example, refused to accept that the expression 'public policy' includes the protection of consumers. By the same token, environmental protection measures to prevent waste, or to reduce discharges into the air or water, will not be considered as protecting the life of humans, animals or plants. They would, therefore, fall outside the exceptions listed in Article 36. In fact, provision for environmental protection within Article 36 is conspicious by its absence.

This omission has, however, been remedied. In the famous *Cassis de Dijon* case,[12] the European Court created a new and non-exhaustive category of measures capable of limiting the principle of free trade. These measures were referred to as 'mandatory requirements' which, the Court said, could justify a restriction on the free movement of goods, provided that there was no Community legislation regulating the issue; that the measure applied equally to domestic and imported products; and that the measure was 'proportional' to the objective to be achieved. In the *Used Oils* case,[13] protection of the environment was held to be a 'mandatory requirement', capable of limiting the free movement of goods. However, it was not until the now famous *Danish Bottles* case, that these principles were applied in practice.

Danish Bottles Case[14]

In 1981, Denmark set up a system under which beer and soft drinks could only be marketed in returnable, re-usable containers. These containers had to be approved by the National Environment Protection Agency which could refuse a new container if, for example, a suitable container of equal capacity was already being used. Exceptionally, non-approved containers (except metal cans) could be used for quantities of up to 3,000 hectolitres per producer, and for drinks sold by foreign producers to test the market. Approved containers could be returned to any retailer while non-approved only to the retailer from which the drink had been bought.

Foreign producers of beer, soft drinks and beverage containers complained to the EC Commission that the Danish rules were discriminatory. They argued that the financial and administrative burdens in establishing collection systems weighed more heavily on them than on domestic producers. Based on this complaint, the EC Commission brought an action against Denmark in the ECJ, alleging violation of the free movement provision of the Treaty (Article 30). Denmark defended the case by arguing that although the collection system did restrict trade, it was justified by a mandatory requirement, namely protection of the environment.

As stated above, Denmark could only rely on protection of the environment if the recycling scheme applied equally to domestic and foreign producers (ie that it was non-discriminatory) and was proportional to the aim in view. The Commission argued that the Danish law did not apply equally to domestic and imported products: imported products were placed at a disadvantage due to the infrastructure needed to set up a collection system and the administrative formalities this would require. However, the Court disagreed.

The Commission also argued that the scheme was disproportionate, in that protection of the environment could be achieved by a means less restrictive of intra-Community trade. In the Commission's view, the mandatory collection system had the effect of 'walling off' the Danish market from imports and was thus too restrictive of trade. In its place, it suggested there should be a system of recycling with selective collection of non-reusable containers. In the Commission's view, what it proposed was a 'more balanced solution', 'in contrast to the absolute priority which

Denmark gives to the protection of the environment, almost totally neglecting the free movement of goods'. The Commission also doubted the sincerity of Denmark's ecological concerns, pointing out that the mandatory collection system did not extend to milk and wine.

Denmark vigorously defended its position. It reiterated its environmental credentials pointing out that milk and wine containers posed an insignificant risk to the environment and for that reason were not covered by the scheme. Denmark confronted the proportionality argument by stating that no other scheme was capable of achieving the same rate of success, namely the return of 99 per cent of bottles which were used up to 30 times each.

The Court found largely in favour of Denmark but did not determine the key issue of who should fix the degree of environmental protection permitted. The Commission, the Advocate-General and the UK (which joined the action in support of the Commission) all took the view that the degree of protection had to be 'reasonable'. Advocate-General Slynn stated that:

> there has to be a balancing of interests between the free movement of goods and environmental protection, even if in achieving the balance the high standard of protection sought has to be reduced. The level of protection sought has to be a reasonable level . . .[15]

The Commission's view was that 'other solutions should be accepted even if they are a little less effective in assuring the aim pursued'.

Denmark declared itself ready to accept alternative solutions to the system it had set up which were equally effective in protecting the environment. However, it hotly contested that, in the absence of any such solution, it could be required to accept 'a weakening of legitimate and effective rules for the protection of the environment'.

Setting a precedent

The Court rejected the Commission's approach although its own position was ambiguous. Its stated view was that it is for the member State to decide the level of environmental protection it wants. However, its ruling that the marketing restrictions of 300ml for non-approved bottles was disproportionate, tended to indicate otherwise. The Court accepted that the system for returning non-approved containers was less effective than for approved containers (approved containers could be returned to any retailer with a 99 per cent recovery rate, non-approved only to the retailer who sold the drink). However, it held that the system for non-approved containers (ie a simple deposit-and-return system) was still capable of protecting the environment.

In spite of this, the Danish Bottles case was a landmark decision. In its ruling, the Court implicity endorsed Denmark's view that,

> the Commission has not followed the increasing ecological awareness which has arisen in recent years throughout Europe and which has led to the giving

of priority to the protection of the environment over the free movement of goods, which, whilst remaining a fundamental and very important objective, is no longer seen as an aim which must be achieved "at any price".

The case was warmly received by environmentalists and those who agreed that in the past too much emphasis had been placed on free trade concerns to the detriment of the consumer and the environment. It established important legal principles which form the framework for balancing trade and environment concerns within the Community order. Although few cases reached the ECJ, during the 1980s the EC Commission regularly conducted this balancing act. Mostly the dilemmas it faced concerned either cars or packaging containers.

At about this time, the German Lander adopted regulations allowing cars fitted with catalytic converters to remain on the roads in the event of a smog alarm, during which all other cars would be banned. The Commission considered that this discriminated against producers of cars from other member States which tended not to be fitted with catalytic converters but which Community legislation had deemed equivalent. The Commission commenced proceedings against Germany but dropped them in 1989 when it decided to enact EC emission standards which would, after all, require the installation of catalytic converters. Similar action contemplated against Denmark, came to a similar end.

In 1988 Italy enacted regulations limiting the phosphate content in detergents so as to combat the eutrophication of waters. The Commission took the view that since it was possible to produce detergents with little, if any, phosphate, and domestic and imported products were equally affected by the provisions, there was no unjustified restriction on trade and infringement of Article 30. At about the same time, Italy banned the marketing of non-biodegradable plastic bags. The ECJ ruled that the ban was permitted within the terms of existing Community legislation and so left open the question of whether it might, in the absence of relevant Community measures, amount to an unjustified restriction on trade. However, given that plastic bags were recognized as posing a considerable environmental hazard, it was thought likely that such a restriction would be justified. Indeed, subsequent provisions taxing these bags and requiring the use of certain materials in their production were considered justifiable on the grounds that no Community provisions were in force and the measures applied equally to domestic and foreign producers. Similarly, German restrictions on the use of lead capsules for wine and spirits clearly affected the marketing of such beverages from other member States. However, on the grounds that domestic and foreign producers were equally affected, that lead capsules could be easily replaced by capsules of other substances, and that the toxicity of lead was well known, the Commission upheld the measures.

In the early 1990s the ECJ finally had the opportunity to re-examine the principles set out in the Danish Bottles case. The occasion for this was the *Wallonian Waste* case, decided in July 1992.

The Wallonian Waste Case[16]

For many years the Wallonian region of Belgium had received waste from abroad. During the 1980s, outcry arose when the local population of Mellery in Wallonia was found to be suffering toxic contamination caused by foreign waste dumped at a nearby site. In response, the Walloon Regional Executive issued a decree,[17] effectively banning imports of waste into Wallonia. Exceptions were allowed in respect of the other Belgian regions such as Flanders and Brussels.

In January 1990 the EC Commission brought an action alleging that the Wallonian ban breached the 1984 Directive on the transfrontier shipment of hazardous waste, and Article 30 of the Treaty guaranteeing free movement of goods. Belgium defended the action on the grounds that waste, because it has no commercial value, could not be considered a 'good' within the meaning of the EEC Treaty, and thus did not fall within the scope of the provisions on the free movement of goods. It further contended that the ban was justified on environmental protection grounds, as consistent with the recently developed principles of self-sufficiency and proximity.[18]

The Court approached its decision in two stages. As regards hazardous waste, the case was clear cut: the system of prior informed consent, set up by the 1984 Directive, was a comprehensive system of harmonization which precluded member States from adopting a global ban on movements of hazardous waste. As regards *hazardous waste*, therefore, the Wallonian ban was illegal.

Having so ruled, the Court had still to consider the legality of the ban on *ordinary* waste to which the 1984 Directive did not apply. At issue here was compatibility with Article 30 of the Treaty relating to the free movement of goods. The Court rejected Belgium's claim that waste for disposal, because it had no positive but only a negative value, could not be 'valued in money' and therefore could not be classed as a 'good'. It also stated that objects transported over frontiers for the purposes of a commercial transaction (be it sale, consumption or even disposal), should always be subject to the free movement provisions. The difficulty in finding a workable distinction between recyclable from non-recyclable waste reinforced this conclusion.

Application of Article 30
Having ruled Article 30 to be applicable, the Court went on to determine whether the Wallonian waste ban in fact violated this fundamental Treaty provision. Applying the principles set out in the Danish Bottles decision, the Court first addressed the question whether the ban was discriminatory

as the Commission alleged. The Advocate General and EC Commission both argued that the Belgian Government could not justify its ban on environmental grounds (ie as a mandatory requirement) because the measure clearly discriminated as between national and imported products. However, the European Court did not share this view. 'In order to evaluate whether the restriction at issue is or is not discriminatory', said the Court, 'it is necessary to take into account the unique nature of waste'.[19]

This required, according to the Court, consideration of the principle that environmental damage should as a priority be rectified at source, which implied that it was for 'each region, commune or other locality to take the appropriate measures to ensure the proper treatment and disposal of their own waste'. The Court then stated that the principle of proximity – that waste disposal should take place as close as possible to its place of production – meant that the Wallonian measures should *not* be considered 'discriminatory'.

A judicial conflict

This reasoning was novel and conflicted with established case law on the legal definition of 'discriminatory'. However, having departed from traditional jurisprudence once, the Court repeated its offence: it made no attempt to apply the proportionality test. It simply concluded that although the Wallonian ban was a restriction on trade, it was justifiable as a measure to protect the environment, and thus did not violate the EC Treaty provisions on the free movement of goods. The Court, therefore, failed to consider whether the environment could have been protected by a measure less restrictive on trade.

The Court had no choice but to find the Wallonian ban in breach of the 1984 Directive. Adopted before the enactment of the Single European Act under the old Articles 100 and 235, the 1984 Directive did not permit member States to adopt national measures more stringent than the harmonized norm. The regime chosen by member States was based on prior notification and clearly precluded outright bans. The argument in relation to Article 30 was less clear cut.

The Danish Bottles decision acknowledged that member States should be permitted to adopt measures to protect the environment, even if they imposed restrictions on trade. But in the Wallonia case the Court was prepared to go to the lengths of manipulating settled jurisprudence to find in favour of the national environmental measures.

The implications of the decision were considerable. First, the motivation behind the judgment seemed to be influenced, at least in part, by political considerations. One month before judgment was given, Denmark voted 'no' to ratifying the Maastricht Treaty. Although the reasons for doing so were varied, many feared that strict Danish environment standards were being watered down by Community compromise. On the debate on 'subsidiarity' which followed, a consensus was formed that the member States should be more free to adopt environment measures which reflected the demands of their own national electorates.

At about the same time, the EC Commission decided another case in favour of the national prerogative. This was the *PCP* case, in which the Commission approved a German request to continue a ban on pentachlorophenol (PCP – a wood, leather and textiles preservative) in spite of subsequent Community legislation which merely restricted PCP use in certain circumstances.[20] The application was made under Article 100(A)(4) of the Treaty (the first of its kind) and required the Commission to consider whether the national measure constituted a means of 'arbitrary discrimination or a disguised restriction on trade'. France has recently brought an action against the EC Commission challenging its decision to uphold the German ban.

The second concrete result of the Wallonian case, was the adoption of a new Regulation on the shipment of waste[21] which expressly provides for national bans on the import of waste for disposal. This became possible once the Court had ruled that such bans did not violate the free movement provisions of the Treaty. This Regulation has been adopted under Article 130S and thus permits member States to take more stringent measures. The result of this is that it becomes difficult, if not impossible, to speak of a Single Market in waste. Indeed the Community seems to have accepted that this is no longer a reality.

In legal terms, the Wallonian decision has muddied waters which the Danish Bottles case appeared to have settled, and left unresolved the question over who is to decide the level of justifiable environmental protection. In the Wallonian case, the Commission did not argue that the same result could have been achieved by less restrictive means (it did not think it was necessary to do so as it anticipated the case would turn on the question of discrimination). Consequently the Court did not question the environmental objective at issue. However, prevailing opinion still seems to suggest that environment concerns should only be allowed to restrict the free movement of goods to the extent that this was 'reasonable'. In the view of Ludwig Kramer, Legal Advisor of DGXI (the environment Directorate of the EC Commission), this implies that, 'in cases of conflict, free-trade considerations prevail over environmental considerations'. Certainly the analysis of the ECJ takes Article 30 as a fundamental provision of the Treaty, upholding a fundamental principle. This principle is subject to limitations in certain narrowly defined circumstances – protection of the environment being one.

In a recently published article,[22] Kramer takes the contrary view. His interpretation of the Treaty suggests that since the Single European Act, the environment has been a accorded privileged position as compared with other Community objectives. Kramer argues that among the Community's numerous objectives only environmental protection is required to be 'a component of other Community policies' (Article 130R(2)). 'Nowhere in the Treaty' writes Kramer, 'is the same said of the free circulation of goods.' Furthermore, environmental proposals which form part of the internal market, must be based on a high level of environmental protection (Article 100A(3)). As Kramer points out, this is 'the only provision in the Treaty which contains quality requirements for the Commission's proposals'. Articles 100A(4) and 130T allow member States, once a Community environmental measure has been taken, to apply or introduce more protective measures at a national level. All this, states Kramer, illustrates the special importance which the Treaty, since the Single European Act, has attached to environmental protection. His conclusion is thus, that in the absence of Community measures, it is for the member States to decide what degree of environmental protection they desire.

Kramer's views are controversial. What is less controversial is the view that once the Maastricht Treaty is ratified and comes into force, the environment will rise a notch in the hierarchy of Community aims. Under the new Treaty, the primary EC objective to promote economic growth (set out in Article 2), will be replaced by the aim to achieve 'sustainable . . . growth respecting the environment'. The methods for achieving these aims, set out in Article 3, would, for the first time, place environment policy alongside the free movement and competition provisions. How this will affect the reasoning of the ECJ remains to be seen. It may mean that the proportionality requirement is dropped and member States are given a freer reign to enact environmental measures to achieve whatever level of protection they deem fit. Other innovations introduced by Maastricht would be the extension of qualified majority voting to most environmental measures (unanimity would be maintained, for example, for planning and taxation proposals). The European Parliament would be granted an even more significant role with the power to veto proposed environmental measures (this is the 'co-decision' procedure). The requirement to integrate environmental concerns into other EC policies would also be strengthened.

THE GATT EXPERIENCE AND RESTRICTIONS ON EXTERNAL COMMUNITY TRADE

So far we have looked at the way the Community tackles restrictions introduced by member States which affect intra-Community trade. These are clearly subject to stricter scrutiny than restrictions on external trade since the ideal of free circulation of goods and the creation of a single or internal market is not applied to non-Community States. However, it is by no means clear that Community measures which regulate trade with third countries would be compatible with existing GATT rules. These measures cover, for example, the trade in wildlife (based on the CITES Convention); trade in seals, whales, tropical timber, dangerous chemicals and CFCs; the use of leghold traps, imports and exports of waste etc. They are intended both to protect the Community environment as well as that of third countries and what are called 'the global commons'. Their adoption is often motivated as much by the wish to protect the internal market as to protect the environment. In other words, if a member State takes a unilateral measure on the grounds of protecting the environment, the Commission will often seek to re-establish the 'level playing field' by proposing parallel Community action.

Examining the compatibility of these measures with the GATT provides an opportunity to review the GATT's attempts to balance trade and environmental concerns while examining in greater detail some of the Community measures in question.

As with the original Treaty of Rome, the GATT contains no provisions specifically geared to protecting the environment. However, in contrast to the Treaty of Rome, public concern about the environment has, to date, not resulted in any amendments to the GATT or the enactment of a code to balance trade and environment concerns. Clearly, amending the GATT is a more onerous process than amending the Treaty, given the number of Contracting Parties and diversity of economic conditions. However, the net result is that in the words of Paul Demaret[23] 'inquiring into the environmental trade justification of a trade restriction seems to exceed, at present, GATT's competence'. These shortcomings are well illustrated by two cases in which the GATT Dispute Settlement Panels attempted to determine trade disputes with an environmental angle. These concerned a Superfund tax and Mexican tuna.

The Superfund Tax Case

In the *Superfund Tax* case, the EC challenged a US tax imposed under the Superfund Act. The tax was levied on certain chemicals to fund the clean-up of hazardous waste created by the use of these substances, which was also imposed on the import of certain chemical derivatives. This tax was presented as a border tax adjustment corresponding to the internal tax. The tax on domestic chemicals was rebated on export. The EC questioned the grounds for the import tax, arguing that it could not really be seen as a border tax adjustment since the domestic products which were taxed were not the same as the imported products. Furthermore, the border tax adjustments were inconsistent with the environmental purpose of the Superfund Act and the polluter pays principle. The imported chemicals would have caused pollution *abroad* (and so may have already been taxed), while chemicals destined for export were exempt even though their production would have caused pollution within the US. The Panel declined to consider the polluter pays principle as it did not consider it a part of GATT law and upheld the Superfund tax.

The Mexican Tuna Case

The facts of the *Mexican Tuna* case are better known. The use of purse-seine nets to fish tuna results in the drowning of dolphins. Under the US Marine Mammal Act, US vessels fishing in the Eastern Tropical Pacific were required to fish using methods which minimized dolphin deaths. In 1988 the US imposed a ban on the import of tuna caught using methods which caused more dolphin deaths than the US average. Mexico complained to the GATT and the panel upheld its complaint. The Panel ruled that a Party was not entitled to restrict imports so as to 'equalize conditions under which a product is produced' domestically and abroad. It also ruled that the ban amounted to a 'quantitative restriction' which could not be justified under either of the GATT exceptions: the measure could not be said to safeguard life or health of humans or plants 'within the jurisdiction of the importing country'. Interpreting Article XX(g), the panel made it clear that trade restrictions could only be enforced to further domestic conservation policies and not those of third countries.

Finally, the panel found that the US had not exhausted all options within the GATT to resolve the dispute, 'in particular . . . the negotiation of an international cooperative agreement'.

Although the panel openly acknowledged that the GATT was ill-equipped to strike a balance between free trade and environment protection, the tuna ruling was still unsatisfactory. Demaret has commented on the inconsistency between these two rulings, and concludes that in the Superfund case 'a trade restriction whose environmental justification was somewhat questionable, was declared compatible with the GATT, whereas in the [tuna fish case] a trade restriction whose environmental justification was certainly stronger, was deemed incompatible with the GATT'.

On the basis of these rulings many of the EC measures mentioned above would be found inconsistent with the GATT. Import restrictions designed to protect the Community's own environment would be lawful, provided they paralleled similar domestic restrictions: for example, restrictions on the import of waste from third countries. However, most of the Community measures referred to above aim at protecting environmental interests *outside* the Community's jurisdiction. These measures, to the extent that they are adopted by the Community alone, would probably be thought inconsistent with the GATT. That would cover the seals Directive[24] and the whales Regulation,[25] although the Community might seek to argue that they paralleled similar prohibitions within the Community. Measures aimed at protecting the global commons would also be unlawful. The only escape would be for measures implemented as a result of international conventions (the Montreal Protocol, CITES, the Basel Convention etc). An interesting case would be the EC's leghold trap Regulation.[26] This raises the same problems as the tuna case, namely that the prohibition relates to production processes rather than the product itself. From 1995 the EC will require skin pelts, produced in third countries, to conform to the same standards as apply to Community production. Under the Tuna case reasoning, this measure might be unlawful.

CONCLUSION

As an institution, the Community has responded to political change. Through a steady progression, environment policy has gained rank within the Community structure. Often this has been at the expense of free trade and the creation of a Single Market. Article 100(A)(4) permits member States to apply national environment rules which are stricter than a Community measure intended to harmonize laws. Although the provision has only been relied on once (the PCP case), its inclusion in the Treaty signals an acceptance on the part of member States that the Single Market should be made subject to environmental concerns. But what it also signals is the continuing tension between the Community and member States. At present the Community lacks the will to resist unilateral national initiatives to protect the environment, regardless of the impact on the Single Market or EC environment policy. Arguably , it has little choice. When the Community loses touch with the prevailing political mood, the institution itself is threatened. The Danish 'no' to Maastricht made this patently clear. The result is seen in overtly political judgments by the ECJ such as the Wallonian waste case. This illustrates an important reality of the Community order: that legal analysis and the rule of law has its limits.

The GATT is not subject to the same political pressures. However, as more countries enact regulations restricting trade on environmental grounds, there is a pressing need to balance trade liberalization and environmental protection on a global scale. The GATT is the only existing body capable of performing such a role. The GATT agreement should thus be revised to expressly include protection of the environment as a possible justification for trade restrictions. It should develop its adjudicatory role so as to assess the validity of trade restrictions, and weed out those which are disguised protectionist tools. The ECJ and its jurisprudence may serve as a model. Trade officials, (among them Mickey Kantor, the US trade representative), have indicated a commitment to ensuring that an environmental and social dimension are included in the next round of trade negotiations. Popular pressure should ensure this commitment is honoured.

7 THE GATT AND THE ENVIRONMENT

James Cameron

INTRODUCTION

It is possible and necessary to re-orient the General Agreement on Tariffs and Trade (GATT)[1] so that this most important international trade institutution can at the very least lend its support to the resolution of global environmental problems. There is a strong perception that the GATT and its trade rules are an impediment to successful solutions to global environmental problems, at least when expressed in law. It is a perception backed by a growing measure of political support. This is likely to mean changes in principle and in process which the institution may find painful to go through. Nonetheless, the GATT cannot escape its environmental responsibilities. To say that GATT is not the right forum for dealing with environmental issues is of no practical use. Of course, it cannot be the sole forum, and it should not be a competing forum, it should be a place for negotiating trade agreements where the ultimate objective is sustainable development.

This chapter considers the extent to which free(er) trade, environmental protection and sustainable development can be mutually supportive in a legal framework yet to be created, but tentatively emerging. Its aim is to communicate the extent to which the institution, with the principal responsibility for regulating international trade agreements, has been affected by arguments arising from, broadly speaking, the environmental community and to pass judgment on the particularly pressing needs for change within that institution. It should be said that that judgment is one coloured by the experience of working with non-governmental organizations, such as the World Wildlife Fund (WWF) and Greenpeace, as well as, in other contexts, developing countries.

The judgment is also part-formed. By that I mean that the judgment is not one set in stone – there is too much still to learn. While it seems clear that change is needed to respond to pressures of an environmentally self-conscious and responsible international institution, for someone with an avowedly internationalist point of view, it is a difficult and dangerous task to propose solutions to environmental problems which do not encourage the more powerful to further limit access to their markets by the weak through tough domestic environmental measures. To the trade experts environmental regulation, perhaps setting standards for products, are *prima facie* barriers to trade and one of the fundamental purposes of the GATT is to remove trade barriers.

As an indicator of the 'greening process' this chapter looks at the language of international legal agreements relating to environment, development and trade. In political and legal discourse language goes with argument. Who wins gets the law on 'their side'. The Uruguay Round process is not yet complete, the package of agreements, in what is known (after the Secretary-General of the GATT) as the Dunkel draft which could be the new law which demonstrates a new commitment to sustainable development is not yet agreed. This means there is much still to play for. So what are we to make of the various positions?

In the development of the rhetoric required to actualize the potential for trade, environmental protection and sustainable development to be mutually supportive, the key players in the international community will want to argue their exclusivity, for their own purposes. Even if there is a widespread consensus that a balance needs to be struck, each player in their turn is pushing for the balance to be struck in a different way. We ought to recognize that not only will there be some diversity in the balancing tests formed by various institutions, such as the GATT, or the European Community (EC), or the fledgeling North American Free Trade Agreement (NAFTA), but in the interpretation of those tests (such as 'proportionality' or 'necessity' discussed below).

International law (the law of international society, the society of all societies) has an important role in enabling these objectives to be mutually supportive. It is possible to imagine law finding, and re-finding, the balance between nature and economy. The law both reflects and promotes the search for such a balance. It creates structures for debate, principles, rules, it distributes resources, above all it transforms natural power into legal power, making all power-holders accountable in law.[2]

UNCED

In 1992, the United Nations Conference on Environment and Development (UNCED), held in Rio de Janeiro in Brazil provided a very significant forum for the debate about trade and environmental issues and their relationship to sustainable development. In my view it has had a significant effect on the future of the GATT. Its most powerful effect was to connect the processes created by UNCED for achieving sustainable development and the regulation of international trade at the GATT. For example in Part A of Chapter 2 of Agenda 21, the international community is called upon to:

ensure that environmental and trade policies are mutually suppotive, with a view to achieving sustainable development.

Part B, 'making trade and environment mutually supportive' includes, under 'objectives', a call to governments to:

strive to meet the following objectives, through relevant multilateral forums, including GATT, UNCED and other international organizations:

to make international trade and environment policies mutually supportive in favour of sustainable development.

Following UNCED, it can be argued that the balance between trade and environment imperatives *is* sustainable development. Sustainable development is a meaningful concept despite its poor usage, precisely because it conveys this sense of balance. The language is a little convoluted for non-lawyers and lawyers alike, but in my view[3] this definition captures much of the debate in the economic, political science and development studies field:

Sustainable development means the progressive economic and social development of human society through maintaining the security of livelihood for all peoples and by enabling them to meet their present needs, together with a quality of life in accordance with their dignity and well being, without compromising the ability of future generations to do likewise.

This applies if the link between trade and environment is through their relationship to development. The key to their resolution is what kind of development is pursued. This is, and should be, a never-ending debate, one that the law, and the institutions in which it operates must continually learn from. Indeed, because sustainable development can be understood as both a principle and a process, tremendous pressure is placed on the the various international organizations, regional, national and local institutions, which have a role to play in giving practical effect to the concept.

UNCED involved a vast new gathering of governmental and non-governmental policy-makers and analysts. The experience of participation in UNCED has helped the progress of distributing the values expressed in, for example the Rio Declaration. I very much doubt whether a larger and more diverse group of human beings has ever gathered to make an international legal agreement. Ideas, learned from the discourse on sustainable development, preoccupied with implementing those agreements have been carried by the many participants to other fora, including the GATT.

Information and the Non-State Actor

To achieve the 'proper' or 'best' balance, information and the process by which it is imparted is the crucial, empowering ingredient. The information upon which the law-making and enforcing system depends is expanding rapidly, introducing new powerful actors in the non-governmental community and continuously altering power relationships.

An example may help to explain. In about March 1992,[4] the WWF, through Charlie Arden Clarke, obtained (note careful choice of word[5]) a draft of the text for the proposed Multilateral Trade Organization (MTO). No one in the non-governmental community had seen it, and until the WWF publicized its contents, very few parliamentarians anywhere in the world had heard of the the MTO. They commissioned a legal and environmental anaylsis.[6] Environmental and development organizations began to exchange the draft and make comments to their members, to the media, to parliamentarians in their home countries. The environmental community had joined the debate about what should or should not be in the Uruguay Round very late. Much at that time seemed beyond further debate. The MTO seemed new and vulnerable.

Campaigns against the MTO began to mobilize. The campaigns were particularly strongly run in the United States, where negotiations for the North America Free Trade Agreement were nearing conclusion. The dominant concern was that international trade rules would challenge national environmental legislation, limiting options to use the law to protect the environment. This was the perception of many environmentalists following the GATT panel ruling in the *US –Mexico Tuna –Dolphin* case,[7] which is described below. Full-page advertisements[8] were taken out in the press, extensive lobbying took place and the international institutions such as the EC and the OECD were engaged. The OECD organized a special meeting of NGOs in September to collect and present their views to member governments. All around the world seminars and conferences bringing together government and non-governmental experts and commentators have been arranged (the process continues apace today).

By early 1993, it can be said that the MTO, as an idea reduced to writing in a negotiating text, is vulnerable. The US Government has not yet commited its support, which is considered vital. Amendments have been informally, or semi-formally, suggested by governments. The US has produced its own text for the administrative mechanism to implement the Uruguay Round, which it has called 'GATT2'. A new more environmentally sensitive Preamble, a committee on trade and environment, perhaps even a free standing article in the agreement providing the institutional authority in the MTO for the expression of environmental or sustainable development policy objectives. Correpondence between the European MEP, Thomas Spencer, and the EC Commissioner responsible for international Trade (External Relations), Sir Leon Britten, has confirmed the EC's interest in making amendments to ensure greater environmental sensitivity in order to retain momentum for the MTO which they strongly support.

My point is not in the details of apparent concessions, but in the observation that the WWF, a well-organized international non-governmental organization, together with many other NGOs around the world have significantly affected the intergovernmental negotiations for a new institutional structure for the administration of GATT Agreements. It started with information. The lack of an effective process has, I believe, led to some of the criticism running out of control. To be more precise, many groups quick to criticise, would be happier with a reformed MTO than none at all.

Institutional Arrangements and the Need for Change

At a private meeting in December 1992[9] with several environmental experts and campaigners to discuss the meaning of a sustainable economy, the issue of international trade and environmental protection was hotly debated. The leader of the Liberal Democratic Party in Britain, Paddy Ashdown, intervened in the debate to ask a simple question: 'are you environmentalists against international trade or against the GATT, as an institution?' In response the room roughly divided – more against the institution than the trade.

Institutional reform is the key to delivering sustainable development through the international trading system. This is, in part, because of the tremendous economic risks associated with restricting international trade, and in part because, as I have argued above, actualized sustainable development is the product of a dialogue between economic and social development and environmental protection. The question, therefore, must be what process will best deliver this product.

Professor David Pearce argues that the dangers associated with restricting international trade are such that environmentalists have 'a difficult assignment' in arguing for the GATT reform; he says their case must pass three tests:

a) they must show that the environmental degradation brought about by free trade is (i) truly brought about by trade rather than some other factor; and (ii) of greater consequence than the losses of of human well-being that would ensue from restricted trade;

b) they must show that production-related damage is a legitimate feature of the importing nation's loss of well-being;

c) they must show that a trade restriction is the most cost-effective way of bringing about the change in the product or process giving rise to the externality[10]

He concludes,

(t)he environmentalists have a case. I doubt if it is a powerful one, but it needs to be heard.

The essence of the argument of this chapter is that the GATT needs to be reformed so that it can be heard. For sustainable development to be an achievable objective within the GATT, procedural devices will have to be carefully drafted to allow the contest between principles which these tests imply.

The GATT has built itself up – even against US opposition for many years following the failure of the US to sign the Havana Charter – into a powerful international institution with wide and widening membership. It is now a big system organized in 'Rounds' of intergovernmental negotiations lasting many years and delivering several agreements. The signs are that even a system with tremendous inertia, such as the GATT, confronted with change induced by events such as UNCED and other elemental changes in human society, is under considerable stress.

It is axiomatic in international negotiations, especially those dealing with environment and economy, that individuals, groups, nations and trading blocks are ever more interconnected. We know that this makes negotiation, agreement and compliance more difficult. There is a genuine fear, often expressed by GATT officials privately or in experts' meetings, that the institution is already in danger of overstretching itself, and having an environmental brief would lead to collapse.

However, if connectedness is part of the problem it is also part of the solution. If we make the bold assumption that the GATT itself would espouse the sustainable development objective, perhaps even in the form suggested in the introduction, then public participation and the widest possible participation of developing countries is essential to the *negotiations* which deliver trade agreements which are sustainable in character.

Institutions exist to solve problems. From time to time the nature of the problem changes, and the institution must adapt to solve the problem as it is perceived or die. A mandate to liberalize world trade is becoming a mandate to liberalize world trade in order to achieve sustainable development. The MTO[11] could still be this institution. There are still good social reasons for its existence. Whilst there is justified scepticism about the dogma of a comparative advantage which dominates GATT thinking, international society needs international trade, you cannot have one without the other. Equally, the good social reasons must not be undermined by the economic or indeed environmental dogma.

In the end, the sum of the institutional argument is that international society is grappling with fiendishly difficult questions of global governance, in which idealogical arguments about the reach of public decision-making into the marketplace are playing a large part. Law and lawyers are as connected to this debate as economics and the economists. The challenge in designing an effective process is to allow our relative ignorance of ecosystems and our relative conviction that capitalism is the most effective economic system for delivering well-being to the society of all human beings. Capitalism and ecosystems share certain characteristics – they are both self-propelled systems, creating and destroying, mutating and adapting, competing, cooperating and selecting survival solutions. Conservationists know that managed ecosystems prosper, that intervention is necessary to conserve; we know also that certain interventions are disastrous. Our best hope lies in educating ourselves towards better judgment. It is trite to say that economists generally agree that management of an economy is necessary, they disagree as to extent, and occasionally as to purposes. Herman Daly has recently observed that the economy is a subsystem of an ecosystem:

> . . . sustainability requires that growth must not exceed the capacity of the larger system to regenerate resources and absorb wastes at sustainable rates and without disrupting other vital natural services, such as photosynthesis, nitrogen fixation, etc.[12]

A SELECTION OF ENVIRONMENTAL CHALLENGES TO FREE TRADE: IN A LEGAL CONTEXT

Principle 12 of the Rio Declaration presents quite nicely the policy issues which set up environmental protection measures as a challenge to international economic law, in the form of the GATT rules:

> States should cooperate to promote a supportive and open international economic system that would lead to economic growth and sustainable development in all countries, to better address the problems of environmental degradation. Trade policy measures for environmental purposes should not constitute a means of arbitrary or unjustifiable discrimination or a disguised restriction on international trade. Unilateral actions to deal with environmental challenges outside the jurisdiction of the importing country should be avoided. Environmental measures addressing transboundary or global environmental issues should, as far as possible, be based on an international consensus.

There are many codes in this language for well established negotiating positions. The text could be very simply interpreted in this way:

- general support for the principles of the GATT and other regional 'free(er)' trade areas such as the EC et al;
- trade measures designed to deal with environmental problems must pass established tests of discrimination and disguised restrictions on trade; and

■ unilateral actions by a single State are clearly discouraged whilst consensus-based multilateral processes are presented as the appropriate means to develop any trade-related environmental measures.

It is an understatement to suggest that the potential for conflict between environment and free trade is great. What follows is a brief selection, with rudimentary legal commentary.

Trade bans based on production processes

That trade instruments can be fundamental for the effectiveness of agreements for the protection of wildlife is demonstrated by the relative success of the Convention on International Trade of Endangered Species (CITES).[13] Although other agreements to protect wildlife contain incidental trade provisions, CITES is the only convention which seeks to protect wildlife solely by the regulation of international trade.

The success of CITES is demonstrated not only by its success in preventing the decline in populations and in some cases the recovery of endangered species, but also by the number of States which are parties:

> The fact that 87 States are now parties to CITES demonstrates the widespread appeal of a treaty which strictly limits international trade in species in genuine need of protection, allows a controlled trade in those able to sustain some exploitation and sets up a system of international cooperation to help achieve its objectives.[14]

This scheme is attractive both to States with and without populations of endangered species within their jurisdiction:

> The Convention is attractive to the 'producer' nations who see controls at the place of import as well as the place of export as essential weapons in their fight to protect their valuable wildlife resources from poachers and illegal traders. The 'consumer' nations support it because without controls their legitimate dealers might have no raw material in which to trade in the generations to come.[15]

Another reason given for the success of CITES is that it contains restrictions on trade with non-parties. This is not only because these restrictions help reinforce the existing system of reciprocal import and export restrictions but:

> The tough line taken in this respect may have contributed to the steadily increasing membership of the Convention since non-Parties may feel that the advantages of being a Party, and therefore in a position to influence the development of the Convention outweigh those of remaining outside where there are even fewer States with which they can freely trade.[16]

Although CITES is the most important international agreement to use trade instruments to protect wildlife, trade restrictions also exist in numerous other agreements. Their use can be justified on environmental grounds by similar reasoning.[17]

Trade restrictions also occur in the context of hazardous waste. Restrictions on import are clearly an important tool for importing States to use in protecting their domestic environment.[18] Restrictions on the export of hazardous waste are also justifiable on other grounds. It is in the long term cheaper to dispose of waste safely, when and where it arises, than to dispose of it unsafely, and then have later to remedy the damage caused. In an increasingly global economy it is in the interest of all States to avoid the waste of resources involved in the unsafe disposal of hazardous waste anywhere.[19] Different considerations apply to agreements intended to protect the global commons, which in particular depend also on trade restrictions with non-Parties.

The benefits of an agreement to protect the global commons accrue to all States. However, in the absence of sanctions on non-Parties, it is only the Parties to an agreement who bear the cost of any measures. Trade restrictions on non-Parties fulfil a double function. First, they seek to prevent free-riders enjoying the benefits of an agreement without contributing to the cost. This argument of equity is a justification in itself. But the prevention of free-riding by sanctions against non-participation also encourages participation in a global agreement. Without such sanctions there will often be greater benefit in remaining a non-Party. Where this is the case, international agreement to protect the global commons is likely to be markedly more difficult.[20]

There are always difficulties when a group of States club together and determine, in the absence of other States, that the absentees' actions are unlawful. This is especially the case when cultural values are associated with relationships between humans and other species. Equally there are dangers in being so relativist about moral arguments in support of law that no judgment is ever made. The entire CITES system works reasonably well because it is focused on the trade and not the act of killing. At the same time there is a high level of understanding that dealing with the trade gets to the cause of the problem which is not the individual death but the decline in conservation status of a species.

Eco-labelling

In many ways, eco-labelling appears to be an effective method of guiding production techniques towards more environmentally-friendly techniques without relying on blunt instruments such as trade bans. The notion of giving the consumer direct influence on this issue appeals to notions of citizen empowerment, and eco-labelling has, in principle, been approved by the GATT Panel in the *Mexican Tuna* case.[21]

Leaving aside a dispute about the effectiveness of labelling schemes,[22] consumer preference is a powerful tool that can easily be exploited for other, more insidious, reasons. The row over Austrian tropical timber labelling reveals just how sensitive this issue can be, particularly when protectionism is suspected to be a hidden motive. An Austrian labelling scheme which would have required displaying to the consumer informa- tion about the 'sustainability' of the forest management of the timber product, was strongly challenged in the GATT. The ASEAN Contracting Parties to the GATT recently stated that the Austrian scheme was inherently protectionist and went on to warn that:

> The quality mark requirement, although not mandatory, is an attempt by Austria to unilaterally decide what constitutes sustainably-managed forests when there is still no international consensus on the criteria and determina- tion of sustainably-managed forests. In doing so, a dangerous precedent has been set and, if left unchecked, may trigger similar actions in other countries and lead to further market access restrictions on tropical timber and tropical timber products.[23]

The Austrians withdrew the scheme and are currently looking to pursue the same environmental objective through the transference of technical and financial resources. The solution to situations such as this may be a propor- tionality test to balance the concerns of economically weaker States against the environmental measures taken by stronger ones. The GATT Working Group on Environmental Measures and International Trade has recently stated:

> A labelling programme could create a trade barrier if it involved requirements which are costly or difficult for foreign firms to meet and favoured domestic products if access to the programme was not equally available to all suppliers. However, transparency of programmes and their criteria, as well as public participation in the establishment of such criteria could help guard against such misuse of labelling programmes.[24]

While this approach is logical in as far as it addresses labelling, it does not address the root causes of developing countries' resentment. In the absence of proper assistance for developing countries, it is clear that conflicts in this area will increase over time. This is simply due to the high stakes for developing countries in their exports. Any measures which they perceive as threatening these exports will be bitterly opposed.

The 'necessity' debate

Article XX(b) of the GATT allows a general exception for GATT obligations if the measures are: '(b) necessary to protect human, animal or plant life or health'. Restrictions on exports of endangered species of plants or animals will fall within Article XX(b) if they can be shown to be 'necessary'. A measure is not 'necessary' if the same level of protection could be achieved by a measure which is less disruptive of international trade.[25] The question is, 'necessary' for what?

The TBT's Agreements (Technical Barriers to Trade) requirement that 'unnecessary' obstacles to trade not be created implies a proportionality test will be used to balance the regulation's objectives against its effects on trade.[26] Equilibrium will be achieved only if dispute panels interpret 'unnecessary' in an environmentally sensitive way. When trade disruptive measures are more likely to achieve environmental objectives than non disruptive ones, such measures should be allowed.

Adoption of the precautionary principle[27] in this context would alleviate the environmental concerns in this regard. In addition to ensuring better environmental protection, such an approach will, to a great extent, permit States to determine their own level of acceptable risk in relation to their environments. Truly international law, the law of international society, not only justifies but encourages the use of law to protect the global commons or the extra-territorial environment. What sort of test could pull these policy goals together and enable consistently fair decisions to be taken in trade tribunals?

The ECJ, in *Commission v Denmark*,[28] in the context of a Danish law requiring all beer and soft drinks containers to be returnable, ruled that in the absence of specific EEC environmental legislation establishing a rule of environmental protection, it will permit national environmental rules to restrict trade between member States provided that:

■ the rules are genuinely intended to protect the environment;
■ the effect on trade is not disproportionate to the objective pursued; and
■ the rules are not discriminatory against producers in third countries.

This may be one of the aspects of EC law which is transferable to the GATT notwithstanding the obvious differences in the social, political and economic make-up of the EC as compared to the GATT.

The trade restrictions in the Montreal Protocol are also subject to limitation by this term. Given the scientific uncertainty about ozone depletion, it is difficult to assert positively that the same level of protection could not be achieved by a less trade disruptive measure. However, given the severe consequences of ozone depletion, it would be rational to adopt a precautionary approach in the face of this scientific uncertainty, and the standard of proof required of the State seeking to justify the measure reduced accordingly.[29]

What is 'arbitrary'?

To fall within either Article XX(b) or (g) it must be shown also that the measures:

are not applied in a manner which would constitute a means of arbitrary or unjustifiable discrimination between countries where the same conditions prevail, or a disguised restriction on international trade.[30]

Provided that export restrictions are justified on ecological grounds and are openly announced, they should not be considered 'disguised restrictions on trade'. And provided the restrictions apply equally to exports to all States, the issue of 'arbitrary or unjustifiable discrimination' should not arise.

A conflict with the GATT may arise, however, where the issue of an export permit is made conditional on the prior issue of an import permit by the State of import. This is the case under CITES for the export of specimens of Appendix I species.[31] Appendix I species are those most in need of protection, and it is for this reason that export is made conditional on the prior grant of an import licence. The grant of an import licence is in turn conditional on the relevant authority in the State of import being satisfied, among other things, that the specimen is not to be used for primarily commercial purposes.[32] In making the grant of an export licence conditional on the prior grant of an import licence, which is in turn conditional on the determination of non-commercial use in the importing State, the State of export may be discriminating between States 'where the same conditions prevail'. Is the fact that an individual specimen will be used for commercial purposes in one State and not in another sufficient to make the two States ones where 'the same conditions [do not] prevail'? If it is not, then the State of export will need to show that discriminating on this basis is not 'arbitrary' or 'unjustifiable'.

This question of compatibility of export restrictions with the GATT, arises under CITES only in relation to exports of specimens of Appendix I species. The export of the less endangered species listed under Appendix II is not conditional on the prior grant of an import permit. It is ironic that restrictions on the export of Appendix I species are less clearly compatible with the GATT than are the restrictions on the export of Appendix II species, since Appendix I species are those which require the greatest protection.

CITES restricts trade not only between Parties, but between Parties and non-Parties. For example, the export of a specimen of an Appendix I species to a non-Party is conditional upon the prior grant of an import permit by the importing non-Party,[33] and the import permit must 'substantially conform with the requirements of' CITES.[34] The import of a specimen of an Appendix I species from a non-Party is also dependent on the grant of an import permit, which will only be granted if the relevant authority in the importing State advises that the import will not be detrimental to the survival of the species.

As the effect of CITES is to impose the same restrictions on trade with non-Parties as on trade with Parties, arguments of 'discrimination' under Article XX and XIII are unlikely to arise, and the same considerations apply as apply to the restrictions on trade with Parties. Restrictions on exports are likely to be justifiable under Articles XX(b) or (g), whereas restrictions on imports are likely be prohibited under Article XI.1 and fall outside the Article XX exceptions.

Many of the agreements in this category [harmful substances] impose different restrictions on trade with non-Parties from those applied to trade with Parties.[35] The Basel Convention requires Parties to prohibit imports of hazardous waste from non-Parties.[36] As hazardous waste produced by non-Parties is intrinsically no more hazardous than that produced by Parties, it could be argued that this discrimination is 'arbitrary'. Similar arguments can be made about the requirement in the Bamako Convention that the African Parties prohibit the import of hazardous waste originating outside Africa, but not that originating inside Africa.[37]

The S&PS Decision[38] contains some similar provisions as the TBT Agreement.[39] It is to be hoped that as with the TBT Agreement, the references in the Decision to 'arbitrary' or 'unjustified' distinctions are interpreted in an environmental manner.[40] Similarly, the requirement that measures be the least trade restrictive should have an environmental proportionality test applied.[41] Finally, assistance to developing countries is affirmed as desirable, but not mandatory.[42]

Like products

When is a product 'like' for the purposes of a technical barrier to trade? Should the manner and process of making the product be relevant, and why? The 1991 TBT Agreement[43] includes measures on processing and production methods (PPM). Article 2.2 acknowledges that protection of human, animal, and plant life or health, and the environment are legitimate objectives for technical regulations. But such regulations can only be legitimately applied if they do not create an unnecessary obstacle to international trade, and if they accord like treatment to like products originating within the country concerned or any other member country.

Although this language is an improvement over the original 1979 TBT Code, it remains unclear how this will impact on the term 'like products', which is fundamental to the GATT system. It is uncertain whether the 1991 Code permits differentiation between like products on the basis of their PPMs – ie when one is produced sustainably and another is not.[44]

A brief examination of EEC and US competition laws provides indications that such a distinction might be supported by commercial reality. Article 86 of the Treaty of Rome controls abusive action by a single commercial organization of its market dominance. For the Article to bite, the relevant organization must have a 'dominant position within the Common Market or in a substantial part of it'.

The practice of interpretation of this provision requires definition of relevant product and geographic markets. In the context of defining product markets, the single most important interpretive tool is the concept of 'substitutability'. This requires consideration of what other products might, in market terms, provide a substitute for the product under consideration, and therefore compete with it. Substitutability may be viewed from the standpoint of the buyer (demand substitution) as well the standpoint of the supplier (supply substitution).

Demand substitutability requires consideration of a product's characteristics, price and intended use. EEC jurisprudence on the subject tends to attach more importance to functional characteristics than the physical or chemical make-up of a product. However, it seems reasonable to accept that where a product falls in an area where buyers' decisions are influenced by environmental factors, including production and processing methods, those environmental factors must be an important factor in assessing relevant product characteristics. The price factor provides a further incentive to distinguish between products on the basis of their production methods. The costs of environmentally sensitive methods of production are often internalized and reflected in a product's price, and those methods of production may be a deciding factor in the buyer's choice of which product to purchase. Similar products which sell at greatly differing prices in the same geographic markets are unlikely to be close substitutes, or, as a corollary, competitors within the same market.

Often, demand substitutability is not looked at in isolation, and is considered in conjunction with supply substitutability. This practice is well-established in the US. One text identifies four main criteria of supply substitutability,[45] which include the following:

- the characteristics of the production technology involved, which includes consideration of whether plants producing other products can be rapidly switched to production of the products in question,
- the presence of barriers to access to the necessary production technology (which might be related to know-how).

The mere fact, taken alone, that considerations of production technology are important factors in the consideration of supply substitutability, indicates that production and processing methods ought to be significant in determining whether products are 'like' or not.

The GATT has objected to the regime of the Montreal Protocol on the grounds that it provides for restrictions on imports to be based not only on the characteristics of products (that they contain ozone-depleting substances), but also on the methods used in the production or processing of products. It is argued that even if quantitative restrictions, intended to protect the extra-jurisdictional environment, are allowed in principle under Article XX, Articles XIII[46] and XX prevent their application in a way which distinguishes between products according to their production methods. Support for this view is found in the Report of the Panel in the US–Mexico Tuna–Dolphin dispute.[47] It is based on the view that the willingness to

113

inflict and suffer environmental degradation is part of a country's competitiveness and should not be restricted under the GATT; products should be treated as 'like' irrespective of the impact on the environment of the process by which they are produced. Two arguments can be advanced against this view. First, even if it is accepted in the case of purely domestic environmental degradation, it should not be accepted where the degradation is of the global commons; the assumption on which it is based, of a sovereign right of States to suffer domestic environmental degradation, does not justify the infliction of environmental degradation on other States through the degradation of the global commons. Secondly, advancing scientific knowledge makes it increasingly unrealistic to speak of purely domestic environmental degradation; the more it can be demonstrated that environmental degradation in one State affects the environment of others, the weaker becomes the argument that the willingness to suffer environmental degradation should be treated as an aspect of a State's competitiveness.

Problems associated with the process of harmonization

The new TBT Agreement[48] encourages the internationalization of regulations and standards.[49] Properly construed, an internationalization policy could make it easier for Parties to adopt effective environmental standards and regulations in order to achieve sustainable development. In its present form, however, the Agreement is unlikely to reduce the pressure on the environment.

Article 2.4 requires that a Party who wishes to go beyond the agreed international norms in order to achieve an environmental objective, must establish that such norms are 'ineffective or inappropriate'. This severely restricts a Party's ability to go beyond those norms and thereby fulfil its particular environmental aims.

The result of this burden of proof on a Party seeking to go beyond international standards is that such international standards provide a ceiling for environmental protection rather than a floor. The examples provided of factors which may determine appropriateness or effectiveness – geographic or climatic – focus exclusively on national concerns, thus failing to account for the transnational nature of many environmental problems. Not only does a Party wishing to exceed international standards have to demonstrate that those standards are ineffective or inappropriate in attaining the environmental objective,[50] but that Party still must comply with the ambiguous provisions on like products and restrictions on trade. In addition, the TBT Agreement places procedural obligations on Parties wishing to exceed international standards[51] or take action where international standards do not exist.[52] Article 2.10 allows for the omission of procedural steps where 'urgent problems of safety, health, environmental protection or national security arise or threaten to arise'. Such an exemption appears to be limited to the case of the individual and does not assist a Party who wishes to unilaterally adopt technical regulations in order to address international or global environmental problems.

This hinderance on Parties' ability is not necessarily suitable to achieving high levels of environmental protection. A properly formulated threshold should allow Parties to go beyond international standards if their objectives are for environmental protection.

The philosophy of sustainable development argues for a very different model for the harmonization of standards. Rather than harmonizing downwards, assistance – financial , technical, and intellectual – should be provided where needed so that standards can be the highest possible. Indeed, in many cases it is desirable, where feasible, to raise international standards from where they currently exist so as to reflect the urgent and irreversible nature of many environmental problems. This is what the EC's Cohesion Fund is, in large part, designed to do – provide resources to assist those less well-off in the Community to meet standards set at a Community/international level.

In contrast to the TBT, Article 100a4 of the Treaty on European Economic Union provides that:

> If, after the adoption of a harmonization measure by the Council acting by a qualified majority, a member State deems it necessary to apply national provisions on grounds . . . relating to protection of the environment . . . it shall notify the Commission of these provisions.
>
> The Commission shall confirm the provisions involved after having verified that they are not a means of arbitrary discrimination or a disguised restriction on trade between member States. . .

This provides an absolute right, subject only to the provisions of the Treaty (which as interpreted by the European Court of Justice includes a proportionality test) for member States to go beyond the agreed norms of Community law, where they, subjectively, consider it necessary to do so for reasons related to protection of the environment. The amendments to the Treaty of Rome proposed by the Treaty on European Economic Union ensure that these provisions exist in the context of a Community of States which recognizes environmental protection as an objective of the Community. Article 130r 2 of the Treaty of Rome, as amended by the Treaty on European Union, provides that:

> Community policy on the environment shall aim at a high level of protection taking into account the diversity of situations in the various regions of the Community. It shall be based on the precautionary principle and on the principles that preventive action shall be taken, that environmental damage should as a priority be rectified at source and that the polluter should pay. Environmental protection requirements must be integrated into the definition and implementation of other Community policies. *In this context, harmonization*

requirements answering these requirements shall include, where appropriate, a safeguard clause allowing member States to take provisional measures, for non-economic environmental reasons, subject to a Community inspection procedure (emphasis added).

As observed above, these provisions exist within the context of a Community of States with relatively similar economic and environmental conditions, unlike those negotiating the Uruguay Round.[53] However, there are differences which revolve around the same broad conceptual conflicts – between environment and development imperatives – which are played out in the negotiation of standards at the European level.

The TBT Agreement does recognize the difficulties which developing countries face in implementing high standards, but no compulsory provision for assistance in this regard is made.[54] In measuring its success in balancing trade and environmental objectives, a useful comparison can be made with the EEC, which expressly encourages members to pursue environmental protection policies based on a high level of environmental protection. The Treaty on European Economic Union supports the attainment of those standards with the establishment of a cohesion fund. In addition, Articles 100, 100a4 and 130t together allow member States an absolute right to adopt more stringent environmental measures than those adopted by the Community as a whole. The Treaty of European Economic Union further allows member States to take provisional environmental protection measures for 'non-economic, environmental reasons'. Finally, Article 130r2 as amended by the Treaty on European Economic Union states that the Community environmental policy is to be based on the precautionary and polluter-pays principles. Community policy-makers are to recognize that preventive action should be taken and environmental damage be rectified at source.

Like the TBT Agreement, the Decision appears to encourage compliance with international standards.[55] Provision is made for departure from these standards, but only if there is a scientific justification or if in compliance with the risk assessment provisions of the Agreement.[56] In any event, departures must not be inconsistent with any other provision of the Decision,[57] including the requirement that scientific evidence support the provision.[58]

THE ELEMENTS OF SUSTAINABLE DEVELOPMENT AND THE FAILURE OF THE GATT/MTO TO ACCOMMODATE THEM

Agenda 21 emphasizes that integration of environmental concerns into decision-making, among other things, is required for sustainable development.[59] Annex IV [MTO] fails to provide the MTO with any commitment to sustainable development. The entire text contains only a single reference to the environment, found in the Preamble. This preambular text contains no legal obligations: it is worded such that the signatories recognize that their relations should be conducted with a view to 'developing the optimal use of resources of the world at sustainable levels'. The concept of optimal use is at variance with sustainable development.

The failure of Annex IV to embrace sustainable development as an objective is in direct opposition to the statute of the European Bank for Reconstruction and Development (EBRD), which has the promotion of sustainable development as one of its functions.[60] In addition, the amendments made by the Maastricht summit to the Treaty of Rome, which establishes the EEC, provide that one of the objectives of the Community is to promote 'sustainable and non-inflationary growth respecting the environment'.[61] The European Union, to be established following the Maastricht summit, carries this objective in all areas of its economic policy and international trade activity.

At issue is the global obsession with growth for growth's sake. A more qualitative approach is what is clearly needed. As Herman Daly recently stated:

> [t]he effort to overcome poverty through further growth in scale of through-put is self-defeating once we have reached the point where growth in scale increases environmental costs faster than it increases production benefits. Beyond this point, which we have in all likelihood already passed, further growth makes us poorer, not richer.[62]

Public participation was identified by the World Commission on Environment and Development, in its report *Our Common Future* (1987) as an important element of policies guided by the concept of sustainable development. The report advised that:

> At the national level, governments, foundations, and industry should greatly extend their cooperation with NGOs in planning, monitoring, and evaluating as well as carrying out projects when they can provide the necessary capabilities on a cost-effective basis. To this end, governments should establish or strengthen procedures for official consultation and more meaningful participation by all NGOs in all relevant organizations.

Indeed, environmentalists consider that some of their greatest successes in influencing policy have come from simply having access to information and being heard.[63]

A further corollary of the principle of sustainable development is the precautionary principle. Both principles emphasize foresight and the need for proaction rather than reaction. The two principles have been linked in a number of international legal documents. The first[64] major document to recognize the link was the Bergen Ministerial Declaration on Sustainable Development in the ECE Region, which explicitly recognized that:

> In order to achieve sustainable development, policies must be based on the precautionary principle. Environmental measures must anticipate, prevent and attack the causes of environmental degradation. Where there are threats of serious or irreversible damage, lack of full scientific certainty should not be used as a reason for postponing measures to prevent environmental degradation.[65]

In its weakest sense, the precautionary principle means that States agree to act with care and foresight when taking decisions which may have an adverse impact on the environment. In a slightly stronger formulation, the principle urges action to regulate activities which may be harmful to the environment *even* if conclusive scientific evidence of their harmfulness is not yet available.[66] At its most profound, the precautionary principle dictates the institutionalization of precaution, which would itself entail the shifting of the burden of proof from those opposing environmental degradation to those engaged in the challenged activity.

It is arguable that sustainable development is possible without implementation of the precautionary principle in its strongest sense. However, given the debate surrounding the environmental effects of some areas of economic activity, and the life-threatening consequences of a failure to achieve sustainable development, implementation of the precautionary principle in its weaker senses must attend the aspiration of sustainable development.

The Report of the GATT Secretariat on Trade and Environment (which, it should be noted, precedes the Draft Final Act of the Uruguay Round), states that:

> These various provisions [ie, Article XX of the GATT, the Subsidies Agreement of the Tokyo Round of the GATT, and the Tokyo Round Agreement on Technical Barriers to Trade] are an attempt to find a reasonable, good faith balance between the desire to avoid distortions to competition and the desire to allow each country sovereignty over measures affecting its natural environment and the health and safety of its residents. This is not an easy task. The issues are among the most sensitive in any society, and the scientific understanding often is such that it comes down to a matter of subjective risk management. Well-informed and fair-minded individuals can differ – sometimes substantially – on where to strike the balance.

The precautionary principle is all about sensible risk management.[67] Given the explicit link between the principles of sustainable development and of precaution, reference to the precautionary principle would be consistent with current international legal practice.

One danger apparent from the S&PS Decision's wording is that it risks being incompatible with the precautionary principle by requiring sanitary and phytosanitary measures to protect human, animal or plant life to be based on 'scientific principles that are not maintained against available scientific evidence'.[68] Over-reliance on scientific evidence is what the precautionary principle warns against. Indeed, in another section, the Decision itself recognizes that risk assessment should be based on, *inter alia*, scientific evidence and environmental conditions.[69] It permits moral and political factors to play an important role in guiding precautionary action. O'Riordan[70] puts it in the following way:

> The principle of precaution in environmental management implies commit-
> ting human activity to investments where the benefits of action cannot at the
> time of expenditure, be justified by conclusive scientific evidence. Other
> grounds for legitimation need to be present – political, ethical, legal as well as
> moral in the sense of playing by the same rules as others in protecting the
> environment. Accordingly, the rationale has to be accounted for in terms that
> are more overtly judgmental.
>
> Precaution, therefore, tests science in the realms where it is most vulner-
> able, namely where adequate data do not exist, or time series trends cannot yet
> be modelled, or where the processes being examined operate in such a manner
> that they are not susceptible to the conventions of prediction and verification.

One of the main tenets of sustainable development is the need to identify and value the environmental effects of economic activity. International practice reveals a growing trend in this regard.[71] For example, the statute of the EBRD at Article 35, provides that: 'The Bank shall report annually on the environmental impact of its activities.' The Framework Convention on Climate Change contains reference to impact assessment by requiring all parties to:

> ... employ appropriate methods, for example impact assessments, formulated
> and determined nationally, with a view to minimizing adverse effects on the
> economy, on public health and on the quality of the environment, of projects
> or measures undertaken by them to mitigate or adapt to climate change;[72]

This is not present in the MTO.

CONCLUSION

The dominant view in the GATT secretariat is that the environmentalists' concerns can be accommodated in the current GATT system. They believe that the system as currently designed can deliver sustainable development.
The recent report of the GATT secretariat describes sustainable

development for example in the following way:

> Although the term means different things to different people, most definitions encompass two basic notions. First, there is a need to place much greater emphasis on assigning values or prices to environmental resources, *with a view to identifying and valuing the environmental effects of economic activity.* Second is the idea that each generation should pass on to the next at least as much capital – environmental and man-made – as it inherited (emphasis added).

The GATT secretariat's report takes the view that neither aspect of sustainable development is intrinsically linked to trade. It states that '*if* the policies necessary for sustainable development are in place, trade promotes development that is sustainable'.

However, the huge assumption that the GATT is neutral on the formation of policies necessary to promote sustainable development renders the second half of the sentence untenable. The spirit of sustainable development at least, must permeate the MTO in its fundamental structure, or the ideological bases for each set of policies will ultimately clash, providing the potential for the descent into chaotic trading conditions which is so feared by the GATT secretariat. To argue that:

> even though the General Agreement does not mention the environment explicitly, non-discriminatory environmental policies ordinarily would not be subject to any GATT constraints

is to dodge the issue. Indeed such an approach is inimical to sustainable development. Furthermore, the Report of the GATT secretariat states that:

> What is needed are multilateral rules to guide countries in formulating their own environmental policies and in responding to domestic complaints about the impact of their own and other countries' policies on international competitiveness.

Sustainable development demands a far more sophisticated understanding of the interconnectedness of international trade policy and environmental regulation whether it is national, regional or global.

What needs to be done? Arguably the leading authority on international trade law, Professor John Jackson has recently written persuasively about 'the clash of cultures' between the environmentalist and trade communities.[73] Professor Jackson belongs unashamedly in the trade community, so his analysis and recommendations are good indicators of the 'greening' of the GATT and its expert actors. He suggests, very wisely, short-term Uruguay Round Greening possibilities and longer-term strategies, based upon the short-term but requiring further study and diplomatic negotiation:

(1) A Waiver[74] for listed environmental agreements which would 'trump'[75] the GATT, along with procedures for adding to the list.
(2) Interpretative notes or resolutions regarding some standard texts including the Uruguay Round drafts, possibly with a few wording changes, to accommodate the idea of permissive higher standards.
(3) Better transparency can be introduced into the GATT dispute settlement processes to be developed by the GATT or MTO Council to carry out the dispute procedure reforms or the Uruguay Round Treaty text proposals.

These proposals would go a long way to resolving some of the conflicts identified above and are very plausible arguments for small step changes now. Covering some of the same ground, I would make the following recommendations for change:

(1) the establishment of sustainable development as an objective of the GATT system;
(2) the recognition of the need to balance environmental protection imperatives with free trade imperatives in any proportionality test for evaluating technical barriers to trade;
(3) the recognition of the importance of taking into account the process behind the product in any evaluation of 'like products', on a case by case basis;
(4) the value (in supporting the public interest) in unilateral measures taken beyond or instead of international standards in order to protect the global commons;
(5) the adoption and implementation of the precautionary principle;
(6) increasing the vital flow of information to the public and interested parties;
(7) increasing the participation of the public and interested parties in decision-making and dispute settlement;
(8) ensuring real separation of powers so that members are accountable in law and disputes are settled through law;
(9) focusing dispute settlements on problem solving (involving full participation of interested parties) through alternative processes such as, for example, mediation;
(10) ensuring that the interests of developing countries are fully taken into account.

A final remark I leave to another famous Professor of (EC) trade law Paul Demaret:

> In the future, GATT will have to mix the promotion of free trade and environmental considerations. In that area it should attempt to become a trusted umpire. This would be in keeping with one of its traditional roles, which is to solve trade disputes and reduce international tension.[76]

8 ENVIRONMENTAL LAW AND POLICY IN ANTARCTICA

Lee Kimball

INTRODUCTION

The greening of Antarctic law and policy began in the era of the 'scientist-conservationists', before there were 'environmentalists'. Having concluded the Antarctic Treaty in 1959 in order to preserve the area for peaceful purposes and the freedom of scientific investigation, its 12 original signatories immediately set about taking measures to conserve its flora and fauna. Their reason – despite the vast continental expanse of nearly 14 million square kilometres (or one-tenth of the Earth's land surface) – only one per cent of Antarctica remains ice-free throughout the year and the transient explorers and scientists who began to settle into permanent research stations found themselves competing for these spaces with the hordes of birds and marine mammals that seasonally breed and raise their young in Antarctica. In deference to these long-time denizens, the nations governing Antarctica adopted general rules of conduct to avoid disturbing them unnecessarily. It was the scientists who took the lead.

The international scientific community was not only present at the creation of the Antarctic Treaty, it played an integral role. During the 1957–58 International Geophysical Year (IGY), the scientists made Antarctica their centrepiece: they installed 40 research stations in the region, and assembled on the continent from 12 countries in numbers that exceeded the sum total of previous visitors. When it was all over, rather than abandon their stations in this inhospitable environment, the countries involved decided to perpetuate this unprecedented research venture and used international scientific cooperation as a cornerstone of the 1959 Treaty. Whether scientist or diplomat took the first step is buried in personal reminiscences. Regardless, science is as intertwined with diplomacy and law in Antarctica as it is with Antarctic conservation.

Laying another cornerstone of the Antarctic Treaty overcame even greater odds. During the height of the Cold War, on the heels of an exchange of gunfire between the United Kingdom and Argentina on the Antarctic Peninsula as recently as 1952, and in the face of fundamentally irreconcilable positions on the territorial status of Antarctica, the countries that signed the Antarctic Treaty agreed to forego any military activities or weapons testing in Antarctica and to 'freeze' their respective positions on Antarctic claims. Of the original signatories, Australia, Argentina, Chile, France, New Zealand, Norway, and the United Kingdom had claimed pie segments of the continent between 1908 and 1943. The claims of Chile, Argentina, and the United Kingdom overlap. To this day Belgium, Japan, Russia, South Africa, and the United States do not recognize any claim to Antarctica, and Russia and the United States maintain that they have a basis for making a claim if they wish to. One pie segment (approximately 15 per cent of the continent) remains unclaimed.

An interesting footnote to its history is when the British laid the first claim to Antarctica (and several outlying islands) in 1908, and thus to some prime whaling grounds, they did so in part to establish a territorial basis for regulating the factories used by whalers. The first land-based whaling station in this area, established in 1904, was followed shortly by others, and by the factory ships which moored immediately offshore. Like the nineteenth century sealers before them, the whalers shunned any notion of 'sustainable' yields. Efforts to curtail overharvesting, however, sought not so much to protect the whale as to protect the industry by stabilizing prices. By 1925, so as to escape restrictions on the licensed factories, the whalers had developed mobile factory ships that could operate well out to sea, beyond the reach of British law. By the 1960s, the industry had destroyed itself. (The International Convention on the Regulation of Whaling, concluded in 1946, governs whaling in the Southern Ocean, where a moratorium has been in effect since 1987.)

The Antarctic Treaty System

The 1959 Antarctic Treaty allows other nations to join, but restricts decision-making rights to the 12 original signatories and those new countries that are conducting 'substantial' scientific research in Antarctica. Today there are 26 'consultative' or decision-making nations, and an additional 15 that take part as observers – the 'non-consultative' parties. A similar distinction is made in the other Antarctic treaties.

The agreements in the Antarctic Treaty System (ATS) comprise the 1959 Treaty, which entered into force in 1961; the 1972 Convention for the Conservation of Antarctic Seals (CCAS), which entered into force in 1978; the 1980 Convention on the Conservation of Antarctic Marine Living Resources (CCAMLR), which entered into force in 1982; the 1988 Convention on the Regulation of Antarctic Mineral Resource Activities (CRAMRA), which has not entered into force and is unlikely to do so; and the 1991 Protocol on Environmental Protection, a supplement to the Antarctic Treaty, which has not yet entered into force.

THE QUIET PURSUIT OF SCIENCE

The first decade of the Antarctic Treaty saw little change. The 12 Contracting Parties established a pattern of meeting every two years, adopting 'recommendations' to reflect their decisions and give substance to the Antarctic Treaty's provisions.[1] These covered everything from the convening of meetings and designation of historic monuments to discussions regarding research, communications, logistics, and conservation. With the spectre of the Cold War hovering – and in order to give effect to the Treaty's prohibition on nuclear explosions and the disposal of radioactive wastes – the governments developed a regular procedure for exchanging information on planned activities in Antarctica, including information on the use of nuclear equipment and techniques such as nuclear energy and radioisotopes. Only the United States made regular use of the Treaty's precedent-setting inspection provisions, which allowed any country, active in Antarctica, to descend unannounced upon another's research station to verify compliance with the Treaty. While the diplomats focused on international cooperation and arms control, they relied on the scientists to maintain their toehold presence in the harsh Antarctic environment and provide some useful research results in the process.

The scientists, meanwhile, decided to establish permanently the non-governmental committee they had formed to organize the IGY. It became the International Council of Scientific Unions' Scientific Committee on Antarctic Research (SCAR). SCAR has since played a vital role in planning Antarctic research and logistics and in designing measures to protect the Antarctic environment and conserve its living resources, which have been adopted by the Parties to the 1959 Antarctic Treaty. These measures recognized early on the vulnerability of the Antarctic ecosystem to human interference, and the fact that Antarctica derives much of its scientific importance from its uncontaminated and undisturbed condition, warranted efforts to stop the deliberate introduction of alien flora and fauna, to restrict and regulate the taking of native mammals, birds, and plants, to protect designated areas and species, and to curb sealing on the open seas.

By 1970, two other issues had arisen: the need to monitor and evaluate the impact of human activities in Antarctica, and the concern that private tourism might disrupt scientific research, station operations, or species protection. At the request of governments, SCAR set about determining the types and extent of human activities impacting Antarctica and the Southern Ocean and how to minimize them. It considered also research programmes that could detect and measure change. These two themes – the effects of human activities in Antarctica, and changes occurring there regardless of origin – became, during the 1980s, a central thrust of Antarctic law-making. In 1972 the Antarctic Treaty nations adopted a measure recognizing that they should assume responsibility for the protection of the environment and 'wise use' of the area covered by the Treaty, and in 1975 a measure recognizing that they should exercise that responsibility 'consistent with the interests of all mankind'. These pronouncements sought to deflect any United Nations interest in Antarctica as the UN was beginning to assert an active role in global environmental issues.

The first commercial tourist venture and the first private adventure/recreation expedition arrived in Antarctica in 1966. Since then, commercial ship and private yacht traffic have increased, and adventure travel is attracting a new clientele to the continent. A short-lived burst of commercial overflight ended tragically in 1979 with the crash of a New Zealand airliner on Mount Erebus that took all 257 lives. In 1987–88, commercial flights recommenced, along with the use of private aircraft to convey adventure travellers into the interior of Antarctica. After a decline from the mid-70s to the mid-80s, the number of Antarctic cruise visitors has grown from approximately 3,000 during the 1988–89 season, to 4,700 in 1990–91 and a projected 6,500 in 1992–93.[2] Since the late 1980s, adventure travellers – such as those wishing to ski in the Ellsworth Mountains – have risen to about 75 in 1990–91. When it enters into force, the 1991 Antarctic Treaty Protocol on Environmental Protection (see below) will subject tourists and tour operators to the same rules for environmental protection and conservation that govern other Antarctic operations. Moreover, the general inclination of these groups to voluntarily avoid detrimental activities has led most of them to assume responsibility for ensuring reasonable and safe operations that do not interfere with research activities nor place emergency rescue demands on research stations and personnel.

THE RESOURCE ISSUES HEAT UP AGAIN

By the late-1960s, concern over renewed resources exploitation focused a different light on Antarctica, exposing again the tenuous compromise upon which the Antarctic Treaty rests. Could the Treaty Parties agree to regulate commercial activities in the face of their different views on Antarctic claims? And could they regulate those activities effectively?

The popular interpretation of the 1959 Treaty's 'freeze' on claims is that they are not a factor in policy debates. Nothing could be further from the truth. The day-to-day management decisions taken in accordance with the Antarctic treaties, any new policies or protocols agreed upon, and the treaties themselves must be crafted to avoid prejudicing the legal positions of claimant and non-claimant nations, as well as those maintaining a basis for claim. The Antarctic Treaty preserves these incompatible views and prevents any action from being used to support, deny, create or extend claims to territorial sovereignty as long as it is in force. Since the natural attributes of sovereignty include the rights to regulate, tax, and adapt and enforce laws within one's territory and with respect to one's citizens, respecting both positions – particularly when it comes to non-governmental activities such as commercial ventures – makes the governance of Antarctica more complex than anywhere else in the world.

Conservation of Antarctic seals

In 1964 it appeared that commercial sealing might begin in the high seas around Antarctica. (The Agreed Measures on the Conservation of Antarctic Fauna and Flora, adopted under the auspices of the Antarctic Treaty in 1964, restrict any taking of seals on the continent and ice shelves.) As SCAR worked out appropriate conservation measures, the Parties to the 1959 Treaty decided that another legal instrument would be necessary to cover high seas sealing. Fishing in the high seas, after all, is one of the freedoms of countries under international law, and both the Antarctic Treaty and the Agreed Measures expressly state that they are without prejudice to the high seas rights of any country under international law in the area covered by the Antarctic Treaty (south of 60 degrees south latitude). In 1972, the Antarctic Treaty members voluntarily entered into a new conservation agreement, the Convention for the Conservation of Antarctic Seals (CCAS). This treaty bans commercial sealing for some species and sets quotas for others, subject to scientific research, educational, and indispensable food supply exemptions. It establishes areas and seasons during which sealing is prohibited as well as three seal reserves, and it sets out reporting requirements for commercial and research activities. If a commercial sealing industry develops, it provides that a regulatory body and a scientific advisory committee may be established; in the meantime, SCAR submits information and views on needed conservation measures. No commercial sealing has occurred since the CCAS was concluded. The treaty is reviewed every five years, and discussions at the last review in 1988 centred on additional study and more detailed reporting. Reflecting similar concerns raised in the International Whaling Commission (IWC), there was agreement that permits issued for scientific research must ensure maximum benefit from any research activities and avoid unnecessary duplication.

Conservation of marine living resources

The challenge of conserving fish in Antarctica proved more difficult. First, by the time the Antarctic Treaty Parties decided to negotiate a third treaty on this subject in 1977, the broader context of international fisheries law was changing. For the major distant water fishing countries like Japan and the Soviet Union, it was apparent that coastal nations would soon gain control over fisheries out to 200 miles off their shores, with the right to exclude foreign fishing vessels. (These negotiations had commenced in 1973 in the Third United Nations Conference on the Law of the Sea and were concluded in 1982.) During the mid-1960s they had begun to test the waters of the Southern Ocean for 'krill' (the Antarctic shrimp) and later finfish. By the time the new Convention on the Conservation of Antarctic Marine Living Resources (CCAMLR) was concluded in 1980 and entered into force in 1982, several species of finfish had already been seriously depleted.

The CCAMLR negotiations were complicated by the changing state of the international law of the sea. The impending extension of coastal nation jurisdiction throughout a 200-mile Exclusive Economic Zone[3] meant that the countries with claims in Antarctica had to consider,

(1) whether they would attempt to exercise their perceived right to exclusive fisheries jurisdiction off their Antarctic claims, and
(2) even if they did not, how to avoid language in the new treaty that would prejudice their legal position.

The non-claimant countries in the Antarctic Treaty had to avoid (1) and likewise ensure (2). While these same issues, in principle, could have arisen in CCAS, the ultimate lack of interest in commercial sealing and the limited three-mile offshore jurisdiction of coastal nations recognized at the time, made them *de facto* irrelevant.

The negotiations were affected also by the multispecies assessments that first emerged in the late 1960s in SCAR. Antarctic krill represented the primary food source for many species of marine mammals, fish, and birds in the Antarctic marine ecosystem. When krill became the initial target of the fishery, there was concern about the effect this would have on the recovery of the great whales. Assumptions that the reduction in whales resulted in a harvestable excess of krill were challenged by research indicating that seal and marine bird populations had undergone a compensatory increase. This relatively unique situation – where krill served as the keystone of the Southern Ocean food web – in the end produced a precedent-setting conservation agreement (see below).

The Long Shadow of Minerals

A final complicating factor in the fisheries negotiations was the prospect of mineral wealth in Antarctica. Inquiries from marine geophysical companies about commercial prospecting led the Antarctic Treaty Parties to discuss, in 1970, the possibility of a legal regime governing minerals activities. The 1972 embargo by the Organization of Petroleum Exporting Countries (OPEC), and circumstantial evidence of hydrocarbons turned up during the deep sea drilling research cruise of the *Glomar Challenger* in 1972–73 in the Ross Sea continental shelf off Antarctica, spurred further discussion among the Treaty nations. SCAR was asked to review and assess environmental and technological aspects of possible mineral development activities.

From the perspective of the fisheries negotiations, it was the conventional wisdom of Antarctic policy-makers that if they could overcome their legal and political differences in the CCAMLR, they had at least a fighting chance to tackle successfully the more difficult negotiations dealing with mineral resource issues. On the fate of the first negotiation would hang not only the conservation of Antarctic marine living resources, but also the ability of the evolving Antarctic Treaty System (ATS) to weather more difficult challenges in the future.

Once the CCAMLR was adopted in 1980, the parties to the Antarctic Treaty, at their 11th Biennial Meeting in 1981, adopted the recommendation calling for a special meeting to negotiate a legally binding agreement to govern the possibility of mineral resources development in Antarctica. That agreement was adopted by consensus in 1988, following a six-year negotiation, but it is unlikely to enter into force in the foreseeable future. Subsequent developments (see below) led to the adoption in October 1991 of a Protocol to the Antarctic Treaty on environmental protection that includes a ban on mineral resource activities. Any modification to that ban must be endorsed by a consensus of the countries with decision-making status under the Antarctic Treaty, or, 50 years after the Protocol enters into force, by the 26 nations that had decision-making status in 1991 when the Protocol was adopted.

No mineral deposits of commercial interest have yet been discovered in Antarctica or its offshore areas. Various studies of economic and technological feasibility indicate that it would take the discovery of either a giant or super-giant oilfield or a significant deposit of high-value minerals of precious or strategic value, such as gold or platinum, to make minerals development in remote and harsh Antarctic conditions attractive. One expert predicts that even if the price of oil were to return to $40 per barrel, this would be insufficient to stimulate Antarctic minerals development in the next few decades, assuming large deposits are even discovered.[4]

ENTER THE ENVIRONMENTALIST

The threat of a resumption of Antarctic sealing prompted environmental organizations like the Sierra Club and Friends of the Earth to become involved in 1970 in national policy discussions on these issues in the United States. By 1975, three years after the Stockholm Conference on the Human Environment, and as the resource issues gained prominence, groups on both sides of the Atlantic began to take an interest in Antarctic law and policy. The Centre for Law and Social Policy (CLASP) in Washington DC was asked to represent the US groups' interests, and the International Institute for Environment and Development (IIED), in London, launched an

Antarctic research project. The US Government invited both the Sierra Club and CLASP to join its delegations to the 1977 Meeting of the Parties of the Antarctic Treaty and to the CCAMLR negotiations. A public advisory committee was formally established by the US State Department in 1978 to receive private sector views, including those of the NGO community. The US practice of inviting NGOs as delegation members for ATS meetings continues to this day. In the early 1980s, the United Kingdom invited an IIED staff member to serve as an expert adviser to the CCAMLR meetings. By the end of the decade, Denmark, Australia, and New Zealand, in addition to the United States, regularly had NGOs on their Antarctic delegations.

Outside the Antarctic Treaty circle, the environmentalists were also active. In 1972 they helped prepare a resolution adopted by the Second World Conference on National Parks, calling for Antarctica to be designated as the first world park under the auspices of the United Nations. The World Conservation Union's (IUCN) Commission on National Parks also took an interest. An initial IUCN General Assembly Resolution in 1977 was followed by more substantial forays into Antarctic policy in 1981 and thereafter. These urged that no minerals development regime be brought into operation until full consideration had been given to complete protection of the Antarctic environment from such activities; they called for NGOs to be invited to participate in ATS meetings in accordance with traditional international practice, and to be consulted by governments in national policy determinations, and invited onto delegations; and endorsed the preparation of a conservation strategy for Antarctica and the Southern Ocean, building on the World Conservation Strategy that the IUCN had prepared in collaboration with UNEP and the World Wildlife Fund (WWF). Ten years in the making, the strategy was published in 1991.

The specific policy recommendations developed by the NGOs helped shape not only Antarctic environmental policies, but also: the opening up of ATS fora to observers from inter-governmental and non-governmental organizations; the improvement of reporting and inspection requirements and regular review of treaty implementation by the governments involved; the public availability of ATS documents; and the institutional development of the ATS (see below).

At the same time, another phenomenon was beginning to gain momentum. The dawning of the computer/telecommunications age granted those able to master it instant accessibility to contacts, documents, and media worldwide. Through the Antarctic specialist in Washington DC, James N Barnes, CLASP sought to develop a worldwide coalition to further NGO objectives and participation in Antarctic policy matters. Joining with NGOs in Australia in 1978, CLASP established the Antarctic and Southern Ocean Coalition (ASOC), which has grown to include members in over 40 countries. In 1983, ASOC's largest member, Greenpeace International, decided to mount a major Antarctic campaign to declare Antarctica off limits to mineral resources development, and to concentrate its substantial assets, including a modern communications system, on that effort.

Through direct action tactics and media-targeted events perfected by Greenpeace – including an international communications network that easily surpassed most governments' in the mid-1980s – ASOC has pressured governments to 'green' their Antarctic policies and activities. Through contacts in the different Antarctic Treaty Parties' governments they have been able to monitor policy developments and contribute useful recommendations. In their boldest move, Greenpeace established a research station in Antarctica in 1986–87. This not only confirmed them as a serious participant in the process, but their visits to other Antarctic stations and the interviews and observations they recorded, offered a new window onto a region where public access to monitor pollutants and harmful practices is severely curtailed by remoteness and harsh conditions. The station was dismantled in 1992 with the completion of the Protocol on Environmental Protection, but Greenpeace continues its periodic inspection tours.

Two events galvanized the environmental community into action in Antarctica in the early 1980s. In addition to the prospect of minerals development in the relatively pristine Antarctic environment, the second issue was the 'French airstrip' controversy. Plans to construct a new airstrip for the French research station at Pointe Geologie entailed major blasting to level several small islands and using the rubble to fill in the space between other islands so that a landing strip, capable of accommodating large transport planes, could be built. The area where construction was initiated in 1982 was a significant habitat for emperor penguins and other birds. As French scientists began leaking information about, and objections to, this project, and questions were raised about the adequacy of environmental impact assessments, the project was put on hold in 1984. But not before Greenpeace and ASOC had mounted a major campaign to stop it and engaged in hand-to-hand scuffles with French Government workers on site. The project recommenced in the late 1980s after additional studies and modifications. On the policy side, Meetings of the Parties to the Antarctic Treaty began to consider substantial improvements to the skeletal guidelines on environmental impact assessment, first adopted in 1975.

THE 1980s: THE DECADE OF THE ENVIRONMENT

Marine Living Resources

The same conservation ethic, permeating the environmental movement, had gained a substantial foothold in governments and in the scientific community. The negotiations of the 1980 CCAMLR produced a dramatic shift in international fisheries management, led by a handful of experts from both quarters. The product they negotiated extends north of the Antarctic Treaty area to cover the whole of the Antarctic marine ecosystem, and it establishes, in international law, an 'ecosystem standard' for conserving marine living resources. The Treaty defines its area of application on the basis of a natural boundary – the 'Antarctic convergence' – which divides the colder, northern-moving Antarctic waters from subtropical waters moving south, and the species common to each. Its principles require that harvesting and associated activities be regulated not only to conserve target fish species, but also to maintain predator/prey relationships and avoid the risk of major changes in the marine ecosystem, taking account of the environmental factors affecting them, and further the restoration of depleted populations. This language builds substantially on related provisions in the 1982 UNCLOS which, with respect to fisheries, were already in final form by the end of 1977.[5]

The CCAMLR's early years of operation have not been without controversy, as the scientists tried to learn more about the elements and relationships of the Antarctic marine ecosystem with limited research funding, and the policy-makers tried to refine reporting and inspection procedures and make do with insufficient information. Resistance to an expanded NGO presence in CCAMLR meetings was somewhat overcome in 1988 when ASOC was invited to attend. (Despite several attempts, Greenpeace has not succeeded in obtaining its own observer seat, and continues to be represented through the coalition.) One criticism often applied to the CCAMLR, that conservation measures adopted by consensus represent the lowest common denominator, is indisputable. More to the point, however, is whether there is an alternative. Given the different national interests at stake – from those of the fishing nations to each country's concern about prejudicing its views on the territorial status of Antarctica as the minerals negotiations loomed on the horizon – there would have been no CCAMLR at all without this safeguard of consensus. Today, the procedures that have evolved under the Treaty for obtaining and evaluating information, and using it to design conservation measures that implement the ecosystem standard, are a useful model for international fisheries management elsewhere. The challenge of applying this concept has yet to be fully realized, and it is only beginning to be considered in other parts of the world.

Antarctic Environmental Protection

Triggered in part by the minerals issue and in part by growing attention to environmental policies generally, the Meetings of the Parties to the Antarctic Treaty between 1983 and 1985 initiated discussion on the following issues:

- strengthening the code governing waste disposal in Antarctica and the surrounding waters;
- developing more specific and detailed guidance for prior assessment of the environmental impacts of activities carried out in Antarctica;
- elaborating and strengthening protected area designations in Antarctica and extending them to cover representative examples of major terrestrial (including glacial and aquatic) and marine ecosystems, and areas not only of special biological, scientific, or historical value but also those of particular environmental, aesthetic, or wilderness value;
- improving environmental monitoring in Antarctica;
- the development of a data management system for Antarctic scientific and environmental data;
- measures to avoid the concentration of scientific stations in the most easily accessible zones of Antarctica; and
- ensuring that the activities governed under the different Antarctic agreements were carried out in a mutually compatible manner.

Following the grounding of the *Bahia Paraiso* in January 1989, new measures were adopted to prevent and contain marine pollution from ships. Moreover, mounting concern over ozone depletion and global climate change led to 1989 measures encouraging environmental monitoring programmes in Antarctica dealing with global phenomena. Also, in the course of the review of comprehensive protection measures during 1990 and 1991, protection for native mammals, birds, and plants in Antarctica (the 1964 Agreed Measures) were strengthened.

As the CRAMRA negotiations proceeded from 1982 to 1988, many of the discussions on environmental protection measures in that forum carried over into the regular biennial Antarctic Treaty meetings. This was assisted by the fact that in most cases, the individuals involved in the two sets of negotiations were the same. Moreover, the vulnerability of the Antarctic environment to damage from possible minerals activities, including associated oil transport, inspired stringent standards and safeguards in the CRAMRA that set the pace for the regular discussions (and, ultimately, the 1991 Protocol), and offered a model for other environmental negotiations. Most significantly, the CRAMRA reversed the burden of proof incorporated into the CCAMLR: where fishing activities could proceed unless conservation restrictions were adopted by consensus, the CRAMRA prohibited minerals exploration and development unless it was authorized by consensus and in accordance with requirements for environmental assessment and other safeguards. This was an important development which was a precursor to the changing approach in other areas of international law, such as the adoption of the precautionary principle (see Chapter 7). Among the CRAMRA's other unique provisions is a requirement that decisions be based upon information sufficient to make the assessments called for; that activities may not proceed unless technology and procedures are available that can give effect to the environmental standards in the Treaty; that any dispute over environmental matters is subject to compulsory, binding settlement procedures; the establishment of an international inspection system answerable to Treaty institutions, rather than individual governments; and an international system for strict liability and emergency response, which, among other things, permits an international institution to pursue liability claims for environmental damage in national courts. Many of these developments are now applied in other regional and global environmental regimes.

As public interest in Antarctica continued to grow, the small circle of scientists and government representatives, traditionally involved in Antarctic matters, were more and more influenced by developments taking place outside the ATS. For example, when it appeared that agreement on revised measures for environmental impact assessment (EIA) would once again be delayed, attention was drawn to the similar EIA measures endorsed by many of the same governments in the UNEP Governing Council, and the Antarctic measures were finally adopted in 1987.[6] The *Bahia Paraiso* and *Exxon Valdez* oil spills, which both occurred in 1989, helped spur agreement in October 1989 on the new Antarctic Treaty measure governing marine pollution from ships. Moreover, that measure urged the Parties to the Antarctic Treaty to ensure that their ships operating in Antarctica were in compliance with six international treaties on marine pollution, administered by the International Maritime Organization (IMO), and led to the designation in 1990 of Antarctic Treaty waters as a 'special area' under one IMO Treaty, subjecting them to more stringent controls for oil pollution and garbage.[7] The latter apply not just to Parties to the Antarctic Treaty, but to any country that is a party to the IMO Treaty whose ships operate in the Antarctic Treaty area south of 60 degrees south latitude. In another linkage between a global treaty and Antarctica, the 1989 Basel Convention on Control of Transboundary Movements of Hazardous Wastes and Their Disposal contains a prohibition on exporting such materials to the Antarctic Treaty area for disposal.

Whatever the improvements taking place in specific environmental measures under the Antarctic Treaty, the conclusion of the CRAMRA in June 1988 opened the door to two lingering questions:

(1) How to ensure improved compliance with measures adopted under the Antarctic Treaty – always difficult in light of conflicting views on territorial sovereignty and enforcement rights?
(2) Whether certain types of activities in Antarctica, such as scientific research, warranted a higher priority or some sort of preference if potential conflicts of use arose?

The Minerals Issue

By mid-1989, it became clear that the Government of Australia was becoming increasingly reluctant to support the CRAMRA, which had been signed by only six States in November 1988, in part due to growing public concern over environmental protection. As a result, the lingering questions about use of Antarctica became intertwined with the debate over the future of the CRAMRA. Chile called for the consideration of comprehensive environmental protection in Antarctica and the United Kingdom's suggestion to convene a special meeting for that purpose was adopted in May 1989. Subsequently, France and Australia jointly proposed a new, comprehensive convention on environmental protection, and France, Australia, and later New Zealand endorsed a ban on mineral resource activities and the establishment of Antarctica as a 'wilderness reserve'. Where France and Australia clearly intended to replace CRAMRA with the new convention, other governments still hoped to conclude comprehensive environmental protection measures, retaining CRAMRA as the regime to govern minerals activities in the future, if any interest were expressed in conducting such activities. All favoured strengthening comprehensive environmental measures and addressing compliance with them; most came to accept the idea of banning minerals activities, although they differed over how best to accomplish that goal.

Within the NGO community, the Cousteau Society is credited with having turned the French Government from its support for CRAMRA to the wilderness option. Greenpeace, which had never wavered from seeking 'world park' status for Antarctica, launched a major effort, together with ASOC, the World Wildlife Fund, and others to support the French / Australian initiative. Within the United Nations General Assembly (UNGA), an about-face occurred. Where initial interest in Antarctica had been triggered by the possibility of sharing in minerals activities (see below), the emerging split among the Antarctic Treaty Parties was seen as a way to dislodge uniform support among them for the ATS as the appropriate forum (as opposed to the United Nations) for considering Antarctic issues. The developing nations in the UN endorsed the idea of a world park and a ban on minerals activities, linking this to their long-standing concern that Antarctic policies should be determined with full participation by all members of the international community. Just as they had maintained that any treaty on Antarctic minerals should be negotiated in the context of the UN, they now advocated a similar course for any new agreement on environmental protection. While they failed to drive a wedge among the Parties to the Antarctic Treaty, this approach buttressed the Antarctic Treaty Parties' intention to conclude a new agreement before outside pressures undermined the foundations upon which the Antarctic Treaty was built – and before the possibility of a review conference after June 1991 might surface.

With remarkable speed, the Antarctic Treaty Parties during 1990–91 agreed on a new Antarctic agreement that designates Antarctica as a 'natural reserve, devoted to peace and science'. In the end, they opted for a Protocol to the 1959 Antarctic Treaty, as opposed to a new treaty. The 1991 Protocol on Environmental Protection substantially strengthens the binding nature of provisions on conservation and environmental protection, and subjects them to compulsory, binding dispute settlement. Detailed annexes incorporate and strengthen the earlier Antarctic Treaty 'recommendations' on EIA, marine pollution, waste disposal, species conservation, and the system of Antarctic protected areas. Moreover, these detailed measures may be updated in a manner that avoids the time-consuming ratification process often necessary for amending a treaty.

As noted earlier, the 1991 Protocol's ban on mineral resource activities may only be altered if all of the decision-making 'consultative' Parties agree, or, after 50 years, if all 26 of today's 'consultative' Parties agree. In addition, the ban may only be lifted if a legally binding regime for mineral resource activities is in force. Nevertheless, if, after 50 years, a proposal to lift the ban, together with a binding regime, has been adopted, and if it has not entered into force within three years of that adoption, any country may withdraw from the Protocol (effective two years later). The proposal to lift the ban does not have to be adopted by consensus. It only takes a simple majority (more than half) of all the countries then party to the Antarctic Treaty – consultative and non-consultative alike – as long as three-quarters of the consultative nations that adopted the Protocol in 1991 (ie 20 of the then 26 consultative Parties) vote with the majority.

When the Antarctic Treaty Parties took up the possibility of minerals development in Antarctica in 1977, they agreed to refrain from such activities as long as timely progress was being made toward adopting an agreed legal regime. With the adoption of the CRAMRA in 1988, they reiterated that commitment and extended it to prospecting activities also, pending timely entry into force of the CRAMRA. With the Protocol, the consultative Parties endorsed 'current constraints' on mineral resource activities, pending entry into force 'which shall take place as soon as possible'. If the 1991 Protocol does not enter into force, renewed questions about 'current' constraints and 'timely' progress are likely to arise.

ACCOUNTABILITY

If the minerals treaty negotiations triggered a decade of environmental concern, they also triggered a major international debate on transparency and accountability, which carried over into the UN Conference on Environment and Development in June 1992. When the minerals treaty negotiations started in 1982, they coincided with the adoption of a legal regime for the deep seabed beyond national jurisdiction, which was based on the 'common heritage of mankind' concept. The idea that minerals development in the international seabed should benefit all nations – who should have the right to participate in decision-making, exploitation, and revenues – was seized upon by the developing nations as an equally valid concept for Antarctica. Malaysia, Antigua and Barbuda led a successful campaign to discuss Antarctic matters in the UN General Assembly in 1983, much to the displeasure of the Parties to the Antarctic Treaty. Today, that debate has deteriorated to a perfunctory exchange where the oversight role of the UN is asserted by one side and rejected by the other.

Nevertheless, the expression of interest in the UN put pressure on the Antarctic Treaty Parties to respond to criticism that their meetings were closed not only to outsiders, but even to the nations that had joined the Antarctic Treaty without full decision-making rights. In 1983, the 'non-consultative' nations were invited to attend treaty meetings as observers, and by 1987, after a four-year struggle, international organizations, including NGOs, were invited to join the ranks of observers. The 1983 Antarctic Treaty meeting also set in motion a series of policy decisions to de-classify and make publicly available ATS documents shortly after they are issued, and to amplify meeting reports and convey them to the UN and other relevant international agencies. Today, the NGOs enjoy rights to participate that parallel those in other inter-governmental fora, and all governments are encouraged to make available Antarctic documents and reports at national contact points. (Some governments give fuller effect to this than others.)

The other side of the accountability coin, of course, is the information coming into the system. Building on the French airstrip case, the NGOs were quick to point out that diplomatic niceties often breed a hands-off approach when there may be a question as to how well a fellow country is complying with its treaty obligations. Moreover, the annual exchange of information and the inspection provisions of the Antarctic Treaty – a first in international confidence-building in 1959 – were relatively incomplete and uninformative as a record of how well countries were implementing treaty measures. They merely existed; they were rarely used to identify or pursue potential problems. To some extent, information exchange helped countries plan cooperative research ventures.

In 1984 the NGOs began to press for improvements in Antarctic Treaty reporting and inspection procedures. Treaty discussions in 1987 reaffirmed the value of exchanging information on national practices to implement Antarctic Treaty decisions and policies as a measure of accountability and in order to assist and inform countries who were just becoming active in Antarctica. At the same time, the delay from 1983 to 1989 in updating and strengthening the code of rules governing waste disposal illustrated the problem: it took an interminable amount of time for governments to pull together information on their current waste disposal practices and problems. Few maintained good records. The results were twofold: not only are the reporting and inspection requirements on environmental matters explicit in the 1991 Protocol, but even before the Protocol was adopted, most of the inspection reports submitted during the late 1980s included information not just on the arms control aspects of the Antarctic Treaty, but also on practices related to waste disposal, siting and concentration of stations, construction projects, and other environmental concerns. Moreover, the 1991 Protocol specifies that national reports and the results of inspections must be considered at Meetings of the Parties to the Antarctic Treaty and then made publicly available. They are not simply to be noted and filed.

Institution-Building

There is one final element crucial to the greening of Antarctic law and policy: the institutional support structure. Since its inception, the Antarctic Treaty has resorted to a simple 'consultative' meeting among its member governments (initially only among those with decision-making standing). The biennial meetings have rotated alphabetically among the consultative group, with the host nation providing secretariat support for the meeting. The US, the depositary government for the Treaty, is responsible for circulating certain formal notices having to do with new Contracting Parties and information on the approval of Antarctic Treaty recommendations. (The United Kingdom is the depositary government for the CCAS, Australia for the CCAMLR, and New Zealand for the CRAMRA.) For over a decade, the governments have discussed – in view of the increase in the number of Antarctic Treaty Parties, the growth of activities in Antarctica by governments and private entities, the frequency and costs of Antarctic meetings, additional demands for documents and inter-sessional communications, and the outpouring of public interest in the region – the merits of establishing a permanent secretariat. The issue was originally controversial for some of the countries with claims in Antarctica, because of the 'internationalization' it would represent of an area they viewed as national territory. Today, there is agreement, in principle, to establish a permanent secretariat, and its terms of reference have been honed, but the location has not yet been agreed. Once established, the secretariat could play a significant role in public information and accountability; it may greatly simplify the circulation and exchange of reports and other documents, including environmental impact assessments and other notifications called for in the Protocol; and it can facilitate responses to governments and private parties seeking practical information and assistance in relation to planned Antarctic activities and help them identify potential collaborators.

The real breakthrough, however, is the provision in the Protocol on a Committee for Environmental Protection. The environmental community

– governmental and non-governmental – had long sought an advisory body for the Antarctic Treaty along the lines of the scientific and technical advisory organs found in many other international agreements, including the CCAMLR. SCAR, as a non-governmental organization of scientists, had played an invaluable role over the years, both informally and in responding to specific Antarctic Treaty requests. But its traditional approach/avoidance anxiety over Antarctic policy questions had left it somewhat on the fringes of hard-headed debates, and its non-governmental character denied it the funds necessary to fully serve Antarctic Treaty needs. Some in the NGO community favoured a free-standing Antarctic Environmental Protection Agency, composed of an independent professional staff, with the power to review, inspect, and conduct hearings on the adequacy of and compliance with environmental requirements. Others accepted the more traditional model of an organ derived from and responsible to the Antarctic Treaty Parties, and composed of government representatives. They believed that its proceedings should be open to NGO observers and its documents publicly available. It is the latter model that has been included in the Protocol. Most controversial was whether the Committee would be a decision-making or an advisory body. The result is that the Committee is to issue a report that fully reflects all views, and to formulate recommendations to the Antarctic Treaty Parties, which bear sole responsibility for policy decisions.

CONCLUSION

Antarctica has, in many ways, served as a microcosm for the evolution of environmental law and policy. On the one hand, the magnitude and diversity of human activity in Antarctica is minimal compared to more habitable climes, which reduces the complexity of environmental measures required. The remoteness of Antarctica from world events has allowed it to develop a system of governance somewhat apart from that for the rest of the world. Yet its very remoteness, and the traditional separateness and uniqueness of the Antarctic Treaty System, have allowed Antarctica to evolve a structure of integrated treaties that may serve as a useful model for other regions. Similarly, the linkages that are developing between Antarctic legal regimes and other international agreements, such as the 1989 Basel Convention and the IMO treaties on ship safety and pollution control, indicate how global and regional agreements may form an interlocking network for global environmental governance.

Equally vital, some of the mechanisms developed in the ATS offer interesting possibilities for application elsewhere. These include procedures to ensure adequate dialogue between the scientists and those responsible for policy decisions, and that the scientists lay out fully the consequences and uncertainties associated with alternative policy decisions, (as in the CCAMLR); mechanisms to address liability for environmental damage (as in the CRAMRA); and the compulsory, binding dispute settlement arrangements in the CRAMRA and the 1991 Protocol. Placing the burden of proof in the CRAMRA on the entity proposing to carry out an activity, to demonstrate that the activity will not have unacceptable environmental effects, and requiring that judgments be based on sufficient information, set other precedents in international environmental law, as do the 1991 Protocol's provisions on exchanging EIAs. The continuing refinement of reporting and inspection procedures, and the use of collective, Treaty-established international institutions to review compliance, parallel more recent mechanisms set out in the Montreal Protocol on Substances that Deplete the Ozone Layer. Additionally, as the greening of international law proceeds, Antarctic regimes will continue to affect the manner in which scientific advisory bodies influence international decision-making, as governments and publics fear that science may be distorted to suit narrow national or political interests.

From another point of view, as the ATS opened its meetings to NGO observers, it became obvious that their contributions to policy discussions at national and international levels grew more focused and relevant. The practice of restricting access to information and documents was not conducive to useful interactions. However, there is one area where the greening of Antarctic law and policy has still some rocky ground to travel. In the mid-1980s, the scientific and environmental communities shared concerns over environmentally-unsound practices in Antarctica and to some extent joined forces to avoid damage to the Antarctic environment. Today there is some fear in the scientific community that over-regulation may occur and may unduly impede research activities. No one questions that certain research can contribute to understanding global cycles and systems as well as local Antarctic phenomena. But it is not always easy to predict the future significance of a research proposal, and a microbiologist may differ with a glaciologist on what is a 'significant' environmental impact. As the 1991 Protocol is implemented in the coming years, some measure of balance will be required to reconcile the thrust for Antarctic environmental protection with the ability to conduct significant research there. The vehicle of science is still a mainstay of Antarctic law and policy, and environmental protection must reinforce it, not oppose it.

9 RADIOACTIVE WASTE DUMPING AT SEA

Remi Parmentier

INTRODUCTION

At their 15th Consultative Meeting, in November 1992, the Parties to the Convention on the Prevention of Marine Pollution by Dumping of Wastes and Other Matter (1972), commonly known until then as the London Dumping Convention (LDC), decided to change their name to the London Convention 1972 (LC 72). In doing so, they sought to show to the international community that, after the UNCED Earth Summit, the time had come to move away from a legal regime which governed sea dumping, and to implement a more precautionary approach designed to protect the marine environment in a more comprehensive and ecologically sound manner.

Even under the current London Convention, however, the dumping at sea of wastes which are as hazardous as Intermediate and Low Level radioactive wastes, is still not legally banned. The dumping of radioactive wastes at sea has been the centre of one of the most drawn-out international political and legal environmental controversies. Dating back to the 1970s and early 1980s, the international legal and political process is expected to culminate with the amendment of the London Convention by November 1994. Although there are numerous reasons to believe that the dumping of any radioactive waste at sea is not in line with current trends and state-of-the-art contemporary environmental policy, a few powerful countries remain reluctant about the prospect of a worldwide, legally-binding ban on the dumping of radioactive wastes at sea.

CURRENT SEA DUMPING REGIME: A HISTORICAL OVERVIEW

The deliberate dumping of wastes at sea, from ships, aircraft, platforms and other man-made structures is regulated worldwide by the Convention on the Prevention of Marine Pollution by Dumping of Wastes and Other

Matter (1972) which entered into force in 1975. The London Convention was adopted shortly after the UN Stockholm Conference on the Human Environment, in the same year that various Western European Governments also adopted a regional instrument – the Oslo Convention – to regulate the deliberate dumping of wastes at sea in the North-East Atlantic region. With 70 Contracting Parties to date, the 1972 London Convention is now one of the main global legal instruments for the prevention of marine pollution world-wide.

While the basic purpose of the Convention is to encourage nations of the world to work together to ensure that the marine environment is protected from the hazards of dumping, the 'protection of the marine environment', broadly defined, is the foundation of the Convention. Article I provides that:

> Contracting Parties shall individually and collectively promote the effective control of all sources of pollution of the marine environment.

Generally speaking, the three major sources of global marine pollution are:

(1) Land-Based Sources (LBS): these include point and non-point sources of terrestrial origin, including pollution inputs from rivers, estuaries, coastal discharges, as well as atmospheric inputs into the sea (these are thought to represent approximately 80 per cent of all marine pollution sources);
(2) Vessel-Source Discharges: represented either by accidental or deliberate discharges into the sea by the shipping industry (they represent approximately 10 per cent of all pollutants entering the marine environment); and
(3) Deliberate dumping of wastes from ships, platforms as well as aircraft (thought to represent the remaining 10 per cent of marine pollution inputs).

While there is no global legal instrument regulating Land-Based Sources (LBS), Vessel-Source Discharges are currently regulated by the International Maritime Organization's (IMO) Convention Marpol 73/78, and the third category, dumping from ships, is the remit of the 1972 London Convention.

The London Convention contains three annexes: Annex I, the so-called 'black list', which includes the substances for which dumping at sea is strictly prohibited; Annex II lists substances for which dumping requires the issuance of special permits; and Annex III establishes criteria governing the issue of dumping permits. The Convention and its annexes can be amended by a two-thirds majority vote of those present at Consultative Meetings.

Contracting Parties to the London Convention hold annual Consultative Meetings, in the headquarters of the International Maritime Organization, the London-based UN Specialized Agency charged with the task of improving maritime safety and limiting the impact of shipping on the marine environment. In 1975, the IMO (then still called IMCO) was designated as the organization responsible for secretariat duties in relation to the Convention. The Office for the London Convention was placed under the auspices of the IMO as a result.

Originally, the Consultative Meetings of the London Convention were designed to do little more than to collect (incomplete) data on dumping activities. However, through the 1980s and early 1990s the Consultative Meetings have had an increasing political importance, in line with the increase of the universal political and social demand for clean seas and a cleaner environment.

The increasingly high political profile of the 1972 London Convention became evident in the first half of the 1980s, when a global political and legal controversy on the permissibility of ocean dumping of radioactive wastes took place under its auspices.

THE RADIOACTIVE WASTE DUMPING CONTROVERSY

At the 7th Consultative Meeting of the London Convention, in February 1983, several countries made proposals to prevent or ban the dumping at sea of all kinds of radioactive wastes, giving rise to an unprecedented political, social, legal, and scientific controversy which – ten years later – continues unabated.

When the London Convention was adopted in 1972, High Level radioactive Wastes (HLW) were placed on the Convention's 'black list' (Annex I), but Intermediate and Low Level radioactive Wastes (ILW and LLW) were placed on Annex II in order to allow the regulated disposal at sea of these inconvenient wastes. However, by 1983 the dumping of radioactive wastes at sea was no longer considered to be an acceptable option for the vast majority of public opinion world-wide, and, as a result, for the majority of the London Convention's Parties. In light of uncertainties over the possible environmental consequences of dumping, as well as the likely impact of this practice on other, legitimate, uses of the sea, such as fisheries and tourism, several countries directly affected decided to raise the issue within the framework of the 1972 London Convention, and proposed that preventive action be taken by the 7th Consultative Meeting. Three separate but related initiatives were undertaken.

Two small island nations from the South Pacific, the Republics of Nauru and Kiribati, concerned by the Japanese and US Governments' plans to resume sea dumping on a vast scale in the Pacific Ocean,[1] put forward a proposal to amend the Convention so that all radioactive wastes (ILW and LLW in addition to HLW) be placed on the 'black list' (Annex I). The five Nordic countries (Denmark, Finland, Iceland, Norway and Sweden) separately presented a proposal by which radioactive waste dumping at sea would be 'phased out' by the year 1990. This proposal was prompted by those countries' concern about the rapid increase in the quantities of radioactive wastes which had been dumped at sea in the early 1980s.[2] Finally, the Government of Spain – severely affected by the proximity of several dump-sites close to its coast (in particular the North-East Atlantic dump site used by eight countries' members of the Nuclear Energy Agency (NEA) of the OECD between 1967 and 1982)[3] – called for an immediate moratorium on all dumping operations.

Opposition to radioactive waste dumping at sea

Summarily stated, those countries' objection to the continuation of sea dumping could be described as follows:

(1) The oceans are a living, interconnected environment that can return radioactive wastes to humans via the ocean's food chain. The objective of radioactive waste management should be to contain those wastes so that they are isolated from the biosphere instead of diluting and dispersing them in the environment, which is the case with ocean dumping.

(2) The ocean is a formidable environment. Pressures and temperatures reach planetary extremes in the seas and the corrosive powers of ocean waters are legendary. The ocean is the most destructive environment for placement of radioactive waste containers.

(3) The oceans are still relatively unknown. New discoveries are made almost on an annual basis. Scientific opinion on the capacity of the seas to absorb wastes is in constant evolution.

(4) The oceans represent a 'global commons' which should be preserved for the benefit of all people and future generations. It is fundamentally unfair for a minority of the planet's population to disproportionately damage shared marine resources and thus deprive the vast majority of their own rights.

(5) Those States which were dumping radioactive wastes at sea were not willing to accept the burden of proving the safety of such a practice – instead preferring the much easier, and more traditional, approach which requires that such a burden rests with these who need to prove that such a practice, is or may be, harmful.

The 'South Pacific' and 'Nordic' proposals were strategic in nature: they were both tabled in order to allow the passage – after a long, acrimonious and hectic debate – of the Spanish proposal, establishing a moratorium, pending the outcome of a meeting of experts on radioactive wastes.[4] Resolution LDC 14(7), by which the moratorium proposed by Spain was established, was adopted by a vote of 19 in favour, six against (Japan, the Netherlands, South Africa, Switzerland, the UK and the USA), and five abstentions (Brazil, the FRG, France, Greece, and the USSR).[5]

Resolution LDC 14(7) was legally non-binding, and the UK and certain other OECD countries planned to ignore it, and to proceed with dumping at sea in the summer of 1983. But the dump ships were forced to stay in port, largely as a result of the strength of political pressure created by public opinion and trade unions from all over Western Europe. The campaign to keep the Atlantic Ocean free from radioactive wastes culminated in the summer of 1983 when the National Union of Seamen (NUS) of the UK and the International Transport Federation (ITF) – with world-wide affiliate members – called upon seamen and transport workers from all over the world not to handle radioactive wastes destined for sea dumping. Their call was heard: the workers did not cooperate, and the planned dumping cruises were cancelled. Instead, the radioactive wastes were stored on land.

Two years later, a report by a 'panel of experts' appointed by the International Atomic Energy Agency (IAEA) and the International Council of Scientific Union (ICSU)[6] was produced. In response, the 9th Consultative Meeting of Contracting Parties (held in September 1985) had to decide whether or not ocean dumping could be resumed. At that time, however, it was obvious to most delegations that the IAEA/ICSU participants in the panel of experts tended, with some exceptions, to be proponents of an obsolescent, but nonetheless influencial scientific perspective that the oceans' 'assimilative capacity' to receive humankind's wastes and other hazardous substances remained limitless. Unsatisfied by the experts panel's response, the Spanish Government proposed another resolution by which 'a suspension of all dumping at sea of radioactive wastes and other radioactive matter' was agreed in order to 'permit time for the further consideration of issues which would provide a broader basis for an informed judgment on proposals for the amendment of the Annexes of the Convention', and requesting that 'additional studies and assessments of the wider political, legal, economic and social aspects of radioactive waste dumping at sea be undertaken'.[7]

This new resolution establishing a moratorium for an indefinite period was adopted by an overwhelming majority of 26 in favour, five against (France, South Africa, Switzerland, the UK and the USA), and seven abstentions (Argentina, Belgium, Greece, Italy, Japan, Portugal and the USSR). Within a period of two years opposition to sea dumping had increased significantly. Resolution LDC 21(9) remains in force today.

Nevertheless, despite two successive resolutions calling for the suspension of radioactive waste dumping at sea, the controversy still continues.

Intergovernmental Panel of Experts

With the exception of illegal dumping activities of wastes from the USSR,[8] officially no radioactive wastes have been dumped at sea since 1983. But the nuclear industry and the military are faced with ever-increasing quantities of wastes and an ever-growing opposition from the public, unhappy about the dumping of wastes in their own backyard. As a result, pressure to resume sea dumping has been maintained, and is expected to grow in the future unless the sea dumping option is definitively and permanently banned.

After the 1985 moratorium Resolution LDC 21(9), the London Convention established an Intergovernmental Panel of Experts on Radioactive Wastes (IGPRAD) to address some of the questions raised by the Resolution. [9] The IAEA was also asked to come up with a series of reports on other relevant issues, including a complete inventory of all radioactive wastes entering the marine environment, and a comparative study of sea dumping with land-based options.

IGPRAD held five sessions between 1988 and 1992, and is expected to hold a final one (effectively to finalize the Panel's report, with no additional substantive discussion) in July of 1993, for presentation to the 16th Consultative Meeting of the London Convention in November 1993.

Clearly, after ten years of thorough review, there is no possible consensus as to whether radioactive waste dumping is or is not an acceptable disposal option, from a scientific, legal, political, economic and/or social point of view. At the end of the day, what the Parties to the London Convention will have to decide is whether it is preferable to let ocean dumping occur, allowing the detriment from radioactive waste generation to be shared and spread within population segments who have not received (or even in some cases have chosen to not receive) the alleged 'benefits' of the nuclear industry, or alternatively whether it is preferable, on the contrary, to rule out ocean dumping completely in order to ensure that the cost of radioactive waste generation is borne by those who have chosen or accepted to generate radioactive wastes. By all accounts, and in particular with due regard to the precautionary principle, the non-dumping option is thought to be preferable by the majority of States, and by the environmental community. It is also important to bear in mind that ocean dumping was considered (until the moratorium) the most expeditious and least costly disposal method in political, social and economic terms; accordingly, the abandonment of this option (for all industrial wastes) represents a significant incentive for the development and implementation of policies which seek to reduce the generation of wastes at source, and – in the case of radioactive wastes specifically – to force governments to take full account in devising and applying their energy policies of the otherwise hidden cost of radioactive wastes.

FUTURE OPTIONS

In light of the substantive differences of opinion between the very small minority of countries who still want to keep open the option of dumping radioactive wastes at sea (principally Japan, the UK, France, and the US), and the majority anti-dumping group, IGPRAD has considered a list of options for the future that will be included in its final report, for the consideration of the Contracting Parties. It is clear that IGPRAD has 'essentially accepted that this range of options should be presented in the final report, with some discussion of their merits and demerits but without a recommendation to the Consultative Meeting necessarily being made'.[10]

The range of options which are being considered for inclusion in the final report of IGPRAD, to be concluded in July 1993, have been summarized as follows:

- **Option 1** – Lift the moratorium, allowing sea disposal of LLW in accordance with existing LC and IAEA rules.
- **Option 2** – Lift the moratorium, allowing sea disposal in accordance with strengthened international rules. This could include revised LC and IAEA rules and any additional guidance agreed to by Contracting Parties.
- **Option 3** – Link action on radioactive waste to the resolution on a phase-out of industrial waste dumping adopted at the 13th Consultative Meeting, by which the dumping of industrial waste is to be phased out by the end of 1995.
- **Option 4** – Continuation of a moratorium, time specific or indefinite.
- **Option 5** – Develop new special consultative procedure governing the sea disposal of radioactive waste.
- **Option 6** – Prohibit disposal of radioactive waste by amending the Convention and/or its Annexes.
- **Option 7** – Prohibit disposal of radioactive waste by amending the Convention and/or its Annexes, with an 'opting out' possibility after a certain agreed upon time, under certain agreed upon conditions, for certain countries who might not be in a position to readily accept an outright immediate ban.[11]

It appears that a resumption of ocean dumping, as described in Options 1 and 2, would be out of step with the current trend of international environmental policy, in particular with the precautionary approach which has become the guiding principle in many international fora, including the London Convention, and which was endorsed in Principle 12 of the Rio Declaration on Environment and Development. In addition, it also appears that Options 1 and 2 would conflict with Agenda 21 adopted by the United Nations Conference on the Environment and Development (UNCED) in June 1992. Indeed, Agenda 21's Chapter 22 entitled 'Promoting the Safe and

Environmentally Sound Management of Radioactive Wastes', includes language directly relevant to the current ocean dumping controversy within the London Convention. Paragraph 22.5(b) of Agenda 21 states that States should:

> Encourage the London Dumping Convention to expedite work to complete studies on replacing the current voluntary moratorium on disposal of low-level radioactive wastes at sea by a ban, taking into account the precautionary approach, with a view to taking a well informed and timely decision on the issue.[12]

Whereas this language does not specifically call for an immediate ban on radioactive waste dumping, because Agenda 21 was the reflection of the lowest common denominator among the 172 countries that participated in the Earth Summit, it is clearly indicative of the global trend against the dumping of radioactive wastes at sea. In particular, it is interesting to note that the purpose acknowledged for the IGPRAD studies is 'to replace the current voluntary moratorium . . . by a ban'. Nowhere is the possibility of a resumption of dumping mentioned in Agenda 21, and it can be said that by not including this option, the Heads of States present in Rio have sent a clear message to the London Convention.

Paragraph 22.5(c) of Agenda 21 was also directly relevent to the London Convention. In it, it is said that States should:

> Not promote or allow the storage or disposal of High level, Intermediate level and Low level radioactive wastes near the marine environment unless they determine that the scientific evidence, consistent with the applicable internationally agreed principles and guidelines, shows that such storage or disposal poses no unacceptable risk to people and the marine environment or does not interfere with other legitimate uses of the sea, making, in the process of consideration, appropriate use of the concept of the precautionary principle.

It should be clear that if States are not to promote or allow disposal near the marine environment, absent compliance with the stringent criteria contained in Paragraph 22.5(c), then they certainly should not do so for disposal in the marine environment. As stated by Greenpeace International at the 5th Session of IGPRAD, any other interpretation, especially when read in combination with Paragraph 22.5(b) would effectively constitute a perversion of the spirit of Rio.

Option 4 of the IGPRAD proposals, continuation of a moratorium (time specific or indefinite) would merely amount to a continuance of the status-quo. Ten years after the first resolution establishing the moratorium was adopted, and after a decade-long thorough review showing that the nuclear industry's biased case in favour of sea dumping could not be technically justified, the re-establishment of a moratorium would be widely perceived as a very limited advancement. Technically, although no one (beside the former USSR) has officially violated the moratorium, it is still non-binding, and the threat of a resumption of this practice would remain. This concern does not preclude the possibility that Resolution LDC 21(9) now reflects a rule of customary international law.

Option 3 would link action on radioactive waste to Resolution LDC 43(13) adopted in 1990 at the 13th Consultative Meeting, and by which the Parties agreed 'that the dumping of industrial wastes shall cease by 31 December 1995 at the latest'. For the purpose of that resolution, 'industrial wastes' was defined as 'waste materials generated by manufacturing or processing operations', and it was agreed that 'the inclusion of radioactive matter in this definition would be considered when the current London Dumping Convention review of issues relating to radioactive waste dumping has been completed'.[13] In light of the inconclusive IGPRAD report, a permanent ban on radioactive waste dumping at sea would be consistent with Resolution LDC 43(13), as long as that resolution is effectively and properly complied with and enforced.

Under Option 5, 'Contracting Parties would not allow sea disposal, except as carried out under a new special procedure agreed by them. The new procedure could be elaborated in an addendum to Annex I, a new annex or protocol, or a new section in Annex II.'[14] The intent of this option is apparently to allow the possibility of dumping under special or exceptional circumstances only, and to develop for such cases a procedure by which decision-making would take place. A nuclear accident causing contamination of considerable areas of land is a case that was mentioned, informally, by some participants to IGPRAD, where sea dumping might be considered to be an 'option of least detriment'. Although it is true that consideration of this approach may have some merits, it is reasonable to question whether it could realistically be implemented. For example, it is doubtful whether 'pro-dumping' governments would agree to a decision-making procedure that would provide that dumping operations could only be allowed on a case-by-case basis with the consensus of all the Parties to the Convention; there are also fears that there might be different interpretations of what constitute a special or an extraordinary circumstance.[15]

In light of these considerations, among others, it appears that the most reasonable and broadly acceptable course of action is that presented by Option 6 – to probibit disposal of radioactive waste by amending the convention and/or its annexes. Indeed, ocean dumping is the disposal option for radioactive wastes that has been the subject of the most thorough critical review. It took over a decade to complete, and the nuclear industry has still not managed to convince the vast majority of Parties to the Convention that there are valid reasons to allow the resumption of this method of disposal. It has even been said that – should the ocean dumping controversy have started in the 1990s rather than the 1980s – its conclusion by the adoption of a permanent ban would have been much faster, and the terms of reference of IGPRAD, as well as the composition of that body, would have been significantly different. [16]

Beside substantive objections, some – in particular the US delegation – have raised two concerns with regard to the applicability of this decision: the need to establish De Minimis levels of radioactivity below which dumping at sea could take place, and the fact that even if the Parties decide this year to amend the Convention, these amendments are unlikely to enter into force for several years, in light of the inherently slow process of ratification. Neither of these concerns provide a reasonable basis for postponing action on the amendments of the 1972 Convention.

De Minimis

The concept of De Minimis levels is based on the fact that, strictly speaking, 'everything' is radioactive, and that, as a result, a level of radioactivity 'below regulatory concern' should be established before the dumping at sea of 'radioactive waste and other matter' is banned. Paradoxically, the advocates of the De Minimis concept who base their reasoning on the need for clarity, are unduly complicating a rather simple issue: already most know what is and what is not commonly known as a 'radioactive waste'.[17] As a matter of fact, the London Convention moratorium has worked very well for ten years without requiring a De Minimis definition and, likewise, several regional legal instruments have banned radioactive waste dumping at sea permanently, without De Minimis definitions.[18] Certainly the adoption of a De Minimis definition would be desirable in relation to a ban on radioactive waste dumping, since such a definition would prevent Parties from exploiting loopholes by relying on overly lax domestic definitions. However, under no circumstances should efforts to agree on such a definition delay the adoption of amendments banning radioactive waste dumping at sea, which can perfectly enter into force without such a definition.

Entry into Force

It is true that amendments to the Convention, adopted by a two-thirds majority of those present, are not binding on those Parties which have not accepted them, and that the others who did not participate in the decision may opt out by making a declaration within 100 days. However, as we have seen that no Party has been able, over the past ten years, to ignore the voluntary moratorium adopted by the resolution in 1983,[19] it is very unlikely that any Party could ignore the amendments by dumping radioactive wastes at sea. In any case, it is less likely that anyone would do so if the Convention does ban the practice than if it does not do so.

At the 5th Session of IGPRAD, in November 1992, where these options were formally considered for the first time, a 7th Option, based on the compromise formula that had been reached in the Convention for the Protection of the Marine Environment of the North-East Atlantic signed at Ministerial level in Paris in September 1992 – a permanent ban with an opt out clause after the passing of a certain amount of time for some countries – was also retained.

THE 1992 PARIS CONVENTION
COMPROMISE FORMULA

The Oslo Convention, which has regulated the dumping at sea in the North-East Atlantic since its adoption a few months before the London Convention was drafted in 1972, excluded radioactive substances from its scope. This early piece of international regulation dates back from the years when there was little public scrutiny and, as a result, little interest on the part of European Governments in putting limits on the development of the nuclear industry. The radioactive waste dump site of the OECD's Nuclear Energy Agency (NEA) was located within the area covered by the Convention but ironically radioactive wastes were not to be talked of within the Oslo Commission.[20]

However, when the Parties to the Oslo and Paris Conventions[21] decided in 1989 that a full review of their past activities should be undertaken, with a view to holding a meeting at Ministerial level in 1992 in order to commemorate the 20th Anniversary of the Oslo Convention, political and social realities, as well as humankind's understanding of environmental priorities, had changed. It was decided that the Oslo and Paris Commissions, which had been sharing a joint Secretariat based in London, should be merged; and for two years delegates met approximately every two months in order to draft a new convention that would be ready for signature by the Ministers in September 1992.

At one of the early preparatory meetings, Spain had put forward a written proposal to include a ban on the dumping of radioactive wastes in the new Convention. The proposal was tabled and not really dealt with for quite a while but, on the other hand, it was agreed that the Annex on Dumping and Incineration at Sea of the new Draft Convention should implement the precautionary principle by establishing a 'reversed listing of substances'. Until recently, all international instruments regulating pollution were listing in their annexes substances that should not be dumped in the sea. By adopting a reverse approach, the new Convention would, for the first time, place the burden of proof on prospective dumpers to show why their substances could and should be dumped.

After it had been agreed that the new framework Convention's Annex on dumping should ban all dumping activities with only a limited number of exceptions,[22] radioactive wastes remained in brackets as a possible exception until the Spanish delegation pushed their proposal forcefully at a meeting of the 'Osparrev' working group held in Madrid in April 1992. At that meeting, all countries with the sole exception of France and the UK were formally on record as supporting the proposed ban on radioactive waste dumping at sea. At the following preparatory meeting, in Oslo in June 1992, an attempt to reach consensus via a weak compromise failed, and, as a result, when the Ministerial Conference opened in Paris on 21 September 1992, the radioactive waste dumping issue remained unresolved.

The French Minister of the Environment, Ms Segolene Royal, felt it to be her duty to prevent a failure of the Conference since her government was acting as host, and she made it known in the preceding weeks that her country would accept a ban for a considerable length of time (50 years were mentioned) as long as some provision for a review after that time was made. As a result, the UK was left isolated on the issue.[23]

The Ministerial Conference was officially open on time on the 21 September, but the Ministers had to spend most of that night, and the entire morning of the 22 September, to reach a compromise. As a result, it was late in the day when they were finally able to sign the new regional Convention. [24]

The alternatives considered ranged from a postponement of the adoption of the Convention and the convening of another conference a few months later, to the signature of the Convention banning radioactive waste dumping at sea by all but the UK. Finally, the UK agreed to an atypical kind of compromise, by which all the Parties accept that the practice of dumping radioactive wastes at sea was banned, but an 'opt out' possibility after 15 to 25 years should be allowed for France and the UK only. Article 3.3 of the Annex on the Prevention and Elimination of Pollution by Dumping or Incineration states that:

3. (a) The dumping of Low and Intermediate level radioactive substances, including wastes, is prohibited.

   (b) As an exception to subparagraph 3(a) of this Article, those Contracting Parties, the United Kingdom and France, who wish to retain the option of an exception to subparagraph 3(a) in any case not before the expiry of a period of 15 years from 1 January 1993, shall report to the meeting of the Commission at Ministerial level in 1997 on the steps taken to explore alternative land-based options.

   (c) Unless, at or before the expiry of this period of 15 years, the Commission decides by a unanimous vote not to continue the exception provided in subparagraph 3(b), it shall take a decision pursuant to Article 13 of the Convention on the prolongation for a period of 10 years after 1 January 2008 of the prohibition, after which another meeting of the Commission at Ministerial level shall be held. Those Contracting Parties mentioned in subparagraph 3(b) of this Article still wishing to retain the option mentioned in subparagraph 3(b) shall report to the Commission meetings to be held at Ministerial level at two yearly intervals from 1999 onwards about the progress in establishing alternative land-based options and on the results of scientific studies which show that any potential dumping operations would not result in hazards to human health, harm to living resources or marine ecosystems, damage to amenities or interference with other legitimate uses of the sea.

Article 13 of the Convention, which is referred in Article 3.3.(c) contains the rules by which decisions and recommendations will be reached:

> Decisions and recommendations shall be adopted by unanimous vote of the Contracting Parties. Should unanimity not be attainable, and unless otherwise provided in the Convention, the Commission may nonetheless adopt decisions or recommendations by a three-quarters majority vote of the Contracting Parties.

The meaning of this convoluted compromise language is that – at a minimum – ocean dumping of radioactive wastes is banned in the North-East Atlantic until the year 2008, and that the ban will most probably be extended for another ten-year period, until 2018, by a three-quarters majority vote.[25] The most important aspect of the compromise solution adopted in Paris is that, for the first time, the UK and France have accepted formally to be legally bound by a measure that bans the dumping of radioactive wastes at sea. In addition, the fact that Article 3.2.(e) bans the dumping of vessels or aircraft from, at the latest, 31 December 2004, and that Article 3.3. bans the dumping of radioactive wastes until at least 2008, the new Convention also represents a formal and definite abandonment of the ocean dumping option for decommissioned nuclear-powered vessels.[26]

Perhaps in the hope that a similar approach could provide a 'face-saving' formula for the 1972 London Convention (in particular for Japan and the US who have not renounced ocean dumping, as well as France and the UK who will resist going beyond the Paris formula), IGPRAD has, at their meeting held two months after the Paris Ministerial Conference, added the formula adopted by the new Paris Convention as a 7th possible Option that Contracting Parties to the London Convention will take into account.

Subseabed Disposal of Radioactive Wastes

After the moratorium on LLW dumping at sea became effective, the Parties to the London Convention turned their attention, in 1984, to plans for the disposal of High Level radioactive Wastes under the seabed, which had been actively considered and researched by various countries' members of the OECD.

From 1973 onward, the OECD's NEA acted as the Secretariat of a 'Seabed Working Group' to coordinate the research of some of their member States with a view to the disposing of HLW under the seabed. This disposal option, which consists of injecting cannisters containing HLW under the seabed from a platform or a vessel, has been considered in the North-East Atlantic near the Canary Islands and Madeira, the Caribbean, and the Pacific Ocean. Those plans included shooting 'suppository-shaped' cannisters that were supposed to penetrate the ocean floor deep enough to prevent the release of radioactivity into the marine environment, and a drilling option, modelled on the engineering experience acquired in the context of the oil and gas off-shore industry.

Although it is true that at least some of those plans are comparable to some of the ideas generated by the worst the movie industry has to offer, the US, France, the UK, Japan, Germany and the Netherlands, among others, have spent millions of dollars of taxpayers' money to try and implement them. At the end of the 1970s and until the mid-1980s, several research vessels cruised several 'reference sites' to study various aspects of the scheme, including site selection and engineering issues.

The nations involved were careful to keep the issue outside of the 1972 London Convention for political reasons. The Convention, as written, prohibits 'disposal at sea' of HLW. Thus, the question arose of whether disposal at sea referred to the final resting place of the wastes, or to the place where the disposal activity occurs?

In 1983, at the 7th Consultative Meeting of the 1972 London Convention, the delegates from Norway and Finland addressed the issue for the first time, and a resolution was adopted calling for a special meeting of legal experts to report to the Contracting Parties on whether or not subseabed disposal was covered by the Convention.[27] The Meeting of Legal Experts took place in December 1983, but no consensus was reached, and it was therefore left to the 8th Consultative Meeting to discuss the issue further.

In February 1984, after a very long and hectic debate, two basic points were agreed by all Parties present at the 8th Consultative Meeting:

(1) the Consultative Meeting of the London Convention is the appropriate international forum to address the question of the disposal of HLW into the seabed, including the question of the compatibility of this type of disposal with the provisions of the Convention; and

(2) no such disposal should take place unless and until it is proven to be technically feasible and environmentally acceptable, including a determination that such waste can be effectively isolated from the marine environment, and a regulatory mechanism is elaborated

in accordance with the provisions of the London Convention to govern the disposal into the seabed of such radioactive wastes.

Beyond this basic agreement, two principal blocks expressed notably different views. The dominant coalition of nations – a large majority of those who stated a position – argued that HLW disposal is covered by the Convention and prohibited. They agreed that, while the express language of the Convention may be unclear, protection of the marine environment required an interpretation that viewed subseabed disposal as 'disposal at sea'. This view was expressed in a draft resolution sponsored by 17 nations, joined by eight more at the 9th Consultative Meeting. On the other hand, France, Japan, the Netherlands, Switzerland, the UK and the USA also submitted a draft resolution which took the opposite view, namely that subseabed disposal was not covered by the text of the Convention, and that it was therefore not prohibited.

Since a number of delegations were concerned about forcing the issue to a formal vote, particularly given the high tension that was experienced at the 1983 meeting with the moratorium on LLW dumping, no vote was called. Instead, both resolutions were attached to the final report of the 8th Consultative Meeting, and tabled.

It is thought that, partly as a result of the debate within the 1972 London Convention, and the moratorium on the dumping of LLW at sea, as well as its extremely high cost, the subseabed disposal programme has been virtually abandoned. However, periodically, in the US in particular, attempts are made in academic circles to revive this option, and get funding for it. As recently as 1992 also, advocates of the subseabed options for HLW were reported as being very active in Russia, possibly trying to establish a programme there.

At the 11th Consultative Meeting, in October 1988, the Irish delegation re-opened the debate on subseabed disposal in light of the UK's plan to develop such a programme for ILW and LLW in coastal areas into repositories either accessed from the sea (via a platform) or from the shore (via a tunnel). A year later, at the 12th Consultative Meeting, the Spanish delegation tabled a draft resolution to establish that subseabed disposal of LLW into repositories accessed from the sea would be a form of dumping currently covered by the moratorium on ocean dumping. It was in 1990, at the 13th Consultative Meeting that this proposal was adopted by an overwhelming vote of 29 in favour, and only four against and four abstentions.[28] As for disposal into repositories accessed from the shore, after the Ad Hoc Group of Legal Experts considered this issue in 1990, no action was taken by the Parties to the Convention, although some argued that this form of disposal could fall within the scope of the London Convention. Since then, the new 1992 Helsinki Convention for the Baltic Sea, and the new Paris Convention for the North-East Atlantic, both consider, as a Land-Base of marine pollution, the damage to the marine environment that could result from this activity.

AMENDMENT CONFERENCE: TOWARD THE 'GREENING' OF THE LONDON CONVENTION

Whilst IGPRAD is about to provide its Report to the 16th Consultative Meeting of the London Convention, which will take place in November 1993, thus technically ending the moratorium on LLW dumping at sea, it is hoped that the now well rehearsed controversy over radioactive waste dumping at sea could be brought to an end.

Pursuant to discussions at their 14th and 15th Consultative Meetings, the Contracting Parties to the Convention have decided to hold an Amendment Conference in 1994, which will be preceded by a special 'Amendments Negotiation Meeting' in July 1993, and the 16th Consultative Meeting in November 1993, at which a decision is needed as to the nature and content of the amendments to be formally adopted by the Conference.[29]

Anticipating this process, the Danish delegation, supported by Norway and Iceland, tabled, prior to the 15th Consultative Meeting, a proposal containing a set of amendments which take into account the controversies of the past decades, and attempt to resolve them.[30] The main features of the Danish proposal, which is expected to form the basis of discussions at the July 1993 negotiations and beyond, consist of:

- including 'the seabed and the subsoil thereof as part of the sea' in the definition of the 'sea' contained in Article III.3 of the Convention (currently 'all marine waters other than the internal waters of States'), with a view to clarifying the status of the disposal of wastes in the subseabed;
- including all radioactive wastes and other radioactive matter in Annex I of the Convention (the 'black list');
- including 'industrial wastes' in Annex I;
- establishing that the incineration at sea of liquid noxious wastes is banned; and
- adding to Annex III a section defining the precautionary approach as the guiding principle of the Convention.

As stated by the Danish delegation in their proposal:

> The substance and principles contained in most of the proposed amendments have already been agreed to in several Resolutions adopted by Consultative Meetings in the last decade . . ... Therefore, the proposal constitutes the much needed incorporation into the Convention of Decisions which already have been taken at past meetings[31]

Yet, from the initial discussions which took place at the 15th Consultative Meeting, it appears that – although the overwhelming majority is in favour of the proposal – a few countries who would rather continue to use the oceans as a dustbin, are likely to prove very obstructive.

For the London Convention, it will be the 'hour of truth'. In the past decade, the London Convention has claimed to be 'greening'. It is perceived as moving away from providing a framework that regulates dumping at sea, and towards a more precautionary and preventive approach. It is true that in the last ten years, the group of countries firmly opposed to dumping at sea has maintained leadership, very much to the annoyance of their opponents – the ever-smaller group of 'pro-dumpers' who 'controlled' the Convention until the mid-1980s. However, it is also true that too few countries, Party to the London Convention, take a real interest and an active part in the work of the Convention. At best, of the 70 countries which are Party to the Convention, no more than 45 ever show up at the Convention's Consultative Meetings; and even among these, many fail to provide adequate reports on their dumping activities (including 'nil' reports when appropriate), despite their legal obligation to do so.

There is a widespread belief that this lack of active involvement is due to the fact that the London Convention is still perceived as a 'dumpers' club', while the majority of Parties are more interested in waste prevention than in ocean diposal techniques. Under these circumstances, the recent decision to drop the word 'dumping' from the name of the London Convention was a step in the right direction. But a deeper and more substantive reform is required for the 1972 London Convention to become an 'anti-dumping regime'.

The amendments proposed by Denmark, if adopted, should send the very positive message that the permissive era, with regard to ocean dumping, has ended. Therefore, it should reinforce the Convention on a broader basis.

CONCLUSION

Beyond the important issue of ocean dumping itself, a lot more could be at stake. Unless the deliberate dumping of industrial and radioactive wastes at sea can be eliminated, there is little hope that the international community ever makes significant global progress towards the elimination of marine pollution from land-based sources – the other 80 per cent of marine pollution inputs worldwide. If the ocean dumping controversy – rather limited in scope – cannot be resolved after a review that has taken a decade, one wonders if the international community will ever be able to come effectively to grips with global marine pollution of terrestrial origin, an issue which is more complicated in technical, legal, political and economic terms. It would seriously hinder hopes of seeing the global oceans becoming clean again.

Votes on Radioactive Waste Dumping Issues at Consultative Meetings of the London Convention (1983–1985)

1983 LLW Moratorium	1984 Legality of Subseabed Disposal	1985 LLW Moratorium	1990 Subseabed LLW Moratorium
In Favour (19)	**Nordic Res Sponsors (25)**	**In Favour (26)**	**In Favour (29)**
Argentina	Argentina	Australia	Argentina
Canada	Brazil	Brazil	Australia
Chile	Canada	Canada	Brazil
Denmark	Chile	Chile	Canada
Finland	Cuba	Cuba	Chile
Iceland	Denmark	Denmark	China
Ireland	Dominican Rep	Dominican Rep	C d'Ivoire
Kiribati	Finland	Finland	Cyprus
Mexico	Fed Rep Germany	Fed Rep Germany	Denmark
Morocco	Haiti	Haiti	Finland
Nauru	Iceland	Honduras	Germany
New Zealand	Ireland	Iceland	Honduras
Nigeria	Kiribati	Ireland	Iceland
Norway	Mexico	Kiribati	Ireland
Papua N Guinea	Nauru	Mexico	Italy
Philippines	New Zealand	Nauru	Malta
Portugal	Norway	Netherlands	Mexico
Spain	Panama	New Zealand	Morocco
Sweden	Poland	Norway	Nauru
	Portugal	Oman	Netherlands
	Spain	Panama	New Zealand
	St Lucia	Papua N Guinea	Nigeria
	Sweden	Philippines	Norway
	Yugoslavia	St Lucia	Oman
	Zaire	Spain	Portugal
		Sweden	Solomon Isl
			Sth Africa
			Spain
			Sweden
Against (6)	**US Spons Res (6)**	**Against (5)**	**Against (4)**
Japan	France	France	France
Netherlands	Japan	South Africa	UK
South Africa	Netherlands	Switzerland	USA
Switzerland	Switzerland	UK	USSR
UK	UK	USA	
USA	USA		
Abstaining (5)		**Abstaining (7)**	**Abstaining (4)**
Brazil		Argentina	Belgium
Fed Rep Germany		Belgium	Greece
France		Greece	Japan
Greece		Italy	Switzerland
USSR		Japan	
		Portugal	
		USSR	

List of Contracting Parties to the London Convention
(at October 1992)

Afghanistan – Antigua and Barbuda – Argentina – Australia – Belgium – Brazil – Belarus – Canada – Cape Verde – Chile – China – Costa Rica – Cote d'Ivoire – Croatia – Cuba – Cyprus – Denmark – Dominican Republic – Egypt – Finland – France – Gabon – Germany – Greece – Guatemala – Haiti – Honduras – Hungary – Iceland – Ireland – Italy – Japan – Jamaica – Jordan – Kenya – Kiribati – Lybian Arab Jamahiriya – Luxembourg – Malta – Mexico – Monaco – Morocco – Nauru – Netherlands – New Zealand – Nigeria – Norway – Oman – Panama – Papua New Guinea – Philippines – Poland – Portugal – Russian Federation – Seychelles – Solomon Islands – South Africa – Spain – Saint Lucia – Suriname – Sweden – Switzerland – Tunisia – Ukraine – United Arab Emirates – United Kingdom – United States – Vanuatu – (Yugoslavia) – Zaire.

10 THE EVOLUTION OF INTERNATIONAL WHALING LAW

Gregory Rose and Saundra Crane

Whales . . . belong to no single nation nor to any group of nations but rather they are the wards of the entire world.[1]

INTRODUCTION

Whales have evolved over millions of years while commercial exploitation of them has taken place for only a few hundred. In those latter years whale populations have been subjected to intensive hunting and some species have been pushed near the point of extinction. International laws for their protection have developed slowly and haltingly, failing to arrest the species' decline. Even today, political and commercial interests continue to impede the progress of legal measures for the whales' protection.

The central international legal arrangement for the protection of whales is provided by the 1946 International Convention for the Regulation of Whaling (ICRW) and the International Whaling Commission (IWC) established thereunder.[2] However, since its signature 47 years ago, the ICRW has become too far removed from the realities of current political needs to adequately meet the needs of whale conservation. The reason that it has survived in its current anachronistic form is simply that its members are divided into two deadlocked camps: pro-whaling and anti-whaling countries. Any change in the balance between them may cause the machinery to collapse and so it remains static and antiquated.

This chapter aims to provide an understanding of the challenges facing the IWC in its attempts to 'manage whale stocks' today. These include deciding what whales are under its jurisdiction; whether to maintain the commercial moratorium; how to formulate 'revised management procedures'; whether to greatly extend the Indian Ocean whale sanctuary; how to properly manage 'scientific', 'pirate' and 'aboriginal' whaling; and how to collaborate with fishery organizations in order to prevent whales from being drowned in fishing nets. A grasp of these issues requires familiarization with the ICRW, some aspects of the international law of the sea and with those political pressures which have shaped the role of the IWC since it was established.

What are Whales?

The question appears deceptively easy but is a source of contention for lawyers attempting to interpret the ICRW. In vernacular usage, one thinks of the great whales – the blue, humpback, sperm whales, etc. However, in scientific terms, the word covers all whales, large and small, including dolphins and porpoises.

Scientifically, there is no distinction between great and small whales. All whales are of the order of Cetacea. They fall into two suborders: baleen (*Mysticetes*) and toothed (*Odontocetes*).[3] Smaller whale species, porpoises and dolphins, tend to be toothed, however, some of the larger whales, such as the sperm whale, are also toothed. Toothed whales consume fish and seals, and some species also feed on other whales and dolphins. Baleen whales feed on plankton and small crustaceans, called krill, at the water's surface. They strain water through their baleen (or 'whalebone') consuming the tiny organisms in large quantities. The blue, right, humpback and bowhead whales are all baleen whales and are great whales. Together with the sperm whale, which is a toothed great whale, and the minke whale, which is a baleen whale of intermediate size, they are among the most highly commercially valued species.

All cetaceans are mammals and must go to the surface of the water to breathe air. Their young are born alive with the calves spending several years with their mothers. Many species form discrete units, called 'pods', composed of females, calves and juveniles. Whales can be classified as belonging to either northern or southern hemisphere populations of the species, since a particular group rarely crosses the equator. For baleen whales, feeding occurs in the cold polar seas where the animals eat intensely for four to five months, living off accumulated fat for the remainder of the year. Breeding and nursing takes place in the warmer equatorial waters. Sperm whales tend to remain in temperate water and feed all year long. Adult males, when not leading a harem of females and their young, may make a solitary venture into colder water.

The minimal descriptions presented here represent more knowledge than commercial hunters possessed when they began massive exploitation of these animals. Yet such information is essential for the rational management and conservation of a species, and is crucial to setting regulations and catch limits for whales. A lack of data concerning migratory patterns, reproductive and breeding behaviours, nutritional requirements and interactions with other marine species remains a major obstacle for the IWC in its attempts to effectively protect whale populations.

Economic History of Whaling

For thousands of years aboriginal hunting of whales has been a subsistence and cultural activity. Commercial whaling began with the Basques in the Bay of Biscay in the eleventh century. Hunted intensively for their meat, oil, and whalebone (for use in furniture and clothing), right whale populations deteriorated rapidly. The Basques extended their hunting grounds to the North Atlantic, where they were joined by British and Dutch hunters. The Basque industry ended in the sixteenth century as a result of stiff competition from the British and Dutch and as a result of the increasing rarity of right whales. The latter also caused a decline in the Dutch industry by the seventeenth century, however, German and French hunters and European settlers in America readily filled the gap with other whale stocks.[4]

An episode illustrative of whaling practices at the time is the story of the grey whales which breed off the coast of southern California in United States waters. Their nursery was discovered in 1851 and commercial whalers proceeded to slaughter the local population to the point of extinction. With the nursery depleted, the whalers destroyed their own industry, in addition to decimating the California grey whale. When the American Civil War limited the US' participation in whaling and the petroleum oil industry emerged, the end of much North American commercial whaling operations came about in the late 1800s.[5]

As target species were depleted, the types of species hunted and the areas they were hunted needed to be continually expanded. In order to remain economically efficient, the industry required larger ships which sailed on longer journeys to the South Pacific and Indian Oceans in search of unexploited stocks. By the 1890s, new technologies had greatly improved efficiency. The Norwegians had invented the harpoon gun, which enabled whalers to hunt the faster swimming whales by firing an explosive shell into the animal, killing it upon detonation.[6] Around this time, steam engines allowed ships to engage in pelagic or high seas whaling as far away as the Antarctic seas. In 1901, approximately 10,000 whales were harvested there.[7] World War I inhibited the industry's operation but, by 1925, the invention of the slip stern ship enabled whalers to pull the captured animal on board for processing. By the end of the 1930s, 85 per cent of the worlds' catch came from the Antarctic, with nearly 55,000 whales killed there in 1938.[8]

Gradual recognition that the industry's future was threatened by a rapid global decline in whale stocks, dawned in the 1930s. An annual catch of 43,219 whales also created a surplus in the whale-oil market which led to lower prices.[9] The industry decided to take measures to protect its commercial interests, in the same manner as cartels would, and steps were taken to limit catches through private agreements.[10] In 1931 a coordinated international effort to establish catch limits was made by the adoption of the Convention for the Regulation of Whaling.[11] These international legal developments need to be seen in the context of the international law of the sea, as it existed then and today.

International Law of the Sea

States have territorial sovereignty over all the resources within their 'territorial seas'. Territorial seas once extended three nautical miles out from the shoreline, but this limit was increased during the 1970s and 1980s to a maximum of 12 nautical miles from the shoreline. Beyond the territorial sea is the 'exclusive economic zone' (EEZ) which coastal States may claim, and it extends to 200 nautical miles from the shoreline. It is different from the territorial sea in that the coastal State has fewer rights over those activities unrelated to economic resource utilization in that area (eg it has less control over the movements of foreign vessels). In the EEZ, the coastal State has exclusive jurisdiction over economic resources, the most important of which is fisheries. An area known as the 'high seas' extends from the outer edge of a State's EEZ (or territorial sea if it has not claimed an EEZ) to the outer edge of another State's EEZ or territorial waters. In its territorial waters and EEZ ('coastal waters'), the coastal State has sovereign rights to exploit the economic resources there. These resources include whales which are, in general, considered a part of the national fishery resource. Any whale conservation measures taken in the territorial seas are voluntary only.

Somewhat more controversial in international law are the international duties to conserve fishery resources in the EEZ. The 1982 UN Convention on the Law of the Sea (UNCLOS) sets out these duties and, although almost all States have signed the Convention, it has not yet come into force. Therefore, one can only say that these conservation duties are still evolving as rules of law outside of UNCLOS and are not yet binding as treaty law. Unless it has signed a voluntary agreement not to do so, the coastal State may legally choose to exploit and deplete the fisheries resources in its EEZ. Even within the terms of UNCLOS, the obligation to conserve fisheries is vague. However, in the cases of marine mammals and highly migratory species – both of which include cetaceans – UNCLOS requires at the least that States cooperate to conserve, manage and study them. Yet, when the Convention comes into force, this obligation will not be compulsory in the sense of being subject to binding decisions by an international tribunal; rather, it will offer political leverage to conservation interests.

On the high seas, all States have equal access to the waters and rights to use the economic resources contained therein. Whales, like other resources in the high seas, belong to no one and are not subject to exclusive control by any State, they are 'free for all'. However, the International Court of Justice has recognized that there is a general obligation for States to cooperate in fisheries conservation on the high seas.[12] Again, however, the duty is vague.

When it comes into force, UNCLOS will require that States cooperate to ensure the conservation of cetaceans and, in relation to the high seas, this obligation is compulsory.

The Failed 1931 Convention

States have taken voluntary measures to conserve whales in both coastal waters and the high seas, beginning multilaterally with the 1931 Convention for the Regulation of Whaling.

The primary purpose of the 1931 Convention was the preservation of the commercial whaling industry, which depended on the abundance of whale populations. It regulated whaling in all waters, including the territorial waters, and prohibited the killing of right whales and the killing of calves, females accompanied by calves, and immature individuals.[13] Implementation of the Convention was limited, however, and the great whales' decline continued. In 1937 the Convention was amended, expanding protective measures to include a ban on the taking of grey whales, the setting of closed seasons, limits on hunting areas, and identifying hunting seasons for all commercial species.[14] This did not prevent 8,000 more whales being killed in 1937 than in the previous year. The following year humpbacks received additional protection and a whale sanctuary was declared (albeit in an area that was not subjected to hunting) in the Convention's 1938 Protocol.

Most attempts to protect whale stocks under the 1931 Convention failed. There were several reasons for this: lack of scientific knowledge resulted in inadequate conservation measures; some major whaling States refused to sign the Convention;[15] and no enforcement mechanisms were in place, leaving it to the individual States to police their own whaling vessels. World War II temporarily interrupted the activities of whaling countries. Following the war, the political climate became increasingly amenable to international supervisory schemes, and the creation of the United Nations established new roles for international organizations such as the IWC.

The Ambivalent 1946 Convention

Following the call by the United States for a conference on the need for a new international convention for the protection of whales, the ICRW was signed by 15 States in 1946. An innovative element of the ICRW was the establishment of the IWC, a central supervisory body with authority to issue binding regulations for the protection of whales.[16] This avoids the need for adoption of protocols to the Convention itself. The Convention's regulations are set out in a Schedule, a document appended to the Convention. While amendments to the ICRW itself can only be made by adoption of protocols to it, under Article III of the ICRW, a three-quarters majority vote is needed to amend the binding regulations in the Schedule. A simple majority is all that is needed for the Commission to set its own procedural rules and resolve on non-binding recommendations. Parties to the Convention are members of the Commission and each member has one vote.

The ICRW reflects the conflicting objectives of its negotiators. First, the Preamble acknowledges the need for conservation of whales with the statement: the 'history of whaling has seen overfishing of one area after another and of one species of whale after another' to near extinction, so that 'it is essential to protect all species of whales from further overfishing'. The Preamble then states, however, that 'increases in the size of whale stocks will permit increases in the number of whales which may be captured. . .'. The tension between conservation of whales and preservation of the whaling industry is inherent.

Under Article V(2) of the ICRW, amendments to the regulations in the Schedule must be those:

> that are necessary to carry out the objectives and purposes of the Convention and to provide for the conservation, development, and optimum utilization of the whale resources.

Amendments to the regulations must be based on scientific findings and take into account the interests of consumers and the whaling industry. The relationship between the dual objectives of the ICRW remains fundamentally unclear. It continues to generate heated debate as whaling nations decry the subversion of the purpose of the ICRW by conservationist interests.

The powers of the ICRW

Ambiguity also surrounds the scope of the ICRW. Article V(1) permits the IWC to adopt regulations fixing:

- protected and unprotected species;
- open and closed seasons;
- open and closed waters, including designation of sanctuary areas;
- size limits for each species;
- time, methods and intensity of whaling (including maximum numbers of whales to be taken in a specific season);
- type and specification of gear and apparatus and appliances which may be used;
- methods of measurement;
- catch returns and other statistical and biological methods; and
- methods of inspection.

The extent of these regulatory powers is not clearly defined. For example, is a total indefinite moratorium on commercial whaling within the scope of the IWC's powers to declare a 'closed season'? Although a closed season would be in keeping with the conservation purposes contained in the Preamble, there is no language concerning the power to impose a closed season of indefinite duration.

An additional tendency to sink into bathos when fixing regulations is generated by the fact that the most of the IWC's work is supported primarily by whaling States. In particular, the IWC relies for its information on the scientific data generated by pro-whaling interests. Much of this information is generated through States' commercial whaling operations and only with their voluntary cooperation can the IWC develop reliably informed conservation and protection measures. Since it must consider this information in order to make its decisions, a failure by the Parties to provide statistical information on whale catches can undermine and even paralyse the promulgation of regulatory measures by the IWC.

Article V(3) establishes an Objections Procedure. Regulations take effect 90 days after all Parties are notified and, upon notification, a Party can object. Parties may opt out of a binding regulation in the Schedule by making such an objection against it. For the past 40 years this procedure has effectively delayed implementation of numerous protective measures because objecting countries undermine common management of a collective resource. At the 1992 annual meeting of the IWC, Norway announced its intention to act upon its objection to the 1982 moratorium decision on commercial whaling, so as to recommence Norwegian commercial whaling in the 1993 season.

There are no prerequisites for becoming a Party to the Convention or to join the Commission. It is not even necessary that Parties be commercial or whaling States. The overriding goal of environmental groups is to stop whaling by obtaining a three-quarters majority in the IWC. Non-whaling countries, with no commercial interest in whales, have therefore been encouraged or assisted to join the IWC, by which means they may gain the politically beneficial label of being 'environmentalist' without suffering any economic cost. As more non-whaling States become Party to the ICRW, increasing pressure is being exerted on the IWC to establish more stringent measures for the protection of whales and to encourage the end of commercial whaling. This has marginalized the pro-whaling States, which have repeatedly threatened to leave the ICRW system. On the other hand, pro-whaling States have now adopted a similar retaliatory strategy; providing development aid to small island States without an interest in commercial whaling or whale conservation, luring them to join the IWC and persuading them to vote for commercial whaling.[17]

These tactics stress the ageing IWC system. They force IWC members into polarized camps, rhetorical language and hypocritical statements. Some frank and constructive dialogues are needed to enable States to negotiatie a way towards more stable solutions to the problems of whale conservation.

ENVIRONMENTAL PRESSURE ON THE IWC

With its initial membership weighted towards pro-whaling governments, the IWC's whale conservation regulations were extremely lax during the 1940s to 1960s. This period was marked by repeated clashes during annual meetings over quotas and seasonal limits. Several members (eg Norway and The Netherlands) frequently threatened to withdraw from the Convention if their demands for quota were not met. This resulted in unsustainably large quotas. For example, in 1964 the Scientific Committee advised a whale-harvest limit of 2,833 Blue Whale Units (BWUs).[18] The IWC disregarded the recommendation and set the quota at 8,000 BWUs.[19] The regulations very not very effective anyway, as no international observer or enforcement mechanism had been established.

In the 1970s, this dismal record was challenged by increasing public awareness. Broad concern over deterioration of the global environment was manifested in the 1972 United Nations Conference on the Human Environment (UNCHE) in Stockholm. Committee II of the Conference, responsible for 'environmental aspects of natural resource management', recommended a ten-year moratorium on commercial whaling to allow time for whale stocks to recover. Evidence of the protectionist tone of the Conference is present in Principle 4 of the Stockholm Declaration which declares man's, 'special responsibility to safeguard and wisely manage the heritage of wildlife.'[20]

Following the Stockholm Declaration, pressure on the IWC to declare a permanent moratorium on whaling grew. Yet, despite arguments that Antarctic whale populations were so depleted that a total ban on commercial whaling for 15 years was necessary for fin whales and 50 years for blue whales to allow them to recover completely,[21] the IWC's Scientific Committee found that 'a blanket moratorium cannot be justified scientifically.'[22]

In 1975, the Commission's work was greatly affected by the entry into force of the Convention on International Trade of Endangered Species of Wild Fauna and Flora (CITES),[23] a powerful tool for the protection of endangered species, including whales. CITES regulates international trade in species which are listed in one of three Appendices to the Convention: commercial trade of Appendix I species is prohibited. By 1983 sperm, fin, sei, blue, humpback, bowhead, right, Bryde's, grey and bottlenose whales and several dolphins had been placed in Appendix I. All cetaceans not listed in Appendix I appear in Appendix II, which imposes conservative controls on trade in listed species.[24] The listing of cetacean species in CITES occurred over time but, eventually, CITES covered more whale species than the IWC. CITES has the advantage of a larger membership and a clearer mandate to protect endangered species than the ICRW. Political pressure was exerted then on the IWC to adopt stronger conservation measures, the sought after objective of many member States being a ban on commercial whaling.

The 1982 UNCLOS created opportunities to adopt stringent conservation measures. Under Article 65 it requires States to:

> cooperate with a view to the conservation of marine mammals and in the case of cetaceans [they] shall in particular work through the appropriate international organizations for their conservation, management and study.

It is noteworthy that this provision specifically addresses conservation of cetaceans without referring to them as a 'resource'. Nor does Article 65 require optimal utilization of whales, as is required for the use of other fisheries under the Convention.[25] Although UNCLOS is not yet in force, some of its provisions already have the effect of international law and, arguably, Article 65 is among those.

Regional pressures

Regional environmental pressures have also affected the IWC. These have occurred in both the northern and southern hemispheres. The Convention on the Conservation of Antarctic Marine Living Resources of 1979 (CCAMLR) has as its primary purpose the protection of Antarctic marine living resources, including their 'rational use'. Article II of the Convention embraces an ecosystemic approach to conservation of resources. It accounts for inter-species relationships and, therefore, protects baleen whales by means including the maintenance of their supplies of krill.[26]

Similarly, the 1979 Berne Convention on Conservation of European Wildlife and Habitats charges signatory States with a duty to conserve wild flora and fauna and their natural habitats, especially those species and habitats whose conservation requires the cooperation of several States.[27] In particular, the signatories agree to provide protection for migratory species. These are listed in Appendix II which contains all small cetacean species regularly present in the North and Baltic Seas. More recently, the Bonn Convention on the Conservation of Migratory Species of Wild Animals has enabled regional conservation measures to be taken,[28] under the Agreement on the Conservation of Small Cetaceans of the Baltic and North Seas. The latter was signed on 17 March 1992 and binds States in the region to maintain a favourable conservation status for small cetaceans.

The 1992 Agreement was formulated following commitments made by Ministers responsible for the protection of the North Sea environment. In March 1990 they and the European Community signed a Memorandum of Understanding on Small Cetaceans in the North Sea. The Memorandum recognized that the intentional taking of small cetaceans was generally forbidden under their national laws and obliged them to cooperate to achieve 'favourable conservation status' for small cetacean populations in the North Sea.

European Community pressures

The initiatives of the European Community should also be noted. In 1981 it adopted a Whale Products Regulation, prohibiting the import, for commercial purposes, of whale products listed in an Annex to the Regulation and requiring a license for non-commercial imports.[29] The Regulation was adopted to conform to the EC's obligations under CITES and is directly binding on all member States without requiring them to implement national legislation in order for it to have effect. The EC's Habitat Directive requires that member States establish measures to protect listed species in their natural range[30] (the listed species include all cetaceans). Member States are to prohibit capture or killing, as well as holding or trading of them.

National pressures

Other than regional developments, national laws have contributed to changes in the management practices of the IWC. The rights of a coastal State, within its EEZ, permit it to ban whaling within 200 miles of its shores. This constitutes a huge area within which whaling is potentially illegal. Some States have imposed bans on commercial whaling in their waters and by vessels under their flag. The United States, Australia and New Zealand are examples. The United States Marine Mammal Protection Act (MMPA) of 1972 emphasizes the international importance of marine mammals for aesthetic, recreational and economic reasons, and sets out management procedures based on scientific information and advice, which does not incorporate industry needs. Exceptions to the prohibitions on intentional killing are made for aboriginal hunting and scientific needs. The Act also prohibits US citizens or US registered vessels from whaling on the high seas. The 1978 MMPA of New Zealand and 1980 Whale Protection Act of Australia go even further by prohibiting their citizens from taking whales from any waters, even when within the coastal zone of another State which permits whaling.[31]

Non-Governmental Organization pressures

Undoubtedly the most important political influence of all is the increasing number of intergovernmental and non-governmental organizations (NGOs) lobbying at the annual meetings of the IWC. They can be accorded observer status under the ICRW, the only qualification being the requirement for the relevant organization to have offices in three countries. A wide range of NGOs, such as Greenpeace, the World Wide Fund for Nature, Whale and Dolphin Conservation Society, International Fund for Animal Welfare and even the International Assembly of Rabbi, are permitted to attend, and their number has increased dramatically – from five organizations in 1965 to more than 50 in the 1980s.[32]

MAINTAINING THE MORATORIUM

The key issue facing the IWC at present, from a conservationist perspective, is the maintenance of the moratorium on commercial whaling. The first call for a moratorium on commercial whaling came out of the 1972 Stockholm Conference. Proposals for a moratorium were defeated at the 1972 and 1973 annual IWC meetings. The Commission, however, agreed to phase-out Antarctic fin whaling by 1976 and at the 1973 meeting defined specific regions within the southern hemisphere which enabled more regulations over individual whale populations. At its 30th meeting in 1979, the IWC heard proposals from the Republic of Seychelles to impose a ban on sperm whaling and to establish a whale sanctuary in the Indian Ocean. These proposals received the necessary three-quarters majority to pass.

In 1982 at its 34th meeting, the IWC took a historic step when it approved a proposal banning commercial whaling indefinitely. As amended, section 10(e) of the Schedule to the ICRW provides:

> Notwithstanding the other provisions of paragraph 10, catch limits for the killing of commercial purposes of whales from all stocks for the 1986 coastal and the 1985/86 pelagic seasons and thereafter shall be zero. This provision will be kept under review based upon the best scientific advice, and by 1990 at the latest, the Commission will undertake a comprehensive assessment of the effects of this decision on whale stocks and consider modifications of this provision and the establishment of other catch limits.

Twenty-five States voted in favour of the amendment, seven voted against and five abstained. Although opposed by active whaling States, the ban acknowledged the threat to whale stocks from continued exploitation, even though insufficient information on populations and their behaviour was available to fully support this position. However, the ICRW itself contains a loophole to the moratorium, in the guise of the Objections Procedure. This enables States opposed to the moratorium to register objections and continue their commercial activities. Japan, Norway, Peru, and the former USSR lodged formal objections; Peru withdrew after threats of unilateral trade sanctions by the US. Japan, after certification by the US under its Pelly Amendment,[33] agreed to comply with the moratorium by 1988. It remains to be seen whether similar action will be taken against Norway, which announced in 1992 that it was to act upon its objection to the moratorium decision and to recommence commercial whaling.

Section 10(e) establishes zero catch limits for commercial whaling. Although Article V of the ICRW authorizes the Commission to set open and closed seasons and quotas for species, there is no language to indicate appropriate limits on the length of closed seasons. Much legal controversy also centres around the ambiguity of the second sentence of section 10(e), which obligates the Commission to initiate a 'comprehensive assessment' of whale stocks by 1990 and to undertake the establishment of new catch limits. Although the undertaking must be commenced by 1990, there is no time set for completion of the assessment. It must be assumed that several years would be necessary to complete sufficient studies to satisfy the requirement that the assessment be comprehensive. As the 1982 moratorium did not take practical effect until 1988, when Japan ceased its commercial hunting of minke and fin whales, assessment of the ban's effectiveness for these species is still inconclusive.

Pro-whaling States argue that section 10(e) does not require an assessment of *all* stocks prior to reopening hunting on specific species. Rather, they assert that as each species is assessed, new catch limits should be issued for those populations capable of sustaining exploitation. To support this claim, whaling States may point to the existing IWC practice of conducting individual stock assessments and emphasize that the second sentence of section 10(e) does not use 'all' to modify 'stocks'. The text, however, is not clear on this point.

The argument available to conservationists is that the IWC's practice of making individual stock assessments is due only to the limited information available on many species and the lack of financial resources available to the Scientific Committee for a series of overall assessments of whale populations. Despite the case-by-case practice, in theory, the Commission has integrated an ecosystem approach into its management schemes. Therefore, 'comprehensive assessment' might be interpreted as requiring an overall determination on the viability of all whale stocks in order to provide accurate information on which species can sustain long-term exploitation and at what levels. In addition, conservationists require that a comprehensive assessment examine environmental factors affecting whale populations. For example, the exposure of Antarctic waters to increased ultra-violet radiation, due the Antarctic atmosphere's ozone layer having been damaged by man-made chemical changes, is said to be damaging the krill upon which the whole ecosystem is based. Given the limited resources available for conducting assessments, a comprehensive assessment would mean that the moratorium is to stay in effect for many years.

The moratorium, as currently formulated, is nevertheless temporary, even if indefinite. Once the 'comprehensive assessment' criterion in section 10(e) is fulfilled, lifting of the moratorium becomes a real probability.

REVISED MANAGEMENT PROCEDURES

As part of its undertaking to establish other catch limits under section 10(e) of the Schedule, the Commission is developing Revised Management Procedures (RMP) for commercial whaling. At its 26th meeting in 1974, the

IWC abandoned the BWU measure for setting catch limits and implemented the New Management Procedures (NMP). The NMP remain on the ICRW Schedule although the 1982 moratorium on commercial whaling is in effect. The concept of ecosystem management, instead of single species management, gained support in the 1970s and the NMP were intended to reflect this trend.

Under the NMP, whales are placed into one of three categories:

(1) Initial Management Stocks, which may be reduced in a controlled way to achieve, but not fall below, optimum harvesting levels.
(2) Sustained Management Stocks, which should be maintained at their optimum levels with commercial whaling permitted.
(3) Protection Stocks which are below optimum levels and require full protection.[34]

Ideally, the NMP were to account not only for numbers of whales, but also for size, weight, reproductive success of individuals and interaction with other species and the influence of variable environmental factors. However, the biological data required to make the NMP work effectively were always unavailable and catch quotas were therefore set at the existing status quo, while whale populations continued to diminish.[35]

The intention behind the current deliberations on the RMP is to remedy these failings. At the Commission's 43rd meeting in Glasgow in 1992, a catch limit algorithm was adopted as a pivotal part of the RMP. This is a mathematical formula designed to account for all the variables affecting stability of whale stock sizes and for setting a catch limit which would ensure that populations are not depleted. It would be applied to particular stocks, once they are comprehensively assessed. As applied to the known stocks in their current depleted conditions, the conservative formula would allow an extremely low limit on those stocks where any catches were permitted at all.

In order to put the RMP into effect, a supporting administrative system needs to be established. At its 1992 annual meeting, the IWC resolved that an integral part of the RMP is to be a 'fully effective' inspection and observation system. This would consist of two vital elements:

(1) population assessment and monitoring; and
(2) an international inspection and observer scheme.

For population assessments, survey standards need to be elaborated and it has been suggested that these need to be conducted at least every five years. For monitoring, linking with the proposed international observer scheme is necessary.[36]

The IWC international observer scheme was established in 1972 and consisted of exchanges between national observers of whaling States placed upon foreign whaling vessels in four regions or types of operation. Observers were made available voluntarily by whaling States in direct proportion to the number of whaling vessels the State had in operation. They were placed upon the vessels of foreign whaling States and were responsible for reporting infractions. The international observer scheme has been in limbo since 1986, during the period of the commercial moratorium. If commercial whaling is reintroduced in future, an observer scheme will be essential to management of the industry. Even at present, there is a possible need for the introduction of some kind of observer scheme for aboriginal whaling.

The 1972 scheme had significant failings, which the RMP could remedy. The RMP observer scheme should consist of a truly multilaterally organized international inspectorate, rather than bilateral exchanges, and observers should be required to meet set standards of competence in the task of whaling management. Competence in communication, or the availability of an interpreter in the language of the State whose national are being monitored, is also essential. The arrangement of bilateral exchanges of observers based upon the sponsoring nation's vessel numbers sometimes resulted in a shortage of observers on the vessels of States with large fleets. A multilateral approach would cover these shortfalls and could be funded through increased IWC membership dues or a State levy based upon the value of the whale products.

Southern Ocean Sanctuary

Whale species are located in geographically distinct areas. Therefore, sanctuaries for different species can be established by cordoning off areas which contain populations of commercial species. Sanctuaries provide indefinite protection of these populations and could possibly render commercial whaling in less populous regions uneconomic. Establishment of whale sanctuaries is provided for in Article V of the ICRW.

The Indian Ocean Sanctuary was created in 1970, initially for a period of ten years. It offers protection to sperm whales, populations of Bryde's whales and other baleen whales. Its period of existence was renewed for another ten years in 1979, for three years in 1989 and indefinitely in 1992, but subject to review in 2002.[37]

At the 44th meeting of the IWC in 1992, France proposed a Southern Ocean Whale Sanctuary.[38] The proposal, as presented, would establish a sanctuary of indefinite duration with a review of its impact on whale stocks ten years after its establishment. This would protect the Antarctic region – where minke whale populations are much sought after and where most recent whaling activity has taken place. The Southern Ocean Whale Sanctuary proposal has therefore received vehement opposition from Japan, which is the main proponent of minke whaling in this region.

In order to give Commission members an opportunity to examine the proposal, its consideration was rescheduled for the 45th meeting in 1993, when a Resolution was adopted which endorsed the concept of that sanctuary and the need to address outstanding issues relating to it.[39] Because Japan has concerns about the non-scientific purposes of a Southern Ocean Sanctuary, (ie that it may fall foul of the requirements that amendments to the Schedule have a scientific basis),[40] the Resolution invited IWC States to enhance their relevant scientific and monitoring activities. Australia will host an intersessional working group to address these concerns and to formulate recommendations for the Commission. It seems possible that the sanctuary might then be adopted by the IWC in 1994, subject to a time limit, and that pro-whaling States may make reservations against its application to them.

Scientific Whaling

There is growing concern over abuse of Article VIII of the ICRW, which provides for the issuance of special permits for the taking of whales for scientific research, 'not withstanding anything contained in the Convention'. The contracting government alone is responsible for imposing catch limit conditions on the permit holder. Thus, the killing or taking of whales under Article VIII is exempt from regulation by the IWC and from the commercial whaling moratorium.

Japan, Norway, the former USSR and Iceland have maximized their use of this provision to continue taking whales. Suspicion that some States were using the exception simply to circumvent the moratorium led the IWC to require that proposed scientific permits be submitted to the IWC Scientific Committee for prior review so that it could issue recommendations on the permit. Several whaling States protested at this suggestion, arguing that the discretion to issue permits falls within the exclusive jurisdiction of the State.

The IWC's initial response was to amend the Scientific Committees's Rules of Procedure so as to enable the Scientific Committee to review and make recommendations on the scientific value of a proposed permit. In 1986 the IWC resolved that specific criteria to promote the comprehensive assessment of the moratorium be applied to the review of permits.[41] The following year, the IWC also adopted a mechanism to review the Scientific Committee's report on proposed permits and to recommend to the Parties that they refrain from issuing permits which fail to meet the IWC's four criteria for scientific value or the IWC's conservation policies.[42] Opposing States question the legality of these IWC resolutions as infringements on the exclusive rights of their governments to issue scientific permits. However, as the resolutions are merely recommendatory, these States are not bound by the decisions of the IWC or its Scientific Committee on this matter.

Legal considerations aside, States which issue scientific whaling permits without an objective scientific justification, undermine the effects of the commercial whaling moratorium and continue to threaten the recovery of depleted whale stocks. For example, in 1992 Norway proposed a special permit for the taking of 382 minke whales in the North Atlantic between 1992 and 1994, notwithstanding the IWC finding that the proposal failed to satisfy all the criteria specified in its 1986 and 1987 resolutions on scientific research.[43]

Pirate Whaling

There are a few nations which are not signatories to the ICRW and which still have vessels which engage in commercial whaling, notably Taiwan and South Korea. Most non-IWC whaling is conducted from shore stations with sperm, sei, fin, and minke as the primary captured species. While most non-members cooperate in data exchange, the failure of some non-members to send catch information to the Bureau of Whaling Statistics (an independent institution based in Norway) results in inaccurate assessments of whale stocks by the IWC. This harms IWC conservation activities, particularly when the population affected is a high seas one in which a number of States have an interest.

'Pirate whaling' is referred to as such because those non-member States involved are knowingly interfering with the conservation policies of the principal international organization for regulation of the industry. Of course, non-parties to the ICRW are not bound by IWC regulations, and so are not in breach of them. However, some signatory States, Japan in particular, have been known to allow circumvention of IWC control by registration of their vessels under the flag of a non-IWC member, such as Taiwan. The IWC, UN Environment Programme and UN Food and Agricultural Organization have each encouraged non-parties to accede to the ICRW so as to close these gaps in the regulatory system.

In 1979, the IWC began compiling a registry of all whaling vessels subject to IWC quotas in order to identify pirate whalers. In 1987 Norway, Iceland and Japan refused to supply further information for the register due to 'terrorist' activites against their vessels by environmental groups. Nevertheless, the register continues in existence and now extends to all whaling vessels and is compiled from publicly available sources of information.

In a further effort to curtail pirate whaling activities, the IWC has passed several resolutions banning not only the importation of whaling products from non-member to member countries, but also the transfer of whaling vessels and expertise to non-member countries.

Aboriginal Whaling

Aboriginal whaling is an ancient practice. There is no distinction between aboriginal and commercial whaling in the ICRW, but exemptions for aboriginal hunting are set forth in section 13 of the Schedule. It provides that seasonal catch limits may be set to satisfy aboriginal subsistence needs. Permits for aboriginal whaling cannot exceed the maximum sustainable yield of the stocks concerned.

As the ICRW does not define 'aboriginal' or 'subsistence', a curious proposal has been put to the IWC by Japan and Norway that coastal communities, which have developed around commercial whaling, should be classified as 'aboriginal', even though the whales caught were not killed for local consumption. This proposal draws attention to the increasing size and sophistication of aboriginal whaling activities elsewhere.

With whale populations severely depleted, aboriginal whaling is receiving greater critical scrutiny, especially from the opponents of whaling. However, the imposition of bans on aboriginal whaling is clearly a sensitive matter, requiring a balance between the cultural and developmental rights of native peoples and the need to protect whales. For example, the Inuit of Alaska, Canada, Greenland and Siberia hunt the bowhead, a protected species under the NMP. In 1977, at the urging of the Scientific Committee, the Commission imposed a ban on all hunting of the bowhead, but for only one season. Because of its existing obligations to native Americans, the US challenged the 1977 ban on the grounds that the ICRW only applies to commercial whaling. A compromise was reached, setting current quotas for the bowhead at 44 for the Alaskan Inuit; the Scientific Committee has estimated that the entire bowhead population stands at only 7,500 animals.

Anti-whaling States with indigenous whaling populations, such as the US, are at a political disadvantage when negotiating with pro-whaling States as the latter can seek concessions from the former in return for permission for aboriginal whaling. Clearly, a balanced formula needs to be struck in order to ensure that this aboriginal whaling proceeds on a rational and conservative basis, without becoming a political hostage to commercial whaling interests.

SMALL CETACEANS

A major issue dividing IWC members is whether IWC competence encompasses the smaller whale species, porpoises and dolphins. Small cetaceans, historically considered by the industry to be under 30 feet, exhibit more coastal and less migratory behaviour than larger species; form bigger social groups; have a more variable reproductive cycle, making them more vulnerable to depletion, pollution, and habitat destruction. The IWC's Scientific Committee has stated that species in danger of imminent extinction include the Indus River dolphin, Mexican vaquita and the baiji (Yangtze River dolphin), all with populations numbering in the low hundreds.

Many States maintain that the IWC lacks the legal competence to regulate smaller cetaceans. Their primary arguments are that small cetaceans are not mentioned in the ICRW and, therefore, were not intended for regulation and that any IWC regulations over certain small cetaceans would intrude upon a State's sovereign rights to control resources in its coastal waters, since many small whales, dolphins, and porpoises occur within 200 miles off shore. In truth, it is the latter which generates coastal State resistance to the inclusion of smaller cetaceans within the IWC's authority. As small cetaceans are often caught, intentionally or incidentally, as part of local fisheries, States are concerned that IWC regulations protecting small cetaceans will impose unwelcome constraints on sectors of their local fishing industries. We will return to this concern shortly.

From a legal point of view, the use of a vernacular interpretation of the term 'whale' may limit the application of the ICRW to small cetaceans. At the time of the ICRW's drafting, only 12 great whale species were recognized as being over-exploited. These species are listed in the Annex of Nomenclature attached to the Final Act of the 1946 Conference which resulted in the signing of the ICRW.[48] The Final Act recommends that the Annex be used as a guide by governments represented at the Conference, but the Final Act is itself not part of the ICRW. Neither the ICRW nor the Final Act of the Conference contain language limiting the IWC's ability to regulate additional species.

On the other hand, a scientific interpretation of the word 'whales' would embrace small cetaceans. The ICRW Preamble does refer to the need to protect 'all species of whales', which might support the broader scientific interpretation. As the intended scope of meaning of the term 'whale' in the ICRW is not clear, we must also look to subsequent IWC practice in interpreting its own mandate. This clearly indicates that small cetaceans be included. For example, regulations on minke whales were adopted by the Convention's Parties, although minke were not included among the great whales in the Annex of Nomenclature. Other small cetacean species have also been individually listed in the Schedule. For example, at the 1977 meeting a Schedule amendment redefining 'small-type whaling'[49] to include some specifically identified small cetaceans was adopted. This concerned information requirements for small type whaling operations. In 1980, the IWC broadened its remit to include in the Schedule a regulation on the actual taking of a small cetacean not listed in the Annex, when killer whales were included in the 1979 ban on pelagic whaling. At its 34th meeting, controversy continued over the IWC's competence to regulate small cetaceans; at that particular meeting, attempts to regulate taking of Baird's beaked whale engendered the debate. The debate is on-going and in 1990 at the 42nd IWC meeting catch limits for Baird's beaked whale in the North Pacific were still unregulated. [50]

The IWC has, in practice, also taken on small cetaceans explicitly and directly as a group, although in the form of recommendations contained in resolutions rather than regulations contained in the ICRW Schedule. In the first instance, in 1973, the Scientific Committee of the IWC recommended that a subcommittee be created to identify areas of research for small cetaceans, analyse small cetacean taxonomy and assess global populations of these species.[51] The Subcommittee's report found that minimal data on most small cetaceans existed. In 1975 the Scientific Committee then proposed that the IWC consider managing direct catches of small cetaceans with the Subcommittee expanding on the proposal in its 1976 report which announced:

[T]here is an urgent need for an international body to manage effectively stocks of all cetaceans not covered by the current IWC Schedule. This body should concern itself with all types of exploitation . . . both incidental and deliberate. All nations involved in the exploitation of small as well as large cetaceans, should be included in such a body . . .[52]

Maintaining its history of making incremental steps in the face of opposition from some of its member States, the IWC responded to the subcommittee by requesting the Scientific Committee to include direct – as opposed to incidental – catches of small cetaceans in its agenda.[53] To facilitate reporting requirements, small cetacean fisheries were divided into three categories: small-type whaling, direct fisheries for small cetaceans, and fisheries with incidental takes of small cetaceans. The compromise language adopted concerned only study of the conservation problems, ie a passive role. Yet many later resolutions have become gradually more proactive, calling upon States to reduce their direct catches of certain small cetaceans. The IWC has recently concerned itself also with indirect catches and has passed a resolution opposing large-scale driftnet fishing[54]

Significant steps toward rational organization of conservative management of small cetaceans were taken in 1992, when a resolution proposed by Brazil was adopted calling for the establishment of a working group to consider a mechanism to address small cetaceans in the IWC.[55] In 1993 a further resolution was adopted extending this group's work, including among its tasks the examination of voluntary funding mechanisms to assist the participation of developing country coastal States in its work.[56]

On the whole, however, it is questionable as to how well placed the IWC is to manage small cetaceans. The main way that small cetaceans die in fisheries is indirectly – ie through their incidental capture in fisheries for other species, such as tuna. For example, dolphin swim above yellow-fin tuna in the south east tropical Pacific Ocean and are caught by fishermen who identify the presence of tuna below the waters' surface by the presence of dolphins above. Small cetaceans, such as Dall's porpoises, are also caught in large-scale gill net or driftnet fishery operations. Current statistics on small cetacean catches are inadequate, largely because reporting requirements are voluntary, and certain IWC members have expressed reservations about supplying the information as a means of reaffirming their opposition to IWC regulation of small cetaceans.

Allowing the IWC to regulate indirect takes of small cetaceans has significant implications for the management of commercial fishing. Several other international and regional fisheries organizations have developed management expertise for complex multispecies coastal and pelagic fisheries. Paragraph 4.16 of the UN Food and Agriculture Organization (FAO) Marine Mammal Action Plan recommends that national governments provide information to the FAO on numbers of marine mammals killed incidental to other activities. Collation and publication of the data is to be done jointly with other organizations concerned with marine resources conservation. The Action Plan recognizes IWC competence with regards to cetacean sanctuaries and specifically urges all non-member IWC States interested in taking cetaceans, particularly large whales, to join the IWC.[57] Yet, it places the study of indirect cetacean catches in its own organization, outside the scope of the IWC. Clearly, information exchange, joint research and coordination of management schemes between the IWC and other fisheries organizations is necessary to ensure that IWC conservation measures for small cetaceans are not devised in isolation from fisheries concerns.

In conclusion, the IWC remains the most knowledgeable international body concerning cetaceans and its practices support competence to regulate direct takes of small cetaceans. At present, its activities concerning indirect takes are mostly confined to information collection and dissemination. In this regard, its expertise on cetaceans can best be utilized in conjunction with other regional fishery organizations.

THREATS TO THE IWC

The IWC is at another crossroads: having achieved little in its attempts to conserve whale stocks in its first years, it has since imposed a full moratorium on commercial whaling. Now, as the pressure to resume commercial whaling continues and the RMP takes shape, the IWC must decide whether its obligations to the whaling industry require the resumption of commercial whaling. The risk of deciding not to permit active commercial whaling in the near future is that pro-whaling States, such as Norway, Russia and Japan, may withdraw from the IWC.

In 1988 Iceland held a meeting in Reykjavik attended by Canada, Japan, Norway, the former USSR, the Faroe Islands and Greenland, to 'discuss their common situation in light of the development in the IWC'.[58] Canada is no longer a member of the IWC and Iceland withdrew in 1992. In its opening Statement at the IWC's 44th meeting, Norway delivered a threat that its continued participation in the IWC depended on a liberal interpretation of proposed RMP for minke whales.[59] At the 45th meeting in 1993, Japan expressed doubts about its future participation but has indicated that it will remain, for the present, in order to lobby against the Southern Ocean Sanctuary proposal.

On 9 April 1992, an agreement was signed by Greenland, the Faroe Islands, Iceland and Norway forming a new organization called the North Atlantic Marine Mammals Conservation Organization (NAMMCO). Its members can produce more whale products than they consume. The largest consumer market remains closed to them since IWC members have agreed by resolution not to import whale products from non-member countries. However, if Japan should leave the IWC and join NAMMCO, both producer and consumer markets would be brought together in an organization outside the auspices of the IWC.

One of the earliest international influences on the IWC was the establishment of the South Pacific Commission (SPC) by Chile, Peru and Ecuador,[60] which had as its objective the management of marine fauna of the waters in their recently declared 200-mile fisheries zones. This undermined the IWC, since the SPC announced it would follow IWC regulations except when they conflicted with 'just needs for national consumption and industrial supplies'. NAMMCO is likely to pose an even more seriously undermining threat, as its participants are likely to be the core of today's pro-whaling States supporting commercial trade in whale products.

Is it legal to form an organization in competition with, and that undermines, the IWC? As noted above, Article 65 of the 1982 UNCLOS mandates that States cooperate in the protection of cetaceans by working with 'appropriate international organizations'. The argument has been put forward by countries such as Iceland that UNCLOS allows States to decide independently whether an international organization is appropriate to the task of managing and conserving marine mammals. Yet this would allow States to operate without real coordination through their own puppet organizations. A much more sensible interpretation of the law is that there must be objective reasons for deciding that an organization is appropriate.

Clearly and objectively, the IWC qualifies as an 'appropriate organization' for the conservation of cetaceans. This fact was recognized by consensus of the international community in Chapter 17 of Agenda 21 of the 1992 UNCED.[61] It reiterates the language of Article 65 and goes further to emphasize:

> States recognize the responsibility of the International Whaling Commission for the conservation and management of whale stocks and regulation of whaling pursuant to the 1946 Convention . . . (Para 17.66(a)).

It is unlikely that NAMMCO is an appropriate organization. It is a fledgeling that lacks the resources and expertise of the IWC.

CONCLUSION

The role of international law in the conservation of whales has been fundamental. Remarkably, the rules set by IWC have usually been observed rather than breached. Many legal controversies and crises have arisen from the ambiguity of its 1946 Convention and, consequently, the proper scope of the mandate of the IWC. Revision of the Convention is necessary in order to deal effectively with these issues. Discussions concerning revision have taken place but amendments require adoption of Protocols and, to be effective, unanimous agreement among the Commission's member countries. Polarization between pro-and anti-whaling States has therefore prevented successful amendment so far. It seems that any substantial conservationist revision to the Convention would result in the withdrawal of pro-whaling countries.

Consequently, we find that the central international legal document for the conservation of whales, the ICRW, has not really been greened in the almost 50 years of its existence. It remains a fishing, rather than a wildlife conservation, convention. However, many of the members of the IWC have succeeded in having it adopt more conservative regulations, resolutions and practices than the ICRW ever originally contemplated. Further, other international laws, such as wildlife treaties, are rapidly filling the legal lacunae and becoming more effective regional tools for conservation. This is especially true in the northern hemisphere where EC and North Sea regional arrangements have been adopted concerning cetacean habitats, trade and protection.

A more politically practical approach to revision of the ICRW than wholesale reformulation is, in the short term, to tinker with it so that it continues to work more efficiently. For example, a Protocol to the ICRW may allow the Commission to deal with the management of small cetaceans in a more rational manner. Although the moratorium is conceived as a temporary measure, there are other options legally available to the IWC within the current Convention to avoid re-instituting commercial whaling. These include the placement of species within the NMP Protected Stock classification (which prohibits hunting), or the adoption of a Revised Management Scheme with very strict or negligible catch limits and strong monitoring and enforcement procedures. As long as the categorization of whale stocks has a scientific basis, the Commission can maintain an 'indefinite' ban for species exhibiting depleted levels. Sanctuaries may also become a primary mechanism for ensuring that sufficient time is given for the recovery of many populations. Yet, a disadvantage in each proposal for any measure other than a full ban on commercial whaling is that some trade in high value whale products would be legitimized and would give cover to increased smuggling by pirate operations.

In the longer term, therefore, States concerned about their image within the international community, may begin to perceive a pro-whaling stance as a political liability. With public support for commercial whaling diminishing while whale-watching in Japan gains popularity,[62] the Japanese Government may soon find itself in the untenable position of supporting an industry unwanted by most of its citizens or the international community. Whaling still provides an economic return in the smaller coastal communities of the pro-whaling countries, but its national economic importance has been marginal.

In contrast, the global economic importance of whale-watching is growing. In 1991, the whale-watching industry world-wide had direct revenues of US$ 75,592,000 and total revenues of US$ 317,881,000. It may be that the Convention can be interpreted or amended to include commercial whale-watching operations as a new branch of the whaling industry to be protected by the IWC. Moves in this direction were renewed in 1993 when a resolution proposed by Great Britain was passed.[63] It requested member States to assess the scientific and economic value of whale-watching, the IWC Secretariat to consolidate a report and a working group to be established on the subject to make recommendations to the next meeting of the IWC.

In its 47 years of existence, the IWC has evolved to embrace various cetacean species and management philosophies. As the scope of its work increases it must work in new ways with other regional organizations, particularly to protect incidental catches of small cetaceans. However, the Commission still remains the most appropriate international organization to regulate whaling. To do its work better it needs more modern and efficient legal machinery than the 1946 Convention. Eventually, it will get it, for one thing is becoming clear: the IWC is suviving its many trials but large-scale commercial whale catching is not.

11 TECHNOLOGY-BASED APPROACHES VERSUS MARKET-BASED APPROACHES

Daniel J Dudek , Richard B Stewart, Jonathan B Wiener

INTRODUCTION

The United States has experience with the two major kinds of tools available for environmental policy: technology-based, command-and-control (CAC) approaches that select a technology for industry to install; and market-based approaches that create economic incentives for industry to reduce harm to the environment, while leaving the choice and innovation of specific technologies and techniques to private actors. In the US, federal and state governments increasingly are employing the market-based approach, with both environmental and economic benefits.

Archetypal CAC regulations rely on uniform, inflexible, technology-based standards issued by the central government. This approach results in high compliance costs, restricts innovation, and discourages efficient use of resources. These rules also require detailed central planning of economic activity. Because the cost of controlling pollution varies among those subject to regulation, a CAC policy requiring them all to meet the same target, or to install the same technology, means that some regulated entities could achieve the same environmental protection through less costly means, or more protection for the same cost. Consequently, a CAC approach forces society to pay for relatively expensive environmental protection. This wastes resources and potentially arouses resistance to further environmental protection measures. In the longer run, CAC, technology-based regulation deters innovation by locking in a chosen technology and eliminating the market's reward for superior techniques; the resulting dearth of better technologies weakens the ability of CAC regulation to prevent environmental degradation.

With a market-based incentive approach, the government still sets firm environmental goals, but defines them in terms of environmental performance, not technology, leaving the choice of specific response and compliance strategies to each individual enterprise. The flexible, market-based approach harnesses the economic self-interest of each business in the service of environmental protection. Unfettered by uniform and technology-based standards, firms creatively meet these goals in the most cost-effective manner, and responses are devised to meet the needs of diverse local circumstances. Economic incentives encourage innovation of new technology and process designs, and efficiency in the use of raw materials and other inputs. Whereas improvements occur under CAC policy only when rules are reviewed and strengthened by government agencies, market-based incentives invite continuous environmental entre-preneurship in the private sector. The lower cost of compliance under market-based incentive approaches enables society to purchase more environmental protection or other desired benefits.

In the US, market-based approaches have been employed with great success in several real-world applications. They have effectively achieved environmental goals while generally cutting the costs of achieving those goals by 25 to 50 per cent or more.[1] Yet the US' CAC-dominated environmental policy of the last two decades has taken its toll, both economically and environmentally. The rediscovery of market-based incentive tools in the last five to ten years has opened the door to better policy here, which we believe should be the model for policy in Eastern Europe.

Support for this proposition begins in the section entitled 'Approaches to Environmental Policy', with a comparison of the attributes of technology-based and market-based environmental policies: their struc-ture and incentive effects, and their impacts on cost, performance, innovation, and government agencies. This section assembles the conceptual case for market incentives. In the following section, 'The Need for Comprehensive Policy', we emphasize the importance of viewing environmental issues comprehensively rather than dividing problems and treating them in narrow, piecemeal fashion. We then build the practical case for market incentives and finally, based on this experience, we suggest consideration as to how best to design environmental policy.

APPROACHES TO ENVIRONMENTAL POLICY

History and Pragmatism

Viewing environmental protection from an historical vantage point, one discerns two distinct phases in US policy.[2] The first, occurring roughly 20 years ago, created the first set of institutions dedicated specifically to the task of environmental protection. This first set of changes saw the transfer of pollution control authority from State and local works agencies to the new US Environmental Protection Agency (EPA), created in 1970;[3] and the enactment of far-reaching, technology-based federal pollution control and waste clean-up laws. The second phase is occurring now, with policy-makers moving from a system of centralized command planning to the use of economic incentives, designed to harness polluters' self-interest in the search for more efficient environmental protection. We are moving from technology-based to market-based policies.

This second stage of development in environmental management is just now blossoming in the US and throughout the world. In the US, policy experiments in this arena began modestly, almost always springing from the need to abate conflicts between economic and environmental goals. For example, the collection of policy tools known as emissions trading was first applied in the late 1970s in economically growing urban areas plagued with severe air pollution.[4] A related set of regulations, allowing trading of lead content reduction credits, was introduced in the early 1980s to reduce the economic impact upon small refiners of phasing out lead in gasoline.[5] These pragmatic exercises have demonstrated success in reducing costs – thus enabling stronger economic growth – while achieving environmental goals.

These successful experiences with market-based approaches are winning adherents all across the political and economic spectrum.[6] Practical experiences with market-based approaches, whether successes or disappointments, have improved our understanding of how best to design these programmes. Every year, new opportunities for the useful application of these incentives are identified.

This two-staged historical development is not preordained and should not be a model for policy development in Eastern Europe. It was, in many ways, an artifact of the way CAC environmental policy arose on the US political agenda in the late 1960s and early 1970s, linked to a distrust of markets as an economic system, and of competition as a cultural system. Today environmental protection is no less cherished, but with the failure of Communist economics, confidence in market mechanisms is renewed. Meanwhile, the practical success of market-based environmental policies is proving their worth.

Other nations need not repeat US history: they can adopt market-based incentive approaches from the outset of their environmental policy formulation. Such approaches are particularly appropriate in nations that are currently in transition from centrally planned to market-based economies.

CAC policies only tend to smother the emerging market economy, raise costs, and thereby raise resistance to environmental protection efforts. They could even offer a backdoor route to central economic control for those in power who resist the transition to democracy. Rather, as we are finding in the US, market-based policy tools should be applied, unless the circumstances demand other policy tools. Experimentation should be used to build practical experience. Market incentive environmental policies should be designed and set in place now to embrace the maturing market economy, and to provide appropriate price signals to guide the actions of increasingly empowered businesses and citizens toward environmentally sound economic growth.

Technology-Based and Market-Based Approaches

The aim of environmental policy interventions is to correct failures of private markets to achieve society's environmental goals. The presumption is that private markets will provide the goods and services that consumers desire. However, private markets alone will not provide adequate environmental protection when market participants treat environmental values as externalities that are not adequately reflected in the prices consumers pay for goods and services, or when participants view environmental values as public goods from which all individuals benefit but in which no individual has an adequate incentive to invest.

The government must first determine which, and to what extent, environmental market failures warrant policy intervention. Then it can decide which policy tool to employ in remedying such market failures; it is in the second decision that the authors hope to assist Eastern European policymakers. Governments (the US included) have traditionally employed CAC regulations, under which the central government typically instructs its pollution control agency to issue uniform technology-based standards. For example, the central agency may be required or authorized to identify the best available control technology (BACT) that industry should use to control pollution.

Several types of CAC, technology-based rules could be fashioned. Indeed, there is a spectrum of policy choices, each of which may be best suited to a particular problem. Under the traditional model, a uniform BACT rule would require all enterprises to employ the same control technology. Alternatively, a rule could require BACT in a separate, case-by-case determination for each enterprise. The latter method allows more attention to the local opportunities at each plant, but it magnifies the amount of central data collection and bureaucracy needed to implement pollution control, and keeps the choice of technologies in the hands of the central government.

A different, somewhat less restrictive approach that stands between the pure CAC and pure market-based ends of the spectrum is a performance standard requiring all plants to meet a uniform or location-specific performance goal, such as an emissions rate. Because a uniform performance standard approach theoretically leaves some flexibility to the private enterprise in the selection of control technologies and methods to achieve the performance goal, it has some attributes of a market-based incentive. In practice, however, performance standards have often been defined so specifically that they require a specific technology for most plants. Additionally, the performance standard is insensitive to differences in the costs and opportunities facing different plants: it still requires every plant to accomplish the same emissions reduction even if the same total reduction could be achieved at less cost by letting some plants control more while others control less.

Since the underlying problem is that private markets are operating imperfectly by producing inadequate environmental protection, the better approach for government action will often be to 'reconstitute' the market:[7] to reorient it by providing incentives that promote the desired environmental outcome. By revising the market's own system of pricing and allocating environmental protection responsibilities, market-based mechanisms turn the power of the marketplace – the indefatigable creativity of diverse and highly motivated market actors – to environmental advantage. Such mechanisms reduce overall social costs because those who can prevent degradation most cheaply have the most incentive to do so. Environmental protection is advanced as the incentives spur innovation in technologies and processes, and as market actors make efficient use of resources to reduce pollutant emissions (such as by conservation of fuels).

Market-based approaches work by attaching a cost to pollution or to other activities that consume social resources. They thus encourage businesses and consumers to avoid products associated with more pollution, because those products bear added costs. The result is better environmental performance among competing producers of goods and services. Meanwhile, market-based approaches do not disturb the flexibility of businesses and consumers to choose the methods by which they achieve that environmental performance in each local situation – through installation of technological controls, process changes, or more efficient use of resource inputs (raw materials). Instead, they stimulate producers to devise newer and better methods of pollution avoidance as businesses and consumers continually seek to avoid the costs imposed on polluting products. Further, market-based approaches allow businesses and consumers to transfer investments in pollution control to those places where pollution control is least expensive – where the most pollution control can be achieved for each unit of resources expended.

Several types of market-based environmental policy tools also exist. These include marketable constraints on the quantity of pollution, such as tradeable allowances or permits; impositions of a tax or charge on pollution, such as emissions fees; a hybrid tool, called a deposit-refund, that requires a deposit on the purchase of some product or the undertaking of some activity, and refunds the actor's deposit when the product or activity is properly handled; and information disclosure rules that require businesses to tell consumers, workers, and others about the risks involved in the company's products or activities. The final section of this chapter surveys several contexts in which US policy has adopted each of these tools.

Both CAC and market-based policies function in an arena of other social rules and systems, such as private property rights, liability for damages caused to others, insurance systems, antitrust law, social custom, and all the features of modern society. It is important in constructing any environmental policy to examine how the policy tools will match the underlying structure of socio-economic activity. For example, tort liability (the system that awards money damages to persons whose property or bodies have been injured by others) may provide powerful incentives to businesses to avoid subjecting others to risks. Tort liability in the US exerts an important influence in many areas, from automobile accidents to medical malpractice to releases of toxic substances. Yet because tort liability is processed through the judicial system, it may be too time-consuming and too expensive a method for resolving some injury claims, and the uncertainties in that process may undercut its effectiveness in guiding risk reduction in advance of potential accidents.

Policies to protect workers from risks, likewise, need to take account of the underlying incentive systems. Most US workers are covered by workers' compensation, a liability system different from tort law, in which an administrative fund (not a court-imposed judgment) compensates injured workers. The fund is collected by charging employers a fee and since the fee amount is based on the accident history of their workplaces, employers have an incentive to prevent accidents in advance by improving workplace safety. Evidence indicates that this system not only provides compensation to injured workers, but if properly designed it can substantially deter accidents (though probably not long-latent risks of disease) as well.[8] Adding additional regulations on accident risks could complement or interfere with this existing system.

A final example of an important underlying system in the US is the market itself. Consumers, workers, and others who know about risks and want to avoid them will generally demand a lower price (or a higher wage) to accept more risk. For example, a worker choosing among jobs will generally take a riskier job only at a higher wage.[9] A family buying a house will generally offer a lower price for a house nearer a noisy railroad or a toxic waste dump. In this way, markets themselves provide some incentives for reducing risks. The limits of such a system become apparent, however, where markets do not provide the public with full or accurate information, or where the public cannot act on that information; in such instances, government intervention may be worthwhile.

Comparing Approaches: Effectiveness and Economy

Most US environmental laws today still employ technology-based approaches such as BACT, but the current second revolution of environmental policy is based on our experience that technology-based approaches are too expensive, short-sighted, and of limited efficacy. Literal-minded federal agencies often require BACT because it gives the impression of accomplishing results. Imposition of technology controls can reduce how much pollution comes out of the 'end of the pipe'. However, the

BACT approach, in our experience, has several important flaws, each of which market-based approaches help to repair.

First, a technology-based approach is insensitive to the costs and benefits of installing a particular control technology at each site. Requiring the same level of control at every site results in substantial cost increases because environmental protection could be achieved at less cost if emissions reductions were produced using the least-cost option at each source. Under a market-based incentive approach, each source is given the freedom to choose the most cost-effective pollution control technology or change in-plant operations suitable to each location in order to achieve its environmental obligations. Moreover, each source can cooperate with other sources to invest in more pollution reduction where it is most cost-effective, rather than achieving the same uniform reduction at every site. The result is the least costly set of responses across the industry. In general, the cost savings of market-based approaches already tried in the US have been quite significant as compared to CAC policies.[10] These cost savings mean that society can achieve its environmental goals and still afford to tackle other social needs or to pursue further environmental protection. The excessive costs of technology-based command planning, by contrast, engender resistance to further efforts at environmental protection.

Second, technology standards discourage innovation in control technologies. When the government designates a technology as 'best' and mandates its adoption, that technology captures the market and forces out other technologies. For example, if the government designates one type of flue gas desulphurization device (scrubber) as BACT, required for installation by all firms, other techniques for sulphur removal have no economic value since they have no market – no firm will buy them. Also, government is generally not as well-placed as industry to identify and develop promising technologies. Once government has chosen a BACT, it is slow to revise its determination in light of new research. Furthermore, once the government has selected a BACT and required its installation everywhere, firms have no incentive to invest in developing a new and better control technology or strategy. Over time, this drawback may seriously impair the ability of technology-based standards to protect the environment. Under a market-based incentive approach, by contrast, each firm is challenged to research and develop its own best technique, and to continue developing better techniques that it can use and that other companies will buy. The result is that environmental protection becomes another opportunity for profit for the firm.[11]

Third, technology-based regulations have typically required the installation of end-of-pipe control devices, mechanisms that treat or scrub the pollutants as they are emitted from the plant or as they are put in disposal sites. CAC rules lead to this end-of-pipe focus because these are the technologies that central regulatory agencies can most generically apply to diverse facilities with varying production processes. These technology-based standards discourage improvements in efficient use of resources (eg, raw materials conservation) because businesses have no incentive to conserve fuels, or otherwise minimize emissions, once the control technology is in place. For example, if a firm is required to install a scrubber as BACT, it has no incentive to switch to cleaner, lower sulphur fuels. Moreover, rather than addressing the total quantity of all pollutants being released into all environmental media, end-of-pipe controls tend to focus separately on each kind of pollution. Market-based approaches, by contrast, set incentives that encourage conservation and pollution prevention measures, such as raw materials choices and efficiency improvements, to reduce the total quantity of pollutants generated.

Fourth, a technology-based approach requires a large centralized government bureaucracy to study industries and choose technologies. Government's limited resources constrain it from expanding and updating its information on useful applications in diverse local settings. Moreover, funding this centralized approach is costly to the public. Since a great deal of decision-making power stays in the hands of central regulators who have less incentive to achieve goals at low cost, this means delay, limited foresight, and diminished creativity.

Fifth, the technology-based approach tends to result in far more stringent controls on new plants than existing plants. Central officials feel pressure from organized, existing facilities not to add burdens. It is easier to respond to environmentalist demands for stringent controls by regulating as yet unidentified new facilities that have no lobbying power. It is economically rational to expect more control at new sources, because the cost of retro-fitting old plants is typically higher than the cost of building controls into new plants. However, new source control rules are often disproportionately stringent, producing several perverse effects. They impose a disincentive on new plants, discouraging capital investment and innovation that is necessary to promote economic growth. Since newer plants are typically cleaner plants, they discourage environmental improvement as well. Meanwhile, new source controls encourage businesses to operate their older, dirtier plants longer, often through modifications that extend the life of the older plants. The net result is that stringent new source controls can actually reduce environmental protection performance. By contrast, using an economic incentive tool to impose a burden on every unit of emissions from every plant, irrespective of its age, reduces emissions without discouraging investment in economic growth, and encourages new clean investment that replaces older, dirtier, less efficient facilities.

Market-based policies usually require fairly complete and accurate information about emissions or discharges, since they tie incentives to ultimate environmental performance. BACT or other technology-based approaches may be useful in those few situations where performance information, such as emissions monitoring data, is extremely difficult to measure or expensive to generate. An example might be controlling methane emissions from cattle; mobile sources whose emissions depend on several complex factors. But if incentives can be provided to encourage industries and others to improve these performance measurements at less cost than the technology-based measure would impose on society, an incentive-based approach will still be preferable. The key is not how much information we have now, but whether the gain from the flexibility of using incentive approaches outweighs the added costs of obtaining the needed performance data.

It should be noted that market-based policies themselves necessarily involve restraints on pollution, and they require government supervision and enforcement to ensure that environmental protection goals are achieved. The benefit of market-based policies is that private enterprises and markets remain relatively free to choose the most efficient means of achieving these goals.[12]

THE NEED FOR COMPREHENSIVE POLICY

Much environmental policy to date has been piecemeal.[13] CAC efforts have, in almost every country, been aimed separately at the air, water, and land media. The major US environmental laws, such as the Clean Air Act (CAA),[14] the Clean Water Act (CWA),[15] and the hazardous waste statutes,[16] were each written to address one environmental medium.[17] Many regulations address one pollutant at a time.

Such piecemeal approaches have too often resulted in solving one environmental problem at the expense of another. They have led to cross-media shifts in residuals, that is, moving pollution from one medium to another without reducing it, and to cross-pollutant shifts. In the heated arena of policy creation, these niceties are often discarded in favour of blunt instruments. Advocates focus on a single issue to the exclusion of all others in the search for a winning political coalition. In the acid rain debates in the US, the environmental community was only too willing to side with high sulphur coal interests to require scrubbers on all plants, despite the fact that requiring scrubbers in order to reduce sulphur dioxide (SO_2) increased another kind of emission – carbon dioxide (CO_2). In contrast, if tradeable allowances rather than technology mandates were implemented, utility CO_2 emissions could be reduced because emissions trading encourages fuel conservation while mandating scrubbers does not.[18] Further, although scrubbers remove sulphur from the air, they create sludge solid wastes that must be disposed of in another medium.[19]

A more ominous piecemeal policy proposal is the drive to control one 'greenhouse' gas, CO_2, to limit global warming. Yet limits on CO_2 alone would induce fuel-switching to natural gas from coal; and natural gas leaks – especially in Eastern Europe – could mean emissions of methane (CH_4) high enough to add more warming potential to the atmosphere than CO_2.[20]

Restrictions on emissions that apply narrowly to one source of a pollutant can also result in compliance strategies that, while adhering to the law, fail to reduce environmental degradation. For example, laws regulating air pollution from stationary sources were written to require that the ambient air quality in the locality of the smokestack not fall below certain levels.[21] One industry response to this approach was to build taller smokestacks, so that pollutant plumes were fed into higher wind currents and were dispersed more widely. Although pollutants were removed from local areas, they often continued to degrade the environment further downwind. The result was that, although the legally diluted pollutants presented reduced threats to human and ecological health, overall pollution was much less reduced than the law had contemplated. Populations downwind received unexpected pollutant loadings in the form of acid rain. Later, the laws were amended to try to prevent such outcomes.[22]

Recognizing the inherent and recurring problems in the piecemeal approach to pollution, the US is now developing and implementing a more comprehensive, integrated strategy to address the difficulties posed by our compartmentalized system of environmental control. It is examining pollution prevention strategies that attempt to decrease risk by reducing the total generation of multiple pollutants that may enter the several environmental media, rather than by focusing solely on the end-of-pipe method. The EPA's Pollution Prevention Strategy encourages firms to reduce total output of several toxic substances across the board.[23] Today's enforcement actions, too, can simultaneously charge violations under several laws in order to achieve a multimedia solution to an area's environmental problems. For example, the US recently brought enforcement actions against industrial facilities along the Grand Calumet River in Northwest Indiana, charging violations of the Clean Air Act,[24] the Resource Conservation and Recovery Act[25] (the law governing hazardous waste management), and the Safe Drinking Water Act.[26] The US is also urging 'comprehensive' approaches in other areas of environmental policy such as climate change.[27]

What is called for are environmental policies that encourage productive investment in new, cleaner production methods that produce less pollution of any kind. Rather than dividing up policies among the several media – even as we have done in the historical examples given in this Article – new policies should address all residuals in concert. For example, instead of enacting separate laws on air emissions, water discharges, and hazardous wastes, a country could draft a law that uses fees or tradeable allowances to address the total pollutants emitted from any source or group of sources, with some variation to account for different risks presented by different substances, the likelihood of human exposure, and other factors. This approach would encourage new technologies that reduce overall pollution, while leaving flexibility to industry to identify the most cost-effective reduction opportunities.

MARKET-BASED APPROACHES IN ACTION

The use of market-based instruments for environmental protection is not just the stuff of theory; it is already a reality in practical application in the US and elsewhere. In several areas of environmental policy, market-based instruments are in place and operating with general, and often great, success. These policy tools may find a useful application in many countries, as well as in international instruments of regional and global application.

Among the several types of economic instruments that might be used to implement environmental policy, current applications have generally employed fees, tradeable allowances, hybrid deposit-refund systems, and information disclosure requirements. A fee can be attached to each unit of emissions, effectively forcing the emitter to internalize – that is, incorporate in its own cost and pricing calculations – the costs that the emissions impose on society. Each emitter will reduce emissions to the point that its marginal costs of control become as expensive as paying the fee. This point will vary for each emitter, but the aggregate emissions reduction will correspond to the size of the fee exacted.

Under a tradeable allowances scheme, a central agency imposes a constraint on the total quantity of emissions. The agency then issues allowances adding up to that total and allows emitters to reallocate allowances among themselves. Alternatively, the agency sets a phase-out schedule and lets firms who achieve reductions ahead of schedule, earn credits that can be traded to other firms. The aggregate emissions cannot exceed the centrally determined total level, but the amount of emissions controlled by any individual emitter may vary so long as it holds allowances for each unit of its emissions. Those who can control emissions more cheaply than others will sell excess allowances at a profit, while those for whom control is more expensive will purchase allowances. The market price of an allowance is, in principle, the same as a fee on emissions to achieve the same reduction, in that it forces purchasers to internalize the costs of their excess emissions. Allowance trading differs, however, in that to achieve the same reduction, the marginal price for a unit of emissions is determined by market interactions rather than by government edict.

A deposit-refund system is like a fee with a rebate: those who generate a waste or purchase a product, must pay a deposit on the item, and when they deliver the item to a designated collection point for proper handling, they receive a refund. A mandatory return rule could induce illegal disposal to avoid the costs of return. However, under a deposit-refund system, the refund should be set to exceed the extra cost of the material (beyond the cost of alternative improper arrangements). Such a refund system would make illegal dumping or inadequate treatment unprofitable.

Information disclosure policies require industry to report information about risks. Such data include the quantity and content of discharges into the environment. In addition to helping society to gauge the severity of environmental threats, this tool can focus public attention on risks and generate incentives for industry to find less-polluting methods of operation. For example, requiring a source to inform a local community of its toxic discharges may encourage the source to reduce those discharges. Similarly, requiring a firm to inform workers of risks they may face on the job – risks they may not have been aware of – can create a job market in which workers make informed choices about which jobs to take at what wages (as mentioned earlier), and in which employers reduce those risks where the cost of doing so is smaller than the wage increase required to retain workers.

The US and other countries have used each of these market-based mechanisms as a tool to implement environmental policy. The following sections provide a picture of the great diversity of contexts in which these tools are applied, and the general features of each programme.[28] This survey is offered to explain experience with these reforms and to identify potentially useful mechanisms and implementation lessons for their application to the environmental needs of individual countries and the international community. Although our discussion is divided according to the environmental media (air, water, land), as indicated above, we urge a more comprehensive, multimedia framework for environmental protection policy.

Air Pollution: Local Atmospheric Pollutants

Urban air quality
In the first attempt to restrain urban air pollution in the US, the Clean Air Act required each region of the country to attain ambient air quality standards.[29] Yet lack of progress toward those goals, and the difficulty of achieving them without high economic costs, created demand for policy reform. Existing, modified, and new sources of emissions were all required to employ emissions controls.[30] The special burdens technology placed on any new sources, discouraged investment in new facilities. The Act also required cities to adhere to the ambient air quality standards or lose federal funding needed for new growth in their local economies. This political pincer on local officials created a demand to ease the painful choice between environmental quality and economic growth. The result was a series of experiments that culminated in the EPA's emissions trading policy.[31]

Through the last decade, the EPA's emissions trading policy has employed several different elements. First, 'offsets' allow new sources of emissions to be added to an area provided they obtain corresponding decreases in emissions from existing sources in the same area. Second, 'netting' allows an existing source to add a modification to a unit in the source facility that produces additional emissions, without having to install the most stringent emissions control technology, if it obtains a corresponding decrease in emissions from other units in the same facility. For example, 'bubbles' allow existing plants with emissions emanating from multiple units (such as several smokestacks) to reallocate emissions among the sites within the plant, and existing plants to reallocate emissions among a set of plants, so long as total emissions from within the bubble do not increase.[32] In addition, a banking programme lets existing sources store excess reductions in emissions for future use.

In each case, firms were given the latitude to expand operations while contributing to improved regional environmental quality. For example, the offset programme allowed a new entrant into a region if it acquired reductions in emissions from some existing polluter in the airshed in an amount at least as great as its proposed additions. In this fashion, both regional economic growth and improved environmental quality were promoted.

Experience has been different under each of these programmes, but, in general, there have been significant cost savings compared to traditional regulation. While keeping the aggregate emissions levels the same as under traditional CAC regulation, the netting and bubble programmes, for example, have achieved savings estimated at several billion dollars in the first seven years of the programme.[33] These substantial savings have been obtained despite the fact that the trading programme introduces a modest degree of flexibility in what remains an overwhelmingly CAC technology design regulatory programme. If trading were liberated from overhanging regulatory constraints, it could operate more effectively and create much larger cost savings.[34] Since 1991 the air management authority for the Los Angeles area – the South Coast Air Quality Management District – has moved to establish a creative new system of marketable permits to reduce urban air pollution from thousands of small sources, such as bakeries, dry cleaners, automobile repair shops, and other businesses.[35]

Appropriate market-based incentives could, likewise, help to solve urban air quality problems in other countries. For example, rather than placing a special restriction on new sources or requiring specific technologies to be installed at facilities, a pollution control policy could tax all emissions from any source or issue emissions allowances that can be marketed among existing or new facilities alike. More concretely, emissions of a toxic substance could be taxed[36] or phased-out using tradeable allowances. These kinds of policies would restrain emissions at least as well as technology-based emissions limits. They would also allow flexibility for industry to choose the least costly means of reducing emissions and enable investment in new, cleaner facilities to spur economic growth.

Lead in gasoline

The 'lead phase-down' in the US since 1981 has resulted in significantly reduced levels of airborne lead and public blood lead over the same period of time.[37] A lead phase-down programme similar to the market-based incentive programme in the US, using trading and banking of lead content reduction credits to minimize the costs of the programme, might thus be used to accomplish a reduction in environmental lead in other countries.[38]

Pursuant to the CAA, the EPA has issued numerous regulations limiting the allowable lead content of gasoline.[39] In 1982, the EPA set new limits on lead content, and instituted trading within and among gasoline refiners: leaded gasoline producers and importers could buy and sell lead content reduction credits freely among themselves, or they could apply such credits to their own gasoline.[40] In 1985, the EPA indicated that the lead trading programme would be terminated at the beginning of 1986, and substantially reduced the lead content limits, requiring the amount of lead to decline in phases – from 1.10 grammes of lead per gallon (gpg) to no more than 0.10 gpg – by the end of 1985.[41] To provide leaded gasoline producers and importers with some flexibility in complying with the new limits, the EPA issued additional regulations later in 1985. Where their gasoline contained less lead than the applicable standard, producers and importers were permitted to bank lead content credits to avoid the expiration of credits. The banking regulations then permitted gasoline producers and importers to withdraw those lead content credits through the end of 1987 and to apply them to help meet the new, more stringent lead content standards that took effect in 1985.[42]

The banking and trading system helped the industry as a whole to comply with the new lead limits, while ensuring that the total amount of lead content did not exceed the maximum that otherwise would have been allowed. Data indicate that banking and trading were active, and that they resulted in cost savings of hundreds of millions of dollars over the few years of the programme,[43] while the lead content of gasoline was reduced over 90 per cent.[44] Moreover, without trading, economic hardship and attendant political resistance would likely have inhibited the phase-down.[45] Internal EPA analysis suggests that the same cost would have been imposed under a non-trading phase-down at a target level of 0.25 gpg, as was imposed with trading at 0.10 gpg.[46] Thus, trading enabled significantly better environmental performance.

The design of the lead phase-down regulations facilitated widespread trading. Firms were not required to apply to the EPA for permission to enter into each trade; they simply reported their trades to the government as part of their regularly required reports of the lead content in their gasoline. Each firm was required to have a net balance of lead content credits (ie, lead credits held, minus the excess lead content of the firm's gasoline over the scheduled phase-down level) greater than or equal to zero in each quarter. In addition, because gasoline refiners and importers were accustomed to trading feedstocks and other commodities with each other, trades in lead content credits among those firms did not require new information networks. In sum, the lead phase-down was highly successful.[47]

Automobiles

CAC regulations focusing on vehicle exhaust emissions have had a number of unfortunate effects on US air quality. First, in a classic example of 'new-old' regulatory distinctions, only the latest generation of vehicles are required to be equipped with the new, and generally high marginal cost, control technologies. This focus precludes the achievement of the most cost-effective emission reductions in the vehicle fleet. Although such reductions could be produced by retrofitting individual high emitting vehicles within the fleet, legislators have yet to pursue this option.

Second, basing automobile emissions policy upon a simple recipe – adding pollutant-removal devices to the exhaust – has had perverse effects upon automobile producers and automobile emissions overall. The current environmental policy strategy is to get the toughest exhaust emission standards that are politically feasible and force the automobile manufacturers to meet these requirements. One result is that design engineers short-sightedly focus on emissions at the exhaust rather than from the vehicle as a system comprised of engine efficiency, fuel use, and other variables that could be influenced to reduce overall emissions at a lower cost. If the engineer is given an overall emissions goal for the entire vehicle, a much more open-ended design challenge, with many more options for current and future emission reductions is created. Under the present exhaust emphasis, the economy loses because the statutes foreclose more cost-effective emission reduction opportunities, and the environment loses because the policy artificially restricts the efforts of creative talent to solve environmental problems.

If environmental statutes gave incentives to companies and engineers to make cost-effective reductions wherever they could be found, the incentives and ability to meet the increasing demands for clean air would be much better aligned. Automobile manufacturers could compete on a much broader basis for cost savings in incrementally improved environmental performance. Innovation in automotive design would be encouraged, not chained to government-selected exhaust devices.

The EPA recently found an opportunity to test a market-based incentive for emissions reductions, revising its CAA programme governing the particulate and nitrogen oxides emissions of heavy-duty truck engines.[48]

For several years, the EPA set an average emissions standard for the line of truck engines produced by each manufacturer, thus affording each manufacturer the internal flexibility to make a range of engines so long as their average cleanliness met the standard. In its new regulation, the EPA allows manufacturers to trade and bank emissions.[49] A manufacturer whose line of engines emits less on average than the standard, will earn credits that can be banked for application to future model years, or traded to other engine manufacturers. Presumably, the greatest emissions reductions will be achieved by those manufacturers who can do so at least cost, reducing the overall social cost of the programme. Instead of simply installing a government-mandated device to comply with pollution reduction requirements, manufacturers will have incentives to reduce emissions as far as they can in order to generate credits to sell at a profit.

In an effort to insure that the trading and banking programme will not impair environmental protection, the EPA is providing that credits will be redeemable at 80 per cent of their face value, reducing by 20 per cent the emissions allowed upon each trade, and increasing somewhat the attractiveness of investment in additional emissions reductions.[50] The EPA forecasts that the profits from credit sales will still be sufficient to stimulate trades and emissions reductions even with the 20 per cent discount.[51] Such a tradeable emissions reduction system, or one that applies to all vehicles, might be used in Eastern Europe as well.

Meanwhile, US law also regulates the fuel efficiency of automobiles. The Corporate Average Fuel Economy (CAFE) rules govern the average efficiency of each manufacturer's entire fleet in each model year.[52] A kind of internal trading (trading within a firm) is thus allowed, giving the manufacturer the flexibility to reach the same aggregate fuel economy while varying the characteristics of each vehicle within its fleet to suit the spectrum of consumer needs and tastes. Even further flexibility in the CAFE rules could result in greater cost savings. For example, fuel economy achievements could be tradeable among manufacturers, that is, a manufacturer who achieved a fleet average efficiency lower than the applicable CAFE rule, could sell its excess as a 'credit' to another manufacturer whose fleet exceeded the rule. The concept could also be expanded to include alternative fuels[53] by counting alternative fuel vehicles in the gasoline fuel economy averages calculated for each fleet; this would give manufacturers an incentive to build alternative fuel vehicles.

Another promising modification of the CAFE system would be to credit manufacturers for retrofitting or repurchasing and retiring old cars now on the roads. Older vehicles with poor gasoline mileage and ageing engines account for a highly disproportionate share of emissions, since newer vehicles are required to be both more efficient and less polluting. Additional controls on new vehicles are progressively more expensive, and by their nature affect only the new vehicles added each year, not the stock of existing vehicles. Reducing emissions could thus be achieved more cost-effectively by fixing or retiring older vehicles, although no organized entity yet has the incentive to do so. Giving automobile manufacturers credit against their CAFE standards for such actions would be a major inducement.

From a cost-effective point of view (abstracting from distributional and political concerns), an even better incentive-based approach to automobile fuel economy and attendant emissions might be to impose a direct fee on fuels. CAFE is a clumsy tool because while it increases the fuel efficiency of the vehicle, it lowers the marginal cost to the driver of driving additional miles. The resulting increase in vehicle miles travelled (VMT) offsets some of the fuel use reduction (and the emissions reduction) that CAFE achieves on each mile driven. Raising the price of fuels, on the other hand, provides a direct incentive to drivers to conserve fuel.

Transboundary Atmospheric Pollution

Air pollutants pose special problems, including the prospect of pollution and damages moving across political boundaries, necessitating joint action among diverse sources and sovereign powers. CAC policies often fail to address these issues, and market-based incentives may be particularly useful in these contexts. Here we highlight two more problems to which the US and other countries have successfully adapted market-based policies.

Acid rain

After over ten years of political impasse over acid rain in the US, Congress adopted a new, creative acid rain programme in the 1990 Amendments to the Clean Air Act.[54] A key feature of new legislation is the use of tradeable emissions allowances. The law sets a permanent cap on emissions of SO_2 from the primary source of SO_2 emissions in the US: fossil fuel-burning electric utilities larger than 25 megawatts. Initially, emissions will be allowed at existing utilities according to a formula that multiplies each plant's historic energy capacity by a target average SO_2 emissions rate that generally is lower than the current actual average emissions rate.[55] Under this formula, plants with higher-than-average emissions would not be allocated enough allowances to cover their historical emissions levels, and by the late 1990s virtually all utilities would face emissions limits below their current levels.

To make up for this shortfall, which will amount to about ten million tons of SO_2 per year by the end of the decade, individual utilities can choose the most cost-effective means to reduce emissions at each source, such as switching to cleaner fuels, installing additional emissions control equipment, or taking conservation measures.[56] Alternatively, a utility could purchase additional allowances to cover its excess emissions. Utilities that can afford to reduce their emissions below their target average emissions rate will be able to sell their unused allowances as credits to other utilities. The market for such credits includes utilities for whom purchasing allowances is cheaper than investing in emissions reductions, and new entrants to the electricity industry who need more allowances than the small percentage reserved by the government and made available at occasional auctions.

The flexibility afforded by the ability to generate credits and sell them or buy them on an allowance trading market will enable industry to achieve most emissions reductions at the facilities where they are least costly. Since the marginal cost of reductions at a given facility varies widely according to the age of the facility, the type of fuel burned, and other variations, the cost savings of this trading plan over a plan not employing trading are substantial, estimated at about 15 to 25 per cent of total costs, or about $1 billion per year.[57] The plan also creates a strong financial incentive for utilities to engage in energy conservation and technological innovation because it permits facilities to choose their own best method of reducing emissions, whereas both would be discouraged by a rule that straightjacketed utilities into adopting specific emissions control mechanisms such as scrubbers.[58]

Stratospheric ozone depletion

In the effort to protect the stratospheric ozone layer, nations all over the world are using both trading and taxes to phase-out chlorofluorocarbons (CFCs) and related substances. The 1987 Montreal Protocol obliges each nation to halve its consumption of CFCs by the year 2000;[59] the 1990 update of the Protocol accelerates that schedule to a total phase-out by the year 2000.[60]

Under the rubric of 'industrial rationalization,' the Protocol allows a small amount of trading among nations in CFC production.[61] To date, little if any trading under this provision has occurred, probably because the Protocol explicitly constrains the extent of the trading to a low percentage of national consumption, and because it restricts trading by defining consumption in terms of production facilities rather than imports.

In the US, in order to implement the first phase of the 1987 Protocol, the EPA has issued regulations requiring the 50 per cent phase-out by the year 2000 to be implemented by allocating progressively reduced allowances to each producer and importer of CFCs. These allowances may be traded among producers, importers, and other interested parties.[62] Thus, just as with the lead phase-down, a producer reducing its output ahead of schedule can sell its excess allowances at a profit. Again, the result is that reductions are achieved fastest where they are least costly.

In addition to issuing CFC allowances, the US has imposed an excise tax on CFC production and importation. Like the allowance trading system, this tax will encourage the transition to higher-priced substitutes for CFCs. The tax is a multiple of the ozone depleting potential (ODP) index value calculated by the Montreal Protocol's scientific assessment panel for each CFC, thus calibrating the tax incentive to the environmental impact of the substance, and helping to discourage the main ozone-depleting CFCs the most.[63]

The efforts at CFC curtailment and stratospheric ozone protection have quickly become major milestones of national and global environmental policy efforts. Both the multilateral Montreal Protocol, one of the most sweeping international environmental agreements ever executed, and the Protocol's domestic implementation programmes demonstrate the growing confidence in market-based incentive programmes for achieving reductions in transboundary environmental pollutants.[64]

Water Resources: Water Quality

In the United States, the Clean Water Act (CWA) has traditionally separated water quality management into different programmes for point and nonpoint source management.[65] Under the CWA, a system was developed that requires a minimum technology-based water treatment level to control industrial discharges both at the point source and at municipal water treatment plants.[66] The programme has also established waste water treatment through publicly owned treatment works (POTWs), although the authority to charge fees on effluents that has been granted to local and regional authorities, is rarely used in practice.[67] As a consequence of this failure to charge fees, POTW facilities have reached capacity quickly, and industrial effluent levels have fallen only slightly, if at all.

This CAC approach to improving water quality by reducing effluents has been costly and has had only modest success. As a result, promising experiments that inject market-based incentives into the problem of water pollution have begun to attract attention. For example, the State of Wisconsin applied market-based approaches to the problem of industrial water pollution. State law regulated the control technologies as well as in-stream ambient standards imposed on several pulp and paper plants along one stretch of the Fox River. Wisconsin adopted a discharge limit system that allowed sources to negotiate individual discharge limits among themselves, so long as the total discharge of all the sources did not exceed the aggregate limit imposed by the State. The system permitted firms to take advantage of differences in the assimilative capacity of the river at the plants' various locations, and differences in the costs related to discharge reduction at each plant.[68]

In principle, the Wisconsin plan established a market for transferable emissions allowances. In practice, however, the system proved cumbersome. Sources held five-year permits authorized by the State; since trades could expire at the close of a permit cycle, the short cycle impaired their use for reallocations involving long-term investments in capital equipment. Further, no allowances or credits were actually issued to sources. Instead, each agreement between sources required the approval of a State agency that determined whether the parties had demonstrated a need to make changes in their permits. Review by the agency could be complex and time-consuming. In short, the programme was never actively exploited, either on the Fox River or elsewhere.[69]

Point source pollution in the US has been pervasively regulated, but at a higher cost than if a market-based incentive system had been used. The use of market-based incentives could cut the costs of achieving better point source control. In Eastern Europe, market-based approaches could, likewise, help achieve cost-effective clean-up, and break the deadlock between industrial interests fearing new regulatory constraints and the public's need for health and environmental protection.

In the US, market-based approaches have been proposed to control the continuing problem of nonpoint sources.[70] For example, in the State of Colorado, discharges were endangering the drinking water supplies in the Dillon Reservoir.[71] Emissions were coming from both point and nonpoint sources. The State government issued restrictive annual discharge allowances to all sources, and allowed point sources to increase their discharges only if they acquired allowances from nonpoint sources at a ratio of two to one.[72] Because control of point sources is about seven times as expensive as control of nonpoint sources, the two-to-one trading ratio provides dischargers considerable opportunities for cost-saving trades. Thus, trading is likely to both save costs and reduce emissions. Similar experiments are being conducted on the Tar-Pimlico watershed in North Carolina.[73]

Water Supply

Water resource supply policies can also exacerbate water quality problems. In the US this has been particularly problematic in the arid West, where water is generally stored in massive publicly financed dams. The water is then bureaucratically allocated to users on the basis of a system of historic entitlements and modern contracts. While this system served the US reasonably well during the period of westward expansion and settlement, it has not been able to adjust to changing social needs, such as the preservation of scarce wetlands, aquatic habitats, fisheries, water-based recreation, and wild and scenic rivers. By offering water at artificially low prices it has created powerful incentives for excessive water use. As a result, farms that own guaranteed supplies are glutted, while water shortages develop in cities and cause impairment of salmon runs, eutrophication, and destruction of natural environments.

In addition to the problems caused by the provision of water at subsidized prices, the laws governing allotment of agricultural water rights in many Western States also tend to discourage conservation and efficiency. In most of these States, each irrigator is entitled to a specific quantity of irrigation water each year, based on its historic level of use. An irrigator who retires farmland may be allowed to sell the unused water, but an irrigator who decides to increase the irrigation efficiency on existing lands is generally not entitled to sell the water freed up by that investment. Worse, in many States the efficient irrigator may be rewarded by having its annual water entitlement reduced by the State and the unused amount made available to competing farmers[74] – a real disincentive to efficiency.

In California, a burgeoning population and a series of droughts have led to some reforms designed to prevent over-use and reallocate water to where it is most needed. The State can and has intervened to restrict water rights where water is being wasted, and current water users can sell conserved water to other users.[75] Better recognition of the right to market conserved water and more easily transferable water rights in all Western States would help provide incentives for efficient use, and help direct water to its most valued uses.

One important remedy for these environmental maladies is to construct market-based incentives for water conservation by letting the price of water, used for irrigation or reservoirs or other purposes, reflect its true market value, not government-set quotas or guaranteed access rights. Ultimately the price of water use should reflect its full social costs, including the costs of increased pollution or overuse imposed by a user, so that those who pollute more or use more must pay more for their water use. Making water use rights transferable helps create that incentive system, because using the water means foregoing the sale price of the right to use that water, and conservation means reaping that sale price.

Solid and Hazardous Wastes: Proper Handling

Prohibiting landfill disposal of hazardous wastes, or mandating disposal at certain designated sites, can lead to 'midnight dumping' and other evasive and environmentally unsound tactics. One market-based option to ensure proper handling or disposal of wastes is the use of deposit-refund systems. A deposit charged on the sale of an item is refunded when the item is delivered to a designated site or treatment facility. This gives the purchaser an incentive to deliver the waste for recycling, incineration, or other proper handling, rather than to discard it randomly. Deposit-refund systems for lead-acid batteries are now operated by the States of Maine and Rhode Island.[76] Deposit-refund systems could also be used to encourage safe disposal or management of used oils, industrial chemicals, and agricultural chemicals.

Similarly, in order to reduce litter and encourage recycling of glass and aluminum beverage containers, several States have enacted 'bottle bills'. These laws institute a deposit-refund system for bottles and cans, in which a deposit (typically five cents per container) is charged at the point of purchase and is refunded upon delivery of the containers to a retailer or recycling depot. Although these programmes may reduce litter, they typically charge the same deposit regardless of the type of container (eg metal or plastic), and thus fail to provide consumers with incentives to choose the material whose disposal is least costly to society. More sophisticated deposit-refund programmes could vary the deposit depending on the type of packaging.

Reducing the Volume of Wastes

The large volume of municipal solid wastes in the US is prompting concern that landfill capacity will run out. As landfills have become scarce, some of the waste stream has been diverted toward incineration, but burning waste poses air pollution problems and generates incinerator ash. Another option might be water disposal in lakes or seas, but tight rules already constrain that possibility. CAC regulations specifying the technology and design of landfills and incinerators can offer some improvements in those facilities, but they do not directly affect the total stream of solid waste, and may simply shift wastes from land disposal to air incineration or water discharge. Similarly, while it may be useful to mandate that residents separate materials for recycling, that does not assure a market for the recyclable materials and does not directly discourage waste generation by residents.

One way to address the over-production of wastes is to impose a fee on the generation of waste that reflects the true social cost of its disposal. Such a fee would provide an incentive to reduce the total volume of wastes produced and would thus alleviate, to some degree, the problem of disposal. The hard questions are how to set the fee and where to assess it. The marginal social cost of disposal may vary from one community to another, so the fee may need to vary across localities, and would be imposed at the curb when wastes are set out for collection. Assessing the fee at the curbside has been successful in cities such as Seattle, Washington and Perkasie, Pennsylvania, where a fee is assessed per container (barrel or bag) of trash that households set out for pickup. These programmes, however, have some difficulty calibrating the fee to the unique disposal costs of each specific material being discarded. This gives little incentive to consumers to avoid excess packaging or other waste at the time a product is purchased, and the products that become solid waste are generally produced and sold in a national retail market.

In a national market, one option is to assess the fee at the point of purchase, by charging a disposal cost on each retail item according to its ingredients and packaging, and reflecting that cost on the receipt the customer receives from the store.[77] This option is facilitated by the use of computerized cash registers and optical scanners that read a bar code printed on the package. The disposal fee can then be programmed into the cash register's computerized price list, and revised periodically or by locality to reflect changing costs.

Fees are also being used to reduce the volume of wastes – in this case, industrial wastes – in the State of Louisiana, which has recently begun to use its tax system to encourage better waste management practices by businesses.[78] The State normally provides large businesses with exemptions from the taxes they would pay on new equipment and other capital expenditures, in order to develop business within the State. At the same time, Louisiana has found itself pursuing many of these companies for violations of waste disposal and other environmental laws. As a means of raising revenues while encouraging cleaner practices, the State now links the size of a business's tax exemption to the environmental record of its plant. The dirtier the plant, the smaller a tax exemption it receives. The State evaluates each application for a tax exemption and assigns the applicant a score from 50 to 100, based on its environmental compliance record. That score is then translated into the percentage of the tax exemption the business may receive.[79]

Information Disclosure Rules

A technique to address emissions into all media – air, land, and water – that could be employed by countries and the international community, is the information disclosure rule. Under the 1986 Amendments to the 'Superfund' hazardous waste clean-up law, businesses in the US are required to report the quantities of toxic substances stored on their premises, and the quantities released into the environment.[80] This simple requirement, without imposing any tax or quantity limit on toxics, and without specifying any technology to reduce toxics, encouraged businesses to make major reductions in measured toxics releases – perhaps more than in all the 25 preceding years of toxics regulation. A key reason was that businesses felt pressure from consumers who would avoid buying products associated with toxics, and from local residents who might protest higher toxic releases.

This information disclosure requirement aims to correct the failure of the market to provide full information to the public, while helping to marshal market forces (consumer and resident preferences) in the protection of the environment. Other US laws require businesses to disclose workplace hazards to workers,[81] or require certain products to be labelled with information about the risks their use may entail.[82] Additionally, some States require that a party selling a piece of land provide prospective buyers with an environmental audit of the site.

Natural Resources: Domestic Land Use Management

The State of New Jersey has successfully used the tradeable allowance approach to prevent excessive development of the Pinelands, a forest zone within the State.[83] In this instance, the allowances are not for emissions, but for development rights. Property in certain areas of the Pinelands is slated for preservation, and development of the land restricted. In return, the owners of that land are issued transferable development rights (TDRs), which they may sell to others seeking to develop land in permitted areas of the Pinelands. Different amounts of TDRs are issued to each owner, depending on the value the State places on preserving that owner's property. In areas where development is permitted, landowners must hold TDRs to develop their property. Thus, the total amount of development in the Pinelands is capped, certain areas remain undeveloped, and the development of permitted properties is left to the market for TDRs. Additionally, no current landowner is entirely deprived of the value of his or her land, because those whose land is slated for preservation receive TDRs they may sell to others. In order to facilitate trades, the government has established a TDR exchange that buys and sells TDRs.

Fisheries Management

Another natural resource under stress in many parts of the world is fishery stocks. Fisheries are often 'public goods': they are available to anyone to harvest, but if too many people are harvesting too much fish and depleting the resource, no one fishery user has an incentive to reduce its fish take because it knows that others will simply 'free ride' on such altruism and continue overfishing. Overfishing has depleted and threatened the sustainability of fishery stocks in many areas. Since free riders will frustrate the attempts of private actors to exercise self-restraint, governments have sought means to preserve mutually beneficial levels of sustainable stocks. The traditional remedy has been to impose restrictions on the number of trips of fishing boats or the size of their nets – essentially technology-based restrictions. A market-based alternative is to issue catch quotas to each fishing company or vessel, and then to allow those quotas to be traded among vessels. Such individual transferable quotas (ITQs) simultaneously protect the shared resource and encourage the most cost-effective firms and techniques. The US has adopted ITQs in certain fisheries.[84] Other nations that have adopted ITQs include Canada, Australia, Iceland, New Zealand, and the United Kingdom.

The New Zealand programme is the most extensive and sophisticated. ITQs, defined as percentages of the annual allowable catch, are distributed to fishing vessel owners and, with very few exceptions, they are freely tradeable among vessel owners. An annual rental fee is charged by the government on each quota. The programme has begun to stabilize the fishery stocks and to rein in an overgrown vessel fleet. Significantly, faced with the opportunity to trade ITQs, fishing firms have recognized that the value of their ITQs is dependent on the health of the fishery stock, and have begun investing in affirmative, voluntary efforts to protect and conserve the fisheries.[85]

RECOMMENDATIONS FOR ENVIRONMENTAL POLICY

The design of environmental policy tools will be critical to their ultimate success. Legal instruments will not, by themselves, necessarily produce environmental quality – there will also need to be sufficient political will to ensure environmental compliance. But to ignore the deeply intertwined susceptibilities of the economy and the environment is to put both at risk. Building public support for environmental protection requires policies that allow economic growth and environmental quality to be pursued in concert. Addressing ourselves now to those who share responsibility for framing environmental policy in individual countries and at the international level, we make the following suggestions to achieve that end.

- *Set risk priorities* – Choosing the right policy tools is not enough; the tools need to be applied to the right goals. Sound environmental policy should identify and prioritize the environmental and health risks it will address. With limited resources, environmental protection agencies cannot attack all problems from all sides at once. Rather, governments will need to define their priorities according to the degree of risk to human health and the environment, their ability to establish policies that will diminish those risks, and the costs associated with those policy options.[86]
- *Create comprehensive, holistic policies* – Ecology provides us with a basic model for environmental institution-building. Environmental policy goals should be developed holistically, recognizing the complexity and interdependence of the natural and social systems being managed. Individual pollutants or media should not be addressed separately; such an approach is cumbersome, often counterproductive, and too often solves one environmental problem at the expense of another.[87]
- *Be pragmatic* – Select environmental policy tools where they will work best, achieving the most benefit at least cost. Market-based tools have powerful advantages, but they are not necessarily ideal in every case. The choice of policy tools should always be a practical, not an ideological, exercise.

- *Develop effective monitoring and enforcement programmes* – Without a credible and legally demonstrable threat of enforcement against polluters, even the most finely crafted environmental protection system may fail. The ultimate economic incentive is legal liability for damages, credibly enforced.
- *Establish a clear system of legal obligations* – Polluters should be able to understand their obligations under the law. Discretionary authorities and conflicting statutes create opportunities for evasion of the law, and frustrate progress toward environmental protection.
- *Give proper authority to relevant agencies* – Agencies charged with environmental protection should have clear legal authority for imposing constraints on polluting offenders. Otherwise, even well-conceived policies may fail.
- *Substitute market-based incentives for bureaucratic whim* – Central planning for the production of goods and services has not worked in Eastern Europe, and central planning for the achievement of environmental quality has been inefficient and sometimes ineffective in the US. Rather than creating layers of bureaucratic instruction on how to operate industrial facilities, farms, small businesses, and individual purchasing choices, new policies should create incentives that channel market behaviour toward environmental protection and stimulate the creative powers of businesses and individuals toward environmentally useful innovations.
- *Leave production decisions to individual businesses, and consumption decisions to individual consumers* – Much potentially productive energy is wasted on attempts to micro-manage the environmental behaviour of individual economic agents. Freedom of choice should be channelled to environmental advantage by creating incentives for private actors to innovate new and better environmental protection measures. Government is not well situated to identify the best new technologies and techniques; it should set incentives for the environmental goals it seeks but leave detailed operational choices to producers and consumers.
- *Facilitate public input* – Governments should work with industry and non-governmental organizations to develop better approaches to difficult problems. Third party advocacy and independent representation of environmental interests has been central to the production of environmental quality in the US. In order to create a credible and responsible enforcement programme, citizens with a real interest in a matter can be given the legal right to bring suit against polluters or agencies charged with protecting the environment. Interested citizens can also be enabled to challenge regulatory actions that are inconsistent with statutory authority. Information itself can be a scarce economic good, and public access to information can improve the functioning of policy-making and of market forces.

- *Avoid repeatedly changing the rules* – In order for market forces to be channelled towards solving environmental problems, a reasonable degree of certainty is required to encourage the necessary private investment. US experience shows that violations of this precept have substantially increased the difficulty of introducing policy innovations, such as SO_2 emissions trading for acid rain control, because industry opposes what it sees as a disruptive upheaval in the rules of the system. Businesses are sceptical that they will be allowed to reap the rewards of their environmental investments. They are asked to make large capital investments and expect, in exchange, to profit from those investments. Unexpected change in the rules can effectively (if not legally) expropriate the value of such investments. Thus, schedules of emissions limits should be announced in advance, and should be geared to deadlines that match turnover rates in capital and process design.
- *Avoid special restrictions on new facilities* – These restrictions discourage investment, encourage dirty, older facilities to operate longer, and fail to restrict pollution directly. Taxes or tradeable allowances on emissions from facilities of any age are a better way to encourage emissions reductions and new economic investment at the same time. At the least, any higher restrictions on new sources should be accompanied by the option for new sources to obtain offsets from existing sources.
- *There is no constituency for efficiency* – Economists who spend their professional and intellectual lives devoted to the pursuit of reform find this a particularly difficult lesson to learn. Because constituents often do not emerge in the absence of incentives for efficient use, policy reforms that ignore this lesson are doomed to stall. Similarly, there is no constituency for comprehensive regulation. Indeed, modern politics tends to reduce issues to sound bites and horse trades. Smart policy design needs to rise above the disfunction of parochial political interests and focus on overall social outcomes.
- *Choose reform targets carefully* – In environmental terms this means selecting a policy tool that matches the special characteristics of the problem to be addressed. For example, in the acid rain case, large-scale emissions trading was made possible by the absence of local 'hotspots' – local harm from local concentrations of emissions. Since the environmental goal was to achieve large reductions in emissions transported over long distances, it mattered little where such reductions were produced within the relevant airshed. Similarly, where several substances contribute to the same environmental problem, such as CFCs or greenhouse gases, it is useful to address the environmental problem as a whole rather than each substance and each source in isolation.
- *Create administrative structures that ease rather than hinder policy* – Such structures should focus on performance, monitoring, and enforcement

measures rather than on planning processes. Elaborate planning processes, such as the State-by-State plans prepared under the CAA, have proven to be cumbersome barriers to change. At a minimum, these planning activities drain resources away from other competing elements of institution building. Frequently, they rely upon doubtful central judgments of 'best technologies' and poor prognostications about the future of the economy. Policy-makers should set incentives, allow markets flexibility in their responses, leave technology planning to private business, and put resources into monitoring and enforcement.

■ *Develop test cases* – If time and resources permit, a very effective way to achieve support for (or realize the flaws in) a policy innovation is to demonstrate its real world application. One of the most difficult obstacles to overcome is the scepticism of environmentalists who perceive threats to environmental quality any time any flexibility is left to industry. Test cases create the opportunity for affected parties as well as the innovators to learn from empirical data. Already, Eastern Europe can look to the US for much of the needed data.

CONCLUSION

We have not tried to produce a recipe for institutional reform: environmental policy tools need to be applied where they are most effective and efficient. Success in developing sound environmental protection can only come from a careful blending of policy options that are crafted to suit circumstances to which they are applied. Traditional CAC strategies need to be supplemented or supplanted by economic incentives that will harness market energies to advance environmental protection.

NOTES AND REFERENCES

INTRODUCTION

1 Allott, P (1990) *Eunomia: New Order for a New World*, Oxford University Press, Oxford, para 17.52.
2 45 *Southern California Law Review* 450 (1972).
3 International Court of Justice, Press Release No 93/20, 19 July 1993, ('Constitution of a Chamber of the Court for Environmental Matters').

1 FROM STOCKHOLM TO RIO: BACK TO THE FUTURE?

1 Resolution 44/228 of the General Assembly of the United Nations (22 December, 1989), *Doc A/RES/44/228*, para 15(d) (1989).
2 *UN Doc A/CONF 48/PC/2*, para 16 (1972).
3 See the excellent analysis of the drafting history of the Stockholm Declaration by Sohn, Louis (1973) 'The Stockholm Declaration on the Human Environment', *Harvard International Law Journal*, pp 423–515, at 425–434.
4 Ibid, at 426–427.
5 *UN Doc A/CONF 48/PC 13*, para 159 (1971).
6 II ILM 1416 (1971).
7 See note 18, infra.
8 As quoted in UNEP's periodical (1982) *Uniterra*, No 2, p 13.
9 UNGA Resolution 37/7, *UN Doc A/37/51*, (1982).
10 World Commission on Environment and Development (1987) *Our Common Future*, Oxford University Press, Oxford, p 332.
11 See Ling, Chee Yoke (1988) 'International Conventions: To What Extent Resource Conservation and Environmental Protection are Safeguarded by Law?', in *Global Development and Environment Crisis: Has Humankind A Future?*, Asia-Pacific Peoples Environment Network/Sahabat Alam, Malaysia, Penang, pp 739–758.
12 *Our Common Future*, supra note 10, p 333.
13 Lammers, J G (ed), (1987) *Environmental Protection and Sustainable Development: Legal Principles and Recommendations*, Graham & Trotman/Nijhoff, London/Dordrecht/Boston. These principles 'have not been approved or considered in detail by the Commission'. They were published and submitted to the UNGA as

scholarly contribution to the debate, without explicit endorsement by the Commission.

14 *UN Doc A/CONF 151/5*, (7 May, 1992).

15 *UN Doc A/CONF 151/PC/WG III/L 33/Rev 1*, (2 April 1992).

16 See eg, Kiss, A (1989) 'Le droit international de l'environnement: formulation et mise en oeuvre universelles', in Postiglione, A (ed) *Per un tribune internazionale dell'ambiente*, published privately, Milano, pp 211–220. This view also seems to have inspired the work of the WCED Experts Group, of which Kiss was a member.

17 Statement by Peter Sand, Principal Legal Officer of the UNCED Secretariat, in an interview with the newsletter (June,1991) *Network '92*, No 7, p 1.

18 For an exhaustive analysis of this principle and its status in international law, see eg, Kiss, A and Shelton, D (1991) *International Environmental Law*, Transnational Publishers, New York/London, pp 129 *et seq*. See also: *Environmental Protection and Sustainable Development*, supra note 13, pp 75–80. For a more critical view questioning the customary character of the principle, see Koskenniemi, M (1990) 'International Liability for Transfrontier Pollution Damage', 2 *International Environmental Affairs*, pp 309–31. A more detailed analysis of the authorities can be found in Pallemaerts, M (1988) 'International Legal Aspects of Long-Range Transboundary Air Pollution', 1 *Hague Yearbook of International Law*, pp 189–224, at 205–206.

19 For a detailed analysis of the drafting history of Principle 21 and of the compromise struck, between sovereignty and responsibility, see Sohn, op cit, pp 485–493.

20 Kiss, op cit, p 129.

21 (18–28 February, 1992) 'Report of the Intergovernmental Committee for Negotiation of a framework agreement on climate change concerning the work of its fifth session' (first part), held in New York, *Doc A/AC 237/18* (Part I), (10 March, 1992), p 24.

22 *UN Doc A/AC 237/18* (Part II)/Add 1, p 2 (15 May, 1992).

23 For an analysis of the relation between environmental protection and human rights, see the collection of essays edited by Kromarek, Pascale (1987), *Environnement et droits de l'homme*, Unesco, Paris.

24 In Resolution 41/128 of 4 December 1986, the UNGA proclaimed that 'the right to development is an inalienable human right'.

25 See Singh, N (1988) 'Right to Environment and Sustainable Development as a Principle of International Law', 41 *Studia Diplomatica*, pp 45–61.

26 Chemillier-Gendreau, M (1987) 'Relations between the Ideology of Development and Development Law', in: Snyder, F and Slinn, P *International Law of Development: Comparitive Perspectives*, Professional Books, Abingdon, pp 57–65, at 59.

27 For a radical critique of established 'development' models and ideologies from the perspective of grass-roots social movements in the Third World, see eg (9–14 November 1984) *Third World: Development or Crisis?*, Declaration and Conclusions of the Third World Conference in Penang, Malaysia, Third World Network, Penang, 1985.

28 *Environmental Protection and Sustainable Development*, op cit, p 38 (Article 1).

29 Ibid, p 40.

30 See eg, EEC Council Directive of 7 June 1990 concerning the right of access to information regarding the environment [90/313/EEC], *Official Journal No L 158*, 23 June 1990, p 56. See also Pallemaerts, M (ed), (1991) *Le droit l'information en matière d'environnement*, E Story-Scientia, Brussels.

31 For a European comparative analysis, see Führ, M and Roller, G (eds), (1991) *Participation and Litigation Rights of Environmental Associations in Europe*, Verlag Peter Lang, Frankfurt.

32 Draft ECE Charter on Environmental Rights and Obligations, adopted at Experts Meeting in Oslo, 29–31 October 1990; *UN Doc ENVWA/R 38*, (1990).

33 See Report of the Ad hoc Meeting on Environmental Rights and Obligations, The Hague, 1–5 July, 1991 *UN Doc ENVWA/AC 7/2*, (10 July, 1991).

34 *Our Common Future*, supra note 10, p 43.

35 A first clear articulation of the concept in an international political document co-authored by IUCN, WWF, UNEP, Unesco and FAO can be found in IUCN/UNEP/WWF, (1980) *World Conservation Strategy*, subtitled 'Living Resource Conservation for Sustainable Development', World Conservation Strategy, Geneva.

36 For an incisive analysis of the ambiguities and pitfalls of the Brundtland concept of 'sustainable development' see Goodland, R, Daly, H, El Serafy, S and Von Droste, B (eds), (1991) *Environmentally Sustainable Economic Development: Building on Brundtland*, Unesco, Paris.

37 Resolution 44/228, para I.3.

38 Ibid, paras I.5–6,.38.22.

39 *Official Journal C 191* (29 July, 1992).

40 Contrast the Fourth ACP-EEC Convention of Lomé, December 1989, between member States of the EEC and associated developing countries of the African, Caribbean and Pacific. It is a legally-binding, multi-lateral instrument negotiated in the aftermath of publication of the Brundtland Report, which contains a title on the environment and includes commitments to sustainable development. However, unthinkable only three years later after Rio, it omits mention of economic growth (cf Article 34).

41 See Goodland et al, op cit. As UNESCO Director-General, Frederico Mayor, points out in his foreword, 'This book makes it clear that unless development is distinguished from economic growth, the turn off towards sustainable development will be missed'.

42 See also EEC Treaty Article 130r(2), as amended by the 1986 Single European Act, and the Treaty on European Union.

43 See eg, Kiss and Shelton, op cit, p 9.

44 16/8/91 GATT Dispute Settlement Panel award, *GATT Doc DS21/R*, 3 September, 1991 (unreported).

45 Paragraph 15(a).

46 Kiss and Shelton, op cit, p 1.

47 For a general overview of this field, see, eg, Feuer, G and Cassan (1985) *Droit International du Developpement*, Dalloz, Paris.

48 Agenda 21, Chapter 39, 'International legal instruments and mechanisms', *Doc A/CONF 151/4* (Part IV), p 54, (27 April, 1992).

49 *UN Doc A/CONF 151/L 3/Add 38*, p 4, para 15, (11 June, 1992).

2 THE RIO DECLARATION: A NEW BASIS FOR INTERNATIONAL COOPERATION

1 Cynics might add that the environment has become trendy, which would explain why movie stars, television personalities, rock stars, Heads of State (past and present), and religious leaders joined the diplomats, bureaucrats, economists, lawyers, and scientists gathered at the Earth Summit. My own view is that the growing popularity of the environment and its problematization deserve much closer attention.

2 The cover of *Time Magazine* of 1 June, 1992, for instance, bears the title 'Rio – Coming Together to Save the Earth' and a naive painting which represents Rio de Janeiro as a tropical paradise.

3 The Conference logo, a schematic drawing of a fragile globe cradled by a dove-like hand, bearing the legend 'In Our Hands', was ubiquitous. It appeared on documents, posters, t-shirts, books, bags, watches and other paraphernalia. See the *Earth Summit Times*, the official daily newspaper of UNCED.

4 See Kennedy, David (1987) *International Legal Structures*, Nomos Verlagsgesellschaft, Baden Baden.

5 (1991)*The Challenge of the Environment*, United Nations Development Programme (UNDP) Annual Report, p 3.

6 The term 'sustainable development' is usually attributed to the Brundtland Commission Report which states: 'Humanity has the ability to make development sustainable – to ensure that it meets the needs of the present without compromising the ability of future generations to meet their own needs. *Our Common Future*, Report of the World Commission on Environment and Development ('the Brundtland Commission Report'), *A/42/427*, para 27.

7 Much of this section is based on my personal observations during the fourth session of the Preparatory Committee of UNCED, held in New York in the Spring of 1992, and during the Earth Summit in Rio de Janeiro in June, 1992.

8 See the three consecutive G-77 proposals: *A/CONF 151/PC/WG III/L 20, L 21 and L 21 Rev 1* (1992).

9 See 'Report of the Panel – United States – Restrictions on Imports of Tuna, General Agreement on Tariffs and Trade, DS21/R', 3 September, 1991 (unreported); see *RECIEL* vol 1:1 pp 28–33. In this context see Principle 12 of the Rio Declaration which provides, *inter alia*, that '[u]nilateral actions to deal with environmental challenges outside the jurisdiction of the importing country should be avoided'.

10 Thus, for instance, the Russian Federation had to choose a side and played an uneasy role within the 'developed country' camp, which came to be known as the 'OECD & Russia Group'.

11 An interesting exception was the Holy See. See letter to the UNCED Preparatory Committee *A/CONF 151/PC/WG III/L 16*.

12 See note 1, supra.

13 This story was told far more eloquently by the delegate for Mozambique during the Rio Declaration negotiations.

14 See, for example, Japan's proposed text: 'In developing countries, the rapid increase in population growth, poverty and the destruction of the environment

constitute a vicious circle and are a serious threat to health and well-being. Accordingly, the issue of environment and development should be considered in this context.' Principle 2, *A/CONF 151/PC/WG III/L 22*.

15 See UNGA Resolution 44/228.

16 The Rio Declaration negotiations took place before the adoption of the Framework Convention on Climate Change, on 9 May, 1992. The Convention's Intergovernmental Negotiating Committee, had however, before the start of the fourth UNCED Preparatory Committee, already approved the inclusion of the concept of 'common but differentiated responsibility' in the Preamble and in the Principles Article of the Framework Convention on Climate Change. See *A/AC 237/18 (Part I) and A/AC 237/18 (Part II)/Add 1*.

17 See in particular Article 130r(2) of the Maastricht Treaty. *'Europe'/Documents No 1759/60*, (7 February, 1992).

18 In addition to their concern to preserve the current understanding of sovereignty, developing countries also insisted on repeating Principle 21 of Stockholm in the Rio Declaration, to ensure the further development of international law concerning liability for transboundary or extra-jurisdictional environmental damage. The G-77 feared its omission might later be interpreted as a decision by the international community that the second prong of Principle 21 was of little consequence.

19 In this regard see the minority response to the critique of rights in the US. Williams, Patricia J (1987) 'Alchemical Notes: Reconstructing Ideals From Deconstructed Rights', *Harvard Civil Rights – Civil Liberties Law Review* 402 *et seq.*

3 DEFENDING THE GLOBAL COMMONS

1 Those interested in a fuller treatment of these two proposals, and others, are referred to my new book, Stone, Christopher D (1993) *The Gnat is Older than Man: Global Environment and Human Agenda*, Princeton University Press, Princeton, NJ.

2 United Nations Convention on the Law of the Sea, done 10 December, 1982, Article 76, reprinted in 21 *International Legal Materials* 1261–1354 (1982). Some 156 nations had signed the Convention by 1986. See Greenville, J and Wasserstein, B (1987) *The Major International Treaties Since 1945*, Methuen, New York, p 498.

3 See Lee Kimball's contribution to this volume, 'Environmental Law and Policy in Antarctica', chapter 8.

4 As explained more fully below, this is the prevailing view, at least as long as there are no substantial spillover effects that spill over across frontiers. In terms of the Stockholm Declaration 'States have, in accordance with the Charter of the United Nations and the principles of international law, the sovereign right to exploit their own resources pursuant to their own environmental policies, and the responsibility to ensure that activities within their jurisdiction or control do not cause damage to the environment of other States or of areas beyond the limits of national jurisdiction.' 1972 Declaration of the United Nations Conference on

the Human Environment, Chapter II, Principle 1, reprinted in 11 *International Legal Materials* 1416–69 (1972).

This position is echoed in the 1992 United Nations Framework Convention on Climate Change, which, while calling for 'the widest possible cooperation by all countries and their participation in an effective and appropriate international response,' makes clear that 'States have the sovereign right to exploit their own resources pursuant to their own environmental and developmental policies ....' Preamble, reprinted in 21 *International Environment Reporter Reference File (BNA)*, 3901–9 (1992).

5   Shortly after Bank President Barber Conable gave a speech in 1987 promising that the Bank would incorporate ecological concerns in its development planning, the institution reviewed, then halted work on the Bapai Dam in Nepal. Plater, Z (1989) 'Multilateral Development Banks, Environmental Diseconomies, and International Reform Pressures on the Lending Process', 9 *Boston College Third World Law Journal*, 169–215, p 204. More often, pressures from outside have been critical in motivating the Bank to account for environmentalist concerns. The National Resources Defense Council (NRDC) of the US, the Environmental Foundation, Ltd (EFL) of Sri Lanka, and US officials convinced the Bank to condition a loan to Sri Lanka for logging on Sri Lanka's undertaking to provide environmental impact statements for the project, and to permit scrutiny by independent environmental groups. See Wirth, David A (1990) 'Legitimacy, Accountability, and Partnership', 100 *Yale Law Journal* , 2645–66 pp 2647–8.

Despite the pressures NGOs have brought to bear, a great deal of dissatisfaction remains. Well-informed critics charge that the Bank's lending practices have not improved generally, and it is still the exceptional case where NGOs and other environmental advocates can overturn a deleterious Bank project. Rich, Bruce (1990) 'The Emperor's New Clothes', 7 *World Policy Journal* , 305–29, p 322. World Bank environmental assessments hardly ever become public; those that have been brought to light suggest a systematic downplaying of environmental threats. See Scott, Dennis J (March/April 1992) 'Making a Bank Turn'; *The Environmental Forum* , 21–5. As of 1990, the World Bank had never suspended loan payments for breach of initial loan covenants, including environmental covenants. See Guyett, Stephanie C (1992) 'Environment and Lending'; 24 *International Law and Politics* 889–919.

6   See Post, Marilyn 'The Debt for Nature Swap: a Longterm Investment for the Economic Stability of Less Developed Countries', 24 *International Lawyer*, 1071–1098.

7   For example, the Biodiversity Convention that issued from Rio declares the conservation of biological diversity to be 'a common concern of humankind'. 1992 United Nations Framework Convention on Biological Diversity, Preamble, reprinted in 21 *International Environment Reporter Reference File (BNA)* , 4001–10 (1992).

8   For example, the 'common concern' language, note 7, supra, is immediately qualified by the principle, 'States have sovereign rights over their own biological resources.' Ibid. This is a long-standing and continuing Third World theme. 'Development is a fundamental right of all peoples and countries.' Kuala Lumpur Declaration on Environment and Development, Article 4, reprinted in 22 *Environmental Policy and Law*, 266–7 (August, 1992). In particular, forests 'are

part of the national patrimony to be managed, conserved and developed by each country in accordance with its national plans and priorities in the exercise of its sovereign rights.' Id at Article 15. The Declaration reaffirms 'the sovereign rights of States to use their biological and genetic resources.' Id at Article 25. '[T]he implementation mechanisms of the [Framework Convention on Climate Change] should fully take into account the sovereign rights of each country to determine its national policies, plans and programmes for sustainable development.' Id at Article 24.

9   *Trail Smelter (US v Canada)*, 3 RIAA 1911 (1941).

10 Springer, A (1983) *The International Law of Pollution*, Qurom Books,Westport, Conn, pp 150-2.

11 Note that the Stockholm Declaration (1972) of the United Nations Conference on the Human Environment, note 4, supra, denounces in the same terms 'damage to the environment of other States' and damage to 'areas beyond the limits of national jurisdiction.' The point of the text is that *in practice* the sameness of treatment is not realized.

12 Special conventions and resolutions are beginning to address such issues, eg, the United Nations General Assembly Resolution on Driftnetting discussed in the text below; as explained more fully in the text, the 'Guardianship' concept advocated herein is not inconsistent with, but should be integrated with, those ongoing efforts.

13 It is worth recalling, in this context, a major if perhaps unfortunate theme in international law: the suggestion that anything not specifically prohibited is *ipso facto* permitted. See *SS Lotus (France v Turkey)* PCIJ Ser A No 10 (1927).

14 See Simon, Stephanie (18 July, 1992) 'Fears over Nazi Weapons Leaking at Bottom of Baltic,'; *Los Angeles Times*, p A3.

15 See (7 May, 1990) 'Atomic Waste Reported Leaking in Ocean Sanctuary off California,'; *New York Times*, p B12 (about one-fourth of 47,500 55 gallon drums dumped between 1947 and 1970 off San Francisco had ruptured, threatening to contaminate local fish resources). How much alarm the potential leakage warrants is controversial. See Holliday, F G T 'The Dumping of Radioactive Waste in the Deep Ocean' in Cooper, David E and Palmer, Joy A (ed) *The Environment in Question*; Routledge, New York pp 51–64, 56–9. In all events, contracting parties to the London Dumping Convention agreed to a moratorium on marine disposal of radioactive wastes in the 1980s; the moratorium is due for revision in 1993. See 'Opponents to Nuclear Waste Dumping Ban Want Global Action, Senior IMO Official Says'; 15 *International Environment Reporter (BNA)* 353 (1992).

16 Tyler, Patrick E (4 May, 1992) 'Soviets' Secret Nuclear Dumping Causes Worry for Arctic Waters'; *Los Angeles Times*, p A1. Impatient Soviet sailors got the canisters to sink more quickly by punching holes in them.

17 Non-governmental organizations were invited to make submissions to early human rights cases before the PCIJ in the 1920s.

18 See 40 CFR (1990) §§ 300.600, 300.615(a)(1).

19 *United States v Montrose Chemicals*, Dkt No CV 90-3122 AAH, DCD Cal 1990.

20 *Seehunde v Bundesrepublik Deutschland* (Verwaltungagericht, Hamburg, 15 August 1988).

21 See Food and Agricultural Organization (1991) *Fishery Statistics 1989*, vol 69 *Food*

and Agricultural Organization, Italy. Tables A-2 and A-4. 'Export value' averaged $1.10 a pound. The figures are for 1989, the most recent year for which reports are available.

22 In 1991, 7 billion barrels of oil and 13.5 trillion cubic feet of natural gas were extracted from offshore sites, worth approximately $160 billion. The global data is not gathered in such a way as to enable us to separate the amount produced within traditional 3 and 12 mile limits from amounts produced within the (extended) reach of the EEZs. Our illustrative calculations are based on the assumption that 50 per cent of the yield is beyond traditional territorial waters. In regard to fish, the only breakdown available is between national fisheries (95 per cent), on the one hand, and the high seas areas beyond (5 per cent), on the other. See Agenda 21, Chapter 17 ('Protection of the Oceans, All Kinds of Seas, Including Enclosed and Semi-Enclosed Seas, and Coastal Areas and the Protection, Rational Use and Development of Their Living Resources')(Draft Version), §17.47, reprinted in 22 *Environmental Policy and Law* 281–90 (1992). Our calculations include all fish. The rationale is explained in the text below.

23 World Resources Institute et al (1990)*World Resources 1988–89,* Oxford University Press, Oxford p 330, Table 22.3.

24 A tax on most uses of the ocean has been proposed, but taxing those who take advantage of the sea just because they *use* it makes no more sense than taxing people for making 'use' of sunlight: as long as the use is non-consumptive and non-rival, why drive people to other, depletable resources? At present, sea traffickers do not fully internalize risks to third parties through oil spills. The 1971 International Oil Pollution Compensation Fund provides for compensation, but only up to $84 million per incident. In any disaster of greater scale, such as the wreck of the *SS Braer* off the Coast of Scotland in January 1993, the taxpayers (British) will presumably be left to foot the balance of the clean-up bill. If ships were charged a full-coverage level of premium, and no more, the charge would not be a naked fee on the privilege of ocean use (and a deadweight loss, see note 24, infra), but would internalize some of the costs of ocean transport; the charge would be earmarked to support emergency clean-up operations as explained elsewhere in the text.

25 Humankind added 8.49 billion metric tons of CO_2 to the atmosphere in 1987. World Resources Institute et al (1990) *World Resources 1990–91,* Oxford University Press, Oxford p 346, Table 24.1. Measuring by mass of carbon dioxide, not carbon, the figure is over 22 billion metric tons. Note that inasmuch as the biosphere continuously withdraws carbon dioxide from the atmosphere, these figures overstate the net annual contribution to atmospheric carbon dioxide attributable to human activities.

26 Annual emission figures for methane and chlorofluorocarbons are found in World Resources Institute et al,(1990) *World Resources 1990–91;* (Oxford University Press, Oxford, p 346, Table 24.1); similar figures for nitrogen oxides from US Environmental Protection Agency (1990) *Policy Options for Stabilizing Global Climate;* USEPA, Washington, DC p II–18. The emission figures were then multiplied by global warming potentials for each greenhouse gas relative to carbon dioxide, using indices from Ellington, R et al (1992) 'The Total Greenhouse Warming Forcing of Technical Systems: Analysis for Decision Making,' 42 *Journal of the Air & Waste Management Association* , 422–28.

27 In the text I have gathered together resources that in fact present quite distinct features from the perspective of tax policy. For example, depositing waste in the sea and atmosphere present negative externalities that the right level of tax would presumably 'correct.' By contrast, seabed oil and minerals, as well as satellite slots (barring congestion) present no pollution externalities, but, depending upon costs of exploitation, afford the potential for considerable economic rents that the State *might* be able to peel off without loss of efficiency. Of course, the authority charged with setting the level and style of charge would have to be sensitive to the traps of 'dead weight loss' that occur in any severance tax context. That is, if the seabed should turn out to be a low-cost source of cobalt, the authority would have to be cautious not to put cobalt, and, in particular, seabed cobalt, at a disadvantage relative to substitutes. The taxation of fisheries or any other regenerative resource presents yet a third type of problem: the right tax will not only raise revenue, but improve the long term yield of the fishery by preventing excessive entry (and do so more efficiently than fishing seasons). These differences would have to be accounted for in any detailed implementation of the GCTF, as would the choice between a tax and alternative policy instruments, for example, auctions of tradeable quotas.

28 And, in part (as regards the levies for resources taken from the EEZs, for example), to compensate other nations for an otherwise unjustifiable unilateral partition of commonly-owned areas.

29 Note that the modest carbon tax proposed for the GCTF is not inconsistent with – in fact, it would leave plenty of room for – stiffer carbon and gasoline taxes that have been proposed in the EC and in the US. Indeed, it ought to be emphasized in general that the two principal proposals in the text are in no way to be understood as displacing various other measures on environmentalists' agenda.

30 'Europeans May Propose Forestry Protocol Under Climate Treaty, EPA Official Says', *International Environment Daily (BNA)*(19 November, 1992).

4 ENFORCING ENVIRONMENTAL SECURITY

1 This article is an adapted version of the chapter on 'Compliance' from Sands, Philippe (1994) *Principles of International Environmental Law*, Manchester University Press, Manchester, UK. Forthcoming.

2 Agenda 21, *UN Doc A/CONF 151/26, I, II, III* United Nations, New York, (12 August, 1992) Chapter 1, Preamble, paragraph 1.1.

3 On the topic of environmental security and international relations, see Matthews, Jessica Tuchman (1989) 'Redefining Security,' 68 *Foreign Affairs*, p 163; Renner, M (1989) *National Security: The Economic and Environmental Dimensions*, Worldwatch Paper 8, Worldwatch Institute; Timoshenko, A 'Ecological Security: Global Change Paradigm', Washington DC, 2 *Colorado Journal of Environmental and International Law and Policy*, p 127; Vinogradov, S (1990) 'International Environmental Security: The Concept and its Implementation,' in Carter, A and Danilenko, G (eds), *Perestroika and International Law*, Graham and Trotman,

London, p 196; Handl, G (1990) 'Environmental Security and Global Change: The Challenge to International Law', 1 *Yearbook of International Environmental Law*, p 3.

4   See note by the President of the UN Security Council on 'The Responsibility of the Security Council in the Maintenance of International Peace and Security,' *UN Doc S/23500* , (31 January, 1992) p 2.

5   UN General Assembly Resolution 44/228 (20 December, 1989).

6   These instruments include Agenda 21; the Rio Declaration on the Environment and Development (Rio Declaration); the Non-Legally Binding Authoritative Statement of Principles for a Global Consensus on the Management, Conservation and Sustainable Development of all Types of Forests (the Forest Principles); the United Nations Framework Convention on Climate Change (Climate Change Convention); and the Convention on Biological Diversity (1992 Biodiversity Convention).

7   Concerning the issue of whether the United States had the right, on conservation grounds, to stop United Kingdom nationals from taking fur seals in areas beyond national jurisdiction, see the Fur Seal Arbitration, *Great Britain v United States* (1893) in *Moore's International Arbitration Awards*, 1, p 755.

8   See for example Trail Smelter Arbitration, *Canada v United States*, 3 *United Nations Reports of International Arbitral Awards*, (1941) p 1905; the Nuclear Test Cases *Australia v France, International Court of Justice Reports (ICJ Reports)*, (1973) p 99; and *New Zealand v France, ICJ Reports* (1974) p 457; Lac Lanoux Arbitration, *ICJ Reports, France v Spain*, 24 *International Law Reports*, (1957) p 101; Fisheries Jurisdiction Case, *United Kingdom v Iceland, ICJ Reports* (1974) p 3; Yellow-Fin Tuna Decision, *Mexico v United States, GATT Doc DS21/R 3* (September, 1991); Case Concerning Certain Phospate Lands In Nauru, *Nauru v Australia, ICJ Reports*, (1992) p 240.

9   'Danube Dam Threatens to Open Floodgates of Hostility', *Financial Times*, 29 October 1992, p 2. A mechanism for consultation and cooperation with regard to emergency situations was adopted at the Berlin Meeting of the Conference on Security and Cooperation in Europe (CSCE), 19–20 June, 1991. The mechanism comprises a process of exchange of information between the concerned States, and, if unsuccessful, may lead to a special meeting of the Committee of Senior Officials, who may then refer the matter to the ministerial level. If this process does not resolve the situation, the dispute may be referred to the Procedure for Peaceful Settlement of Disputes, involving the Conflict Prevention Center. See CSCE, 30 *Summary of Conclusion of the Berlin Meeting in International Legal Materials*, (1991) p 1348, Annex 2 and Annex 3. On 22 October 1992, Hungary formally filed an application with the ICJ to prevent the construction of the Grabcikovo Dam.

10   Non-compliance with international environmental obligations can occur for a variety of reasons, including a lack of institutional, financial or human resources, and differing interpretations as to the meaning or requirements of a particular obligation.

11   Principle 21 provides, in relevant part, that States accept 'the responsibility to ensure that activities within their jurisdiction or control do not cause damage to the environment of other States or of areas beyond the limits of national jurisdiction.' The same language is now found in Principle 2 of the Rio Declara-

tion (June 1992), which was adopted by 176 States and the European Community at the UN Conference for the Environment and Development (UNCED).

12 Several thousand bilateral and multilateral treaties concerning the environment have been adopted since the late eighteenth century. The more important ones may be found in the United Nations Environmental Programme (UNEP), *Selected Multilateral Treaties in the Field of the Environment*, vol 1 (1983); vol 2 (1991).

13 See for example Convention on the Conservation of the Living Resources of the Southeast Atlantic (1969) Article X (1); Convention on the Prevention of Marine Pollution by Dumping of Wastes and Other Matter (1972 London Dumping Convention) Article VII (1); Convention on the Control of Transboundary Movements of Hazardous Wastes and their Disposal (1989 Basel Convention) Article 4 (4); Protocol on Environmental Protection to the Antarctic Treaty (1991 Antarctic Protocol) Article 13.

14 Convention on the Regulation of Antarctic Mineral Resource Activities (CRAMRA) (1988) Article 7 (1).

15 See 1989 Basel Convention, Article 5.

16 For examples of measures within a State's jurisdiction or control, see 1972 Convention for the Prevention of Marine Pollution by Dumping from Ships and Aircraft (1972 Oslo Convention) Article 15(1); 1973 Convention on International Trade in Endangered Species (CITES) Article VIII (1). For examples of application of sanctions or other punitive measures, see 1946 International Convention for the Regulation of Whaling (1946 Whaling Convention) Articles IX(1) and IX(3); 1972 Oslo Convention, Article X(3); 1972 London Dumping Convention, Article VII (2); 1989 Basel Convention.

17 See 1987 Montreal Protocol, Article 7 and 1990 Amendments, Article 7; 1946 Whaling Convention, Article VIII (1); 1972 London Dumping Convention, Articles VI (4) and VIII (3); 1989 Basel Convention, Articles 13 (2) (c)(d) and 13 (3)(c); and 1992 Climate Change Convention, Article 12 (1).

18 A recent report prepared for the US Committee on Environment and Public Works considered, *inter alia*, six environmental treaties that require parties to submit periodic reports, and found wide variations in compliance with reporting requirements. See US General Accounting Office, *International Environment: International Agreements Are Not Well Monitored*, Report to Congressional Requesters, *GAO Doc GAO/RCED-92-43* (1992). Some treaties revealed a strong record. All six parties to the International Whaling Convention required to submit information on their 1989 whale harvests did so, and 16 of the 17 parties to the Protocol Concerning the Control of Emissions of Nitrogen Oxides or their Transboundary Fluxes (1988 NOX Protocol) submitted their 1990 reports on their emissions in 1987 or other years. By October 1990, 52 of the then 65 parties to the 1987 Montreal Protocol had responded to the requirement to report information on their consumption of controlled substances in 1986, of which 29 (representing 85 per cent of world consumption) submitted complete data. At the other end of the scale, however, only 19 of the 64 parties to the 1972 London Dumping Convention reported on the number and types of dumping permits they issued in 1987, and only 13 of the 57 parties (representing only about 27 per cent of the world's gross shipping tonnage) to the 1973 International Convention for the Prevention of Pollution from Ships, amended in 1978 (MARPOL 73/78)

submitted reports summarizing violations and penalties they had imposed in 1989. Finally, just 25 of the 104 parties to CITES submitted reports summarizing their 1989 import and export certificates for listed endangered species.

19 The question of who may enforce environmental obligations at the national level lies beyond the scope of this article. Recent international developments concerning this issue include Principle 10 of the Rio Declaration, which calls on States to provide 'effective access to judicial and administrative proceedings, including redress and remedy'; also recent attempts by the EC Commission to develop legislation allowing citizens to seek injunctive relief for environmental damage. See 'Proposal for a Council Directive on Civil Liability for Damage Caused by Waste', COM(89) 282 final, *Official Journal of the European Community* (1989) C 251/3.

20 See 'European Commission on Human Rights, European Convention for the Protection of Human Rights and Fundamental Freedoms' (1950) Article 24.

21 The global commons includes the high seas, the seabed beyond national jurisdiction, outer space and the Antarctic.

22 On the suggestion that a coastal State is obliged to the world at large to prevent pollution of the territorial seas, see O'Connell, Daniel (1984) *The International Law of the Sea*, Oxford University Press, Oxford, 2, pp 988–89.

23 See Sands, Philippe (1988) *Chernobyl: International Law and Communication*, Grotius, Cambridge, UK, pp 26–30.

24 See Sands, Philippe 'Environment, Community and International Law,' 30 *Harvard International Law Journal*, (1989) p 393.

25 See Reparations for Injuries Case, *ICJ Reports* (1949) p 174. The ICJ found in an advisory opinion that the United Nations had an 'undeniable right' to 'demand that its Members fulfill the obligations entered into by them in the interest of the good working of the Organization,' and the capacity to claim adequate reparation for a breach of these obligations. It also held that 'fifty States, representing the vast majority of the members of the international community, had the power, in conformity with international law, to bring into being an entity possessing objective international personality and not merely personality recognized by them alone, together with the capacity to bring international claims…'.

26 See for example Treaty on the Prohibition of the Emplacement of Nuclear Weapons and Other Weapons of Mass Destruction on the Sea-Bed and the Ocean Floor and in the Subsoil Thereof (1963) Article III (4); Convention on the Prohibition of the Development, Production and Stockpiling of Bacteriological and Toxic Weapons and on Their Destruction, London, Washington, Moscow (1972) Article VI.

27 See for example Convention on the Conservation of European Wildlife and Natural Habitats (1979) Article 14 (1); 1992 Climate Change Convention, Article 7 (2).

28 The EC Commission has the power to enforce compliance of environmental obligations among EC member States, including ensuring proper implementation of their Community obligations. See Treaty Establishing the European Economic Community (1957 EEC Treaty) Article 155.

29 Ibid.

30 Northeast Atlantic Marine Convention, Article 22; reprinted in London Dumping Convention, *International Marine Organization (IMO) Doc IS/INF 11* (20

October, 1992) Annex I.

31 Under some of the regional human rights treaties, individual victims, including non-governmental organizations, may bring complaints directly to an international body. See European Convention on Human Rights (1950); American Convention on Human Rights (1969) Articles 44, 45; African Charter on Human and Peoples' Rights (1981) Article 55. Similar provisions can be found in the First Optional Protocol to the International Covenant on Civil and Political Rights, UN General Assembly Resolution 2200 (1966).

32 See for example the Convention on Fishing and Conservation of the Living Resources of the High Seas (1958) Article 9 (1), specifically referring to Article 33 of the UN Charter.

33 See for example the Convention on Nature Protection and Wildlife Preservation in the Western Hemisphere (1940) and the 1946 Whaling Convention.

34 In the context of a dispute over international fisheries jurisdiction, the ICJ has laid out the objectives underlying negotiation as an appropriate method for the solution of a dispute. See Fisheries Jurisdiction case, *ICJ Reports*, p 31.

35 See for example CITES, Article XVIII.1; 1972 Space Liability Convention, Article IX; Convention on Long-Range Transboundary Air Pollution (1979 Air Pollution Convention) Article 13; 1985 Convention for the Protection of the Ozone Layer (1985 Ozone Convention) Article 11 (1); 1992 Climate Change Convention, Article 14; 1992 Biodiversity Convention, Article 27 (1).

36 See for example 1979 Air Pollution Convention, Article 5; 1991 Convention on Environmental Impact Assessment in a Transboundary Context, Article 5.

37 See for example 1968 African Nature Convention Article XVIII [referring disputes to the Commission of Mediation, Conciliation and Arbitration of the Organization for African Unity (OAU)]; 1976 European Convention for the Protection of Animals Kept for Farming Purposes, Article 10; UN Convention on the Law of the Sea (1982 UNCLOS) Article 284 and Annex V, Section 1; 1985 Ozone Convention, Article 11 (2).

38 See for example 1963 Vienna Convention on Civil Liability for Nuclear Damage, Optional Protocol Concerning the Compulsory Settlement of Disputes, Article III; 1974 Paris Convention, Article 21 (conciliation by the Commission); 1985 Ozone Convention, Articles 11 (4)–11 (5) (providing for the establishment of a conciliation commission); 1992 Biodiversity Convention, Article 27 (4) and Annex II, Part 2; 1992 Climate Change Convention, Articles 14 (6)–14 (7).

39 See for example 1949 Agreement for the Establishment of a General Fisheries Council for the Mediterranean, Article XIII; 1951 International Plant Protection Convention, Article IX; International Convention for the High Seas Fisheries of the North Pacific Ocean Protocol (1952) paragraphs 4 and 5.

40 See for example Regional Convention for the Conservation of the Red Sea and Gulf of Aden Environment (1982) Article XXIV (2); Agreement on the Network of Aquaculture Centres in Asia and the Pacific (1988) Article 19 (1).

41 See for example Fur Seal Arbitration, Trail Smelter Arbitration and Lac Lanoux Arbitration.

42 Jurisdiction of the ICJ over a particular dispute depends on whether the Court has been invoked in a contentious case between two or more States or to give an advisory opinion. In relation to contentious cases, it is important to recall that 'only States may be parties in cases before the Court'. UN Charter, Article 34 (1).

43 See for example Convention on Civil Liability for Nuclear Damage, Optional Protocol Concerning the Compulsory Settlement of Disputes (1963) Article I (not yet in force).

44 See for example 1959 Antarctic Treaty, Article XI (2); 1974 Baltic Convention, Article 18 (2).

45 See Nuclear Tests cases, note 7, supra.

46 *ICJ Reports* (1949) p 4.

47 It is relied upon by Hungary in its application of 22 October 1992 to the ICJ concerning the dispute over the construction of the Grabcikovo Dam. See note 8, supra.

48 Statute of the ICJ, Article 96 (1).

49 Ibid, Article 96 (2). The UN Economic and Social Council (ECOSOC), the Trusteeship Council and 15 of the specialized agencies have been authorized by the General Assembly, as has the International Atomic Energy Agency (IAEA), the Interim Committee of the General Assembly and the Committee for Applications for Review of the UN Administrative Tribunal. UNEP has not been so authorized by the General Assembly.

50 EEC Treaty, Article 164.

51 Ibid, Article 189.

52 See for example Case 91/79, *Commission of the European Communities* v *Italy*, *European Court Reports* (1980) p 1099, rejecting Italy's defences that the national legislation already contained provisions that to a large extent secured the realization of the objects of the Directive; that the Directive was *ultra vires*; and that implementation was 'thwarted by the vicissitudes which were a feature of the brief existence of the seventh legislature of the Italian Parliament, and particularly its premature end.' Ibid, p 1105.

53 See for example Cases 30 to 41/81, *Commission of the European Communities* v *Italian Republic*, *European Court Reports* (1981) p 3379; Case 134/86, *Commission of the European Communities* v *Belgium*, *European Court Reports* (1987) p 2415.

54 See for example Cases 96 and 97/81, *Commission of the European Communities* v *Netherlands*, *European Court Reports* (1982) pp 1791 and 1819.

55 The ECJ also has jurisdiction under Article 175 of the EEC Treaty, under similar conditions as Article 173, to challenge the failure of the EC Council or Commission to have acted in pursuance of its environmental obligations under the treaty. To date no environmental case appears to have been brought under this provision.

56 See for example Case 182/89, *Commission of the European Communities* v *France*, 1 *Yearbook of International Environmental Law*, (1990) p 274. The ECJ held that France had infringed Article 10.1 (b) of EC Council Regulation No 3626/82 on the implementation of CITES by granting import licenses for skins of certain feline animals originating in Bolivia.

57 See for example Case C-75/91, *Commission* v *Netherlands* (as yet unreported). Under Article 170 of the EEC Treaty, a member State that believes another member State has breached its obligations has a similar right to bring a matter before the ECJ. To date, however, no case concerning alleged breaches of environmental obligations have been brought under this head.

58 1982 UNCLOS, Articles 213, 214, 216 and 222.

59 Ibid, Article 287 (1).

60 See Decision II/5 (non-compliance) of UNEP, Report of the Second Meeting of the Parties to the Montreal Protocol on Substances that Deplete the Ozone Layer, *UNEP Doc OzL Pro 2/3* (29 June, 1990) Annex III, paras 1–5.

61 Ibid, paras 6 and 7.

62 *Report of the Fourth Meeting of the Parties to the Montreal Protocol, UNEP Doc OzL Pro 4/15* (25 November, 1992) Annex 5. The measures envisaged include, for the first time in an international environmental instrument: issuing cautions and suspending specific rights and privileges under the Protocol, including those related to the trade, technology transfer and the availability of resources under the financial mechanism.

63 1992 Climate Change Convention, Articles 10 and 13.

64 See note 7, supra.

65 Ibid.

66 Sands, Philippe and Bedecarré, Al 'CITES: The Role of Public Interest Non-Governmental Organizations in Ensuring the Effective Enforcement of the Ivory Trade Ban', 17 *Boston College Environmental Affairs Law Review*, (1990) p 799.

67 Rio Declaration, Principles 10, 11 and 26.

68 Ibid, paras 38.22(h); 38.24 and 38.25(a).

69 Ibid, para 38.13(f). The Commission on Sustainable Development was formally established by UN General Assembly Resolution 47/191 in December 1992.

70 Ibid, para 39.3(h).

71 Ibid, para 39.9.

5 GREENING BRETTON WOODS

1 The term 'World Bank' or 'World Bank group' as used here loosely refers to the International Bank for Reconstruction and Development (IBRD), the International Development Association (IDA), the International Finance Corporation (IFC), and the Multilateral Investment Guarantee Agency (MIGA). The term 'Bretton Woods' institutions, used here interchangeably with the 'World Bank' often includes the General Agreement on Tariffs and Trade (GATT), not covered in this discussion, but touched upon in Chapter 7.

2 See, eg, (April, 1992) *The World Bank's Greenwash: Touting Environmentalism While Trashing the Planet*, Greenpeace (hereinafter 'Trashing the Planet'); and Statement of Bruce M Rich on Behalf of Environmental Defense Fund and the Sierra Club Before the Subcommittee on Foreign Operations, Export Financing, and Related Matters, Committee on Appropriations, United States House of Representatives, 1 March, 1993.

3 (1987) *Our Common Future: The Report of the World Commission on Environment and Development*, Oxford University Press, Oxford, at 317 (hereinafter WCED).

4 Agreement Between the UN and the IBRD, 15 November, 1947, Article I (2), I (3), Article IV(3).

5 Articles of Agreement of the IBRD, as amended 17 February, 1989, Article III (4) vii.

6 Wapenhans, Willi A et al (1 July, 1992) *Report of the Portfolio Management Task Force*, (internal Bank document), at 4 . According to the Bank's own criteria, 37.5

per cent of the Bank's recently evaluated projects are failures.

7   With the addition of Macedonia in March 1993, UN membership included 180 States; as of March 1993, the World Bank had 174 members.

8   See, eg WCED, at 310, *et seq*; Thacher, P (1992) 'The Role of the United Nations', (hereinafter Thacher) in Hurrell, A and Kingsbury, B *The International Politics of the Environment*, Oxford University Press, Oxford 204–205 (hereinafter Hurrell and Kingsbury).

9   Staffed by fewer than half a dozen people, asked to screen 250–300 projects annually through the 1980s it is not surprising that the process was subject to criticism. Murgatroyd, C (1 July, 1990) *The World Bank and Environmental Protection*, a long essay for the LL M degree.

10 Piddington, K 'The Role of the World Bank' in Hurrell and Kingsbury supra note 8, at 220 (hereinafter Piddington).

11 *The World Bank and the Environment: Fiscal 1992*, World Bank, 1992 at 14.

12 See Goodland and Daly (1992) *Approaching Global Environmental Sustainability: a World Bank Environmental Working Paper No.*

13 Statement of Lori Udall, Staff Attorney, Environmental Defence Fund, on Behalf of Environmental Defence Fund and Sierra Club Before the Subcommittee on Foreign Operations, Export Financing, and Related Matters, Committee on Appropriations, United States House of Representatives, 1 March, 1993 (hereinafter Udall testimony).

14 WCED at 337.

15 Piddington at 216.

16 *Environment Bulletin: A Newsletter of the World Bank Environment Community*, vol 5, No 1, Winter 1992/1993.

17 Thacher at 192.

18 WCED at 338.

19 Agenda 21; 38.17.

20 Rich, B *Memorandum: The Role of the World Bank After UNCED: The Need for Institutional Reform* at 5.

21 Morse, B and Berger, T (1992) *Sardar Sarorat: Report of the Independent Review*, Resource Futures International, Ottowa, Canada at 36.

22 'India to drop World Bank dam loans',*Financial Times*, 30 March, 1993, at 6 col 1.

23 For a full discussion of these principles see Chapter 2.

24 Rio Declaration, Principle 27; 2; 13; 24.

25 Rio Declaration, Principle 2; Stockholm Declaration, Principle 21.

26 Thacher at 205.

27 WWF, (February, 1993) *The Southern Green Fund: Views from the South on the Global Environment Facility* .

28 Rio Declaration, Principle 7.

29 Ibid, Principle 10.

30 Agenda 21, 38.2.

31 Agenda 21, 38.40.

32 UNGA Resolution 47/191, para 3.a; Agenda 21, 38.12.

33 Ibid, para 23.

34 Agenda 21, 38.43.

35 WCED, at 338, 342.

36 Resolution of the Board of Executive Directors of the IBRD, 14 March, 1991.

37 (May, 1992) *The Global Environment Facility: Beyond the Pilot Phase*, Working Paper Series Number 1, 2–4 (Beyond the Pilot Phase), pp 8–9.
38 Ibid, at 3.
39 Ibid.
40 Ibid, at 9.
41 Udall testimony.
42 'Trashing the Planet', at 2.
43 UN Framework Convention on Climate Change, (hereinafter Convention) Article 11(4).
44 Ibid, Article 11(1).
45 The Convention expressly describes regular reporting by the FM's operating entity as 'consistent with the requirement for accountability'. Article 11(3)(b).
46 Article 11(3)(a), (3)(b).
47 The GEF has given every indication that its membership will be made universal in conformity with the GEF's own public statements with Agenda 21 and with the Convention. *Beyond the Pilot Phase* (May, 1992) at 5, paragraph 2.05, (BAP); GEF Chairman's Summary of the Abidjan Meeting, at 1, para 6; Agenda 21, Chapter 33.

6 GREENING THE EEC TREATY

1 Council Directive 67/548, *Official Journal 1967 L196/1*.
2 Council Directives 70/157, *Official Journal 1970 L42/6* and 70/220, *Official Journal 1970 L76/1*.
3 See, for example, Johnson and Corcelle (1989) *The Environment Policy of the European Communities*, Graham & Trotman, London.
4 Articles 130R–T
5 Article 130S provides for: '[a]ction by the Community relating to the environment [having] the following objectives:
   - to preserve, protect and improve the quality of the environment;
   - to contribute towards protecting human health;
   - to ensure a prudent and rational utilization of natural resources.'
6 See Case 300/89 *Commission* v *Council* and Case 155/91 *Commission* v *Council* [155/91 is the Waste Directive case going 'the other way'].
7 Article 34 imposes the same prohibition in relation to exports.
8 Case 8/74 *Dassonville* [1974] ECR 837.
9 Case 261/81 *Rau* [1982] ECR 3961.
10 Case 220/81 *Robertson* [1982] ECR 2349.
11 Case 50/85 *Schloh* [1987] 1 CMLR 450.
12 Case 120/78 *Rewe* v *Zentralverwaltung* [1979] ECR 649.
13 Case 240/83 *Procureur de la République* v *Association de Défence des Bruleurs d'Huiles Usagées* [1985] ECR 531.
14 Case 302/86 *Commission* v *Denmark* [1988] ECR 4607.
15 See Advocate-General's Opinion in Case 302/86 delivered on 24 May, 1988.
16 Case 2/90 *Commission* v *Belgium* , judgment of 10 June 1991 (unreported).
17 Decree of 19 March 1987 concerning the disposal of certain waste products in the

Region of Wallonia (Moniteur Belge of 28 March 1987, p 4671) as amended by Decree of 23 July 1987 (Moniteur Belge of 29 September 1987, p 14078).

18 Set out in the 1989 Basel Convention and endorsed by the EC Council of Ministers in its Resolution of 7 May 1990 on EC waste policy.

19 This is a rough translation from the French, which to date, is the only language version of the ECJ's decision.

20 Directive 91/173 *Official Journal 1991 L85.*

21 Regulation (EEC) No 259/93 on the supervision and control of shipments of waste within, into and out of the European Community, *Official Journal 1993 L30.*

22 Kramer, Ludwig *Environment Protection and Article 30 EEC Treaty,* 30 CMLR 111.

23 Demaret, Paul 'Trade-related environmental measures (TREMs) in the external relations of the European Community' published in Maresceau, M (ed) *The European Community's commercial policy after 1992: the legal dimension 1992,* Martinus Nijhoff, Dordrecht.

24 Council Directive 83/129 concerning the importation into member States of skins of certain seal pups and products derived therefrom, *Official Journal 1983 L91/30.*

25 Council Regulation 348/81 on common rules for imports of whales and other cetcean products, *Official Journal 1981 L39/1.*

26 Council Regulation 3254/91 of 4 November, 1991 prohibiting the use of leghold traps in the Community and the introduction into the Community of pelts and manufactured goods of certain wild animal species originating in countries which catch them by means of leghold traps or trapping methods which do not meet international humane standards, *Official Journal 1991 L308/1.*

7 THE GATT AND THE ENVIRONMENT

(The author is grateful to Richard Tarasofsky and Halina Ward for their research and assistance.)

1 The General Agreement on Tariffs and Trade has 106 Contracting Parties and a Secretariat servicing the government delegations and the some 200 treaties and agreements which form part of the GATT system, see Jackson, John H (1989) *The World Trading System: Law and Policy of International Economic Relations,* MIT Press, Cambridge, Massachusetts..

2 Allott, P (1990) *Eunomia,* Oxford University Press, Oxford.

3 Not an objective point of view since FIELD (Fahana Yamin and myself) drafted this for the GLOBE Convention on the Conservation and Wise Use of Forests, available from GLOBE, 50 Rue de Taciturne, 1040 Brussels, Belgium.

4 Interestingly the draft was soon to be overtaken by a new draft, 27 May, 1992, so that for some time research was being carried out on out-of-date information, until the May draft was obtained.

5 These documents are not public.

6 Cameron, James and Ward, Halina (1992) *The MTO: A Legal and Environmental Assessment,* WWF Research Paper, WWF, Gland, Switzerland.

7 *GATT Doc DS21/R,* (3 September, 1991).

8 'SABOTAGE! of America's Health, Food Safety and Environmental Laws', *New York Times* , 20 April, 1992.

9   Organized by the Liberal Democratic Party and held at Kings College London.
10 The externality which gives rise to the environmental damage.
11 Draft Final Act Embodying the Results of the Uruguay Round of Multilateral Trade Negotiations (MTN TNC/W/FA), 20 December 1991, Annex IV.
12 Daly, H in *Network 92 Special Networks Supplement: Reviews of Agenda 21*, No 1, Centre for Our Common Future, Geneva, Switzerland.
13 Convention on International Trade in Endangered Species of Wild Fauna and Flora (1973, Washington) 993 UNTS 243; 12 ILM 1085 (1973).
14 Lyster (1985) *International Wildlife Law*, Grotius Publications Limited, Cambridge, at 241.
15 Lyster at 241.
16 Lyster at 256.
17 See, for example, in relation to wild plants, de Klemm, C (1990) *Wild Plant Conservation and the Law*, Chapter 4.3, IUCN, Switzerland.
18 Eg, Article 39 of the Fourth ACP-EEC Lome Convention (Lome IV) [29 ILM 783 (1990) 52] provides: 'The Contracting Parties undertake, for their part, to make every effort to ensure that international movements of hazardous waste and radioactive waste are generally controlled, and they emphasize the importance of efficient international cooperation in this area.'

Similarly the preamble to the Resolution on an African Common Position on the Basel Convention of the OAU Pan-African Conference on Environment and Sustainable Development [Bamako, Mali, 23–30 January 1991] states that: 'Regional and International Cooperation is necessary for an effective control of the transboundary movements of hazardous wastes and their elimination.'
19 This is affirmed in Rio Principle 14.
20 As regards participation of developing countries it is imperative that the making of the agreement is legitimized by their participation. That participation needs to be entirely encouraged through funding mechanisms. Thereafter, developing countries invariably need to be assisted to comply with obligations, through direct funding or through transfer of technology or both.
21 (3 September, 1991) 'Report of the Panel, US – Restrictions on Imports of Tuna', *GATT Doc No DS21/R*.
22 This dispute I learned from Ed Barbier at University College London.
23 *GATT Doc L/7110*, (23 October, 1992).
24 *GATT Doc No TRE/W/3*, (29 September, 1992).
25 See (7 November, 1990) 'Report of the Panel, Thailand – Restrictions on Importation of, and Internal Taxes on, Cigarettes'.
26 Article 2.2.
27 See infra notes 64–67 and accompanying text. Official references to the precautionary principle include: 'In order to protect the environment, the precautionary approach shall be widely applied by States according to their capabilities. Where there are threats of serious or irreversible damage, lack of full scientific certainty should not be used as a reason for postponing cost-effective measures to prevent environmental degradation.' (Rio Declaration, June 1992); 'Dealing cautiously with risk implies that where considerable uncertainty surrounds a proposed action, the decision should lean on the side of caution. This does not mean that development should not proceed whenever we cannot be certain of its ecological impact. It does mean that the need for particular

caution needs to influence the balance between a need to preserve natural capital and a need to proceed.' (1992 Australian ESD Intersectoral Issues Report,p 40); 'in order to protect the North Sea from possibly damaging effects of the most dangerous substances a precautionary approach is necessary which may require action to control inputs of such substances even before a causal link has been established by absolutely clear scientific evidence.' (Ministerial Declaration, Second International Conference on the Protection of the North Sea, 1987); see also: Treaty on European Union (Maastricht 1992), Article 130r, para 2; The Noordwijk Declaration on Atmospheric Pollution and Climate Change, 7 November, 1990; Preamble to the Montreal Protocol to the Vienna Convention for the Protection of the Ozone Layer, 1987.

28 *Commission of the European Communities* v *Kingdom of Denmark* (1988) ECR.
29 For a discussion of the precautionary principle, see Cameron, J and Abouchar, J (1991) 'The Precautionary Principle: A Fundamental Principle of Law and Policy for the Protection of the Global Environment'*Boston College International and Comparative Law Review*, vol XIV No 1.
30 GATT Article XX. Article XIII also contains a general requirement that quantitative restrictions be applied in a non-discriminatory way.
31 CITES Article III.2 (d).
32 CITES Article III.3 (c).
33 CITES Article III.
34 CITES Article X.
35 eg 1989 Basel Convention.
36 Basel Convention, supra note 33, Article 4.5.
37 Bamako Convention, supra note 33, Article 4.1.
38 Decision by Contracting Parties on the Application of Sanitary and Phytosanitary Measures, Draft Final Act of the Uruguay Round, supra note 11.
39 Agreement on Technical Barriers to Trade, 1979, adopted following the Tokyo Round of Trade Negotiations, BISD26S/8.
40 See eg Article 20.
41 Article 21.
42 Article 29 and 30. Although the Decision does require access to be facilitated (Article 29).
43 Agreement (1991) on Technical Barriers to Trade, Section G Draft Final Act of the Uruguay Round, supra note 11.
44 Article 2.1 simply requires no less favourable treatment for like products.
45 Ritter, Braun and Rawlinson (1991) *EEC Competition Law: a Practitioners Guide*, Kluwer, Deventer.
46 Article XIII Non-discriminatory Administration of Quantitative Restrictions.
47 Supra note 21.
48 Supra note 43.
49 Article 2.4.
50 Article 2.5.
51 Article 2.5.
52 Article 2.9.
53 Article 75 of the European Economic Agreement is identical to Article 130t of the Treaty of Rome, as amended by the Treaty on European Union. Articles 112–114 of the Agreement contain safeguard provisions which may be applied 'if serious

... environmental difficulties of a sectorial or regional nature liable to persist are arising'.

54 Articles 11.5 and 12.

55 Article 9.

56 Article 11.

57 Article 11.

58 The relationship between Article 6 and 17 is unclear. While it appears that environmental factors are to be taken into account on a similar footing as scientific evidence in Article 17, Article 6 seems to require scientific justification alone.

59 Para 2.6.

60 Article 2.

61 Article 2, Treaty on European Union (Maastricht 1992), *Agence Europe Documents No 1759/60*, (17 February, 1992).

62 Daly, H (29 February, 1992) *From Adjustment to Sustainable Development: The Obstacle of Free Trade*, transcript of a presentation given at Loyola Law School, 9–10, cited in Housman, R 'A Kantian Approach to Trade and the Environment', 49 *Washington and Lee Law Review* 1373, at 1382–83.

63 See Housman, R *A Kantian Approach . . .* ; Goldman, P 'Resolving the Trade and Environment Debate: In search of a Neutral Forum and Neutral Principles', 49 *Washington and Lee Law Review* 1279.

64 More recently, the link between sustainable development and the precautionary principle has been recognized in the Treaty on European Union. This provides that: '**Article B** The Union shall set itself the following objectives: – to promote economic and social progress which is *balanced and sustainable* . . .' (emphasis added), and in an amendment to the Treaty of Rome, a revised Article 130r, section 2, states that: 'Community policy on the environment shall aim at a high level of protection taking into account the diversity of situations in the various regions of the Community. *It shall be based on the precautionary principle and on the principles that preventive action should be taken, that environmental damage should as a priority be rectified at source and that the polluter should pay.*' (emphasis added).

65 Subsequent Conventions have endorsed the precautionary principle, see, for example: United Nations Framework Convention on Climate Change, A/AC 237/18; Convention on the Transboundary Effects of Industrial Accidents (Helsinki), 17 March, 1992; Convention on the Protection and Use of Transboundary Watercourses and International Lakes (Helsinki), 17 March, 1992.

66 This is the approach reflected in Rio Principle 15.

67 For further exposition of the nature of the precautionary principle, see, *inter alia*, Cameron, J and Abouchar, J (winter, 1991) 'The Precautionary Principle: A Fundamental Principle of Law and Policy for the Protection of the Global Environment', *Boston College International & Comparative Law Review*, vol XIV, No. 1; Cameron, J and Wade-Gery, W (1992) *Addressing Uncertainty: Law, Policy and the Precaustionary Principle*, European Science Foundation; O'Riordan, T (1992) *The Precaution Principle in Environmental Management*, Centre for Social Economic Research on the Global Environment, University of East Anglia and University College, London, GEC 92–03; Cameron, J and Werksman, J D 'The Precautionary Principle: a Policy for Action in the Face of Uncertainty', *CIEL*

Background Papers on International Environmental Law No.1/1991, Foundation for International Environmental Law and Development. See also supra note 18.
68 Article 6.
69 Article 17.
70 'The Precaution Principle in Environmental Management', supra note 67.
71 See Rio Principle 14.
72 Article 4 (1) (f).
73 Jackson, John (1992) 'World Trade Rules and Environmental Policies: Congruence or conflict?' 49 *Washington and Lee Law Review* 1227. In addition Professor Jackson contributed a shorter paper on Greening the GATT to a seminar on International Trade and environmental protection hosted by FIELD in London, 24 April 1993.
74 Contracting Parties can agree individually or collectively to waive their strict legal rights under the GATT rules in order to allow for favoured exceptions.
75 Article 104 of NAFTA does this for the Basel Convention, CITES and the Montreal Protocol.
76 Demaret, P TREMS, Multilateralism, Unilaterlaism and the GATT, seminar paper for FIELD, 23/24 April, 1993, to be published.

8 ENVIRONMENTAL LAW AND POLICY IN ANTARCTICA

1 'Recommendations' are adopted by the Contracting Parties under Article IX of the 1959 Antarctic Treaty.
2 Drawn from Enzenbacher, Deborah N (1992) *Polar Record*, 28/164, and a personal communication from the US National Science Foundation.
3 Under Articles 55–75 of the 1982 UN Convention on the Law of the Sea.
4 Behrendt, John C (1987) 'Scientific Studies Relevant to the Question of Antarctica's Petroleum Resource Potential' in Tingey, RJ (ed) *Geology of Antarctica*, Oxford University Press, Oxford.
5 Articles 61, 116–119 of the UN Convention on the Law of the Sea.
6 'Goals and Principles of Environmental Impact Assessment', *UNEP/GC 14/17*, (2 April, 1987).
7 International Convention for the Prevention of Pollution from Ships, 1973, and the Protocol of 1978 relating thereto, with Annexes I, II, III, and V (MARPOL 73/78).

9 RADIOACTIVE WASTE DUMPING AT SEA

1 In 1979, both Japan and the USA announced their intention to initiate new programmes of radioactive waste dumping at sea. Japan has been planning to dump up to 100,000 curies per year into a Pacific Ocean site 600 miles North of the Northern Marianas. The US considered a plan to scuttle ageing nuclear submarines in the Atlantic and Pacific Oceans. As many as 100 old nuclear

submarines would have been involved in this dumping programme, each representing 50,000 curies of radioactive wastes. In addition, the US Department of Defense is still hoping to find ways to dump at sea thousands of cubic metres of radioactively contaminated soils dating back from the early years of their nuclear weapons programme in the 1940s, the so-called 'Manhattan Project' which preceded the bombing of Hiroshima and Nagasaki.

2   In the summer of 1982, the largest dumping operation ever undertaken officially took place on the NEA North-East Atlantic dump-site: four ships were involved in dumping 10,000 tons of wastes from the UK, the Netherlands, Belgium and Switzerland, representing nearly 130,000 curies of radioactivity.

3   Ocean dumping operations were coordinated by the OECD's NEA and were taking place in a designated dump site 700km off the North-west coast of Spain, in the NE Atlantic Ocean, between 1967 and 1982. A total of 1,030,000 curies were officially dumped on this site. Other dump sites in the NE Atlantic and the Gulf of Gascony were also used in the 1950s and 1960s.

4   Resolution LDC 14(7), 'Disposal of Radioactive Wastes and Other Radioactive Matter at Sea', in Report of the 7th Consultative Meeting of the London Dumping Convention, Annex 3, *Doc LDC 7/12*.

5   Greenpeace International (January, 1989) *Briefing on Radioactive Waste Dumping at Sea – The Controversy Over Ocean Dumping of Radioactive Wastes: The London Dumping Convention,* Greenpeace International, Amsterdam.

6   The International Atomic Energy Agency (IAEA) is the Vienna-based agency created in 1957 to 'seek to accelerate and enlarge the contribution of atomic energy to peace, health and prosperity throughout the world' (Article II of the IAEA Statute), and the International Council of Scientific Union (ICSU) is a UN-based advisory scientific body.

7   Resolution LDC 21(9), 'Dumping of Radioactive Wastes at Sea', in Report of the 9th Consultative Meeting of the London Dumping Convention, Annex 4, *Doc LDC 9/14*.

8   In 1991 and 1992, Greenpeace revealed that the USSR had secretly been dumping LLW as well as HLW (nuclear reactors with spent nuclear fuel) in the Kara and Barents Seas until at least 1986 (See Greenpeace International 'Necessary Correction to IAEA's Inventory of Radioactive Wastes in the Marine Environment: Soviet/Russian Dumping Activities', submitted to the 15th Consultative Meeting of the London Convention, 1992, *Doc LDC 15/INF 18*.

9   Resolution LDC 28(10) 'Studies and Assessments pursuant to Resolution LDC 21(9)', in Report of the 10th Consultative Meeting of the London Dumping Convention, Annex 11, *Doc LDC 10/15*.

10 Report of the the 15th Consutative Meeting of the London Convention, Paragraph 11.2., *Doc LC 15/16*, (3 December, 1992).

11 'Options Paper on the Sea Disposal of Radioactive Wastes', Submitted to the 5th Session of IGPRAD, *Doc LDC/IGPRAD 5/6*, and Report of the 5th Session of IGPRAD.

12 Agenda 21, UN Conference on Environment and Development (UNCED). On the implication of Agenda 21 for the London Convention, see: Greenpeace International 'Political Aspects of Radioactive Waste Disposal at Sea in the 1990s and Beyond', submitted to the 5th Session of IGPRAD, *Doc LDC/IGPRAD 5/2/1*, and: Greenpeace International 'Review of the Outcome of the UNCED',

submitted to the 15th Consultative Meeting of the London Convention, *Doc LDC 15/3/1*.

13 Resolution LDC 43(13) in Report of the 13th Consultative Meeting of the LDC, Annex 9.

14 *Doc LDC/IGPRAD 5/6*, op cit.

15 The decommissioning of nuclear installations, which are bound to become radioactive wastes themselves, may be portrayed as a special circumstance by the industry, although it is clear that it is not because it was forseeable when decision to build those installations took place. Likewise, the recent implosion of the Soviet Union and future political and economic disorders in other regions could be seen as special circumstances, and, in effect, pervert the intent of the Parties to the Convention.

16 The predominant role of the IAEA in the IGPRAD process has led some participants to question the entire exercise; also in the first years, NGOs were deliberately excluded from the meeting; it is only in 1992 at the 5th Session that Greenpeace was allowed to participate fully in the proceedings; NGO input until then had been limited to written contributions with no discussion with their authors.

17 The Bamako Convention on the Ban of the Import into Africa and the Control of Transboundary Movement and Management of Hazardous Wastes within Africa (1991) of the Organization of African Unity (OAU) contains, for example, a very good definition of 'radioactive wastes'.

18 The Paris Convention for the Protection of the North-East Atlantic (1992), the Bamako Convention (1991), the Barcelona Convention for the Protection of the Mediterranean (1973), the South Pacific Regional Environmental Programme (SPREP), among others.

19 Although it points out to deficiencies in the enforcement of the Convention, the case of the former USSR is a very special one.

20 Two years later, when the Paris Convention (1974) for the Prevention of Pollution from Land-Based Sources in the North-East Atlantic was signed by the Parties to the Oslo Convention, radioactive substances were included, but they remained outside the remit of the Oslo (dumping) Convention.

21 Belgium, Denmark, the EEC, France, Germany, Iceland, Ireland, the Netherlands, Norway, Portugal, Spain, Sweden, and the UK are members of the Paris Commission. All of them, plus Finland, are also members of the Oslo Commission.

22 The finally agreed text establishes exceptions for: 'dredged material, inert material of natural origin that is solid, chemically unprocessed geological material the chemical constituents of which are unlikely to be released into the marine environment, sewage sludge until 31 December 1998, fish waste from industrial processing operations, vessels or aircraft until, at the latest, 31 December 2004'.

23 The Minister's brief for the Conference, which was leaked by the British press a few days before the conference indicated that the UK was ready to threaten the conference that it would not sign the new convention unless it got away with an exemption allowing radioactive waste dumping at sea (see, for example, *The Observer*, 20 September, 1992).

24 The new Convention was signed by all the members of the Paris and Oslo

Conventions, plus Switzerland and Luxembourg.

25 The UK accompanied its signature of the following statement: 'The Government of the United Kingdom of Great Britain and Northern Ireland declares its understanding of the effect of the paragraph 3 of Article 3 of Annex II to the Convention to be amongst other things that, where the Commission takes a decision pursuant to Article 13 of the Convention, on the prolongation of the prohibition set out in subparagraph (3)(a), those Contracting Parties who wish to retain the option of the exception to that prohibition as provided for in subparagraph (3)(b) may retain that option, provided that they are not bound, under paragraph 2 of Article 13, by that decision.' Article 13.2. states that: 'A decision shall be binding on the expiry of a period of two hundred days after its adoption for those Contracting Parties that voted for it and have not, within that period, notified the Executive Secretary in writing that they are unable to accept the decision, provided that at the expiry of that period three- quarters of the Contracting Parties have either voted for the deicision and not withdrawn their acceptance or notified the Executive Secretary in writing that they are able to accept the decision. (. . .)' It is conceivable that the UK Government may be technically right from a legalistic point of view. However, whether they are politically realistic remains to be seen, given that they were already forced to renounce to ocean dumping after a non- binding resolution of the London Convention, in 1983.

26 Ten British nuclear submarines are expected to be decommissioned in the UK by the year 2000, and France's oldest nuclear submarine has also been decommissioned recently. Until the adoption of the new Paris Convention, UK's Ministry of Defence was keeping ocean dumping as their preferred disposal option for these inconvenient bulky radioactive wastes.

27 Report of the 7th Consultative Meeting of the LDC, February 1983.

28 Resolution LDC 41(13) in Annex 7 of the Report of the 13th Consultative Meeting of the LDC, October 1990.

29 The 9th and 10th Consultative Meetings adopted resolutions on the 'Procedures for the Circulation of Proposed Amendments of the LDC' and 'Procedure for Preparation and Consideration of Amendments to Annexes to the LDC' respectively. The rule adopted suggests that amendments must be adopted 'in principle' by a meeting that will designate a future meeting for the formal adoption of these amendments.

30 In addition to the radioactive waste dumping issue, the London Convention has adopted non-binding resolutions for the Phasing-Out of the Incineration at Sea of Liquid Noxious Wastes (Resolution LDC 35(11)), the Phasing-Out (by 31 December 1995) of the Dumping of Industrial Wastes (Resolution LDC 43(13), and on the Application of the Precautionary Approach (Resolution LDC 44(14)).

31 'Proposal for a Draft Resolution on the Convening of a Conference in 1993 for Amending the London Dumping Convention and Proposals for Amendments to the Convention', submitted by Denmark to the 15th Consultative Meeting of the London Convention, *Doc LDC 15/5/1*.

10 THE EVOLUTION OF INTERNATIONAL WHALING LAW

(The authors are grateful to Julie Pruitt for her research assistance.)

1   Dean Acheson, acting US Secretary of State, Opening Address, IWC/11, 1946, 1.

2   International Convention for the Regulation of Whaling with Schedule of Whaling Regulations, 2 December, 1946, 161 UNTS 72 (entry into force 10 November, 1948). Article III establishes the International Whaling Commission.

The IWC is run by three permanent committees: the Scientific Committee, the Technical Committee, and the Finance and Administration Committee. The Scientific Committee is charged with reviewing catch data and recommending research areas, quotas, and rate of stock depletion (IWC Rules of Procedure, Rule 12). The Technical Committee drafts amendments for consideration by the IWC and reviews infractions of IWC rules. These two committees often have contrary objectives resulting in internal disputes regarding proper catch limits and areas of IWC competence.

3   The following description about whale behaviour is taken from *IWC Fact Sheet 1.5, The Lives of Whales*, as extracted in Birnie, Patricia (1985) 'International Regulation of Whaling: From Conservation of Whaling to Conservation of Whales and Regulation of Whale Watching', Oceana, New York, [hereinafter 'Birnie 1985'].

4   Smith, Gare (1984) 'The International Whaling Commission: Analysis of the Past and Reflections on the Future', 16 *Natural Resources Journal*, 901, 904.

5   Ibid.

6   Birnie, Patricia (1989) 'International Legal Issues in the Management and Protection of Whales: A Review of Four Decades of Experience,' in 29 *Natural Resources Journal*, 901, 904 [hereinafter 'Birnie 1989'].

7   D'Amato A and Chopra, S K (1991) 'Whales: Their Emerging Right to Life,' in 85 *American Journal of International Law*, 21, 29.

8   Andresen, Steiner (1989) 'Science and Politics in the International Management of Whales', in 13 *Marine Policy* 99, 101.

9   D'Amato, A and Chopra, S K, supra note 7, at 31.

10 Birnie 1985, supra note 3, at 118–123.

11 Convention for the Regulation of Whaling, 24 September, 1931, 49 Stat 3079, TS No 880, 155 LNTS 349.

12 *Fisheries Jurisdiction* case [1973] *ICJ Report 3*.

13 1931 Convention, Articles IV and V.

14 Agreement for the Regulation of Whaling and Final Act, 8 June, 1937, 52 Stat 1460, TS No 933, 190 LNTS 79.

15 D'Amato, A and Chopra, S K, supra note 7, at 32; Birnie 1989, supra note 3, at 66.

16 Article III.

17 The 39 IWC member States as at June 1993 are: Antigua and Barbuda, Argentina, Australia, Brazil, Chile, The People's Republic of China, Costa Rica, Denmark, Dominica, Ecuador, Finland, France, Germany, Grenada, India, Ireland, Japan, Kenya, The Republic of Korea, Mexico, Monaco, Netherlands, New Zealand, Norway, Oman, Peru, Russian Federation, St Kitts and Nevis, St Lucia, St Vincent and Grenada, Senegal, Seychelles, South Africa, Spain, Sweden,

Switzerland, United Kingdom, United States, Venezuela.

18 Blue Whale Units were the original measurement unit for setting catch limits. One blue whale equals two fin or two and one-half humpback or six sei whales. Devised by the whaling industry, the measurement was incorporated in the private agreements of the 1930s, M'Gonigle, R Michael (1981) 'The Economizing of Ecology: Why Big, Rare Whales Still Die', in 9 *Ecology Law Quarterly* 119, 132.

19 Valeria, Neale Spencer (1991) 'Domestic Enforcement of International Law: The International Convention for the Regulation of Whaling,' in 2 *Colorado Journal of International Environmental Law & Policy*, 109 at 112.

20 *UN Doc A/Conf 48/14/Rev 1* , 1992.

21 D'Amato, A and Chopra, S K, supra note 7, at 39.

22 IWC, 23rd Report (1973) 38.

23 6 March, 1973, 27 UST 1087, TIAS No 8249, 993 UNTS 243.

24 Lyster, Simon (1985) *International Wildlife Law*, Grotius Publications Ltd, Cambridge, 36.

25 Davis, Kimberly (1985) 'International Management of Cetaceans Under the New Law of the Sea Convention', in 3 *Boston University International Law Journal*, 477, 501.

26 CCAMLR, 20 May 1980, 33 UNTS 3476, reprinted 19 ILM 837 (1980) (entry into force 7 April, 1982).

27 Europe T S No 104; UKTS No 56 (1982), Cmnd 8734.

28 19 ILM 15 (1979).

29 Regulation on Common Rules for the Import of Whales and Other Cetacean Products, EEC Council Regulation No 348/81, 20 January 1981, *Official Journal*. L39, 12 February, 1981.

30 Directive on the Conservation of natural habitats of wild fauna and flora, EEC Council Directive No 92/43, 21 May 1992, *Official Journal* L206, 22 July, 1992 p 7.

31 Lyster, supra note 24, at 33.

32 Andresen, supra note 8, at 109.

33 The 'Pelly Amendment' to the Fisherman's Protective Act 1967 (22 USC Sec 1978 Supp V 1981) requires the US Administration to ban importation of fishing products from countries whose fishing activities undermine an international fishery conservation programme or jeopardize an international programme for endangered species. Of note also is the 'Packwood-Magnuson Amendment' to the Fishery Conservation and Management Act (16 USC Sec 1821(e)(2) Supp V 1981) which imposes a mandatory 50 per cent cut on a nation's fishing quota in US waters upon certification if it 'directly or indirectly' diminishes the effectiveness of the IWC. These sanctions provide the US with a powerful economic tool for compelling recalcitrant States to abide by the ICRW regulations.

34 ICRW Schedule, section 10, para s (a),(b) & (c).

35 Young, Nina M (1992) *Understandiang the RMP*, Centre for Marine Conservation, Washington DC, 1.

36 Id 55.

37 IWC 38th Report (39th Meeting, 1988) App 1, p 27.

38 IWC/44/19.

39 IWC/45/35.

40 See ICRW Article V.2(b).

41 Birnie 1989, supra note 6, at 932.

42 Ibid.
43 IWC/44/24 Resolution on Norwegian Proposal for Special Permits, July 1992..
44 1977 Chairman's Report IWC Special Meeting, pp 3–5, at 11–13.
45 Birnie 1989, supra note 3, at 930.
46 Carlson, Cynthia (1984) 'The International Regulation of Small Cetaceans', in 21 *San Diego Law Review*, 577, 581.
47 Scharff, J (1977) 'The International Managment of Whales Dolphins and Porpoises: An Interdisciplinary Assessment', 6 *Ecology Law Quarterly* 323, 375–6.
48 Birnie 1989, supra note 6, at 911.
49 Small-type whaling is defined as 'catching operations using powered vessels with mounted harpoon guns exclusively for minke, bottlenose, beaked, pilot or killer whales'. ICRW Schedule, para 1(C). Pilot whales are considered small cetaceans.
50 Chairman's Report of the 42nd IWC Annual Meeting, 1990.
51 Carlson, supra note 46, at 586.
52 Report of the Sub-Committee on Small Cetaceans IWC/SC/28 Report 3 Annex L (1976), reprinted in IWC 27th Report (th Meeting, 1977) 480.
53 IWC 27th Report (29th Meeting, 1977) 25, in Carlson, supra note 46, at 597. It was agreed that all cetaceans taken for their own value would be considered by the Scientific Committee with four species in need of immediate action: northern bottlenose whale, striped dolphin, Dall's porpoise, and the harbour porpoise.
54 IWC/44/28 endorsingUNGA Resolution 44/225 (22 December, 1989).
55 IWC/44/25.
56 IWC/45/29.
57 (15–16 October, 1990) Ad hoc Working Group on Legal Arrangements for Marine Mammals, Draft Global Plan of Action for the Conservation of Marine Mammals', Bonn, 22.
58 Andresen, supra note 8, at 114.
59 IWC/44/OS Norway, 44th Meeting, IWC 1992.
60 Agreement Relating to the Organization of Permanent Commission of the Conference on Exploitation and Conservation of the Marine Resources of the South Pacific, 18 August 1952, 1006 UNTS 331; cf: Birnie 1985, supra note 6, at 273.
61 Agenda 21 Chapter 17 'Protection of Oceans, All Kinds of Seas Including Enclosed and Semi-enclosed Seas, Coastal Areas and their Protection, Rational Use and Development of Their Living Resources', United Nations Conference on Environment and Development, 4th Sess Prep Comm, Chapter 17, 1992. See paras 17.50, 17.80.
62 Karl Schoenberger, 'Friends for Whales in Japan,' *Los Angeles Times*, 4 January, 1991.
63 IWC/45/29.

11 TECHNOLOGY-BASED APPROACHES VERSUS MARKET-BASED APPROACHES

1 See generally Hahn, Robert W and Hester, Gordon L (1989) 'Marketable Permits: Lessons for Theory and Practice', 16 *Ecology Law Quarterly*, 361.

2   It has been argued that there have been three stages of environmentalism. See Krupp, Frederic D (20 November, 1986) 'New Environmentalism Factors in Economic Needs', *Wall Street Journal*, § 1, at 34. Krupp places the first stage roughly around 1900, when a resource conservation movement appeared that was concerned with the availability of raw materials such as timber. This conservation movement is perhaps best known for public investments in a series of national parks and forests.

3   Reorganisation Plan No 3 of 1970, 35 Federal Register 15,623 (1970) (codified as amended at 42 USC §§ 4321-70(a) (1988)).

4   See 51 Federal Register 43,814 (1986) (originally issued at 44 Federal Register 71,779 (1979)).

5   See infra notes 48–51 and accompanying text.

6   See Hahn, Robert and Stavins, Robert (1991) 'Incentive-Based Environmental Regulation: A New Era from an Old Idea?', 18 *Ecology Law Quarterly* 1. Major reports on the use of market incentives, such as Project 88 and Project 88 – Round II, see Stavins, Robert N (January–February, 1988) 'Harnessing Market Forces to Protect the Environment', *Environment*, at 5 (summary of Project 88); (May, 1991) Project 88 – Round II, Incentives for Action: Designing Market-Based Environmental Strategies, Washington, DC , and major legislation embodying market incentives such as the 1990 Clean Air Act Amendments, have received broad support from Democrats, Republicans, industry, environmentalists, universities, and other sectors of society.

    Eastern Europe has already experimented with pollution fees; but they have typically been so low, and imposed on command economies so insensitive to prices, that these fees have had little impact.

7   See Stewart, Richard B (1986) 'Reconstitutive Law', 46 *Maryland Law Review* 86 (describing as 'reconstitutive' regulatory law that repairs market failure by introducing incentives to steer market processes towards socially desired outcomes).

8   See Kip Viscusi,W (1989) 'Toward a Diminished Role for Tort Liability: Social Insurance, Government Regulation, and Contemporary Risks to Health and Safety', 6 *Yale Journal on Regulations* 65.

9   See Kip Viscusi, W (1983) *Risk by Choice: Regulating Health and Safety in the Workplace* , Harvard University Press, Cambridge, Massachusetts.

10 See for example, Hahn and Hester, supra note 1.

11 Market incentives do not require each polluting business to 'reinvent the wheel' of pollution control in isolation. If certain pollution control techniques are widely applicable and there are economics of scale in their research or production, private market actors facing appropriate incentives will invest specifically in that large-scale production and marketing effort. Indeed, the prospect of inventing a new pollution control technique that one can sell to many other firms is one of the key factors driving improved pollution control under market-based incentive policies.

12 Market-based incentives are not a soft substitute for tough enforcement programmes. The US chlorofluorocarbons phase-out programme, a tradeable allowance system, see infra notes 76–81 and accompanying text, presents a good example of vigorous enforcement efforts, since its success depends on preventing producers from producing more pollutants than their allowances permit. In

1990 and 1991 the US brought the first enforcement actions by any government worldwide, so far as we know, to enforce compliance with obligations under the Montreal Protocol. The US sued companies for importing CFCs without obtaining allowances; the violators were required to purchase allowances on the open market and, in addition, to pay penalties.

13 See generally (1991) *US Interagency Task Force, A Comprehensive Approach to Addressing Potential Climate Change* , 46–59 [hereinafter Comprehensive Approach]; Stewart, Richard B and Wiener, Jonathan B (November–December, 1990) 'A Comprehensive Approach to Climate Change', *American Enterprise*, at 75.

14 42 USCA §§ 7401–7671 (West Supplement 1991).

15 33 USC §§ 1251–1387 (1988).

16 Resource Conservation and Recovery Act (RCRA), 42 USC §§6901–92 (1988); Comprehensive Environmental Response, Compensation, and Liability Act (CERCLA), 42 USC §§ 9601–75 (1988).

17 See for example, Guruswamy, Lakshman (1991) 'The Case for Integrated Pollution Control', 54 *Law and Contemporary Problems* 41. Indeed, the examples of market-based policies given in this Article are divided by medium, because that is how the structure of environmental law has developed in the US. Yet we do not recommend that such a medium-by-medium approach be employed in the future.

18 See Dudek, Daniel J et al, (1990) *Environmental Defense Fund, SO2 and CO2: Consistent Policymaking in a Greenhouse*.

19 Reducing SO2 emissions by ten million tons per year through scrubbing could generate 45 million tons per year of sludge – about one-third the current total municipal solid waste volume in the US. *See* Harrington, Winston (1989) *Acid Rain: Science and Policy* ,16.

20 See 'Comprehensive Approach', supra note 13, at 50–52; Stewart and Wiener, supra note 13, at 78.

21 See CAA Amendments of 1970, Public Law No 91–604, § 4, 84 Stat at 1678–89 (current version at 42 USCA §§ 7407–16 (West Supplement 1991)).

22 See 42 USC § 7423 (1988).

23 See generally EPA, Pollution Prevention Strategy (January, 1991). See also Pollution Prevention Act of 1990, Public Law No 101–508, §§ 6601–10, 104 Stat 1388, 1388–321 to 1388–327 (codified at 42 USCA §§ 13101–09 (West Supplement 1991)); EPA, Environmental Stewardship: EPA's First Two Years in the Bush Administration 4–5 (May, 1991) (describing '33/50' Pollution Prevention Programme).

24 42 USCA §§ 7401–7671 (West Supplement 1991).

25 42 USC §§ 6901–92 (1988).

26 42 USC §§ 300(f)–(j)(26) (1988).

27 See Stewart and Wiener, supra note 13, at 79–80. See generally 'Comprehensive Approach', supra note 13.

28 For further detail on certain of these programmes, see generally Opschoor, Johannes B and Vos, Hans B (1989) *Organisation for Economic Co-operation and Development, Economic Instruments for Environmental Protection*; Ackerman, Bruce A and Stewart, Richard B (1988) 'Reforming Environmental Law: The Democratic Case for Market Incentives', 13 *Columbian Journal of Environmental Law,*

171; Hahn and Hester, supra note 1; Tripp, James TB and Dudek, Daniel J (1989) 'Institutional Guidelines for Designing Successful Transferable Rights Programmes', 6 *Yale Journal on Registration* 369.

29 Air Quality Act of 1967, Public Law No 90–148, § 108, 81 Stat 485, 491–97 (current version at 42 USC § 7409(b) (1988)).

30 CAA Amendments of 1977, Public Law No 95–95, § 109(a), 91 Stat 685, 697 (current version at 42 USC § 7411(a) (1988)). New and modified sources generally must meet more stringent standards than sources that were 'existing' as of passage of the 1977 CAA. 42 USC § 7411(a)(1) (1988).

31 See EPA Emissions Trading Policy Statement, 51 Federal Register 43, 814 (1986) (final policy statement, revised version of 1979 statement); Tietenberg, Thomas H (1985) *Resources for the Future, Emissions Trading: An Exercise in Reforming Pollution Policy.*

32 For a fuller discussion of bubbles, netting, and offsets, see Hahn and Hester, supra note 1, at 368–73; Liroff, Richard (1986) *Reforming Air Pollution Regulation: The Toil and Trouble of EPA's Bubble* 1–18.

33 Hahn and Hester, supra note 1, at 373–76.

34 See Dwyer, John (26–27 June, 1991) *California's Tradeable Emissions Policy and Its Application to the Control of Greenhouse Gases,* Paper Presented at the OECD Workshop on Emissions Trading of Greenhouse Gases, Paris. The most notable shortcomings of the current scheme are the central choice of control technology, the limits on full inter-firm trading, the arbitrary distinction between mobile and stationary sources, and the separate, more demanding regulation of any 'new' source. This latter strategy has increased the political feasibility of environmental legislation by lessening the resistance from existing facility owners. As explained above, since 'new' facility owners do not yet exist as an identified group, they are not heard to complain. But this has had the pernicious effect of extending the economic life of old high polluting facilities, and thereby has increased emissions over time. It has posed obstacles to investment in new, often cleaner facilities. It has also led to a hopelessly tortured legal debate over when a facility has been so 'modified' as to be 'new'. This is a classic example of the failure of command environmental policies to engage dynamic behavioural forces. In contrast, providing an incentive to limit pollution at all sources, treating all old and new sources alike, and allowing inter-firm trading could better achieve environmental goals without impeding economic growth.

35 See South Coast Air Quality Management District, Draft Concept Proposal for a Marketable Permit Programme (January, 1991).

36 The tax rate could depend on the amount emitted, its potency as a hazard, and the likelihood of exposure to humans and other life forms, so that the most dangerous emissions would be discouraged most.

37 Portney, Paul R (1990) 'Air Pollution Policy', in *Public Policies for Environmental Protection* 27, 48 (Portney, Paul R (ed), *Resources for the Future* 1990) (airborne lead fell 89 per cent from 1980 to 1987).

38 The effectiveness of an Eastern European lead phase-down would depend to some extent on Eastern Europe's ability to influence the refineries that produce petrol for Eastern Europe. Action taken in concert with the European Community ('EC') or the Soviet Republics might be needed. The EC began making unleaded petrol widely available only as recently as 1989, but with no target date

for a full phase-out of leaded petrol. The United Kingdom, aiming to move faster than the full EC, introduced a market-based incentive: a tax on leaded fuels imposed in 1986 and raised in 1988. The tax is paid at the filling station by petrol consumers. The combination of the tax incentive and regulations on vehicle manufacture raised the use of unleaded petrol in the UK from 4 per cent of petrol sales in January 1989 to about 40 per cent in late 1990. See *Air Quality Division, UK Department of Environment, Unleaded Petrol: The UK. Position* (February, 1991). Both the UK and EC programmes are still far behind the near-100 per cent phase-out of leaded gasoline in the US by 1987.

39 See generally Nussbaum, Barry D (9 December, 1991) *EPA, Unleaded Gasoline Transition in the US: The Use of Mandates and Incentives* , EPA working paper; 47 Federal Register 49,322–34 (describing background and historical context of the regulations).

40 40 CFR § 80.20(a), (d) (1983).

41 40 CFR § 80.20(a), (d)(4) (1991). See 50 Federal Register 9,386–90 (1985) (describing background of the regulations).

42 40 CFR § 80.20(e) (1991). See 50 Federal Register 13,116–18 (1985) (describing background of the regulations).

43 Hahn and Hester, supra note 1, at 387.

44 The lead content of gasoline was reduced from 1.10 gpg to 0.10 gpg. Nussbaum, supra note 39, at 35. Note that the UK standard of 0.13 grammes per litre is almost five times the US standard. See UK Department of Environment, supra note 38.

45 Nussbaum, supra note 39, at 10.

46 Interview with Barry D Nussbaum, Chief of the Operations and Compliance Policy Branch, Field Operations and Support Division, Office of Mobile Sources, Office of Air and Radiation, EPA (9 December, 1991).

47 The US Government backed the gasoline lead phase-down with a continually more vigorous enforcement effort. Now broader, multi-source lead content reductions are being sought. In July 1991, the Justice Department and EPA announced a nationwide Lead Enforcement Initiative aimed at lead pollution in air, water, land, and buildings. The initiative contains 36 enforcement lawsuits 'in the most sweeping enforcement action ever taken against sources of a single pollutant.' Weisskopf, Michael (1 August, 1991) 'US Cracks Down on Lead Pollution', *Washington Post*, at A4. The effort was designed both to correct violations and to deter potential future polluters.

48 40 CFR § 86.090-15 (1991).

49 Id.

50 Id.

51 See 55 Federal Register 30,584 (1990).

52 First authorized by the Energy Policy and Conservation Act of 1975, Public Law No 94–163, Title V, §§ 501–02, 89 Stat 871, 902–04 (codified as amended at 15 USCA §§ 2001–02 (West Supplement 1991)).

53 Such as ethanol, methanol, mixed fuels, liquified natural gas, and perhaps hydrogen and electric powered vehicles.

54 Public Law No 101–549, Title IV, §§ 401–16, 104 Stat at 2584–631 (1990) (codified at 42 USCA § 7651(a)–(o) (West Supplement 1991)).

55 See id §§ 403–04, 104 Stat at 2589–605 (codified at 42 USCA § 7651(b)–(c) (West

Supplement 1991)). This rate will be lowered to about 50 per cent of current emissions by 1999. Id.

56 The law does not prescribe specific technology to achieve SO2 emissions, leaving precise response techniques up to each manager. See id; Dudek, Daniel J (November, 1989) 'Emissions Trading: Environmental Perestroika or Flim-flam?', *Electricity Journal,*at 32, 40, 42.

57 See (November, 1991) *National Acid Rain Precipitation Assessment Programme, 1990 Integrated Assessment Report* 433.

58 Indeed, before trading was proposed, BACT requirements for new sources went up to 90 per cent SO2 removal – the highest thought technically feasible. Now, with trading and performance incentives, industry is ordering newly devised technologies that remove 95 per cent or even 98 per cent of SO2. Presentation by Brian McLean, Director of the Acid Rain Division, Office of Atmospheric and Indoor Air Programmes, Office of Air and Radiation, EPA (9 December, 1991).

59 Montreal Protocol on Substances that Deplete the Ozone Layer, 16 September, 1987, Article 2, § 4, 26 ILM 1550, 1552 (entered into force 1 January, 1989). CFC consumption is defined as production plus imports minus exports. Id Article 1, § 6, 26 ILM at 1551.

60 'Report of the Second Meeting of the Parties to the Montreal Protocol on Substances that Deplete the Ozone Layer', UN Environmental Programme, *UN Doc EP/OzL Pro 2/3 (1990)*. The update also added several substances to the phase-out programme.

61 Montreal Protocol, supra note 59, Articles 2, § 5, 26 ILM at 1553.

62 See 53 Federal Register 30, 566 (1988) (codified as amended at 40 CFR § 82 (1991)).

63 See Seidel, Stephen R and Blank, Daniel P (November–December, 1990) 'Closing an Ozone Loophole', *Environmental Forum*, at 18, 20. Another important issue in protecting the earth's ozone layer is the large reservoir of CFCs remaining stored in coolant systems such as refrigerators, automobile air conditioners, and other end use products. The tax and tradeable allowance systems will provide some incentive to recover and recycle old CFCs, but a direct refund might be offered to encourage more affirmative steps at recovery by those who own, or can find, abandoned and leaking CFC systems.

64 The trading of CFCs, both nationally and internationally, might serve as a model for additional national or global greenhouse gas policies, if reductions in greenhouse gases are warranted in light of their likely costs and benefits. See Grubb, Michael (1989) *The Greenhouse Effect: Negotiating Targets,* Royal Institute of International Affairs, London; Stewart and Wiener, supra note 13; Dudek, Daniel J (1990) *Environmental Defense Fund, International Trading in Greenhouse Gas Permits* , Policy Paper prepared for Project 88 – Round II; Dudek, Daniel J (7–11 July, 1987) *Marketable Instruments for Managing Global Atmospheric Problems, Economic Frontiers in Environmental Policy*, Paper Presented at Annual Meeting of the Western Economics Association, Vancouver, British Columbia (describing options for the design of greenhouse gas trading programmes); Haites, Erik (May, 1990) *Tradeable Allowances and Carbon Taxes: Cost Effective Policy Responses to Global Warming* (unpublished manuscript).

65 Point sources are generally sources discharging effluents (water pollutants) out of single discharge sites such as pipes carrying effluent from a factory to a stream. 33 USC § 1362(14) (1988). Nonpoint sources are generally sources whose

operations entail diffuse multiple discharges spread over a large area, such as 'runoff' from agricultural fields or city parking lots.

66 Clean Water Act § 301(b), 33 USC § 1311(b) (1988). See generally Freeman, A Myrick, III, 'Water Pollution Policy', in *Public Policies for Environmental Protection* 97, 105-20 (Portney, Paul R (ed), *Resources for the Future*, 1990).

67 See 33 USC § 1311(b)(1)(B) (1988); Freeman, supra note 66, at 119–20 (suggesting the need to charge effluent fees).

68 A few States issue waste discharge permits that vary by month. These allow firms to adjust discharges according to seasonal changes in water flows and temperatures as well as the seasonably variable assimilative capacity of the waterway. Inter-firm trading, however, is not currently permitted.

69 See Hahn and Hester, supra note 1, at 391–93; Tripp and Dudek, supra note 28, at 386–88.

70 See Wendell, Heidi and Dudek, Daniel J (18–22 September, 1989) *The Design and Legality of Innovative Approaches to Nonpoint Source Control, Proceedings of the American Water Resources Association Annual Meeting*, Tampa, Florida.

71 See Hahn and Hester, supra note 1; Tripp and Dudek, supra note 28.

72 That is, 2 units of effluent reduction had to be obtained from a nonpoint source to allow the point source to increase by 1 unit. This ratio was applied to ensure real pollution reductions during trades, but if the cost ratio were not greater than 2:1 in favour of nonpoint sources, the 2:1 allowance trading ratio would inhibit trades.

73 See Apogee Research Inc, (1991) *Nutrient Trading in the Tar-Pimlico River Basin*.

74 See Tarlock, A Dan (1991) *Law of Water Rights and Resources*, § 5.05[5]; Weatherford, Gary D et al (eds) (1982) *Water and Agriculture in the Western US: Conservation, Reallocation and Markets*, 215–223 Westview Press, Boulder, Colorado.

75 California Water Code §§ 1011(a),(b) (West Supplement 1992). Open water markets remain constrained by subsidized federal water supplies, 'area of origin' requirements, and the absence of readily available systems to convey water from one basin to another. See O'Brien, Kevin M (1988) 'Water Marketing in California', 19 Pacific Law Journal 1165; Willey, Zach and Graff, Tom (1988) 'Federal Water Policy in the United States – An Agenda for Economic and Environmental Reform', 13 *Columbian Journal of Environmental Law* 325 . Still, some major water deals are occurring. For example, in 1988 the Los Angeles Metropolitan Water District (MWD) and the Imperial Irrigation District (IID) agreed on a $233 million arrangement to conserve and transfer water from farmers in the IID to urban users in the MWD (who face marginal water costs up to 20 times higher than the farmers). See Hahn and Stavins, supra note 6, at 18–19.

76 See (March, 1991) *EPA, Economic Incentives: Options for Environmental Protection* 2.18–.21 EPA, Washington DC. One possible difficulty with offering a refund on returned batteries is that it might encourage theft of batteries; various measures, such as lockable battery cases, or requiring a receipt to be presented with the battery, could be used to deter theft. Moreover, there is a market price for lead in batteries today, but few battery thefts to lend credence to this concern.

77 See Menell, Peter, 'Beyond the Throw-Away Society: An Incentive to Regulating Municipal Solid Waste', 17 *Ecology Law Quarterly* 655 (1990).

78 See Schneider, Keith 'Louisiana's New Environmental Tool: Using Taxes to

Discourage Pollution', *New York Times*, at A24 (27 February, 1991).

79 Id. The Louisiana tax programme applies to all environmental residuals, not only solid and hazardous wastes, and in that aspect is a good example of a multimedia policy as recommended above in 'The Need for Comprehensive Policy'.

80 42 USC §§ 11001–50 (1988).

81 See, for example, OSHA Hazard Communication Rule, 29 CFR § 1910.1200 (1991).

82 See, for example, Federal Insecticide, Fungicide, and Rodenticide Act of 1947 (FIFRA), 7 USC § 136–136y (1988).

83 See Tripp and Dudek, supra note 28, at 378–82.

84 See Fishery Management Plan for the Atlantic Surf Clam and Ocean Quahog Fishery, 50 CFR § 652 (1991).

85 See generally Pearse, Peter H (July, 1991) *New Zealand Ministry of Agriculture and Fisheries, Building on Progress: Fisheries Policy Development in New Zealand*). Drawing on the land use and fisheries examples, dwindling global forest resources could be protected through tradeable forest protection obligations. Under such a regime, each nation enjoying the biodiversity benefits of forests would be obliged to contribute to a joint protection effort, and could 'trade' in the sense of achieving its obligation by investing in protection efforts in cooperation with other resource holders as well as on its own lands. This kind of flexibility would direct investments in forest protection to their most cost-effective uses, while simultaneously serving as a vehicle for investment flows to those nations, chiefly developing nations, which have major forest resources.

86 See (1990) Science Advisory Board, EPA, *Publication No SAB EC 90 021, Reducing Risk: Setting Priorities and Strategies for Environmental Protection*, 1–2.

87 See 'Comprehensive Approach', supra note 13, at 1–2; Stewart and Wiener, supra note 13, at 75–76. A project is now underway at the Harvard Center for Risk Analysis to analyze examples of such risk tradeoffs in several areas of public policy. Graham, J (ed) *Harvard Center for Risk Analysis, Weighing the Risks: Risk Tradeoffs in Public Policy* (forthcoming 1992).

GLOSSARY

ACC	–	(UN) Administrative Coordination Committee
ASOC	–	Antarctic and Southern Ocean Coalition
ATS	–	Antarctic Treaty System
BACT	–	Best Available Control Technique
BWUs	–	Blue Whale Units
CAA	–	Clean Air Act
CAC	–	Command-and-Control
CAFE	–	Corporate Average Fuel Economy
CCAMLR	–	Convention on the Conservation of Antarctic Marine Living Resources
CCAS	–	Convention on the Conservation of Antarctic Seals
CIDIE	–	Committee of International Development Institutions on the Environment
CITES	–	Convention on International Trade of Endangered Species
CLASP	–	Centre for Law and Social Policy
COP	–	Convention of the Parties
CRAMRA	–	Convention for the Regulation of Antarctic Mineral Resource Activities
CSD	–	Commission on Sustainable Development
CSCE	–	Conference on Security and Cooperation in Europe
CWA	–	Clean Water Act
EA	–	Environmental Assessment
EBRD	–	European Bank for Reconstruction and Development
EC	–	European Community
ECE	–	Economic Commission for Europe
ECJ	–	European Court of Justice
ECOSOC	–	UN Economic and Social Council
ECR	–	European Court Reports
EIA	–	Environmental Impact Assessment
EPA	–	Environmental Protection Agency
FAO	–	Food and Agriculture Organization
FIFRA	–	Federal Insecticide, Fungicide, and Rodenticide Act
FM	–	Financial Mechanism
GATT	–	General Agreement on Tariffs and Trade
GEF	–	Global Environmental Facility
GESAMP	–	Joint Group of Experts on the Scientific Aspects of Marine Pollution
HLW	–	High Level Waste
IAEA	–	International Atomic Energy Agency
IBRD	–	International Bank for Reconstruction and Development

ICJ	–	International Court of Justice
ICJ Reps	–	Reports of the International Court of Justice
ICRW	–	International Convention for the Regulation of Whaling
ICSU	–	International Council of Scientific Union
IDA	–	International Development Association
IFC	–	International Finance Corporation
IGPRAD	–	Intergovernmental Panel of Experts on Radioactive Wastes
IGY	–	International Geophysical Year
IIED	–	International Institute for Environment and Development
ILW	–	Intermediate Level Waste
IMO	–	International Maritime Organization
ITF	–	International Transport Federation
ITQ	–	Individual Transferable Quotas
IUCN	–	World Conservation Union
IWC	–	International Whaling Commission
LC 72	–	London Convention 1972 (previously known as LDC)
LDC	–	London Dumping Convention
LLW	–	Low Level Wastes
MIGA	–	Multilateral Investment Guarantee Agency
MMPA	–	Marine Mammal Protection Act
MTO	–	Multilateral Trade Organization
NAFTA	–	North American Free Trade Organization
NAMMCO	–	North Atlantic Marine Mammals Conservation Organization
NEA	–	Nuclear Energy Agency
NGO	–	Non-Governmental Organization
NMP	–	New Management Procedures
NOAA	–	National Oceanic and Atmospheric Administration
NUS	–	National Union of Seamen
OAU	–	Organization of African Unity
OEA	–	Office of Environmental Affairs
OECD	–	Organization of Economic Cooperation and Development
OPEC	–	Organization of Petroleum Exporting Countries
PA	–	Participants' Assembly
PCIJ	–	Permanent Court of International Justice
POTW	–	Publicity Owned Treatment Works
PPM	–	Process and Production Methods
RIAA	–	Reports of International Arbitral Awards
RIIA	–	Royal Institute of International Affairs
RMP	–	Revised Management Procedures
SCAR	–	Scientific Committee on Antarctic Research
SPC	–	South Pacific Commission
SPREP	–	South Pacific Regional Environmental Programme
STAP	–	Scientific and Technical Advisory Panel
TBT	–	Technical Barriers to Trade
TDR	–	Transferable Development Sites
UNCED	–	United Nations Conference on Environment and Development
UNCHE	–	United Nations Conference on the Human Environment
UNCLOS	–	United Nations Convention on the Law of the Sea

UNESCO	–	United Nations Education Scientific and Cultural Organization
UNDP	–	United Nations Development Programme
UNEP	–	United Nations Environment Programme
UNGA	–	United Nations General Assembly
WCED	–	World Commission on Environment and Development
WWF	–	World Wildlife Fund for Nature
YIEL	–	Yearbook of International Environmental Law

LIST OF TREATIES AND OTHER INTERNATIONAL ACTS

1940 Convention on Nature Protection and Wildlife Preservation in the Western Hemisphere, Washington DC, 12 October 1940, in force 1 May 1942: 222.

1945 Charter of the United Nations, San Francisco, 26 June 1945, in force 24 October 1945: 55–6, 58, 63–4, 67, 222.

1946 International Convention for the Regulation of Whaling, Washington DC, 2 December 1946, in force 10 November 1948: 123, 159–61, 163–76, 179–80, 220, 222, 235–7, 245.

1947 General Agreement on Tariffs and Trade, Geneva, 30 October 1947, not yet in force (in force provisionally since 1 January 1948 under the 1947 Protocol of Provisional Application): 23, 59, 62, 85, 96–106, 108–16, 118–21, 213, 219, 224, 227–9, 231, 245.

1949 FAO Agreement for the Establishment of a General Fisheries Council for the Mediterranean, Rome, 24 September 1949, in force 3 December 1963: 222.

1950 European Convention for the Protection of Human Rights and Fundamental Freedoms, Rome, 4 November 1950, in force 3 September 1953: 221–2.

1951 FAO International Plant Protection Convention, Rome, 6 December 1951, in force 3 April 1952: 222.

1952 International Convention for the High Seas Fisheries of the North Pacific Ocean, Tokyo, 9 May: 222.

1952 Agreement Relating to the Organization of Permanent Commission of the Conference on Exploitation and Conservation of Marine Resources of the South Pacific, 18 August 1952: 237.

1958 Treaty Establishing the European Economic Community, Rome, 25 March 1957, in force 1 January 1958: 15, 55, 58, 85–90, 92–7, 99, 112, 115–17, 221, 223, 227, 230.

1958 Convention on Fishing and Conservation of the Living Resources of the High Seas, Geneva, 29 April 1958, in force 20 March 1966: 222.

1959 Antarctic Treaty, Washington, 1 December 1959, in force 23 June 1961: 122–31, 133–9, 223, 231, 245.

1963 Convention on Civil Liability for Nuclear Damage, Vienna, 29 May 1963, in force 12 November 1977.

1963 Optional Protocol Concerning the Compulsory Settlement of Disputes, Vienna, 29 May 1963, not in force: 222.

1966 International Covenant on Civil and Political Rights, 16 December 1966, in force 23 March 1976, Optional Protocol to the 1966 ICCPR, 16 December 1966, in force 23 March 1976: 222.

1968 African Convention on the Conservation of Nature and Natural Resource, Algiers, 15 September 1968, in force 9 October 1969 (or June 1969): 222.

1969 American Convention on Human Rights, San Jose, 22 November 1969, in force 18 July 1978: 222.

1969 FAO Convention on the Conservation of the Living Resources of the South-East Atlantic, Rome, 23 October 1969, in force 24 October 1971: 220.

1971 Treaty on the Prohibition of the Emplacement of Nuclear Weapons and Other Weapons of Mass Destruction on the Sea-Bed and the Ocean Floor and in the Sub-Soil Thereof, 11 February 1971, in force 18 May 1972: 221.

1972 Convention for the Prevention of Marine Pollution by Dumping from Ships and Aircraft, Oslo, 15 February 1972, in force 7 April 1974: 141, 150, 220, 233, 234.

1972 Convention for the Conservation of Antarctic Seals, London, 1 June 1972, in force 11 March 1978: 123, 126–7, 137, 245.

1972 Convention on the Prohibition of the Development, Production and Stockpiling of Bacteriological (Biological) and Toxic Weapons, and on their Destruction, London, Washington, Moscow, 10 April 1972, in force 28 March 1975: 221.

1972 Convention on the Prevention of Marine Pollution by Dumping of Wastes and Other Matter, London, Mexico City, Moscow, Washington DC, 29 December 1972, in force 30 August 1975: 39–40, 47, 140–50, 152–8, 216, 220–1, 232–3, 235, 246.

1973 Convention on International Trade in Endangered Species of Wild Fauna and Flora, Washington, 3 March 1973, in force 1 July 1975: 47, 62–3, 97, 99, 107–8, 111, 166, 168, 220–4, 228–9, 245.

1973 International Convention for the Prevention of Pollution by Ships, London, 2 November 1973, not in force (see 1978 Protocol): 220, 231.

1974 Nordic Convention on the Protection of the Environment, Stockholm, 19 February 1974, in force 5 October 1976: 225.

1974 Convention on the Protection of the Marine Environment of the Baltic Sea Area, Helsinki, 22 March 1974, in force 3 May 1980: 223.

1974 Convention for the Prevention of Marine Pollution from Land-Based Sources, Paris, 4 June 1974, in force 6 May 1978: 222, 233–4.

1974 Barcelona Convention for the Protection of the Mediterranean, Barcelona, 6 February 1976, in force 12 February 1978: 233.

1976 European Convention for the Protection of Animals Kept for Farming Purposes, Strasbourg, 10 March 1976, in force 10 September 1978: 222.

1978 Protocol Relating to the 1973 International Convention for the Prevention of Pollution from Ships, London, 17 February 1978, in force 2 October 1983: 231.

1979 Convention on the Conservation of Migratory Species of Wild Animals, Bonn,

23 June 1979, in force 1 November 1983: 167.

1979 Convention on the Conservation of European Wildlife and Natural Habitats, Berne, 19 September 1979, in force 1 June 1982: 167, 221.

1979 Convention on Long-Range Transboundary Air Pollution, Geneva, 13 November 1979, in force 16 March 1983: 222.

1980 Convention on the Conservation of Antarctic Marine Living Resources, Canberra, 20 May 1980, in force 7 April 1982: 123, 126–32, 137–9, 167, 236, 245.

1981 African Charter on Human Rights and Peoples' Rights, Banjul, 27 June 1981, in force 21 October 1986: 222

1982 Regional Convention for the Conservation of the Red Sea and Gulf of Aden Environment, Jeddah, 14 February 1982, in force 20 August 1985: 222.

1982 United Nations Convention on the Law of the Sea, Montego Bay, 10 December 1982, not in force: 57, 59, 127, 131, 162, 167, 179, 222–3, 231, 236, 246.

1985 Convention for the Protection of the Ozone Layer, Vienna, 22 March 1985, in force 22 September 1988: 39, 222.

1985 Protocol on the Reduction of Sulphur Emissions or Their Transboundary Fluxes by at Least 30 per cent, Helsinki, 8 July 1985, in force 2 September 1987: 220.

1986 Single European Act, 17 February 1986, in force 1 July 1987: 15, 94–6, 88.

1987 Protocol on Substances that Deplete the Ozone Layer, Montreal, 16 September 1987, in force 1 January 1989: 51, 60–1, 99, 110, 113, 139, 199–200, 220, 223–4, 229, 231, 239, 242.

1988 Protocol Concerning the Control of Emissions of Nitrogen Oxides or their Transboundary Fluxes, Sofia, 31 October 1988, in force 14 February 1991: 220.

1989 Convention on the Control of Transboundary Movement of Hazardous Wastes and their Disposal, Basel, in force 24 May 1992: 47, 99, 112, 133, 138, 220, 227–8, 229.

1989 African, Caribbean and Pacific States – European Economic Community: Fourth Lomé Convention, 15 December 1989, in force 1991: 228.

1991 Convention on the Ban of Imports into Africa and the Control of Transboundary Movement and Management of Hazardous Wastes within Africa, Bamako, 29 January 1991, not in force: 112, 229, 233.

1991 Convention on Environmental Impact Assessment in a Transboundary Context, Espoo, 25 February 1991, not in force: 222.

1991 Protocol on Environmental Protection to the Antarctic Treaty, Madrid, 4 October 1991, not in force: 123, 125, 128, 130, 135, 139.

1992 Treaty on European Union, Maastricht, 17 February 1992, not in force: 15–16, 94–6, 99, 115, 116, 117, 214, 221, 229, 230.

1992 Convention on the Protection and Use of Transboundary Watercourses and International Lakes, Helsinki, 17 March 1992, not in force: 230.

1992 Agreement on the Conservation of Small Cetaceans of the Baltic and North Seas, 17 March 1992: 167.

1992 UN/ECE Convention on the Transboundary Effects of Industrial Accidents, Helsinki, 17 March 1992, not in force: 230.

1992 Convention on the Protection of the Marine Environment of the Baltic Sea Area, Helsinki, 9 April 1992, not in force: 154.

1992 United Nations Framework Convention on Climate Change, New York, 9 May 1992, not in force: 1, 6–7, 10, 28, 40, 50–1, 57, 61, 63, 67, 74, 81, 83–4, 119, 211, 214, 215–16, 218–22, 224, 230.

1992 Convention on Biological Diversity, Rio de Janeiro, 5 June 1992, not in force: 1, 7, 51, 57, 63, 74, 215, 219, 222, 226.

1992 Convention for the Protection of the Marine Environment of the North-East Atlantic, Paris, 22 September 1992, not in force: 55, 150–2, 154, 233, 234.

1992 North American Free Trade Agreement, Washington, Ottawa and Mexico City, 8, 11, 14, 17 December 1992, not in force: 101, 103, 231.

NON-BINDING INSTRUMENTS

Stockholm Declaration, Stockholm (1972): 1–13, 16, 18, 52–3, 58, 72, 166, 210–11.

World Charter for Nature, UNGA (1982): 1, 12–13, 16.

Agenda 21, Rio de Janeiro (1992): 1, 13, 19, 22, 50, 59, 63–4, 74–6, 79–84, 101–2, 116, 146, 147, 179, 217–18, 225, 237.

Rio Declaration on Environment and Development, Rio de Janeiro (1992): 1–2, 4–13, 16–19, 20–32, 59, 63, 74–8, 102, 106, 146, 213–14, 218–19, 221, 224–5, 228, 230, 231.

Statement of Principles on Forests, Rio de Janeiro (1992): 1, 7–8, 10, 18, 219.

LIST OF CASES

Permanent Court of International Justice

SS Lotus (*France* v *Turkey*) 1927 PCIJ (Ser A) No 10: 216.

International Court of Justice

Corfu Channel Case, 1949 ICJ Reports 4: 58, 223.
Reparations for Injuries Case, 1949 ICJ Reports 174: 221.
Nuclear Test Case (*Australia* v *France*), 1973 ICJ Reports 99: 219, 223.
Fisheries Jurisdiction Case (*United Kingdom* v *Iceland*), 1974 ICJ Reports 3: 219.
Nuclear Test Case (*New Zealand* v *France*), 1974 ICJ Reports 457: 219, 223.
Case Concerning Certain Phosphate Lands in Nauru (*Nauru* v *Australia*), 1992 ICJ
Reports 240: 60, 219.

European Court of Justice

Case 8/74, *Dassonville*, 1974, ECR 837: 226.
Case 120/78, *Rewe* v *Zentralverwaltung*, 1979 ECR 649: 89, 226.
Case 91/79, *Commission* v *Italy*, 1980 ECR 1099: 223.
Cases 30–41/81, *Commission* v *Italy*, 1981 ECR 3379: 223.
Case 96/81, *Commission* v *Netherlands*, 1982 ECR 1791: 223.
Case 97/81, *Commission* v *Netherlands*, 1982 ECR 1819: 223.
Case 220/81, *Robertson*, 1982 ECR 2349: 226.
Case 261/81 *Rau*, 1982 ECR 3961: 226.
Case 240/83, *Procureur de la République* v *Association de Défence des Bruleurs D'Huiles
Usagées* (*Used Oils*), 1985 ECR 531: 90, 226.
Case 50/85 *Schloh*, 1 CMLR 450 (1987): 226.
Case 134/86, *Commission* v *Belgium*, 1987 ECR 2415: 223.
Case 302/86, *Commission* v *Denmark* (*Danish Bottles*), 1988 ECR 4607: 90–5, 110, 226,
228.
Case 182/89, *Commission* v *France*, 1 YIEL 274 (1990): 223.
Case 300/89, *Commission* v *Council*: 226.
Case 2/90, *Commission* v *Belgium*, judgement of 10 June 1991 (unreported): 93, 95,
226.
Case C-75/91, *Commission* v *Netherlands* (unreported): 223.
Case 155/91, *Commission* v *Council* (unreported): 226.

GATT Panel Decisions

Superfund Tax Case, Report of the Panel, GATT Doc BISD/345/16T (17 June 1987):
97.
Yellow-Fin Tuna Decision (*Mexico* v *US*), GATT Doc DS21/R, (3 September 1991),
62, 85, 98, 99, 103, 108, 113, 219, 227, 228.

Arbitration

Pacific Fur Seals (*Great Britain* v *United States*), 1 Moore's International Arbitration Awards 755 (1893): 219.
Trail Smelter (*United States* v *Canada*), 3 RIAA 1905 (1941): 37, 219.
Lac Lanoux Arbitration (*France* v *Spain*), 24 ILR 101 (1957): 219.

National Courts

Germany
Veehunde v *Bundesrepublik Deutschland* (Verwaltungagericht, Hamburg, 15 August 1988): 41–2, 216.
United States
United States v *Montrose Chemicals*, No CV 90–3122 (DDC Cal 1990): 41, 216.

INDEX

Administrative Procedure Act, the
42
Agenda 21 *see* UNCED
Agreement on the Conservation of
Small Cetaceans of the Baltic and
North Seas 167
Alaska 47
Antarctica 35, 47, 122, 124, 129–30,
133, 134, 136, 161, 170
Agreed Measures on the Conserva-
tion of Antarctic Fauna and Flora,
the 126
Antarctic and Southern Ocean
Coalition (ASOC) 129–30, 134
Antarctic Environmental Protection
Agency 138
Antarctic Treaty, the 122, 126–7,
129–30, 133–8
history 124–5
signatories 123
Antarctic Treaty Protocol on
Environmental Protection, the
123, 125, 128, 130, 135, 137
Antarctic Treaty System (ATS) 39,
127–9, 133
claims 123
Convention on the Conservation of
Antarctic Marine Living Resources
(CCAMLR) 123, 127, 129–31, 137–
9, 167
adoption 128
Article 2 167
Convention of the Conservation of
Antarctic Seals (CCAS) 123, 126–
7, 137
Convention on the Regulation of
Antarctic Mineral Resources
Activities (CRAMRA) 123, 131–2,
133–5, 137, 139
International Council of Scientific
Unions' Scientific Committee on
Antarctic Research (SCAR) 124,
126–7, 138
Ross Sea continental shelf 123

Antigua and Barbuda 136
Arctic Sea 39
Argentina 122, 123, 144
Ashdown, Paddy 104
Association of South Asian Nations
(ASEAN) 109
Atmosphere
in environmental security 59
and taxation for GCTF 45
Australia 60, 123, 129, 134, 168, 205
Whale Protection Act 168

Bahia Paraiso 132–3
Bamako Convention 112
Barnes, James N 129
Basel Convention on the Movement of
Transboundary Wastes, the 47,
99, 112, 133, 138
Bay of Biscay 161
Bergen Ministerial Declaration on
Sustainable Development in the
ECE Region 118
Belgium 85, 123, 144
Wallonian Waste Case 93, 95
Berne Convention on Conservation of
European Wildlife and Habitats
167
Biodiversity
and taxation for GCTF 7, 46–7
Bonn Convention on the Conservation
of Migratory Species of Wild
Animals 167
Brazil 46, 144, 177
Bretton Woods 65–6, 72, 79, 81, 84
Brittan, Sir Leon, 103
Brundtland
Commission, the 14
Gro Harlem 14
Report, the 3–4, 13, 15, 26
Bush, George 63

Canada 19, 37, 178, 205
Canary Islands, the 153
Caribbean, the 153

Centre for Law and Social Policy (CLASP), the 128–9
Charter of Environmental Rights and Obligations 11
Chemillier-Gendreau, Monique 10
Chernobyl 54
Chile 123, 134, 179
China 63
  and the Climate Change Convention 6
  and the Rio Declaration 22
Chloroflorocarbons (CFCs) 199–200, 208
Clarke, Charlie Arden 103
Clean Air Act (CCA) *see* Environmental Policy
Clean Water Act (CWA) *see* Environmental Policy
Columbia 46
Committee on International Development Institutions on the Environment (CIDIE) 72
Common Heritage of Humankind 46
Commonwealth of Independent States, the (CIS) 60
Conable, Barbara 71
Conference on the Security and Cooperation in Europe (CSCE) 51
Convention on Biological Diversity *see* UNCED
Convention on Climate Change *see* UNCED
Convention on International Trade in Endangered Species (CITES) 47, 62–3, 97, 99, 107–8, 168
  Appendix 1 111, 166
  Appendix 2 111, 166
  conflict with GATT 111
  Lausanne meeting 62
  and trade bans 107–8, 111
Convention on the Prevention of Marine Pollution by Dumping Wastes and other Matter *see* London Dumping Convention
Convention for the Protection of the Marine Environment of the North-East Atlantic *see* the Paris Convention
Cousteau Society, the 134
Czech Republic, the 51

Daly, Herman 106, 117
Debt for nature swap 35
Declaration of Environmental Policies and Procedures Relating to Economic Development, the 69, 72
Declaration on the Human Environment *see* Stockholm Declaration
Demaret, Paul 97–8, 121
Denmark 129, 143, 155–6
  Danish Bottles Case 90–4
Differentiated responsibilities
  Rio Declaration definition 29
Dillion Reservoir, the 201

Earth Summit '92 *see* UNCED
Economic Commission for Europe (ECE) 11
Ecuador 179
El-Ashry, Mohammed 84
Ellsworth Mountains 125
Environmental conflicts, international
  defined 52
  dispute settlement 56–9
  enforcement, international 53–5
  enforcement, national 53
  enforcement, NGO 55–6
  enforcement, State 54
  and trade 61–2
Environmental obligations, international
  defined 53
Environmental policy
  Best Available Control Technology (BACT) 185, 187–90
  Clean Air Act (CAA), the 190–1, 193, 195, 198, 209
  Clean Water Act (CWA), the 190, 200
  Command and Control regulations (CAC) 182–90, 194, 196, 198, 200, 203, 209
  comparisons 187–90
  Corporate Average Fuel Economy rules (CAFE) 197–8
  history 183–7
  market-based approaches 186, 192–3, 201
  market-based tools 186–7, 192
  recommendations 206–9
  technology-based approaches 185, 187

Transferable Development Rights
(TDAs) 205
US law 190
Environmental Protection Agency
(EPA)
emissions trading policy 194
lead regulations 195
origin 183
Pollution Prevention Strategy 191
regulations 197
Environmental security 50–64
cases 60–3
challenges 59–63
concerns with compliance 51
controversial issues 51
Erebus, Mount 125
European Bank for Reconstruction
and Development (EBRD) 117
Article 35 of the statute 119
European Community (EC) 15, 58,
63, 88, 97–9, 103, 106, 110, 168, 180
Commission 55, 58, 87–8, 90–3, 112
European Economic Community
(EEC) 16, 30, 85, 110, 113, 116–
17
European Economic Union, the
Treaty on 115, 116
Single European Act, the 15, 94–6
described 88
Treaty (The Treaty of Rome) 15,
55, 58, 97, 115, 117
Article 2 15
Article 30 89–90, 92–6
Article 36 89
Article 86 112
Article 100 87–8, 94–6, 99, 115, 116
Article 103 115
Article 130R 88, 116
Article 130S 88, 95
Article 130T 88, 96, 116
Article 169 58
Article 173 58
Article 235 87, 94
Cohesion Fund 115
establishment 85
history 85–90
Memorandum of Understanding
on Small Cetaceans in the North
Sea 167
European Court of Justice (ECJ) 57–
9, 88–9, 95, 99, 110, 115

Danish Bottles Case 90–3
Wallonian Waste Case 93–6
Exclusive Economic Zone (EEZ) 35,
45, 47–8, 127, 168
and whaling 162
Exxon Valdez 133

Faroe Islands, the 178–9
Finland 143, 153
Fox River, the 200–1
France 85, 123, 134, 144, 146, 151–4,
172
Friends of the Earth 128

Gandhi, Rajiv 48
General Agreement on Tariffs and
Trade (GATT) 23, 59, 62, 85, 99,
100–1, 106, 110–11, 114, 119–21
Article XI.1 112
Article XIII 111–13
Article XX 18, 109, 111–13
GATT 2, 103
Mexican Tuna Case 98–9, 108
and Montreal Protocol 113
recommendations to 121
reform 104–6
Report of the GATT Secretariat on
Trade and Environment, the 118
Superfund Tax Case 97–8
Technical Barriers to Trade (TBT)
110
and UNCED 101–6
Uruguay Round, the 101, 103
Germany 85–7, 92, 144, 153
pollution of the North and Baltic
Seas 41–3
Global Commons 36, 110, 114
defined 35
responsibility 38–9
Global Commons Guardians 39–41
establishment 40
examples 40–1
legislative function 40–1
recognition 43
Global Commons Trust Fund (GCTF)
34, 43–9
examples 47
implementation 44
objections 48
projections 45–7
Global Environmental Facility (GEF)

63, 66–7, 69
Conference of the Parties (COP) 83–4
criticisms 82
described 81–4
financial accountability 83
as a Global Commons Trust Fund (GCTF) 44
Participants Assembly (PA) 82–3
problems 44
Global Guardianships 34, 43
Glomar Challenger 127
Grand Calumet River, the 191
Greece 144
Greenhouse gases (GHGs) 190
and taxation for GCTF 45
Greenland 178–9
Greenpeace 49, 63, 100, 129–31, 134, 147, 168
as a Global Commons Guardian 40
Group of 77 (G–77) 24
Rio Declaration 22–3, 31
Group of Experts on the Scientific Aspects of Marine Pollution (GESAMP), the Joint 40

Havana Charter, the 105
Helsinki Convention for the Baltic Sea, the 154
Hong Kong 62–3
Human Rights
and Economic Commission for Europe (ECE) 11
and the Rio Declaration 10
and Stockholm Declaration 8–9
and World Commission on Environment and Development (WCED) 10–11
Hungary 51

Iceland 143, 155, 173–4, 178–9, 205
India
and the Climate Change Convention 6
Narmada Dam Project 66, 73–9
Individual Transferable Quotas (ITQs) 205–6
Intergovernmental Panel of Experts on Radioactive Wastes (IGPRAD) 145, 152, 155
proposals 146–50

International Atomic Energy Agency (IAEA) 144–6
International Convention for the Regulation of Whaling (ICRW) 123, 159–60, 163–6, 168, 174, 176, 180
Article 3 163
Article 5 164, 169, 172
Article 8 173
Section 13 175
International Council of Scientific Union (ICSU) 144
International Court of Justice (ICJ) 51, 57–60, 64, 162
International Development Agency 49
International Fund for Animal Welfare 168
International Geophysical Year (IGY) 122
International Institute for Environment and Development (IIED) 129
International Maritime Organization (IMO) 133, 138, 141–2
International Transportation Federation (ITF) 144
International Whaling Convention (IWC) 39, 126, 159–60, 163–6, 168, 173–81
Moratorium on Commercial Whaling 169, 178
Scientific Committee's Rules of Procedure 173
Section 10(e) 169–72
whale sanctuaries 172, 178
Inuit, the 175
Italy 92, 144

Japan 39, 123, 126, 144, 146, 152–4, 169–70, 172–5, 178, 180
Jackson, John 120

Kantor, Mickey 99
Kiribati 142
Korea 39
Kramer, Ludwig 95–6

Liability and compensation 8, 60
London Convention on the Prevention of Marine Pollution by Dumping

of Wastes (LDC), the   39–40, 47,
140–2, 146–7, 149–50, 152–6
Annex 1   141–3, 148, 155
Annex 2   141–2
Annex 3   141, 155
List of Parties   157
Resolution 14(7)   144
Resolution 21(9)   144–5, 148
Resolution 43(13)   148
Votes on radioactive waste dump-
ing   158

Maastricht, The Treaty of   15, 94, 117
Article B   16
Article 2   96
Article 3   96
Madeira   153
Marshall Plan   86
Mexico   23, 61–2, 85, 98–9, 103
Mobutu, President   3
Montreal Protocol on Substances that
Deplete the Ozone Layer, the   51,
60–1, 99, 110, 113, 139, 199–200
Morse Commission Report, the   73
Multilateral Trade Organization
(MTO)   103, 116, 119–20
Annex 4   116–17

National Oceanic and Atmospheric
Administration (NOAA)
as Global Commons Guardian   41
National Union of Seamen (NUS)   144
Narmada Dam *see* India
Nauru   60, 142
Netherlands, the   11, 144, 153–4, 166
New Zealand   123, 125, 129, 134, 137,
168, 205
Marine Mammal Protection Act 168
North Atlantic Marine Mammals
Conservation Organization
(NAMMCO)   179
North American Free Trade Agree-
ment (NAFTA)   101, 103
Norway   11, 14, 123, 143, 153, 155,
165–6, 169, 173–5, 178–9
Bureau of Whaling Statistics   174

Oceans
Indian   159, 161, 169
Pacific   142, 153, 177
and taxation for GCTF   45

South Pacific   142–3, 161
Southern   123–4, 127, 129
Organization for Economic Coopera-
tion and Development (OECD)
103, 144
Nuclear Energy Agency (NEA)
143, 150
Organization of Petroleum Exporting
Countries (OPEC)   127
Oslo Convention, the   141, 150
Ozone Agreements, the   40

Paris Convention, the   55, 150, 154
Article 3   152
Article 13   152
Paris Resolution, the   87
Pearce, Professor David   104
Pelly Amendment   169
Peru   169, 179
Poland   42
Polluter Pays Principle   97, 116
Principle 16 of UNCED   21
Portugal   144
Precautionary Principle   116–19, 132
adoption   110
O'Riordan's definition   119
Principle 15 of UNCED   21
Prevention and Elimination of Pollu-
tion by Dumping or Incineration,
the
Article 3.2   152
Article 3.3   151–2

Resource Conservation and Recovery
Act, the   191
Rio Conference *see* UNCED
Rio Declaration *see* UNCED
Royal, Segolene   151
Russia   123, 154

SCAR *see* International Council of
Scientific Unions Scientific Com-
mittee on Antarctic Research
Safe Drinking Water Act, the   191
Scientific and Technical Advisory
Panel (STAP)   82
Sierra Club, the   128–9
Seals
German court case   41–3
Seas
Arctic   39

Baltic 41, 167
North 41, 167, 180
North Atlantic 174
North-East Atlantic 141, 150, 152–3
dump site 143
Seychelles, the Republic of 169
Slovakia 51
Slynn, Advocate–General Sir Gordan 91
South Africa 123, 144
South Coast Air Quality Management District, the 194
South Korea 174
South Pacific Commission (SPC) 179
Sovereignty of States 5, 7, 36–7, 43, 64, 76
developing country concerns 31–3
in Rio Declaration 75, 77
territorial 35, 55
US 37
Soviet Union 126
Chernobyl 54
Space
and taxation for GCTF 45
Spain 143, 150
Spencer, Thomas 103
Statement of Principles on Forests *see* UNCED
Stockholm Conference on the Human Environment 128, 141, 166, 169
Stockholm Declaration 1, 11–12, 16, 51, 55, 63, 72, 79
description 2
Principle 1 8, 10, 12
Principle 4 13, 166
Principle 8 16
Principle 9 16
Principle 10 16
Principle 21 2, 5–7, 30, 52–3, 58
Principle 22 8
Principle 23 18
Suitability 112–13
Superfund Legislation, the 41, 204
Sustainable Development 1, 10, 14–16, 18–19, 25, 28, 32–3, 65–6, 74, 77, 79, 101–2, 104, 116–21
Bergen Declaration 118
Brundtland Report definition 13
differentiated responsibilities 29
Rio Declaration interpretation 26–7
Sustainable forest use 18

Sustainable growth 13–14, 16
in the European Community 15
Sweden 143
Switzerland 47, 144, 154

Taiwan 39, 174
Technical Barriers to Trade (TBT) Agreement 110, 112, 114–16
Article 2.2 112
Article 2.4 114
Article 2.10 114
Thatcher, Margaret 87
Tonga 46
Transboundary environmental harm
State responsibility 5–6, 8
Transparency principle
defined 77
and the GEF 82

United Nations Charter 58, 63–4, 67
Article 33 56
United Nations Commission on Sustainable Development 19, 63–4, 79–80
United Nations Conference on Environment and Development (UNCED) 1, 8–9, 11, 14–15, 17, 19, 20–2, 24, 28–9, 50–2, 56–7, 64–7, 69–73, 135, 140
Agenda 21 1, 13, 22, 50, 59, 63–4, 74, 76, 79–84, 116
Chapter 2 101
Chapter 17 179
Chapter 22 146–7
Chapter 39 19, 75
described 79
and GATT 101–6
Convention on Biological Diversity 1, 7, 51, 57, 63, 74
Development lending 74–9
Framework Convention on Climate Change 1, 6–7, 10, 28, 51, 57, 61, 63, 67, 81, 83, 119
Article 11 83–4
Human Rights 10–11
Objectives 14, 50
Rio Declaration on Environment and Development 4–5, 16–28, 30, 32, 59, 63, 74, 76–8, 102
Principle 1 9, 12–13, 21, 24, 26
Principle 2 5–8, 31–2, 75

Principle 3   9–10, 12, 24–5
Principle 4   17, 24–5, 26
Principle 5   26
Principle 7   13, 17, 28, 29–30
Principle 8   26–7
Principle 9   21
Principle 10   11–12
Principle 11   17–18, 30
Principle 12   16, 18, 21, 106, 146
Principle 13   8
Principle 15   21
Principle 16   21
Principle 18   21
Principle 19   21
Principle 25   21
Principle 26   21
Principle 27   19
State aims   1
Statement of Principles on Forests
    1, 7–8, 10, 18
United Nations Conference on the
    Human Environment (UNCHE)
    1, 69, 72, 86
United Nations Convention on the
    Law of the Sea (UNCLOS)   57, 59,
    127, 131
    Article 65   167, 179
    Part 15   59
    and whaling   167, 179
United Nations Development Pro-
    gramme (UNDP)   63, 66
    and GEF   81–2
United Nations Environmental
    Programme (UNEP)   3, 14, 45, 63,
    66, 72, 129, 133, 174
    as Global Commons Guardian   40
    and GEF   81–2
United Nations Food and Agriculture
    Organization (FAO)   174
    Marine Mammal Action Plan   178
United Nations General Assembly
    (UNGA)   68, 83, 134, 136
    Resolution 44/228   4, 12
    Resolution against driftnetting   39,
    47
United States of America (USA)   11,
    23, 37, 42, 63, 103, 105, 112–13, 123–
    4, 129, 137, 142, 144, 146, 149, 152–
    4, 161, 175, 182–3, 187, 191–3, 195,
    197, 199, 201, 203–4, 207–8
    Climate Change Convention   37

Marine Mammal Protection Act
    (MMPA)   168
    Article 20(G)   98
Tuna dispute   61–2, 85, 98–9, 103,
    113
United Kingdom (UK)   11, 60, 62–3,
    87, 91, 122–3, 129, 134, 137, 144,
    146, 151–4, 205
Uruguay Round, the   101, 103,
    116, 120
USSR   144–5, 148, 169, 173, 178

Vienna Convention on Substances that
    Deplete the Ozone Layer, the   39

Whale and Dolphin Conservation
    Society   168
Whale Products Regulation   168
World Bank   23, 35, 44, 63, 65–6, 74,
    77, 79
    environmental concerns   69–74
    Environmental Guidelines   70
    and the GEF   81–4
    Office of Environmental Affairs
        (OEA)   70
    Operational description   67–9
    Operational Directive on Environ-
        mental Assessment (EA)   70
    restructuring   71
World Charter for Nature   1, 12–13,
    16
World Commission on Environment
    and Development (WCED)   3–4,
    13–14, 70, 72, 81, 117
    and human rights   10–11
World Conference on Natural Parks
    129
World Conference on Ozone Protec-
    tion   87
World Conservation Union (IUCN)
    Commission on National Parks   3,
    129
World Meteorological Organization
    (WMO)
    as Global Commons Guardians   40
Worldwide Fund for Nature (WWF)
    62, 100, 103–4, 129, 134, 168
    as Global Commons Guardians   40

Zaire   3
Zimbabwe   63